802.11 Wireless Network Site Surveying and Installation

Bruce E. Alexander

Cisco Press

Cisco Press
800 East 96th Street
Indianapolis, IN 46240 USA

802.11 Wireless Network Site Surveying and Installation

Copyright© 2005 Cisco Network Systems, Inc.

Published by:

Cisco Press

800 East 96th Street

Indianapolis, IN 46240 USA

Printed in the United States of America   2 3 4 5 6 7 8 9 0

Second Printing April 2006

Library of Congress Cataloging-in-Publication Number: 2003108615

ISBN: 1-58705-164-8

Warning and Disclaimer

This book is designed to provide information about performing site surveys and installation for 802.11 wireless LANS, as well as about selecting the proper components. Every effort has been made to make this book as complete and as accurate as possible, but no warranty or fitness is implied.

The information is provided on an "as is" basis. The author, Cisco Press, and Cisco Systems, Inc., shall have neither liability nor responsibility to any person or entity with respect to any loss or damages arising from the information contained in this book or from the use of the discs or programs that may accompany it.

The opinions expressed in this book belong to the author and are not necessarily those of Cisco Systems, Inc.

Trademark Acknowledgments

All terms mentioned in this book that are known to be trademarks or service marks have been appropriately capitalized. Cisco Press or Cisco Systems, Inc., cannot attest to the accuracy of this information. Use of a term in this book should not be regarded as affecting the validity of any trademark or service mark.

Corporate and Government Sales

Cisco Press offers excellent discounts on this book when ordered in quantity for bulk purchases or special sales.

For more information, please contact: **U.S. Corporate and Government Sales** 1-800-382-3419 or corpsales@pearsontechgroup.com

For sales outside the U.S., please contact: **International Sales** international@pearsoned.com

Feedback Information

At Cisco Press, our goal is to create in-depth technical books of the highest quality and value. Each book is crafted with care and precision, undergoing rigorous development that involves the unique expertise of members from the professional technical community.

Readers' feedback is a natural continuation of this process. If you have any comments regarding how we could improve the quality of this book, or otherwise alter it to better suit your needs, you can contact us through e-mail at feedback@ciscopress.com. Please make sure to include the book title and ISBN in your message.

We greatly appreciate your assistance.

Publisher	John Wait
Editor-in-Chief	John Kane
Executive Editor	Jim Schachterle
Cisco Representative	Anthony Wolfenden
Cisco Press Program Manager	Nannette M. Noble
Production Manager	Patrick Kanouse
Development Editor	Dayna Isley
Technical Editors	John Elliott, Larry Ross, Charles Sablatura
Team Coordinator	Tammi Barnett
Cover Designer	Louisa Adair
Copy Editor	Keith Cline
Indexer	Christine Karpeles
Composition	Tolman Creek Design
Proofreader	Tonya Cupp

CISCO SYSTEMS

Corporate Headquarters
Cisco Systems, Inc.
170 West Tasman Drive
San Jose, CA 95134-1706
USA
www.cisco.com
Tel: 408 526-4000
    800 553-NETS (6387)
Fax: 408 526-4100

European Headquarters
Cisco Systems International BV
Haarlerbergpark
Haarlerbergweg 13-19
1101 CH Amsterdam
The Netherlands
www-europe.cisco.com
Tel: 31 0 20 357 1000
Fax: 31 0 20 357 1100

Americas Headquarters
Cisco Systems, Inc.
170 West Tasman Drive
San Jose, CA 95134-1706
USA
www.cisco.com
Tel: 408 526-7660
Fax: 408 527-0883

Asia Pacific Headquarters
Cisco Systems, Inc.
Capital Tower
168 Robinson Road
#22-01 to #29-01
Singapore 068912
www.cisco.com
Tel: +65 6317 7777
Fax: +65 6317 7799

Cisco Systems has more than 200 offices in the following countries and regions. Addresses, phone numbers, and fax numbers are listed on the
Cisco.com Web site at www.cisco.com/go/offices.

Argentina • Australia • Austria • Belgium • Brazil • Bulgaria • Canada • Chile • China PRC • Colombia • Costa Rica • Croatia • Czech Republic
Denmark • Dubai, UAE • Finland • France • Germany • Greece • Hong Kong SAR • Hungary • India • Indonesia • Ireland • Israel • Italy
Japan • Korea • Luxembourg • Malaysia • Mexico • The Netherlands • New Zealand • Norway • Peru • Philippines • Poland • Portugal
Puerto Rico • Romania • Russia • Saudi Arabia • Scotland • Singapore • Slovakia • Slovenia • South Africa • Spain • Sweden
Switzerland • Taiwan • Thailand • Turkey • Ukraine • United Kingdom • United States • Venezuela • Vietnam • Zimbabwe

About the Author

Bruce Alexander is the technical marketing manager for Cisco Systems Wireless Networking Business Unit. Bruce joined Cisco as a result of the Cisco acquisition of Aironet Wireless Communication, where he was director of technical support. Bruce has been working in the RF technology area for more than 30 years, has held an amateur radio license since 1978, and has been working in RF WLAN technology for the past 18 years. Previous duties include working in both software and hardware areas of the RF engineering group at Telxon, senior instructor for National Education Centers, and cofounder of Ameritron Amateur Radio Company. Bruce attended Akron University where he majored in computer programming and business administration.

About the Technical Reviewers

John Elliott, CCIE No. 2095, is a consulting system engineer at Cisco Systems, Inc., where he has been employed since 1996. John's previous work with radio networks led him to specialize in Aironet products from the initial acquisition by Cisco. Previously, John was a software engineer for 10 years developing communications code for diverse systems—including phone switches, minicomputers, and embedded systems—and later spent five years deploying large networks around the globe using technologies from dial to high-speed leased lines. He is a graduate of the University of Arkansas with a bachelor of science degree in computer science.

Charles Sablatura has more than 23 years of experience with wide-area and local-area wireless network sales and support. In addition to being one of the founding partners and vice president of training services for GigaWave Technologies, Charles is a wireless training specialist for GigaWave Technologies and is a certified Cisco Systems instructor. Since May 2000, he has conducted training for Cisco Systems Aironet Wireless LAN 802.11a, 802.11b, and 802.11g product set. Throughout his career, Charles has performed more than 250 site surveys and 200 hundred installations involving WLAN and bridging equipment from various vendors. These site surveys and installations have been in a wide variety of environments such as electrical generation plants, chemical refineries, steel mills, aluminum smelting plants, hospitals, retail, distribution, pharmaceutical manufacturing, ISP last mile, and education.

Dedications

This book is dedicated to my wife, Shelley, to the entire team from the old Aironet wireless customer support group, and to Belle. Thanks to you all for keeping me motivated and inspired.

Acknowledgments

I want to give special recognition to Larry Ross, Fred Niehaus, Matthew Stein, Mike Adler, Navdeep Johar, and Stacey Albert, all members of the Cisco WNBU TME team; as well as to Charles Sablatura and John Elliot for providing their support, input, and technical knowledge in developing and editing this book. As usual, they are not afraid to tell you when you're wrong, and they have a combined wealth of knowledge about WLANs second to none.

Thanks also to Ron Seide and Neil Reid for getting my feet wet in writing material for publication and for their support (and push) to do this book.

A thank you must also go out to the production team for this book. Jim Schachterle and Dayna Isley have been incredibly professional and a pleasure to work with. Their drive (and subtle motivation) helped to get me through some tough times in this project. Also thanks to Keith Cline, Patrick Kanouse, Christine Karpeles, and Christopher Cleveland. Their behind-the-scenes work made this book a reality.

Contents at a Glance

Introduction   xviii

Part I   **Understanding the Prerequisites of a Site Survey**   1
Chapter 1   Defining a Wireless Network's Protocols and Components   3
Chapter 2   Understanding RF Fundamentals   25
Chapter 3   Regulating the Use of 802.11 WLANs   55
Chapter 4   WLAN Applications and Services   83
Chapter 5   Selecting the WLAN Architecture and Hardware   111

Part II   **The Site Survey**   141
Chapter 6   Preparing for a Site Survey   143
Chapter 7   Site Surveying Equipment   157
Chapter 8   Discovering Site-Specific Requirements   177
Chapter 9   Discovering Wired Network Requirements   191
Chapter 10   Using Site Survey Tools   217
Chapter 11   Performing a WLAN Site Survey   249

Part III   **Installing WLAN Components**   283
Chapter 12   Installing WLAN Products   285
Chapter 13   Preparing the Proper Documentation   303
Chapter 14   Outdoor Bridge Deployments   313

Part IV   **Appendixes**   337
Appendix A   WLAN Product References   339
Appendix B   Antenna Radiation Patterns   347
Appendix C   Alternative Antennas   365
Appendix D   Sample Forms   373
Glossary   395
Index   417

Table of Contents

Introduction   xviii

Part I   Understanding the Prerequisites of a Site Survey   1

Chapter 1   Defining a Wireless Network's Protocols and Components   3

The Evolution of Wireless Standards   3
The First Proprietary WLANs   4
Standards-Based WLAN Systems   5

Introducing 802.11   6
Direct-Sequence Spread Spectrum   7
IEEE 802.11b Direct-Sequence Channels   8
Frequency Hopping   8
802.11 Working Groups   9
802.11a   10
802.11b   11
802.11g   11

Additional Wireless Standards   11
Bluetooth   12
HiperLAN   13
Home RF   13
Ultra Wideband   13

Wi-Fi Alliance   14
Other Wi-Fi Certifications   14
Wi-Fi Capabilities Label   14

WLAN Components   15
Access Points   16
Client Devices   17
Bridges   18
Accessories   21

Summary   23

Chapter 2   Understanding RF Fundamentals   25

Understanding RF Components   25
Frequency   25
Modulation   26
Amplitude Modulation   28
Frequency Modulation   29

Phase Modulation   29
    Binary Phase Shift Keying   30
    Quadrature Phase Shift Keying   31
    Complementary Code Keying   31
    Quadrature Amplitude Modulation   31
    Orthogonal Frequency Division Multiplexing   32
Modulation Methods for 802.11 Technologies   33
Signal Strength   34

Understanding RF Power Values   34
    Decibels   35
    Power Ratings   35

Antennas   36
    Gain   37
    Directional Properties   38
        Omni-Directional Antennas   38
        Directional Antennas   40
    Polarization   40
    Antenna Examples   40
        Patch Antenna   41
        Panel Antenna   41
        Yagi Antenna   41
        Dish Antennas   41
    Diversity   42

Connectors   45

Cables   45

Understanding RF Site Propagation   46
    Frequency Versus Coverage   47
    Material Absorption, Reflection, and Refraction   47
    Reflection   47
    Signal Strength, Noise, and Signal-to-Noise Ratio   48
    Coverage Versus Bandwidth   49
    Modulation Versus Coverage   50
    Outdoor RF Issues   50
        Propagation and Losses   51
        Earth Bulge and Fresnel Zone   51

Summary   52

Chapter 3   Regulating the Use of 802.11 WLANs   55

    Early Spread-Spectrum Regulations   55

    RF Regulatory Domains   57

WLAN Frequencies of Operation   58
　　900-MHz Frequency Band   59
　　2.4-GHz Frequency Band   60
　　5-GHz Frequency Band   62

Dynamic Frequency Selection and Transmitter Power Control with 801.11h   64

Regulatory Channel Selections   65
　　North American Domain Channel Scheme   65
　　　　2.4 GHz (NA)   65
　　　　5 GHz (NA)   66
　　ETSI Domain Channel Scheme   66
　　　　2.4 GHz (ETSI)   66
　　　　5 GHz (ETSI)   67
　　Japan Channel Scheme   67
　　　　2.4 GHz (Japan)   67
　　　　5 GHz (Japan)   67
　　Other Regulatory Domain Frequency Limits   67

Maximum Transmitter Power Levels   67
　　EIRP   68
　　North American Regulatory Power Levels   68
　　　　2.4-GHz Power Levels for the North American Regulatory Domain   68
　　　　5-GHz Power Levels (NA)   71
　　ETSI Regulatory Power Levels   72
　　　　2.4-GHz Power Levels (ETSI)   72
　　　　5-GHz Power Levels (ETSI)   73
　　Japan Domain Power Levels   73
　　　　2.4 GHz (Japan)   73
　　　　5 GHz (Japan)   74
　　World Mode (802.11d)   74

Amplifiers   75

Antenna Connectors and Remote Antennas   76

Health and Safety   77

Plenum Locations   79

Summary   79

Recommended Reading   79

Chapter 4   WLAN Applications and Services   83

Typical WLAN Environments   83
　　Retail/Bar Coding   84
　　　　Retail   85

Warehousing   88
Enterprise Offices   89
Health Care   91
Education   93
Manufacturing   95
Hotel, Conventions, and Hospitality   97
Public Hotspots   98
SOHO   99

Defining the WLAN Requirements   100

Defining Your Technology Requirements   101

Selecting Necessary WLAN Services   105
VLANs   105
Quality of Service   105
IP Subnet Roaming   106
Security   106
Load Balancing   107
Interoperability   107

Building-to-Building Connectivity   107

Summary   108

Chapter 5   Selecting the WLAN Architecture and Hardware   111

Key Features of a WLAN   111
Software Upgrade Capabilities   112
Rogue AP Detection   112
Flexible and Secure Mobility   113
Assisted Survey and Installation Tools   113
Self-Healing Systems   114
Remote Debugging   114

Various WLAN Architectures   114
Distributed Intelligence   115
Centralized Intelligence   117
Core Device Architecture   118
Comparing Packet Flows of Distributed and Centralized Intelligence
  Systems   120
Edge Device Architecture   123
Switched Antenna Systems   124
    Phased Array Antenna Technology   125
    Phased Array Antenna Extends Range   126
Mesh Networking   129
Free-Space Optics (Laser)   130

Selecting the Access Point   131
    Single- or Dual-Radio Architecture   131
    AP Radio Styles   134

Selecting the Client Products   136

Summary   139

Part II   **The Site Survey**   141

Chapter 6   Preparing for a Site Survey   143

Pre-Site Survey Form Information   143
    Customer Information   145
    Site Survey Location   146
    Current Network and Communications Information   147
    WLAN Equipment Requirements   148
    Site Information   149
    Survey Personnel Requirements   152
    Scope of Work   152
    Coverage Map   152
    Outdoor Bridge Links   153

User Input   154

Balancing Wants, Needs, and Capabilities   154

Summary   155

Chapter 7   Site Surveying Equipment   157

WLAN Equipment   157
    Access Points   158
    Client Devices   160
    Connectors   162
    Antennas   163
    Cables   165
    Attenuators   166
    Physical Measuring Devices   167
    RF Analyzers   168
      Spectrum Analyzer   169
      Portable Analyzer Tools   169
    Two-Way Radios   170
    Outdoor Tools   170
    Battery Packs   170
    Digital Camera   172
    Mounting Hardware   172

Site Survey Kits   173

Summary   175

Chapter 8   Discovering Site-Specific Requirements   177

Recommended Facility Documentation   177
   Site Map   178
   Building Construction   179
   Building Contents   180
   Defined User Areas and Densities   184

Limitations Affecting Equipment Installations   185
   Customer Restrictions   186
   Regulatory Limitations   186
   Environmental Concerns   187

Using Cookie Cutter Designs   188

Summary   189

Chapter 9   Discovering Wired Network Requirements   191

Switches, Routers, and Hubs   191

Roaming   192
   Developing a Policy for Device Roaming   193
      802.11f IAPP   194
      Association of Clients   195
   Layer 2 Roaming   196
   Layer 3 Roaming   197
      The Nomadic-Node Approach   198
      The Mobile-Node Approach   198
   Mobile IP   198
      Mobile IP Disadvantages   200
      Proxy Mobile IP   200
   Layer 3 Wireless Switching   202

Deploying VLANs over Wireless   203

QoS for WLANs   206
   Wireless QoS Deployment Schemes   206
   Downstream and Upstream QoS   207
   QoS and Network Performance   207

Cabling Requirements   208
   Power over Ethernet   208
   802.3af   211
   Proprietary PoE Methods   212

Summary   214

References   214

Chapter 10   Discovering Wired Network Requirements   217

    Types of Site Surveys 218
        Manual 218
        Automated 218
        Assisted 219
        Theoretical Surveys 220

    Manual Site Survey Tools 221
        Cisco Systems Aironet Client Utility 221
        Cisco Systems Aironet Desktop Utility 226
        Intel Centrino Utility 228
        ORiNOCO Survey Utility 230
        Netgear Clients 231
        Wireless 802.11 Phones 232
        AirMagnet 233
        AirMagnet Site Survey Utility (SiteViewer) 237
        DOS and Other Systems That Do Not Support Standard Utilities 242

    Automatic and Assisted Site Survey Tools 243
        Aruba 243
        Cisco Assisted Survey Utility 244

    Theoretical Site Survey Tools 245

    Summary 246

Chapter 11   Performing a WLAN Site Survey   249

    Steps in the Site Survey Process   249
        Obtain a Floor Plan or Facility Blueprint   250
        Inspect the Facility   250
        Identify User Areas on the Diagram   251
        Identify Potential Problems Areas on the Diagram   251
        Identify AP Locations and Antenna Types   253
            RF Issues in the Site   253
            Detecting Interference   255
            The Walkabout Test   258
                Defining the Cell Boundaries   258
                Overlapping Cell Coverage   262
        Performing a Manual Survey   263
        Documenting the Site Survey   270

    Surveying with the AirMagnet Tool   270

    Assisted Site Surveys   273
        Performing a User-Density Test   274
        Using the Assisted Site Survey Tool   276
        RF Configuration Parameters   276

Site Surveying for Repeater Usage   277

Dual-Band Surveys   278

Site Surveys for Voice   278

Final Verification   279

Summary   280

Part III   **Installing WLAN Components**   283

Chapter 12   Installing WLAN Products   285

Understanding Installation Issues   285
    Facility Construction   286
    Aesthetics   286
    Physical Security   289
    Environment   290
    Building Codes   291

Proper AP Mounting   293
    Wall Mounting   294
    Ceiling Mounting   296

Proper Antenna Mounting   296

Ethernet Considerations   300

Summary   301

Chapter 13   Preparing the Proper Documentation   303

Final Site Survey Report   303

Documenting the Work   305

Site Survey Report-Generation Programs   309

Summary   310

Chapter 14   Outdoor Bridge Deployments   313

Understanding Bridge System Characteristics   313

Understanding Bridge Topologies   314

Using Common Applications over Bridges   315
    VLANs   316
    QoS   317
    Voice over IP   317
    Security   318

Feasibility Study   318
    Determining Line of Sight   319
    Environmental Issues   322

Fresnel Zone   322
Determining the Possible Coverage Distance   325

Interference Study   326

Installing Bridges   326
Lightning Protection   327
Indoor Testing Before Installation: Understanding Maximum Operational Receive
 Level   331
Aligning the Antenna   332
Weatherproofing the Connectors   332
Parallel Bridge Links for Increased Throughput   333

Summary   334

Part IV   **Appendixes**   337

Appendix A   WLAN Product References   339

Appendix B   Antenna Radiation Patterns   347

Appendix C   Alternative Antennas   365

Appendix D   Sample Forms   373

Glossary   395

Index   417

Icons Used in This Book

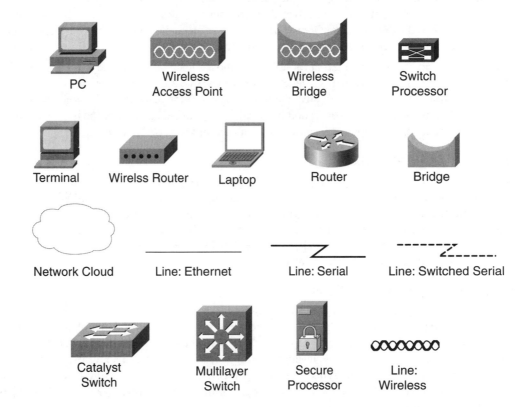

PC

Wireless Access Point

Wireless Bridge

Switch Processor

Terminal

Wirelss Router

Laptop

Router

Bridge

Network Cloud

Line: Ethernet

Line: Serial

Line: Switched Serial

Catalyst Switch

Multilayer Switch

Secure Processor

Line: Wireless

Command Syntax Conventions

The conventions used to present command syntax in this book are the same conventions used in the IOS Command Reference. The Command Reference describes these conventions as follows:

- **Boldface** indicates commands and keywords that are entered literally as shown. In actual configuration examples and output (not general command syntax), boldface indicates commands that are manually input by the user (such as a show command).
- *Italics* indicate arguments for which you supply actual values.
- Vertical bars (l) separate alternative, mutually exclusive elements.
- Square brackets [ ] indicate optional elements.
- Braces { } indicate a required choice.
- Braces within brackets [{ }] indicate a required choice within an optional element.

Introduction

WLANs, as we know them today, were introduced as early as 1986 for use in barcode scanning. These often basic ad hoc systems were used for either temporary systems or very simplified "unwired" systems. As WLANs began to become more popular, a need arose for some type of installation guidelines. However, every installation was unique, and a cookie cutter design guide was difficult to write.

To provide a good, stable installation for a WLAN, most sites require an independent evaluation. This book addresses how to perform this evaluation, or survey, of a site. It also provides guidelines for selecting the technology and products to meet the requirements of the desired applications. As you will learn in this book, however, the heart of a good installation is an understanding of the tools and methods that can be used to determine optimal installation locations for the WLAN products.

Goals and Methods

WLANs have evolved at a very fast pace over the past decade, and changes have led to many new ways to resolve some of the most common issues surrounding where and how to install WLAN devices. The most important and somewhat obvious goal of this book is to help you understand the methods of 802.11 WLAN site surveys and installations and the tools needed for completing these tasks. A secondary goal of this book is to help you understand the decisions needed to select the proper components and architectures that compose an 802.11 WLAN.

Who Should Read This Book?

This book is not designed to be a general-purpose 802.11 WLAN design book. Instead, it is intended to assist in understanding the available systems, architectures, components, and tools and how to use all of these in completing a design for an 802.11 WLAN. In most cases, separate individuals set down the WLAN design, perform the survey, install the products, and configure the devices. This book assists engineers who are not only surveying or installing WLANs, but also those defining and designing them. After all, to prepare an efficient and reliable design, some level of knowledge about site surveys and installation is required.

How This Book Is Organized

This book has been arranged to match the chronological order of the final design, survey, and installation procedures of an 802.11 WLAN project. It is designed to be read in order, because one chapter builds upon the others.

The book is divided into four parts, as follows:

- Part I, "Understanding the Prerequisites of a Site Survey," describes the pre-site survey considerations:

  —Chapter 1, "Defining a Wireless Network's Protocols and Components," defines WLAN standards and devices.

  —Chapter 2, "Understanding RF Fundamentals," provides a basic-level understanding of RF characteristics required for surveying and installing WLANs.

  —Chapter 3, "Regulating the Use of 802.11 WLANs," describes various regulations that you must adhere to when installing WLANs.

- —Chapter 4, "WLAN Applications and Services," outlines WLAN common applications, required services needed for supporting these applications, and how they affect the design, site survey, and installation.

- —Chapter 5, "Selecting the WLAN Architecture and Hardware," discusses WLAN architecture and component selections so that the survey can be correctly planned and performed.

- Part II, "The Site Survey," describes the procedures and requirements involved in performing a site survey:

  - —Chapter 6, "Preparing for a Site Survey," covers presurvey information, including what is necessary before any on-site work is performed.

  - —Chapter 7, "Site Surveying Equipment," compares the various site-specific tools and details the benefits of each for different situations.

  - —Chapter 8, "Discovering Site-Specific Requirements," describes building construction and contents and the effect they have on a WLAN.

  - —Chapter 9, "Discovering Wired Network Requirements," covers characteristics of existing wired networks and their impact on WLANs.

  - —Chapter 10, "Using Site Surveying Tools," describes how to use the site survey utilities.

  - —Chapter 11, "Performing a WLAN Site Survey," provides guidelines for a successful WLAN site survey.

- Part III, "Installing WLAN Components," covers the final stages of the site survey and installation process:

  - —Chapter 12, "Installing WLAN Products," focuses on the issues that can arise during the installation process.

  - —Chapter 13, "Preparing the Proper Documentation," emphasizes the importance of thorough documentation.

  - —Chapter 14, "Outdoor Bridge Deployments," covers building-to-building WLANs.

- Part IV, "Appendixes," includes the following supplemental information:

  - —Appendix A, "WLAN Product References," describes popular WLAN manufacturers and their products.

  - —Appendix B, "Antenna Radiation Patterns," shows radiation patterns for some popular WLAN antennas.

  - —Appendix C, "Alternative Antennas," identifies antennas that you can use (provided that they meet local regulatory standards) when standard antennas do not meet the needs of a certain environment.

  - —Appendix D, "Sample Forms," provides examples of pre-site survey documentation and a final site survey form.

At the end of the book, you can find an extensive glossary that defines many common WLAN concepts.

PART I

Understanding the Prerequisites of a Site Survey

Chapter 1   Defining a Wireless Network's Protocols and Components

Chapter 2   Understanding RF Fundamentals

Chapter 3   Regulating the Use of 802.11 WLANs

Chapter 4   WLAN Applications and Services

Chapter 5   Selecting the WLAN Architecture and Hardware

This chapter covers the following topics:

- The Evolution of Wireless Standards
- Introducing 802.11
- Additional Wireless Standards
- Wi-Fi Alliance
- WLAN Components

CHAPTER 1

Defining a Wireless Network's Protocols and Components

So you have decided to add a wireless system to your network. Where do you start? What products do you need? You know that a *wireless LAN* (WLAN) can provide overall productivity improvements, based on user mobility and resulting improvements in organizational and individual efficiency. All of this is, however, is based on selecting the proper components, the proper WLAN architecture, and proper installation. As network administrators rush to integrate wireless LANs across enterprise networks, they often underestimate and oversimplify the technology.

A properly selected and installed Wi-Fi, or *wireless fidelity*, network can provide a dramatic increase in productivity at the individual level, which in the end relates to the bottom line for the company or organization. However, selecting the wrong components or the wrong architecture, or installing the WLAN using improper guidelines, can cause you to just as easily end up with a system the users hate because of arcane access and use rules. Or you will have a system that causes the network to become unbearably slow, insecure, or extremely unstable.

This book covers many aspects of properly selecting your WLAN components (including the WLAN architecture), assists in the design stages, and covers many details of site survey steps and proper installation techniques. Remember, a well-deployed WLAN is like a drug: When users get a taste of it, they are addicted. So you have to prepare for expansion, and continued growth (unless, of course, you enable everyone the first day!).

This chapter focuses on the protocols that make up today's WLANs and the evolution of the technology. Understanding the migration path from early systems through what is available today will help you relate to issues and problems that arise with WLANs.

Later chapters cover different WLAN architectures from which you can select one that meets your application needs, stays within budget, and allows for proper installation and expansion.

The Evolution of Wireless Standards

Standards define by law what certain values are, such as the pound or kilogram, gallon or liter, dollar or euro. Standards also define the specifics of a product or technology and enable suppliers of such to claim, use, and adhere to well-defined standards.

Many of us do not really think about standards too much, unless they are relatively new and in the forefront of the media. Most IT professionals and network engineers never consider the actual protocol of the 802.3 standard and how it operates. Rather, it is typically thought of more as just "Ethernet." Without the underlying standard, however, the simplicity of just plugging in a cable to a switch or hub and it working would not be possible. In the communications industry, standards reduce the number of challenges with information exchange and product interoperability.

The more broadly adopted a standard is, the wider the market for providers of that technology. And providers using the most preferred standard, meaning one that has been ratified on a global basis, tend to capture more of the market share. This also tends to assist in driving costs down and improving quality. International standards are far more difficult in practice than in theory, however, and with wireless standards this is probably even more true.

The wireless world has many standards. They have been in place since the beginning of wireless. Without these standards, everyday things that are used in every facet of our life would not be possible. Think for a minute how often you use some form of wireless in your life today. Did you watch the news this morning? Remember the TV is receiving a signal that is wireless somewhere in the system (satellite to the cable company, or perhaps wireless all the way to your set). What about that remote control you used to turn the TV on or change the channel? Of course, that signal is likely infrared, but it is still considered wireless. Then there is the garage-door opener that you used to close your door as you backed out of the drive. And did you listen to the radio on the way to work? Was that an AM or FM radio? Or perhaps a satellite radio? You may have also used the technology with the biggest growth of wireless in history: your cell phone.

Without standards, mainstream adoption of these well-known wireless technologies would have occurred more slowly, if at all. This book restricts its discussion to mainly WLAN standards and focuses on the key 802.11 technologies.

The First Proprietary WLANs

To get a good understanding of 802.11, let's take a look at the evolution of WLAN technologies. The earliest WLAN systems were proprietary systems used mainly for bar code systems. These systems typically used what is called *narrowband radio* and were based in the UHF spectrum. A popular frequency band was 450 MHz, and the radios that were used were originally designed for voice communication. Just as a phone line was designed for voice and migrated to data with modem, so did voice-type radios. Whereas the radios followed a standard for communication at the *radio frequency* (RF) level, the data that was sent over them was proprietary to each and every vendor. One drawback to using these "voice-grade" radios was bandwidth. It was limited to about 9600 bps per system, and would only support up to perhaps 30 users for the entire system. A secondary problem was that these radio systems had to be licensed. In large cities such as Chicago or New York, most of the available frequencies were already spoken for.

In 1986, and with the need for more speed, more users, and license-free systems, eyes turned to the recently "declassified" spread-spectrum technologies. The *Federal Communications Commission* (FCC) had opened up several new unlicensed frequency bands for use with this new technology, and it promised to improve WLAN capabilities tenfold. The three new bands were defined as the ISM bands, indicating they were intended for *industrial, scientific, and medical* uses.

The first such band to be used was 900 MHz. It provided for data rates in the 1-Mbps range. But one issue with the early 900-MHz WLAN was the limited number of countries that allowed for the use of this type of equipment. The 900-MHz band could not be used in Europe and most Asia Pacific and South American countries.

Companies such as Ford Motor Company and IBM wanted a system that could be used in all their corporate locations, and because 900-MHz was limited to a handful of countries, there was a push from customers for a more widely acceptable solution.

In part because of these reasons (speed and global usage), the 2.4-GHz ISM band became the choice for innovative WLAN vendors. By the early 1990s, 2.4-GHz systems started to appear in the WLAN market, and the speed increased to an average of 2 Mbps. (One wireless LAN vendor, Breezecom, even pushed this limit to 3 Mbps.) The 2.4-GHz technology was permitted in more than 60 countries at that time; because of the higher speed and global availability, WLANs started moving into more mainstream networking.

Standards-Based WLAN Systems

There was still one drawback to investing in WLAN systems. There was no standard, and therefore WLANs were all proprietary and single-source products. A single-vendor implementation was, and still is, something most large users have a strong desire to avoid because, in part, they want to ensure equipment availability, service, and support in the event the vendor that sold them the equipment became unavailable or indifferent. Indeed some who chose to implement early WLANs ended up with a proprietary system that worked only with a single vendor's product line. Another risk in this approach was one of scaling, or in other words, expansion. If the vendor dropped the product line (which happened on more than one occasion) or worse, went out of business, you were left with a system that you could not expand or update, or in some cases, you could not even continue to get support for. This meant only one thing—R&R—rip and replace! The industry and the *Institute of Electrical and Electronics Engineers* (IEEE) saw a need to compile standards for WLANs to follow that would allow interoperation across vendor platforms. The result was the formation of 802.11 Working Group within the IEEE. This new IEEE group started working on the WLAN standard in 1991. Even though it was six long years before the IEEE completed the standard, the standard has affected tremendously the adoption of 802.11 equipment by customers both large and small.

In lieu of any completed industry standard, one company, Proxim, tried to develop an industry de facto standard known as the *Wireless LAN Interoperability Forum* (WLIF). The WLIF specification was completed and in place while the IEEE was working on the 802.11

standard. WLIF was based on the Proxim frequency-hopping radio design that provided a maximum data rate of 1.6 Mbps in the 2.4-GHz band. Many of the Proxim partners and customers joined the WLIF, and this forum was a dominant force in the WLAN community for several years, even with the limited bandwidth available with WLIF.

When the IEEE completed the 802.11 standard in 1997, there was more confusion. The standard supported two totally incompatible RF implementations: *frequency hopping* (FH) and *direct sequence* (DS). Some users again did not know which implementation to install. A philosophical war broke out between FH and DS vendors and customers, much like the debates that occurred between the VHS and Beta technology in the videotape arena. This confusion also prompted many potential WLAN customers to wait to install because they did not know which path to follow, FH or DS.

The new 802.11 systems had defined data rates only up to 2 Mbps, so the data rate advantage over the WLIF format was minimal, and therefore products based on the 802.11 took a little while to catch on. The main advantage of 802.11 was that it was an *industry* standard. Unlike WLIF, which was a standard clustered around a single company, 802.11 was intended to provide interoperability (and in many cases it did). However, there were still many issues with getting Vendor A to work with Vendor B, and users had to take the word of their potential vendors as to the level of interoperability. This again stalled the event of widespread WLAN adoption.

By the time the 802.11 products started to take hold in the industry, users were screaming for more and more bandwidth. Just two years after the first 802.11 standard was completed, the industry made a huge jump to 11 Mbps with the completion of the 802.11b standard and the introduction of 11-Mbps products based on the standard. As 802.11b devices started coming to fruition, there was still some skepticism about interoperability among vendors. This was the main reason that Wi-Fi certification was started. Known at that time as *Wireless Ethernet Compatibility Alliance* (WECA), the organization developed a program to assure users that Vendor A products would now have a minimum degree of interoperability with Vendor B products. The certification from this group was known as the *Wi-Fi certification*. The certification program was such a success that the term *Wi-Fi* was the unofficial wireless standard; in 2003, WECA even changed their name to the *Wi-Fi Alliance* (WFA).

Introducing 802.11

IEEE 802.11 is the Working Group within the IEEE responsible for wireless LAN standards. IEEE 802.11 became a standard in July 1997, and defined two RF technologies operating in 2.4-GHz band:

- **Direct-sequence spread spectrum (DSSS)**— 1 Mbps and 2 Mbps
- **Frequency-hopping spread spectrum (FHSS)**— 1 Mbps and 2 Mbps

Each of these two different technologies relies on a similar MAC layer protocol, but the physical layer differs drastically. Although they use the same frequency band, their approach to utilizing the actual RF is miles apart.

Because 802.11b and 802.11a operate in different frequency bands, the two standards have different propagation characteristics. A thorough understanding of how performance is affected when moving from one band to another or from one standard to another is essential to a successful design. Details such as capacity, data rates, throughputs, performance, and ranges and their varying effects when moving between 802.11b and 802.11a technologies need to be understood. Do not assume that you can just replace 802.11b products with 802.11a devices without other system implications. RF engineering is a very complex field of study, and this book outlines the necessary information for a solid understanding of the required RF basics.

Direct-Sequence Spread Spectrum

The DSSS approach involves encoding redundant information into the RF signal. Every data bit is expanded to a string of chips called a *chipping sequence* or *Barker sequence*. The chipping rate as mandated by the IEEE 802.11 is 11 chips (Bipolar Phase Shift Keying [BPSK]/Quadrature Phase Shift Keying [QPSK]) at the 1- and 2-Mbps rates. At these rates, 11 bits are transmitted for every 1 bit of data. The chipping sequence is transmitted in parallel across the spread-spectrum frequency range. The rationale here is that because the energy is so spread across the band, the signal looks more like noise to standard RF receivers, and with the information spread across a wide spectrum, it tends to be more immune to interference than a signal with a narrow spectrum. For this reason, DS is considered to have good *interference immunity*. Chapter 2, "Understanding RF Fundamentals," covers DS in more detail.

The DS protocol transmits out multiple "chips," or bits, for every data bit from the information. In Figure 1-1, the data of 1001 needs to be transmitted. Each bit is then converted into 11 chips. A 1 and a 0 will have unique codes. This permits some of the "chips" to be lost in transmission. When the receiver gets the 11-chip code, it can determine whether the resultant bit was a 1 or a 0, even if some of the chips are missing.

Figure 1-1   *Direct-Sequence Chipping Sequence*

If the Data Bit Was: 1001

Chipping Code Is: 1=00110011011   0=11001100100

Transmitted Data Would Be:

00110011011   11001100100   11001100100   00110011011

     1   0   0   1

After Transmission: ⌐———— Missed Chips ————⌐

00110X11XX1   110X10X100   1100XXX0100   00X10011X11

IEEE 802.11b Direct-Sequence Channels

Fourteen channels are now defined in the IEEE 802.11 *direct-sequence* (DS) channel set. Each DS channel as transmitted is 22 MHz wide; however, the channel separation is only 5 MHz. This leads to channel overlap such that signals from neighboring channels can interfere with each other. In a 13-channel DS system (11 usable in the U.S.), only three nonoverlapping (and hence, noninterfering) channels 25 MHz apart are possible (for example, Channels 1, 6, and 11). For the 14-channel systems (Japan only), there are 4 possible nonoverlapping channels (1, 6, 11, and 14).

This channel spacing governs the use and allocation of channels in a multi-*access point* (AP) environment such as an office or campus. APs are usually deployed in "cellular" fashion within an enterprise where adjacent APs are allocated nonoverlapping channels. Alternatively, APs can be collocated (placed in the same physical area) using Channels 1, 6, and 11 to deliver 33-Mbps bandwidth to a single area (but only 11 Mbps to a single client). Figure 1-2 shows the channel-allocation scheme.

There are up to 14 22-MHz-wide channels, with only 3 nonoverlapping channels (1, 6, and 11 in the U.S. and 1, 7, 13 in Europe). This allows three APs to occupy the same space for a total of 33-Mbps aggregate throughput. (Each channel supports an 11-Mbps data rate.)

Figure 1-2 *802.11 2.4-GHz DS Channel Scheme*

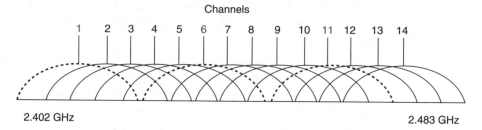

Frequency Hopping

The *frequency-hopping* (FH) approach to data transmission is basically what the name implies. The transmitting signal "hops" or moves around the band on a predetermined sequence. The receiver must also have the same sequence in order to "follow" the transmitter. The 802.11 standard specifies 78 different sequences or *hopping patterns*. In the face of interference, the radio just transmits the data packets, and if they do not reach the intended destination (as verified by an *acknowledgment* [ACK] sent back after successful reception of the packet), the transmitter just retransmits the packets on the next frequency, which is theoretically free of interference. For this reason, FH is said to have good *interference avoidance*.

Figure 1-3 is an example of FH in action. Packet 1 is sent out at a frequency near the bottom edge of the band, followed in time by packet 2. Notice that this second packet is located at a higher frequency in the band. Each successive packet in time is transmitted on a different frequency. In the actual FH implementation, the transmitter may send out multiple packets on the same frequency before moving to another frequency, but the amount of time that it is permitted to reside on any one frequency is limited to 400 *milliseconds* (ms).

Figure 1-3   *Frequency-Hopping Scheme*

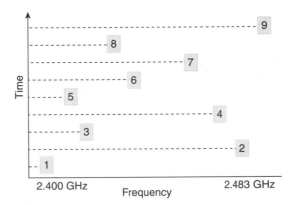

802.11 Working Groups

Within the 802.11 Working Group, a number of different Task Groups are responsible for various elements of the 802.11 WLAN standard. Table 1-1 details the various Task Groups within 802.11.

Table 1-1   *802.11 Working Group Task Groups*

Task Group	Project	Status (June 2004)
MAC	Develop one common MAC for WLANs in conjunction with PHY Task Group	Complete
PHY	Develop three WLAN physical layers (PHY): infrared, 2.4-GHz FHSS, 2.4-GHz DSSS	Complete
802.11a	Develop PHY for 5-GHz UNII band	Complete
802.11b	Develop higher-rate PHY in 2.4-GHz band	Complete

continues

Table 1-1   *802.11 Working Group Task Groups (Continued)*

Task Group	Project	Status (June 2004)
802.11b-cor1	Correct MIB deficiencies in 802.11b	Ongoing
802.11c	Cover bridge operation with 802.11 MACs (spanning tree)	Complete (802.11d)
802.11d	Define physical layer requirements for 802.11 operation in other regulatory domains (countries)	Complete
802.11e	Enhance 802.11 MAC for QoS	Estimated completion spring 2005
802.11f	Develop recommended practices for Inter-Access Point Protocol (IAPP) for multivendor use	Ongoing
802.11g	Develop higher-speed PHY extension to 802.11b (54 Mbps)	Complete
802.11h	Enhance 802.11 MAC and 802.11a PHY-dynamic frequency selection and transmit-power control	Complete
802.11i	Enhance 802.11 MAC security and authentication mechanisms	Complete
802.11j	Additional channels in Japan	Complete
802.11k	Radio measurement	Ongoing
802.11n	Develop higher-speed PHY extension (greater than 100 Mbps)	Ongoing

802.11a, b, and g represent the different radio technologies of the 802.11 specification. A good understanding of the advantages and disadvantages of these technologies will assist you in making the proper product-selection decision for your WLAN. The following sections focus on the important facets of these three technologies.

802.11a

In 1999, the IEEE released two new specifications for higher-bandwidth WLANs. One of these was the 802.11a specification, which identified a protocol that permitted data rates up to 54 Mbps, using the 5-GHz frequency band. At the time, very little in the way of development was being done in that RF band, which delayed the introduction of this technology into the market place for several years. In 2001, the first products based on the 802.11a standard started to appear on the market, and by 2002, most WLAN vendors were shipping some type of 802.11a products.

802.11b

The 802.11b standard was released at the same time as the 802.11a standard, but because of development that was already in place in the 2.4-GHz band, this technology hit the market much sooner. In fact, one vendor, Aironet Wireless Communication (now part of Cisco Systems), released their first 802.11b-designed product almost nine months before the standard was completed.

This new 802.11b standard used the same band as previous 802.11 standards—that is, 2.4 GHz—but increased the data rate to 11 Mbps. This provided the much-needed bandwidth to utilize standard office application over the wireless link, and many users started to consider implementation in the standard networks.

When the 11-Mbps standard was completed, all of the main WLAN vendors jumped into development; within a year, the WLAN market had shifted to an 802.11b market.

802.11g

With the push for higher and higher bandwidth and for backward compatibility to the industry "standard" of 802.11b, a new standard was needed. The goal of more than 20 Mbps was initially set by the Task Group, but because there was already much development around 802.11a and 54 Mbps, it was finally decided (after many months of debate in the Task Group) to move this data rate to 54 Mbps, similar to 802.11a. This permitted many vendors to utilize some of the same components for the new 802.11g technology that they had used in their 802.11a devices.

One requirement for 802.11g was that the devices must be backward compatible to 802.11b. This means any devices that meet the new standard would be able to communicate with an existing 802.11b device, at the 802.11b data rates. This enabled users to migrate from 802.11b to 802.11g without a complete replacement of all devices at once.

802.11g was completed in June 2003. Some prestandard products were already shipping at that point, but many companies were waiting for the completion of the standard before making final design changes and beginning production.

Additional Wireless Standards

Many other standards apply to the WLAN arena, most notably Bluetooth, HiperLAN, and Home RF. Each of these is unique. Some are designed for WLANs, whereas others are better suited for *wireless personal-area networks* (WPANs).

Other products also utilize 802.11 standards or proprietary standards for usage as a MAN or WAN.

Table 1-2 shows many of the network types that wireless products are included in, as well as typical usages for these various networks.

Table 1-2 *Wireless Technologies Compared*

	PAN	LAN	MAN	WAN
Standards	Bluetooth	802.11a, 802.11b, 802.11g HiperLAN/2	802.11 MMDS, LMDS	GSM, GPRS CDMA, 2.5–3G
Speed	<1 Mbps	2–54 Mbps	22+ Mbps	10–384 Mbps
Range	Short	Medium	Medium-Long	Long
Application	Peer to peer Device to device	Enterprise networks	Fixed, last-mile access	PDAs, mobile phones, cellular

This book deals mainly with WLAN systems, with some attention to MAN/WAN systems that can be implemented using products modeled after the 802.11 specifications.

Bluetooth

Bluetooth in its initial conception was intended as a design that could be completed in a single US$5 silicon chip providing 10 kbps, for 10 feet, sufficient as a cable replacement. This was thought to be the wireless interface for all the desktop devices, including your laptop, phone, PDA, printer, and so on. Bluetooth meant no more cables. And 10 kbps was fast enough for most of these devices at the time of conception.

During development, data rates increased to 1 Mbps, and ranges increased to average around 30 feet. Although not true WLAN capabilities, some users have tried to use Bluetooth as an 802.11b replacement. However, Bluetooth has been limited to a cable replacement and is most common in technologies such as cell phone headsets and portable printer connections.

Bluetooth radios use a spread-spectrum, frequency-hopping, full-duplex signal at up to 1600 hops/sec. The signal hops among 79 frequencies at 1-MHz intervals to give a high degree of interference immunity. Up to seven simultaneous connections can be established and maintained.

HiperLAN

The HiperLAN standards provide features and capabilities similar to those of the 802.11a WLAN standards. HiperLAN/1 provides communications at up to 20 Mbps on the 5-GHz band while HiperLAN/2 operates at speeds up to 54 Mbps in the same RF band. HiperLAN/2 is compatible with *third-generation* (3G) WLAN systems for sending and receiving data, images, and voice communications.

With the adoption rate of 802.11a and the advancements in that technology, the HiperLAN/2 technology has been slow to gain a foothold.

Home RF

A group called the Home RF Working Group developed a single specification, the *Shared Wireless Access Protocol* (SWAP), for a broad range of interoperable consumer devices. SWAP was an open industry specification that allowed PCs, peripherals, cordless telephones, and other consumer devices to share and communicate voice and data in and around the home without the complication and expense of running new wires. The technology behind the specification was frequency hopping and was limited to 2 Mbps.

The membership of the group exceeded 100 companies, but because of the limited acceptance of FH products (after the introduction of 802.11a, b, and now g products), and the user requirement of higher data rates, the group was officially disbanded in January 2003.

Ultra Wideband

Of all the technologies and standards, ultra wideband seems to have some very good potential, although its usage as a WLAN product hasn't been widely exploited. Much like spread spectrum in the 1980s, the technology for ultra wideband is one that for decades was the province of military labs. In the past few years, startups, information technology companies, and consumer electronics giants have begun pushing ultra wideband beyond the radarlike systems the military pioneered and into applications that could transform the home. Two companies are both pursuing the possibility of using ultra wideband transmission to wirelessly link DVD players, stereos, and TVs in home-entertainment systems. In the future, ultra wideband links could distribute extremely information-rich content, endowing a home or office with high-resolution 3D virtual-reality simulation.

The technology uses a very low-power transmitter and spreads the signal out over a very wide (much wider than DS) spectrum. As a result of these two features, the overall energy level is very hard to detect by a normal receiver and looks like noise to most receivers. However, its capability to transmit over long distances is also hampered by these requirements. Hence, its usage is limited to more of WPAN-type applications.

Wi-Fi Alliance

Wi-Fi (pronounced "why-phy") is a trade name developed by WFA and has come to mean WLAN for many users. The group is responsible for the term *Wi-Fi* (which is meant to be a truncation of wireless fidelity) and, more importantly, independent testing to verify interoperability.

Wi-Fi describes WLAN products that are based on IEEE 802.11 standards and is meant to be a more user-friendly name in the same way that Ethernet and Token Ring are more user friendly than IEEE 802.3 and 802.5, respectively. No other organization has done so much to drive the adoption of the WLAN technologies. With the goal of interoperability among devices based on the 802.11b standard, the WFA started a program to certify interoperability among devices. Founded in August 1999 by 3Com, Aironet Wireless Communications, Harris Semiconductor (now Intersil), Lucent Technologies (later Agere), Nokia, and Symbol Technologies, the WFA has grown to well over 200 members. Products such as bar code scanners, PCMCIA cards, embedded radio modules, APs, and wireless entertainment systems have successfully passed Wi-Fi interoperability testing and earned the right to carry the Wi-Fi label.

The Wi-Fi certification label ensures customers of at least a base level of interoperability. Wi-Fi testing, which is conducted at a third-party testing lab, is fairly stringent.

Other Wi-Fi Certifications

Other testing has also started to take place at the WFA. There is now a security specification called *Wi-Fi Protected Access* (WPA) that follows the 802.11i security specification and provides a test to ensure interoperability among devices when using WPA.

There is also a QoS interoperability certification available from WFA, known as Wi-Fi Multimedia (WMM), which uses some features identified by the 802.11e task group.

Wi-Fi Capabilities Label

Originally, *Wi-Fi* was meant to describe only 11-Mbps (maximum) devices that operate in the 2.4-GHz portion of the frequency spectrum and that conform to the IEEE 802.11b specification. It was later decided that Wi-Fi should be expanded to include 54-Mbps (maximum) data rate products operating in both the 2.4-GHz and 5-GHz portions of the frequency spectrum that are based on the IEEE 802.11g and 802.11a specifications. Testing for all three technologies provides for certification in all areas but creates some confusion for the customer.

Today a Wi-Fi device carries a Wi-Fi certification logo, and the packaging also carries a capabilities label (see Figure 1-4). This label defines which certification the device has passed, such as 802.11a, 802.11b, WPA, and so on. A customer implementing a multi-vendor WLAN network is advised to demand that all devices in the WLAN have passed interoperability testing and verification and have received the Wi-Fi logo.

Figure 1-4   *Wi-Fi Capabilities Label*

WLAN Components

This section briefly reviews some key points in WLAN product evolution. In the beginning, all WLANs were very vendor-specific and proprietary systems. Data rates started at 10 kbps and approached 1 Mbps with the advent of spread spectrum, with radios transmitting in the 900-MHz ISM band. Product availability was limited to APs, ISA cards, and to a lesser degree, PCMCIA cards. For PCMCIA cards, the overall power consumption of the WLAN client was high, and in many cases exceeded the capability of the device it was being used in. The high power consumption also reduced available battery run time, which therefore limited the degree to which a user could be truly untethered from an AC power source.

These early WLANs were used mainly by retail and warehouse systems for bar coding and inventory control. The required bandwidth for such application was, and in many cases still is today, comparatively low, as were overall transaction rates. The total number of users on this type of system is typically low, on the order of several to perhaps 30 for an entire system, so the limited availability of bandwidth was generally acceptable.

The convenience of being untethered prompted users to develop new ideas about how wireless might be used. Initially, the radio devices that were attached to the network were all proprietary, both in the RF protocol area and on the network connection side. Many devices used special *remote transceiver antenna* assemblies, attached back to some form of protocol converter over RS 232 or RS 485 interfaces. Proprietary cabling was used to provide connection and permit the radio device to be located in the area that the users needed connection.

As time moved on, demand increased to move the network-side RF device to a standard networking interconnection such as Ethernet or Token Ring. (Yes, there were loud cries for Token Ring devices at the time.)

A basic WLAN consists of a device that is attached to the network (AP), an antenna, and a device that is portable (commonly referred to as the client) and its associated antenna. The next sections examine these devices a little closer.

Access Points

The device that provides access to the network by the remote or portable radio devices is called the *access point* (AP); some vendors call it an *access port*. For the small office, or home use, the AP is often referred to as a *wireless gateway*. This device typically uses a standard network connection (Ethernet being the most common) that ties back to a network switch, router, or hub.

Figure 1-5 shows some of the popular APs available on the market today.

Figure 1-5   *Access Point Examples*

The AP is essentially a bridge between the wired network protocol (such as 802.3) and the RF protocol (802.11). It also provides the 802.11 protocol RF connection requirements, providing all features defined by the standard such as 802.11 association and 802.11 authentication, packet acknowledgment, handoff notification, and so on.

APs communicate on a one-to-many basis with wireless clients. For all purposes, they are the wireless hub for that particular RF area.

APs come with different features, functions, and performance levels, as well as in various physical form factors. The differences between these are discussed throughout various chapters of this book.

The AP also requires connection to power and an antenna of some sort. These two features in particular can make a difference in the product you choose for the network. The particulars of this topic are discussed in Chapter 2, "Understanding RF Fundamentals," and Chapter 9, "Discovering Wired Network Requirements."

Client Devices

The client device is the remote or portable device that communicates to the AP. Many of the early devices were specialty devices, such as bar code scanners, lift-truck mounted terminals, and point-of-sale devices. Virtually all of these devices were proprietary. Figure 1-6 shows some of the popular form factors of wireless clients, including bar code scanners, PCI cards, PCMCIA cards, compact Flash radios, and standalone USB or Ethernet radios.

Figure 1-6   *Client Device Examples*

Wireless ISA cards, available since in the early 1990s, were the first industry-standard devices geared for general computer use. PCMCIA cards followed, as did Ethernet standalone devices (sometimes called *workgroup bridges* or *wireless hubs*).

More recently, a form factor called *miniPCI* has been introduced; it is a style used in many laptop computers. This permits the client radio device to be embedded inside the computer, leaving the USB and Ethernet ports and the PCMCIA slots available for other devices, and making the WLAN client an integral part of the computer (see Figure 1-7).

Figure 1-7 *MiniPCI Radio Card*

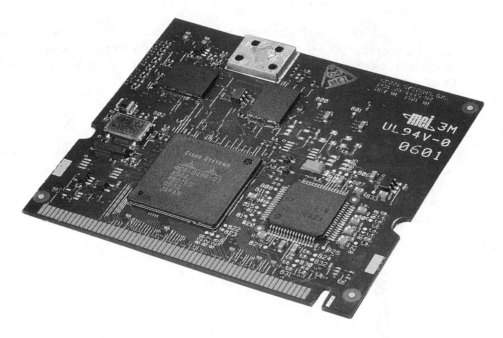

Bridges

The term *bridge* in the WLAN lexicon usually indicates a wireless device that connects a group of computers or devices to another group of computers or devices over a single RF link. Most commonly found in building-to-building connections, bridges many times follow the 802.11 specification, even though they are not actually included in the specification. As depicted by Figure 1-8, bridges enable you to connect multiple buildings (or networks) together, eliminating the need for cable runs or leased lines.

Figure 1-8   *Wireless Bridging*

Multipoint Bridging

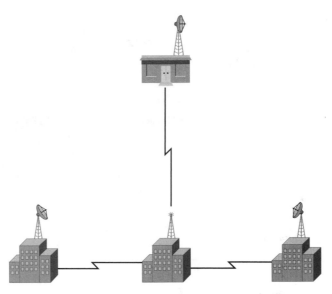

NOTE	The 802.11 specification was intended for wireless *local*-area networks, with the imperative word here being *local*. Because of certain laws in the physics of RF, and certain timing constraints invoked to keep performance at a maximum, the local distance is set for approximately 1000 feet. Although it may work fine at distances beyond this, longer distances are not covered under the 802.11 specification.
	Some devices enable you to alter timing to provide for longer distances by stretching timing parameters, such as ACK wait times and slot times, beyond the specification.

Bridges come in two main architectures or topologies, as follows:

- Point-to-point (PTP)
- Point-to-multipoint (PMP)

PTP systems permit connection between only two points, whereas PMP systems permit a central-site communication to multiple remote sites. Any PMP system will function as a PTP system as well.

Figure 1-9 and Figure 1-10 show the differences between a PTP and PTM system.

Figure 1-9 *Point-to-Point Link*

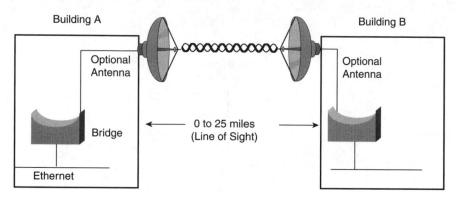

Figure 1-10 *Point-to-Multipoint Link*

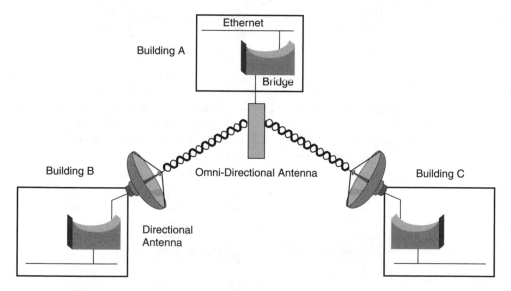

When you are setting up a bridge, many things play an important part. Features that you need to research include available antennas and cables, indoor/outdoor transmitter design, transmitter power, and so on.

Accessories

With any type of networking, there are the main devices, and then there are the accessories that make design and installation possible. The same is true for WLAN systems.

Accessories such as mounting brackets, inline power injectors, lightning arrestors, proper RF cables, and weatherproof enclosures can make the difference between a system that you can just design and one that you can design *and* install. For example, Figure 1-11 shows a mounting bracket for an Oronoco AP1000. Although mounting brackets are not necessarily thought of as technical, a bracket similar to the one shown (with multiple features and mounting options) can make the installation task much simpler.

Figure 1-11 *Access Point Mounting Bracket*

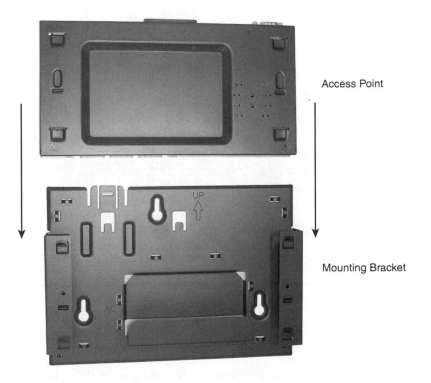

Per the FCC (and most approval agencies), WLAN device antennas must be certified with the particular transmitter. Some vendors offer a wide variety of antennas, whereas others offer only a very limited selection (leaving the feasibility of using certain types of antennas in question).

When using an RF cable on a WLAN system, a significant amount of loss occurs in the cable. To offset this, the cable has to be physically large. In some cases, the connection to the radio may be a PCMCIA card antenna port, limiting the cable size, which can affect performance as well as offer a point of failure.

Utilities that come with the WLAN systems are also a vital part of the product. If you select an AP that lists SNMP support, verify the *Management Information Base* (MIB). A few APs on the market do support SNMP, but the MIB has a total of only four parameters supported.

Some devices provide utilities for measuring RF link quality, verifying status of the devices, and displaying historical data concerning the devices. Some even include site survey tools. Figure 1-12 shows one such utility. The more feature rich your devices, the easier the installation and support.

Figure 1-12 *Site Survey Utility*

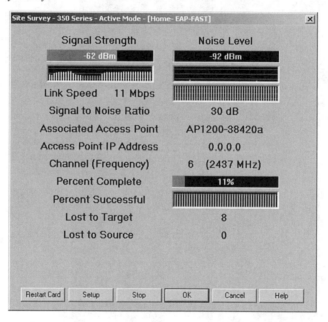

Make certain that the devices you select have an assortment of accessories that enable you to use the device in your situation.

Summary

Before you can start a WLAN design or install a WLAN system, you need a general understanding of WLAN protocols, specifications, and components. This understanding will enable you to make the proper decisions about the technology that you need.

Knowledge of the available WLAN components will enable you to efficiently pick what works for your application and system design. You should also have a good understanding of the differences between available products and what each offers.

At this point, it is time to start thinking about the particulars discussed in this chapter that may affect your initial design. As you progress through this book, you will encounter topics such as RF fundamentals, antennas, and site propagation; these topics provide the foundation for your understanding of the effects of RF in your facility. This book also covers relevant regulations, an understanding of which will assist you in determining whether your initial design will work as desired.

This chapter covers the following topics:

- Understanding RF Components
- Understanding RF Power Values
- Antennas
- Connectors
- Cables
- Understanding RF Site Propagation

CHAPTER 2

Understanding RF Fundamentals

A grasp of the basics of *radio frequency* (RF) helps to form a solid basis for understanding and resolving problems and concerns that can arise when working with WLANs. In this chapter, you will learn the fundamentals of RF. This will include areas that directly affect the design and installation of WLANs such as RF fundamentals, modulation schemes, signal and RF power levels, antenna concepts, data rates versus coverage relationships, and outdoor RF issues.

Understanding RF Components

RF is, by many, still considered black magic. In reality it is no more magic than the electrical current that travels down the wires in your house to light a lamp or sound a doorbell. The one difference is *how* the energy is moved from one location to another.

To efficiently and properly use RF to perform useful work, you need to be aware of various aspects and factors surrounding RF technologies. In most cases, these characteristics are interrelated, and understanding how one characteristic affects another can help in selection of the proper technology and proper installation techniques. Frequency is a characteristic that relates to the physical relationship of the transmitted signal and time, whereas modulation deals with how information is carried on that signal. Signal strength and RF power are parameters that determine the energy level that is being received or transmitted.

Frequency

Back in 1864, the Scottish theoretician James Clerk Maxwell first developed the idea that electromagnetic waves arose as an electric current and changed direction. In the 1880s, Heinrich Hertz used this idea to develop the first RF device that sent and then received electromagnetic waves over the air. This radio was capable of increasing the number or frequency of waves produced in a given period of time and how fast they changed. Based on this discovery, his name became a common unit of measure for frequency, where 1 *hertz* (Hz) means one complete oscillation, or cycle, per second. In radio, *kilohertz* (kHz) means thousands of these waves per second, *megahertz* (MHz) means millions of waves per second, and so on through *gigahertz* (GHz).

These waves are called *sine waves* because of their shape (see Figure 2-1). Sine waves have several properties that make up the information that is carried on them. These properties are known as *amplitude*, *frequency*, and *phase*. The method in which these properties carry the information on a sine wave is known as *modulation*, which significantly affects data output and other key RF attributes.

Figure 2-1 *Sine Wave*

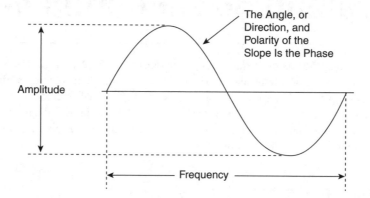

Throughout the years, technology has pushed frequencies higher and higher. The initial WLANs were designed using radios that were converted from voice-type radios (land mobile walkie-talkies) that utilized the 450-MHz range.

With the need for unlicensed spectrum and higher data rates, there was a move to 900 MHz in the late 1980s. Within a few years, the WLAN industry had moved to 2.4 GHz, and in 2000, this was moved even higher with the release of WLAN products in the 5-GHz range. You learn more about the frequency spectrum in Chapter 3, "Regulating the Use of 802.11 WLANs."

Modulation

Modulation is a process by which information signals—analog or digital—are transformed into waveforms suitable for transmission across some medium or channel. For WLANs, the medium or channel is the RF carrier, which has embedded digital information. The RF carrier will have a particular set of frequencies, with some minimum and maximum range. The overall amount of frequency spectrum used by a channel is known as the *RF bandwidth*. Modulation and RF bandwidth are fundamental components of a digital communication system. Modulation can be accomplished by changing the amplitude, frequency, or phase of the carrier in accordance with the incoming bits. These techniques are called *amplitude modulation* (AM), *frequency modulation* (FM), and *phase modulation* (PM), and *orthogonal frequency division modulation* (OFDM).

In some cases, as the modulation is increased (more information is placed on the RF carrier), the RF bandwidth will also increase, consuming more RF spectrum. Figure 2-2 illustrates this phenomenon.

Figure 2-2   *Increasing Bandwidth*

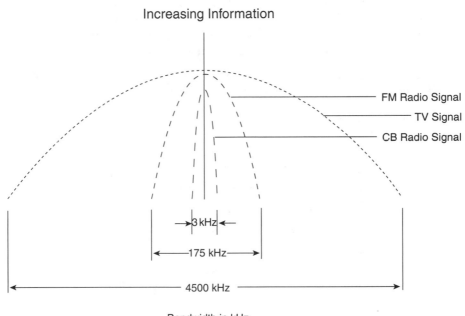

Bandwidth in kHz

There are two basic ways to increase the amount of information that is carried on a RF wave. One is just to use more spectrum. An FM broadcast radio has much better quality (more information) than a CB radio. And a TV transmission includes a picture (again, more information). In each case, they consume more RF spectrum. Because the overall available RF spectrum (and therefore the number of channels) is limited, you soon run out of frequency spectrum to use.

The second method to get more information onto an RF wave is to compress the data. Years ago, a computer modem was able to communicate over your phone lines at 300 baud. Today, a 56-kbps modem gets much higher speeds over the same phone line as the 300-baud modem. This increase in speed results in the modem compressing the data into the same amount of space (or spectrum in the case of RF) and using the same overall bandwidth of the phone line as the 300-baud modem used.

One problem that may arise is that any noise on the phone line will reduce the modem speed. As the data is further compressed, it requires a stronger signal as compared to the noise level. More noise means slower speed for the data to be received correctly.

The same is true in radio. As a receiver moves farther from a transmitter, the signal gets weaker, and the difference between the signal and noise decreases. At some point, the signal cannot be distinguished from the noise, and loss of communication occurs. The amount of compression (or modulation type) at which the signal is transmitted determines the amount of signal needed to be clearly received through the noise.

As transmission or modulation schemes (compression) become more complex and data rates go up, immunity to noise decreases, and coverage goes down (see Figure 2-3).

Figure 2-3   *Compressing Data Reduces Range*

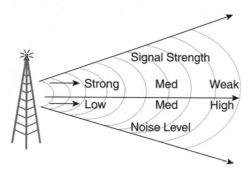

Amplitude Modulation

Amplitude modulation occurs when the output power of the transmitter is varied while the frequency and phase of the sine wave remains constant (see Figure 2-4).

Figure 2-4   *Amplitude Modulation*

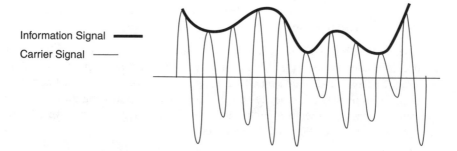

Frequency Modulation

Frequency modulation occurs when the output power and phase remain constant while the frequency is varied over a small range (see Figure 2-5).

Figure 2-5   *Frequency Modulation*

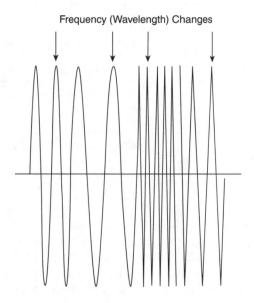

Frequency (Wavelength) Changes

Phase Modulation

Phase modulation occurs when the amplitude and frequency remain constant but the phase within the carrier frequency changes over a small range (see Figure 2-6). A change in phase (polarity or direction of wave travel) is related directly to the digital information comprising the transmitted information.

Figure 2-6   *Phase Modulation*

Phase or Polarity of Wave Changes

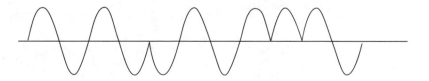

Although you will find many different modulation schemes in use today, this discussion describes only those used in WLANS (see Table 2-1).

Table 2-1   *Modulation Schemes Used in WLANs*

Symbol	Modulation Scheme
CW	Continuous wave (telegraphy)
DSSS	Direct-sequence spread spectrum
FHSS	Frequency-hopping spread spectrum
BPSK	Bipolar Phase Shift Keying
QPSK	Quadrature Phase Shift Keying
CCK	Complementary Code Keying
QAM	Quadrature amplitude modulation
PBCC	Packet Binary Convolutional Coding

Radios following the 2.4-GHz IEEE 802.11b standard use two different types of modulation, depending upon the data rates—BPSK and QPSK. There are two types of codings: Barker code and CCK. Some people count the CCK as a third type of modulation, but it is, in fact, a particular type of coding (converting desired information into a particular digital algorithm), which is applied to a QPSK modulated signal.

The difference between BPSK and QPSK enables twice the information from the same number of cycles (or sine waves), keeping the RF bandwidth identical for twice the overall data rate transmitted.

Binary Phase Shift Keying

BPSK uses one phase to represent a binary 1 and another phase to represent a binary 0 for a total of 2 bits of binary data (see Figure 2-7). BPSK is used to transmit data at 1 Mbps.

Figure 2-7   *BPSK Modulation*

BPSK Modulation

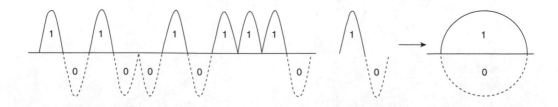

Quadrature Phase Shift Keying

With QPSK, the carrier can have four changes in phase or overall direction of the sine wave movement (increasing positive, decreasing positive, increasing negative, or decreasing negative). When compared to the overall 360 degrees of a circle, this is comparable to the 4 quadrants of 0–90 degrees, 90–180 degrees, 180–270 degrees, or 270–360 degrees. These 4 separate portions of the signal represent 4 binary bits of data (see Figure 2-8). QPSK is used to transmit data at 2 Mbps.

Figure 2-8   *QPSK Modulation*

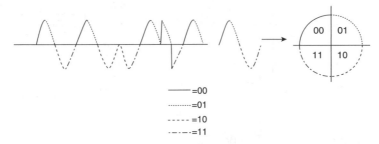

———— =00
·········· =01
----- =10
-·-·-·=11

Polarity and Direction of Slope Define Value

Complementary Code Keying

CCK modulation uses a complex set of functions known as *complementary codes* to send more data. CCK is based on in-phase (I) and quadrature (Q) architecture using complex codes, and replaces the Barker code used at the lower data rates. This provides for higher data rate while maintaining the same required RF bandwidth, as well as providing a path for interoperability with existing IEEE 802.11 lower data rate systems (by maintaining the same RF bandwidth and incorporating the existing physical [PHY] layer structure).

Quadrature Amplitude Modulation

Instead of using the CCK modulation type as specified by 802.11b for higher data rates, 802.11a and 802.11g specify QAM, which encodes via both changes in phase (as is the case with BPSK and QPSK) and changes in amplitude (see Figure 2-9). When encoding a single bit, two possible messages or symbols are possible (0 or 1). When encoding 2 bits, 4 symbols are possible. Working the exponential progression of this, when encoding 4 bits, 16 symbols are possible and when encoding 6 bits, 64 symbols are possible. A 16-QAM encodes 4 bits and provides for either 24-Mbps or 36-Mbps data rates, depending upon the rate of encoding. A 64-QAM encodes 6 bits and provides for either 48-Mbps or 64-Mbps data rates, depending on the rate of encoding. As is the case with 802.11b, increases in data rate are achieved by modulating an increasingly larger number of bits, not by increasing bandwidth. As a greater number of bits are encoded (particularly a greater number of bits than are encoded by 11-Mbps data rate) you can see that the "price" paid for the higher data rates provided by 802.11a and 802.11g is figured in terms of range.

Figure 2-9 *QAM Modulation*

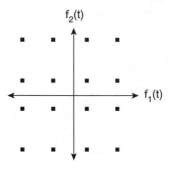

M=2^N	Bits (N)
16-ary	4
32-ary	5
64-ary	6
128-ary	7
256-ary	8

Orthogonal Frequency Division Multiplexing

OFDM is one of the key factors in 802.11a and 802.11g standards. This section briefly describes the key advantages and how it works. In FDM, the available bandwidth is divided into multiple data carriers. The data to be transmitted is then divided between these sub-carriers. Because each carrier is treated independently of the others, a frequency guard band (an area of frequency between each of the carriers) must be placed around it (see Figure 2-10). This guard band lowers the bandwidth efficiency because frequency is not used to carry any useful information. In some FDM systems, up to 50 percent of the available bandwidth is wasted. In most FDM systems, individual users are segmented to a particular subcarrier; therefore, their burst rate cannot exceed the capacity of that subcarrier. If some subcarriers are idle, their bandwidth cannot be shared with other subcarriers.

Figure 2-10 *FDM Discrete Carriers*

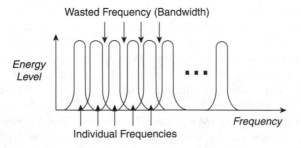

The OFDM spread-spectrum technique spreads the transmitted data over a large number of RF carriers that are spaced apart at particular frequencies. This orthogonal (mutually independent or well-separated) relationship between carriers prevents the receivers demodulators from "hearing" frequencies other than their own.

OFDM carries with it many advantages. As an RF signal is transmitted, it can be reflected by objects in the environment, providing multiple signals to the receiver in varying time frames and signal strengths. This is known as *multipath fading*. Because OFDM is a multiple-carrier system, it has built-in frequency diversity (achieved by using multiple frequencies in parallel), which provides greater immunity to multipath environments. It is very unlikely that two frequencies will reflect (or fade) simultaneously in the same environment, so one of the signals will inevitably be successfully received. OFDM also provides higher data rates and high spectral efficiency (more information in the same amount of frequency spectrum) and helps in fighting a signal's delay spread of a signal, which can limit the data rate.

Combined, these features result in OFDM systems providing better tolerance to noise, interference, and multipath situations, which in turn provides improved range and overall performance (when compared to other modulation schemes for the same frequencies).

Modulation Methods for 802.11 Technologies

The 5-GHz IEEE 802.11a specification and the 2.4-GHz 802.11g specification provide for a variety of data rates (see Table 2-2).

Table 2-2   *Data Rate Versus Modulation Type*

Data Rate in Mbps	Modulation Type	Number of Bits Encoded
6	BPSK	1
9	BPSK	1
12	QPSK	2
18	QPSK	2
24	16-QAM	4
36	16-QAM	4
48	64-QAM	6
54	64-QAM	6

Note that with 802.11a and 802.11g, the BPSK and QPSK modulation types used for 802.11 are again employed, encoding 1 and 2 bits respectively. Note, however, that with 802.11a and 802.11g, when using BPSK modulation, the data rate achieved is not 1 Mbps, as is the case with 802.11b, but rather 6 Mbps or 9 Mbps (depending upon the rate at which the encoding takes place). The difference between a 1-Mbps and 6-Mbps data rate is attributed to the greater efficiency of OFDM relative to DSSS. Similarly, with 802.11a and 802.11g, QPSK modulation yields not the 2-Mbps data rate, as is the case with 802.11b, but rather 12 Mbps or 18 Mbps when transmitting via OFDM, as specified by 802.11a and 802.11g.

Signal Strength

Another characteristic that needs to be discussed is the signal strength of an RF signal. Signal strength can be thought of as the volume of a signal. As an RF signal travels, it interacts with its surroundings (air molecules, walls, moisture, and so on) and loses some of its energy. The receiving device has a lower limit, called a *receive threshold*, that defines the amount of energy needed to receive the signal and be able to read the information that it contains.

If a signal strength is lower than the receive threshold, the information contained in the signal cannot be properly decoded and is useless. Maintaining a certain level of signal strength above the receiver threshold is desirable. The actual amount of signal strength recommended for a good communication link is discussed in Chapter 12, "Installing WLAN Products," and depends on frequency, modulation schemes, and data rates.

When deciding on a WLAN product, it is a good idea to also review the receiver performance as well as the transmitter. Sensitivity, adjacent-channel rejection, and spread delay are a few of the parameters that vary among receivers. A good receiver can improve coverage by a significant amount.

Understanding RF Power Values

RF signals are subject to various losses and gains as they pass from a transmitter through the cable to its antenna, then through the air (and other obstructions such as walls and doors), to the receiving antenna, through that cable, and finally to the receiving radio. With the exception of the walls and other obstructions, most of these signal-loss factors are known and can be used in the design process to determine whether an RF system such as a WLAN will work. To understand how to evaluate systems, a good understanding of how RF parameters are measured is important. The following sections discuss measurement values such as decibels and RF power, as well as antennas, cables, and RF propagation in a WLAN environment.

Decibels

The *decibel* (dB) scale is a logarithmic scale used to denote the ratio of one power value to another:

$$dB = 10 \log_{10}(\text{Power A} / \text{Power B})$$

An increase of 3 dB indicates a doubling (2×) of power. An increase of 6 dB indicates a quadrupling (4×) of power. Conversely, a decrease of 3 dB is a halving (1/2) of power, and a decrease of 6 dB is a quarter (1/4) the power. Table 2-3 shows some examples.

Table 2-3   *Decibel Values and Corresponding Factors*

Increase	Factor	Decrease	Factor
0 dB	1× (same)	0 dB	1× (same)
1 dB	1.25×	−1 dB	0.8×
3 dB	2×	−3 dB	0.5×
6 dB	4×	−6 dB	0.25×
10 dB	10×	−10 dB	0.10×
12 dB	16×	−12 dB	0.06×
20 dB	100×	−20 dB	0.01×
30 dB	1000×	−30 dB	0.001×
40 dB	10,000×	−40 dB	0.0001×

Power Ratings

The transmitter power rating of most WLAN equipment is usually specified in decibels compared to known values such as mW or watts.

Transmit power and receive sensitivity are specified in dBm, where *m* means 1 *milliWatt* (mW). A value of 0 dBm is equal to 1 mW. From there you can use the previously mentioned 3-dB rule and calculate that 3 dBm is equal to 2 mW, 6 dBm is equal to 4 mW, and so on. For example, a radio with a rating of 100-mW transmit power is equal to a radio specified at 20-dBm transmit power.

Common mW values to dBm values are shown in Table 2-4.

Table 2-4   *Common mW to dBm Values (Approximate)*

dBm	mW	dBm	mW
0 dBm	1 mW	0 dBm	1 mW
1 dBm	1.25 mW	–1 dBm	0.8 mW
3 dBm	2 mW	–3 dBm	0.5 mW
6 dBm	4 mW	–6 dBm	0.25 mW
7 dBm	5 mW	–7 dBm	0.20 mW
10 dBm	10 mW	–10 dBm	0.10 mW
12 dBm	16 mW	–12 dBm	0.06 mW
13 dBm	20 mW	–13 dBm	0.05 mW
15 dBm	32 mW	–15 dBm	0.03 mW
17 dBm	50 mW	–17 dBm	0.02 mw
20 dBm	100 mW	–20 dBm	0.01 mW
30 dBm	1000 mW (1 W)	–30 dBm	0.001 mW
40 dBm	10,000 mW (10 W)	–40 dBm	0.0001 mW

Antennas

The proper use of antennas can improve the performance of a WLAN dramatically. In fact, antennas are probably the single easiest way to refine the performance of a WLAN. But it is important to have an understanding of the basics of antenna theory, as well as the various types that are available for use in WLANs.

All antennas have the three fundamental properties:

- **Gain**—A measure of increase in power
- **Direction**—The shape of the transmission pattern
- **Polarization**—The angle at which the energy is emitted into the air

All three of these properties are discussed in detail in the following sections.

Gain

Gain is the amount of increase in energy that an antenna *appears* to add to an RF signal. There are different methods for measuring gain, depending on the reference point chosen.

Basic antenna gain is rated in comparison to isotropic or dipole antennas. An *isotropic antenna* is a theoretical antenna with a uniform three-dimensional radiation pattern (similar to a light bulb with no reflector). The dBi rating is used to compare the power level of a given antenna to the theoretical isotropic antenna (hence the use of the *i* in dBi). The FCC, as well as many other regulatory bodies, use dBi for defining power levels in the rules and regulations covering WLAN antennas. Most mathematical calculations that include antennas and path loss also use the dBi rating. An isotropic antenna is said to have a power rating of 0 dBi (that is, zero gain/loss when compared to itself).

Unlike isotropic antennas, *dipole antennas* are physical antennas that are standard on many WLAN products. Dipole antennas have a different radiation pattern when compared to an isotropic antenna. The dipole radiation pattern is 360 degrees in the horizontal plane and usually about 75 degrees in the vertical plane (assuming the dipole antenna is standing vertically) and resembles a bowtie in shape (see Figure 2-11). Because the beam is *slightly* concentrated, dipole antennas have a gain over isotropic antennas in the horizontal plane. Dipole antennas are said to have a gain of 2.14 dBi (in comparison to an isotropic antenna).

Figure 2-11 *Dipole Radiation Pattern*

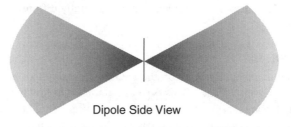

Dipole Side View

Some antennas are rated in comparison to dipole antennas. This is denoted by the suffix dBd. Hence, dipole antennas have a gain of 0 dBd (0 dBd = 2.14 dBi).

NOTE   Note that many WLAN vendors' documentation refers to dipole antennas as having a gain of 2.2 dBi. The actual figure is 2.14 dBi, but is often rounded up.

To ensure a common understanding, many WLAN vendors have standardized on dBi (which is gain using a theoretical isotropic antenna as a reference point) to specify gain measurements. However, some antenna vendors still rate their products in dBd, instead of dBi, as the reference point. To convert any number from dBd to dBi, just add 2.14 to the dBd number. For instance a 3-dBd antenna would have a rating of 5.14 dBi (or rounded up to 5.2 dBi).

Directional Properties

Any antenna, except for an isotropic antenna (theoretical perfect antenna that radiates equally in all directions), has some sort of radiation pattern. That means that it radiates energy in certain directions more than others. A good analogy for antenna directionality is that of a reflector in a flashlight. The reflector concentrates and intensifies the light beam in a particular direction. This is very similar to what a dish antenna does to an RF signal.

In RF, you usually have to give up one thing to gain something else. In antenna gain, this comes in the form of coverage area or what is known as *beamwidth*. As the gain of an antenna goes up, the beamwidth (usually) goes down.

An isotropic antenna's coverage can be thought of as a perfect round balloon. It extends in all directions equally. The size of the balloon represents the amount of RF energy that the transmitter is sending to the antennas, and the antenna is converting the energy to radiated RF energy. As you learn about other antenna types, you will see that the overall energy radiated from the antenna is not increased, it is just redirected. As was the case with the dipole antenna discussed earlier in this chapter, this perfect round balloon of energy that an isotropic antenna provides becomes something totally different in shape.

Omni-Directional Antennas

An omni antenna is designed to provide a 360-degree radiation pattern (on one plane, usually the horizontal plane). This type of antenna is used when coverage in all directions surrounding the antennas on that one plane is required. The standard 2.14-dBi Rubber Duck is one of the most common omni antennas. When an omni antenna is designed to have higher gain, it results in loss of coverage in certain areas.

Imagine again, the balloon of energy for an isotropic antenna, which extends from the antenna equally in all directions. Now imagine pressing in on the top and bottom of the balloon. This causes the balloon to expand in an outward direction, covering more area in the horizontal pattern, but reducing the coverage area above and below the antenna. This yields a higher gain, as the antenna *appears* to extend to a larger coverage area. The higher the gain on an antenna means the smaller the vertical beamwidth.

If you continue to push in on the ends of the balloon, it results in a pancake effect with very narrow vertical beamwidth, but very large horizontal coverage (see Figure 2-12). This type of antenna design can deliver very long communications distances, but has one drawback: poor coverage below the antenna.

Figure 2-12 *High Gain Omni-Directional Radiation Pattern*

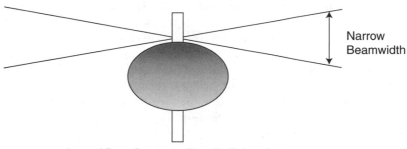

Narrow
Beamwidth

Area of Poor Coverage Directly Below Antenna

In some cases, the gain of an antenna can be high enough and the radiation patterns so small, that even small motions of the antenna (from wind, for instance) can cause the signal to move away from the intended target and lose communication. For this reason, extremely high-gain antennas are typically mounted to a very strong and permanent structure and almost never used in a mobile or portable environment.

With high-gain omni antennas, this problem can be partially solved by designing in something called *downtilt*. An antenna that uses downtilt is designed to radiate at a slight angle rather that at 90 degrees from the vertical element. Downtilt helps for local coverage, but reduces effectiveness of the long-range capability (see Figure 2-13). Cellular antennas use downtilt.

Figure 2-13 *Antenna Downtilt*

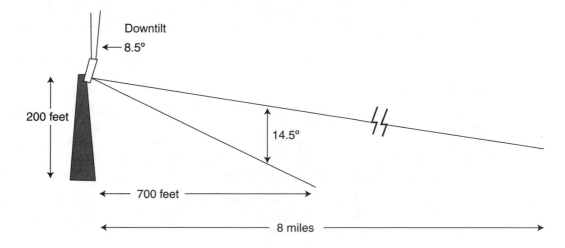

Downtilt
← 8.5°

200 feet

14.5°

700 feet

8 miles

Directional Antennas

Directional antennas can be used to provide farther range in certain directions and to isolate the radios for other signals. You can choose from a wide assortment of available directional antennas, from short-range wide-coverage areas to very focused and narrow coverage areas. As stated earlier, an antenna does not add any additional power to the signal; instead, it redirects energy from one direction and focuses energy in a particular direction. This results in more energy on certain directions and less energy radiating on other directions. As the gain of a directional antenna increases, the overall coverage area usually decreases. Common form factors for WLAN directional antennas include dish antennas, patch antennas, and Yagi antennas.

Consider the common Mag-Lite flashlight (one of the adjustable-beam-focus flashlights). There are only two batteries, and the one light bulb, but the intensity and width of the light beam can be changed. Moving the back reflector and directing the light in tighter or wider angles accomplishes this. As the beam gets wider, the intensity in the center decreases, and it travels a shorter distance. The same is true of a directional antenna. The same power is reaching the antenna, but by building it in certain ways, the RF energy can be directed in tighter and stronger waves, or wider and less-intense waves, just as with the flashlight.

Polarization

Two planes are used in RF radiations: the E and the H plane. The E plane (electric field) defines the orientation of the radio waves as they are radiated from the antenna. If the E is perpendicular to the Earth's surface, it is referred to as *vertically polarized*. In WLAN systems, for instance, an omni-directional antenna is usually a vertically polarized antenna.

Horizontally polarized (linear) antennas have their electric field parallel to the Earth's surface. WLANs seldom use horizontally polarized antennas, except in certain outdoor, point-to-point systems.

Antenna Examples

You can choose from a wide variety of antennas for use with WLAN equipment. The use of different antennas can simplify the installation of a WLAN system, and in some cases reduce the overall cost of the system. A thorough understanding of different antenna types available will enable the survey engineer and installer to provide a WLAN that not only provides adequate coverage but also helps to stay within budgetary constraints.

Appendix B, "Antenna Radiation Patterns," provides an assortment of WLAN antennas and the associated polar plots. The polar plot is the common method to define an antenna's beamwidth, or radiation pattern, and gain factors.

Patch Antenna

A patch antenna is typically small and somewhat flat and is usually designed to mount against a wall or on a small bracket. It has a beamwidth that is less than 180 degrees, and is sometimes referred to as a *hemispherical antenna*.

Panel Antenna

A panel antenna (sometimes also referred to as a *sectorized antenna*) is similar to a patch antenna, but is generally a higher gain and physically larger. Many times a panel antenna has an adjustable back reflector that can be used to change the beamwidth as well as mounting brackets that can be adjusted for downtilt.

Panel antennas are usually used outdoors and can have gains ranging from as little as 5 dBi to more than 20 dBi. They can be used as a single antenna or in multiples to cover a larger area.

Yagi Antenna

A Yagi antenna has a series of small elements, referred to as *reflectors* or *directors*, and an active element. These are placed in a straight line and direct the energy in a given direction. Generally Yagi antennas have fairly high gain. The more reflectors and directors a Yagi has, the higher the gain. Due to the short wavelength for frequencies used in WLAN systems, the elements are fairly small, and most Yagis used for 2.4-GHz or 5-GHz contain some type of cover to protect the antenna's components from the weather and to provide more structural strength. Yagi antennas can range in gain from as low as 5 dBi to as high as 17 dBi or more.

Dish Antennas

There are really two main types of dish antennas: the parabolic and the grid dish. The parabolic dish contains a reflector that is solid in construction, and a driven or active element supported in the center of the reflector. These are similar to what you would find for a standard satellite TV dish antenna, except the placement of the active element is typically centralized on the WLAN antenna.

The grid dish antenna is very similar to the parabolic antenna, except the reflector is not solid. It is made of a grid-type structure to permit wind and rain to flow through it. This provides less wind resistance and therefore requires a smaller mounting structure. Chapter 14, "Outdoor Bridge Deployments," provides more information about outdoor mounting.

Diversity

Diversity antenna systems are used to overcoming a phenomenon known as *multipath distortion* or *multipath fading*. It uses two identical antennas, located a small distance apart, to provide coverage to the same physical area.

To understand diversity, it is important to give you an overview of multipath distortion as well as an understanding of how this can occur. Multipath distortion is a form of RF interference that can occur when a radio signal has more then one path between the transmitting antenna and the receiving antennas. Environments with a high probability of multipath interference include such places as airport hangars, steel mills, manufacturing areas, distribution centers, and other locations where the antenna is exposed to metal walls, ceilings, racks, shelving, or other metallic items that reflect radio signals and create this multipath condition (see Figure 2-14).

Figure 2-14 *Multiple Signal Paths*

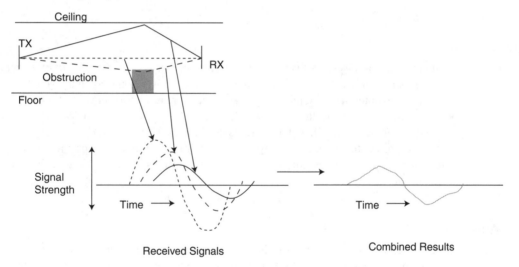

When an antenna transmits, it radiates RF energy in more than one definite direction. This causes RF to move between the transmitting and receiving antenna in the most direct (desired) path while reflecting or bouncing off metallic and other RF-reflective surfaces. The process of reflecting the RF waves causes several things to occur. First, the reflected RF waves traveled farther than the desired direct RF wave. This means the reflected waves will get to the receiving antenna later in time. Second, because of the longer transmission route, the reflected signal loses more RF energy while traveling than the direct route signal. Third, the signal will lose some energy as a result of the reflection or bounce. In the end, the desired wave, along with many reflective waves, are combined in the receiver. As these different waveforms combine, they cause distortion to the desired waveform and can affect receiver-decoding capability.

When these reflected signals are combined at the receiver, although RF energy (signal strength) may be high, the data would be unrecoverable. Changing the location of the antenna can change these reflections and diminish the chance of multipath interference. You have likely encountered multipath distortion with common products such as televisions and radios. For example, when an indoor antenna is used on a television set, it is possible to see images of the same picture slightly offset or distorted. This ghost, or fuzzy picture, is the result of the transmitted television signal reflecting off metal items in the home such as a refrigerator or a filing cabinet. You can usually fix this multipath interference just by adjusting or moving the antenna. Because an *access point* (AP) can't physically move its antenna, many have been designed with two antenna ports. The radio performs an assessment of each antenna port and selects to use the antenna with the best reception.

Another example of multipath interference occurs while listening to the radio when driving an automobile. As you pull up to a stop sign, the radio station might appear distorted, or you may even lose the signal altogether as a result of a radio null, which is also referred to as a *dead spot*. As you move the car forward a few inches or feet, the radio reception starts to come in clearer. As you move the vehicle, you are actually moving the antenna slightly, out of the point where the multiple signals converge. In all probability, the radio signal was reflecting off another vehicle or metal object nearby.

In some cases, if signals are received in equal strength, yet delayed in such a manner that they are opposite in polarity, they will actually cancel each other out completely, creating a total absence of received signal by the receiver. This is known as a *multipath null*.

Many do not understand the method of how a diversity antenna system works, and this lack of understanding often leads to confusion and improper installation. The diversity antenna system includes two antennas that are connected to an RF switch, which in turn connects to the receiver (see Figure 2-15). The receiver actually switches between antennas on a regular basis as it listens for a valid signal.

Figure 2-15 *Diversity Antenna Switch*

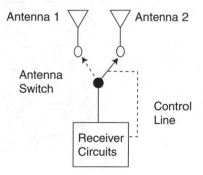

Theoretical View of Diversity Antenna Switch

Note that this switching occurs extremely fast. The AP samples part of the radio header and determines and utilizes the best antenna to receive the client's data and then uses that very same antenna when transmitting back to the client. If the client doesn't respond, the AP will then try sending the data out the other antenna port.

Improper Diversity Deployment Example

A golf course with an electronic scoring application used an AP with an outdoor antenna to cover the front nine holes of the golf course. Originally the AP was placed in the clubhouse, and one outdoor antenna was used to cover the front nine of the course. Because there was little multipath interference (few things outside to reflect the radio signal), one antenna was sufficient and communication seemed to be fine. In this case, the customer had used a directional Yagi antenna. This antenna was chosen for its distance characteristics and ease of installation.

Later it was determined that coverage was needed on the back nine of the golf course as well. Instead of adding another AP, the customer decided just to connect another directional Yagi antenna to the other antenna port and point it off in another direction (the back nine), as shown in Figure 2-16. While driving around in the golf cart, performing a survey, the customer had no issues with coverage.

Figure 2-16 *Improper Diversity Installation*

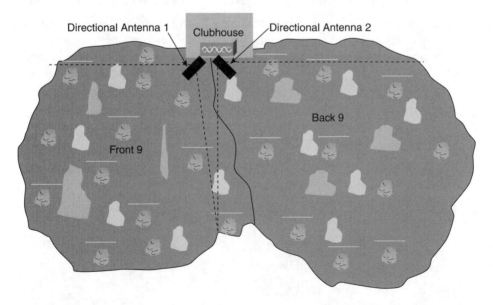

But as the tournament started and many users were added, they encountered difficulty. When the first users (clients on the front nine of the course) registered to the AP, the AP sampled both antennas (one at a time) and selected the antenna pointing to the front section.

When users started migrating to the back nine, and more users entered the front nine, problems started popping up. As the AP was communicating to the users on the front section of the course users on the back section could not hear that RF traffic because the back-nine antenna was being used at that instant. Therefore, the back users tried to send their own traffic, which was not heard by the AP.

In the case of the golf course, two methods could resolve this problem. One method is to replace the directional Yagi antenna with a similar-gain omni antenna. The AP's radio would then be able to work in all directions rather than the limited directional pattern of the Yagi.

Another method is to add an AP to cover the other radio cell. This way both APs could properly handle the RF traffic, and each AP could use the higher-gain Yagi antenna to cover each area.

Connectors

To prevent improper usage of antennas that can create interference or violate the U.S. regulations, the FCC added a regulation requiring connectors used on WLAN equipment manufactured after June 1994 to be of a "unique and non-standard" format. Canada followed suit with a similar regulation. Most WLAN vendors such as Cisco worked with connector companies to produce connectors that, while maintaining a quality 50-ohm low-loss connection, met this regulation. Several companies started using a version of the popular TNC (*threaded Neill-Concelman*) connector that has a center conductor component reversed between the plug and jack of a regular TNC connector. This is known as a *reverse-polarity TNC* (RP-TNC). Although they are similar to the standard TNC connectors, they cannot be mated with a standard connector. Therefore, you need to verify that all components you are purchasing (antennas, cables, and so on) are supplied with the same connector format.

Cables

The antenna should be mounted at a location that utilizes its radiation pattern to maximum performance for the users. In some cases, this is not an ideal location to mount the AP. Therefore, it is sometimes desired to separate the antenna from the AP or radio device. This can be due to the necessity to mount the antenna outdoors and keep the AP indoors, or to mount the AP in the ceiling and mount the antenna below the ceiling. Sometimes customers may even want to keep the AP in a wiring closet and place the antenna out in the user area.

Although this seems like a trivial matter, it really is not. As stated earlier in the section "Understanding RF Power Values," cabling introduces losses into the system, lowering signal level from the transmitter to the antenna, as well as reducing the signal level moving from the antenna to the receiver. In both cases, this has a dramatic effect on the RF coverage area.

Cable designed carrying RF for WLAN is a coaxial cable and must be selected to match the impedance of the transmitter and antenna. Virtually all WLAN systems utilize 50-ohm antenna system impedance, and the cable selected must match this value.

A wave traveling down either a wire or in the open air has a distinctive physical characteristic to it: its length. One relationship that occurs in RF is that as the oscillations or frequency of a wave becomes faster, the overall length of the associated wave (called *wavelength*) becomes shorter.

As frequencies of signals change, they are affected differently by the surroundings. In a wire, as electrons travel down the conductor, they have opposition called *resistance*. As the frequency of that electrical signal increases, the electrons in the wire are moving faster and faster. They tend to move toward the surface of the conductor, which is called *skin effect*. This actually increases the resistance to electron travel (because they use only the skin, or outside portion, of the cable), and therefore reduces the amount of energy reaching the end of the wire. To offset this skin effect, many coax cables, designed for microwave frequencies and higher use cables of significant physical diameter, for lower loss.

Many cable types appropriate for WLAN environments are available today. Table 2-5 shows some of the typical type cables that can be used and the values of attenuation (energy losses) that are associated with these cables.

Table 2-5   *Typical WLAN Cable Attenuation Values*

Cable Number	Size (Inches)	Attenuation/100 Ft.	
		2.4 GHz	5.8 GHz
LMR400	0.405	6.8	10.8
LMR600	0.5	5.48	8.9
LMR900	0.87	2.98	4.9

Information from *Times Microwave*

Understanding RF Site Propagation

As RF waves travel through the air, they also have resistance or opposition to movement known as *path loss*. As the frequency changes, so does the wavelength. These are inversely proportional and can actually be measured by the following formula:

Wavelength (meters) = 300 / Frequency in MHz

As the frequency increases into the *ultrahigh frequency* (UHF) range and then into micro-wave frequencies (which are used for WLANs), the opposition offered by the atmosphere increases, which in turn reduces the energy being transferred. The end result is shorter radio range. This is the main reason that a 5-GHz WLAN signal utilizing the same transmitter power and antenna gain as a 2.4-GHz WLAN has less range.

As you progress through this book, you will learn about many issues that you should consider before the site survey portion of the WLAN project can begin. One such parameter is the frequency that will be used. Another factor that you need to determine is the minimum acceptable data rate for the users. Both of these parameters will affect the site survey and overall coverage capabilities.

Frequency Versus Coverage

Naturally, transmission range is an important consideration when judging wireless technology. With all other things being equal, as frequency increases, range decreases. First of all, the higher the frequency, the shorter the wavelength of the signal. The shorter the wavelength, the higher the attenuation caused by the atmosphere. Second, higher-frequency waves are more vulnerable to absorption by building materials, such as drywall and concrete. Other factors come into play as well, such as antenna selection, modulation schemes, data rates, transmitter power, and receiver sensitivity.

Material Absorption, Reflection, and Refraction

Other factors that drastically affect the range include signal absorption, signal reflection, and signal refraction. Many materials actually absorb RF energy. At 2.4 GHz, material that contains a high level of moisture (such as bulk paper and cardboard) absorbs the signal. Facilities that contain a significant number of metal objects (such as a steel warehouse) experience reflections that can either assist or hinder coverage based on the multipath created.

Many times, materials are totally out of your sight and beyond your knowledge, such as steel reinforcement in the concrete walls and flooring, certain types of tinting on windows that contain metal properties, or even some types of insulations used in walls. The only true way to discover how the material in a facility will affect the signal and coverage is to perform a site survey, which you learn more about in Part III, "Installing WLAN Components," of this book.

Reflection

Reflection is the signal bouncing back in the general direction from which it came. Consider a smooth metallic surface as an interface. As RF hits this surface, much of its energy is bounced or reflected.

Radio waves also reflect when entering different media. Radio waves can bounce off of different layers of the atmosphere. The reflecting properties of the area where the WLAN is to be installed are extremely important and can determine whether a WLAN works or fails. Furthermore, the connectors at both ends of the transmission line going to the antenna should be properly designed and installed so that no reflection of radio waves takes place. If the line and connectors are not properly matched, some energy will be thrown back as an echo and will constitute a loss in power from the system.

Signal Strength, Noise, and Signal-to-Noise Ratio

When performing a site survey, you will want to be concerned with several items to determine whether you have adequate coverage. Three of these things are signal strength, noise level, and the signal-to-noise ratio.

Signal strength, as defined earlier, is the value of the signal (usually expressed in dBm for receiver levels in WLAN systems) that is getting to the receiver. Most receivers have some method of displaying this value. Whereas some products only provide a level in general terms (percentage, or possibly good, fair, or poor), some actually provide a reading in dBm. It is important to understand and define the minimum signal strength that you want for your particular application, data rates, and radio devices being used. You will read more about this topic later in Part III of this book.

Ambient RF noise, referred to as the *noise floor*, occurs in the atmosphere. As you continue to add electronic devices to your environment (even computers now have bus speeds that run in the GHz range and give off unwanted RF signals), you will gradually increase the ambient RF noise levels. To properly receive a signal, the desired signal must have a signal strength greater than the noise floor by a defined amount, which will vary from one receiver type to another and from one data rate to another.

The *signal-to-noise ratio* (SNR) can be compared to trying to listen to another person speak in a noisy environment. Based on the surrounding noise, the speaker will have to raise his voice to a level that is strong enough to be heard over the other surrounding noise. This would be the signal-to-noise ratio. SNR is just that, a ratio between the desired signal (signal strength) and the ambient RF noise (noise floor). It is expressed in dB, and the required SNR will vary based on modulation, data rate, and quality of the receiver.

Figure 2-17 shows an output screen from a WLAN device showing signal strength, noise floor, and SNR.

Figure 2-17 *SNR Example*

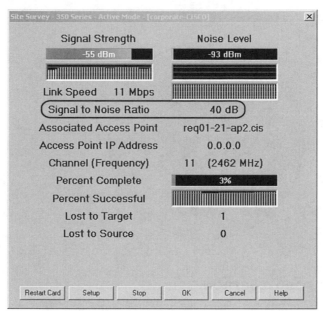

Coverage Versus Bandwidth

APs offer clients multiple data rates for the wireless link. For 802.11b, the range is from 1 to 11 Mbps in four increments: 1, 2, 5.5, and 11 Mbps. The 802.11a range is 6 to 54 Mbps in eight increments: 6, 9, 12, 18, 24, 36, 48, and 54 Mbps. 802.11g products include all of these rates. (It is backward compatible to 802.11b, but more on this in Chapter 4, "WLAN Applications and Services.") Because data rates affect range, selecting data rates during the design stage is extremely important. The client cards will automatically switch to the fastest possible rate of the AP; how this is done varies from vendor to vendor.

Because each data rate has a unique cell of coverage (the higher the data rate, the smaller the cell), the minimum data rate must be determined at the design stage. Cell sizes at given data rate can be thought of as concentric circles with higher data-rate circles nested within the coverage area of the immediately higher data rate. Selecting only the highest data rate will require a greater number of APs to cover a given area; therefore, care must be taken to develop a compromise between required aggregate data rate and overall system cost.

An example of data rate versus range is shown in Figure 2-18.

Figure 2-18 *Data Rate Versus Range*

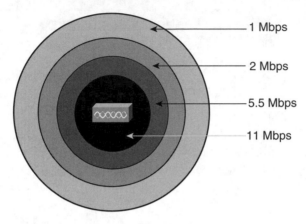

Modulation Versus Coverage

Another factor that can affect range and coverage is the modulation scheme. Certain modulation schemes such as OFDM have better performance in certain areas. Take a highly reflective environment, for instance, where there is a lot of multipath signal interference. OFDM offers a better performance in this type of environment due to its multicarrier format.

Under the 802.11 specifications, modulation techniques are defined and related to data rates. Therefore, a site survey should be done using the data rates intended for use in the specific environment.

Outdoor RF Issues

When using WLAN systems in an outdoor environment, many other factors come into play. Most WLAN devices are not geared to mount directly outdoors. Therefore, either a weatherproof enclosure must be used, or the AP will be placed indoors (and a cable will be used to attach the antenna). As stated earlier in this chapter, the use of cables can dramatically reduce the available power reaching the antenna and can affect overall ranges.

Another factor to consider with outdoor installations is lightning. Because you are now placing conductors outside, there is the possibility that the system may be exposed to lightning. Chapter 14 discusses lightning protection for both the antennas and the network.

Propagation and Losses

Outdoor RF links have different propagation characteristics than those indoors. Calculations can provide accurate information on possible performance and distance. The following are included in calculations for determining outdoor coverage performance:

- Antenna gain
- Transmitter power
- Receiver performance
- Cable losses
- Environmental structures

All of these parameters are known *values* and are easily determined. However, environmental structures, such as buildings, trees, and so on, and basically anything in the line of sight between one antenna and the other, can cause major issues for outdoor RF links. For long-distance communications using WLAN frequencies, a line of sight between the antennas is necessary to maintain quality RF links (see Figure 2-19).

Figure 2-19 *Line of Sight*

Earth Bulge and Fresnel Zone

Two other factors that affect outdoor links are the Fresnel zone and Earth bulge. Wireless links that carry data over long distances require additional care to ensure proper clearance. Christopher Columbus sailed the Atlantic Ocean and taught us that the world is not flat, but rather that the Earth has a curvature at the approximate rate of 12 feet for every 18 miles. It is important to make sure your antennas have proper height to maintain line of sight.

While observing these calculations, it's important to remember that this accounts only for Earth bulge. You must add the elevation of other objects (such as buildings, trees, hills, and so on) into this formula.

Another factor to consider at long distances is the Fresnel zone (pronounced "frennel"), which is an elliptical area immediately surrounding the visual path (see Figure 2-20). It varies depending on the length of the signal path and the frequency of the signal. The Fresnel zone can be calculated, and it must be taken into account when designing a wireless link. If the Fresnel zone is obstructed, required line of sight is not clear and the link may be unreliable.

Figure 2-20 *Fresnel Zone*

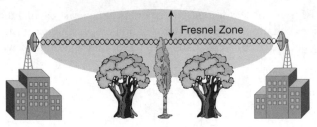

The industry standard is to keep 60 percent of the first Fresnel zone clear from obstacles. Therefore, the result of this calculation can be reduced by up to 60 percent without appreciable interference. This calculation should be considered as a reference only and does not account for the phenomenon of refraction from highly reflective surfaces.

Chapter 14 covers this topic in more detail when outdoor RF links are covered in depth.

Summary

As always, obtaining a good understanding of the technology that drives a system is helpful if you intend to do more than just use the system. To properly select components, design, install, utilize, and troubleshot a WLAN, a basic understanding of RF technologies and associated topics is important. Starting with this understanding, you can make educated decisions about which technology will work best for you, what products fill the needs, and how they will react in your environment.

Next you will learn about the regulations that surround WLANs, and then finally move on to selecting the proper WLAN architecture and components for your system.

This chapter covers the following topics:

- Early Spread-Spectrum Regulations
- RF Regulatory Domains
- WLAN Frequencies of Operation
- Dynamic Frequency Selection and Transmitter Power Control with 801.11h
- Regulatory Channel Selections
- Maximum Transmitter Power Levels
- Amplifiers
- Antenna Connectors and Remote Antennas
- Health and Safety
- Plenum Locations

CHAPTER 3

Regulating the Use of 802.11 WLANs

802.11 WLAN devices are typically certified and used in an unlicensed mode of operation, meaning they do not require an operator's license or station license to be put into use. However, unlicensed does not mean unregulated. In fact, with levels that vary on a country-by-country basis, 802.11 WLAN operation is subject to a variety of regulations that impact range, scalability, portability, and a host of other factors that affect the overall usability of WLANs.

In 1985, the United States *Federal Communications Commission* (FCC) enacted standards for the commercial use of spread-spectrum technology in the *Industrial, Scientific and Medical* (ISM) frequency bands. These bands included 900-MHz, 2.4-GHz, and 5-GHz areas. Shortly thereafter, the Canadian regulatory body, *Industry Canada* (IC; once called the *Department of Communication*, or DoC) followed suit, and many other countries started to enact regulations surrounding spread spectrum and the use of these frequency bands for commercial applications. Today many countries permit the use of WLANs in at least some of these bands; however, regulations vary from country to country; therefore, is important to review, understand, and abide by the regulations covering the country of installation.

Most countries set limitations covering areas of frequency use, transmitter power, antenna gain, *Effective Isotropic Radiated Power* (EIRP) limits, modulation techniques, and other criteria related to radio transmissions.

Other regulations also affect WLAN usage, besides those set forth by the authorities governing the RF frequencies and transmitters. Some regulations relate to the absorption of RF by the human body, other regulations relate to usage in health-care and hospital facilities, and still others relate to installation locations. This chapter covers many of these regulations that can impact your WLAN project.

Early Spread-Spectrum Regulations

Prior to 1985, the use of spread-spectrum modulation was not permitted in the United States (and most countries) for commercial communication. Its use was limited mainly to experimental and military use. In 1985, the FCC changed Part 15 of the Code of Federal Regulations to permit the use of spread-spectrum modulation in certain ISM bands. The FCC rules tend to discourage use of amplifiers, high-gain antennas, and other means of increasing RF radiation significantly. The rules are further intended to discourage systems that are installed by inexperienced users and that either intentionally or unintentionally do not comply with FCC regulations for use in the ISM band. The rationale behind the strict regulations is to enable multiple RF networks to coexist with minimum impact on one another by exploiting the properties of spread-spectrum technology.

Basically, these rules seek to limit RF communications in the ISM band to a well-defined region (that is, wireless *local*-area network), while ensuring multiple systems can operate with minimum impact on one another. These two needs are addressed by limiting the transmitter power and the type and gain of antennas used with a given system, and by requiring a greater degree of RF energy efficiency or *spreading*.

The IC followed the FCC rules very closely, and in many cases adopted the FCC regulations on a word-for-word basis. The rest of the world soon followed suit, enacting regulations to govern the growing number of WLAN products. You will read more about these regulations throughout this chapter.

Intentional Versus Unintentional Radiators

In the discussion of the regulations throughout this chapter, a distinction is made between intentional and unintentional radiators. A spread-spectrum transmitter is designed to send out (or emit) an RF signal. This (or any radio transmitter for that matter) is known as an *intentional radiator*. Intentional radiators emit signals that are wanted (or intended for emission).

Although this chapter focuses on the intentional emissions of 802.11 transmitting devices—in other words, the radio energy produced to transmit information—certain regulations refer to unintentional radiators. Practically any electronic device also emits unintentional RF emissions of some level of energy that can impact the operation of other devices. *Unintentional radiators* are devices that emit radio signals typically not designed for transmission. (These are, in most cases, unwanted signals.)

These unintentional radiations are also subject to regulation. In the FCC regulatory domain, the level of unintentional emissions falls into two general categories: Class A or Class B. The FCC Class A device allows for a higher emission amount, and regulations of this class apply to devices designed for operation in industrial, office, and similar commercial environments. The FCC Class B device must meet a more stringent standard that applies to operation in residential environments and commercial environments representing a superset of the two.

A similar set of dual standards exists in the *European Telecommunication Standards Institute* (ETSI) domain, which falls under the *Conférence Européene des Administrations des Postes et des Télécommunications Administrations* (translated to European Conference of Postal and Telecommunications [CEPT]). The document #EN-55022 describes these standards. ETSI follows similar naming conventions in that it has a Class A for commercial use and a Class B for residential operation, although the classes do not identically match the FCC Class A and Class B in terms of emission allowances.

A common benefit of 802.11 is that it enables users to have connectivity in a variety of environments—home, office, and even public areas such as hotels, airports, coffee shops, and restaurants. Because these 802.11 devices are used in various types of environments, they must comply with FCC Class B regulations. The 802.11 *access point* (AP) and bridge devices are typically static, or permanently mounted, and can therefore be designed with a particular operating environment in mind (residential or commercial). Oddly, the higher-performance, higher-cost APs designed for operation in the enterprise are subject to the more forgiving emissions standard (Class A) than their lower-cost counterparts designed for installation in the home. It is typical for enterprise-destined APs to be FCC Class B certified, even though it is not an absolute requirement—it just shows a generally higher level of quality.

Almost all electronic devices, including 802.11 devices as well as your computers, televisions, video game machines, radios receivers, and so on, have a Class A or Class B rating.

RF Regulatory Domains

Although every country in the world today has the authority to create and enforce technology regulations specific unto itself, most countries adopt such regulations that are uniform with other (typically larger) countries. Countries (usually adjoining) that share a common set of regulations are referred to in the 802.11 specification as *regulatory domains*. That said, three major regulatory bodies exercise authority over the vast majority of the world's technology regulations, as follows:

- **FCC**—As mentioned in the preceding section, the first regulatory bodies to police spread spectrum and WLANs were the FCC and IC, which have jurisdiction over the United States and Canadian RF regulations, respectively. Although referred to as the *FCC domain* in the 802.11 specifications, the FCC and IC are commonly called (as in this book, too) the *North American regulatory domain*.

- **ETSI**—ETSI is more of an advisory body than a regulatory body (unlike the FCC and TELEC), and makes recommendations for regulations instead of enacting them itself. As the name implies, the ETSI was developed with the European countries in mind; however, many other countries worldwide follow the ETSI recommendations.

- **TELEC**—In Japan, the *Telecom Engineering Center* (TELEC), part of the Japanese Ministry of Posts and Telecommunications, defines the regulations for WLAN and other radio services. These regulations tend to be used only in Japan.

Each of these domains has different parameters for antenna gain, transmit power, channel selection, and so on that must be followed. In addition, many countries may follow one of the standards in its entirety, or may use one of the standards just as a guideline and apply their own unique changes. Thankfully, only a few countries fall into this latter category today.

Table 3-1 *Regulatory Domains*

Regulatory Domain	Geographic Area
North American (FCC)	North, South, and Central America; Australia and New Zealand; various parts of Asia
ETSI	Europe; Middle East; Africa; various parts of Asia
TELEC	Japan

WLAN Frequencies of Operation

As mentioned previously, unlicensed WLANs fall into three basic frequency bands: 900 MHz, 2.4 GHz, and 5 GHz. Each has its own advantages and disadvantages, and each is broken down into channels or channel groups. The different regulatory domains have defined which frequencies and channels may be used, and these channels are in an ever-changing state. These bands are often referred to as the *Industrial, Scientific, and Medical* (ISM) *bands*. Figure 3-1 shows where these bands fall in the overall frequency spectrum.

Figure 3-1 *ISM Bands*

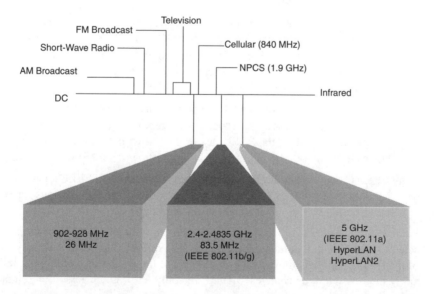

900-MHz Frequency Band

The 900-MHz band was the first area for which spread-spectrum WLANs were developed. A nearby neighbor of the 900-MHz band was the cellular phone band. This helped the early development of the WLAN industry in the 900-MHz band because of the availability of inexpensive, small RF components developed for use in that industry. Because the WLAN and cellular phone frequencies were very close, many components could be "borrowed" from the fast-growing cellular industry.

The 900-MHz band had a couple of major drawbacks, however. It was limited in its use worldwide, with only North America, some parts of South America, Australia, and a handful of other smaller countries permitting WLAN usage in the 900-MHz band. Another disadvantage of the 900-MHz band was the limited bandwidth. Data rates were limited to 1 and 2 Mbps maximum because of the limited frequency span that was available. Figure 3-2 depicts the overall bandwidth requirement at 900 MHz when running the various data rates. As you can see, running the higher data rates limits the number of channels to one that incorporates the entire band and severely limits scalability.

Figure 3-2   *900-MHz Channel Scheme*

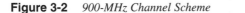
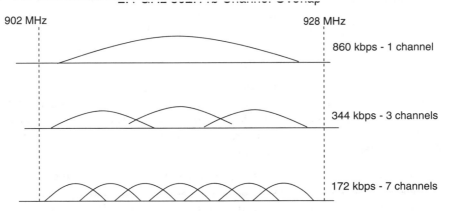

As the IEEE 802.11 specification was being developed, the IEEE recognized the deficiencies of this band and chose not to include it in the standard. For the same reason, this book concentrates on the 2.4- and 5-GHz bands, using the 900-MHz band only as a reference for historical information.

2.4-GHz Frequency Band

The desire for higher data rates, more scalability, and greater global deployment drove the development in the 2.4-GHz band. This band was generally available in almost every major country worldwide. Although it initially provided for data rates of only up to 2 Mbps, it did offer more channel capability. Development of 2.4-GHz devices was encouraged by the fact that the 2.4-GHz band had neighbors in the *Personal Communication Services* (PCS) wireless systems as well as some radar systems. The close frequencies meant that some of the RF component and development costs could be shared among the different technologies. As the industry started to invest into the 2.4-GHz technology, the IEEE was developing a specification to provide interoperability for the new WLAN market.

In 1997, the IEEE completed the 802.11 specification, defining data rates up to 2 Mbps for the 2.4-GHz band and setting down a channel scheme that provided three nonoverlapping and noninterfering channels. In the North American domain, there was a need to limit the upper channels because of a very tight restriction for RF signals that fell outside the band at the top end of the band. Therefore, there were only 11 channels specified. For the ETSI domain, the upper-band restriction was not an issue, and 13 channels were defined. In Japan, a very strict regulation limited WLAN usage to only a narrow section and limited the number of channels to 1, and that channel was incompatible with any of the ETSI or North American channels. Several years later, the Japan TELEC changed the regulations, permitting operation of the 13 ETSI channels plus the old single Japan channel, thus providing for 14 channels under the Japan domain.

Because of the demand for higher data rates, the IEEE added an amendment in 1999 to increase the data rate for 2.4-GHz *direct sequence* (DS) systems to include 5.5 Mbps and 11 Mbps, which is known as the *802.11b specification*. The number of channels did not change, and the new specification required that products be backward compatible to the older 1-Mbps and 2-Mbps 802.11 products.

Likewise, in 2003, the IEEE added another part to the 802.11 specifications. The 802.11g standard is yet another, even higher data-rate scheme in the 2.4-GHz band yielding rates as high as 54 Mbps, and again, requiring backward compatibility to the 802.11b specification.

Because the frequency scheme is identical between the initial 2.4-GHz 802.11, the 802.11b, and the 802.11g specifications, most countries that permitted operation for the early 2.4-GHz 802.11 devices also permitted the 802.11b and 802.11g products.

The 802.11 specification defines the channel scheme as being 22 MHz wide, starting with the center frequency of the first channel at 2.412 GHz. The center frequencies for the channels are spaced at 5-MHz intervals; this channel scheme results in two overlapping channels, as shown in Figure 3-3.

Figure 3-3   *2.4-GHz 802.11 Channel Overlap*

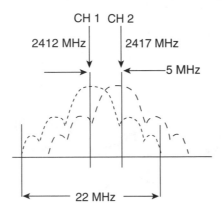

The 2.4-GHz channel overlap results in much confusion for many users. To many, the fact that there are 11 (or 13 or 14) channels available logically indicates that you can use a WLAN system on one channel in the same vicinity as another system on a different channel. Although this is true, the design engineer must be certain to use channels that are not overlapping.

Based on the defined channel scheme for both ETSI and North America, three nonoverlapping channels can be used in the same area with no interference between them. Although you may see papers written on the ability to use four or even five separate channels in the same area, by using channels that are slightly overlapping, the WLAN industry in general recommends the use of the three nonoverlapping channel scheme (see Figure 3-4).

Figure 3-4   *2.4-GHz 802.11 Channel Scheme*

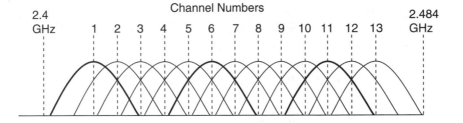

Using the three nonoverlapping channels, you can reuse the channels in a rotating scheme and carefully define adjacent cells on channels that are noninterfering (see Figure 3-5).

Figure 3-5 *2.4-GHz Channel Reuse*

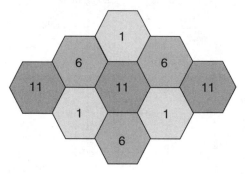

5-GHz Frequency Band

The 5-GHz band was initially used in Europe for the ETSI HiperLAN specification, but traction for this technology never seemed to take a good foothold, and it was overtaken by the development of a competing 802.11 standard from the IEEE. The 802.11a specification, which was completed in 1999, defined several different channel groups within the 5-GHz band. Because of many varying regulations around the world with 5 GHz, the channel groups and area of permitted operation must be reviewed carefully.

There has been a lot of activity in the regulatory bodies concerning the 5-GHz WLAN bands recently. In 2003, there was a meeting of the world's regulatory bodies that discussed reworking many of these regulations and opening up new frequencies.

As mentioned, the 5-GHz band is broken down into several different channel groups. In the United States, these are referred to as the *Unlicensed National Information Infrastructure* (UNII) *bands*. The three bands or groups—UNII1, UNII2, and UNII3—permit operation in the 5.215- to 5.225-GHz, 5.225- to 5.235-GHz, and 5.725- to 5.825-GHz frequency ranges, respectively. After the recent changes in regulations, a new band of frequencies are now available ranging from 5.470 to 5.725 GHz (see Figure 3-6).

Figure 3-6   *5-GHz 802.11a Channel Scheme*

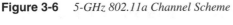
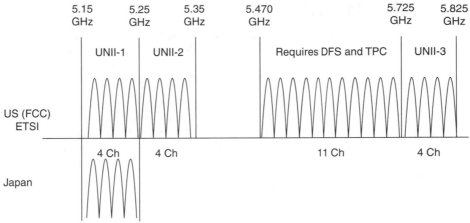

When compared to 2.4 GHz, the 5 GHz offers at minimum eight channels. Although there is a slight overlap in the sidebands, the channels are typically referred to as nonoverlapping. Some installers believe it is fine to use adjacent channels in adjacent cells; however, it is recommended that when possible (and with the number of channels available, it is usually possible) to avoid adjacent channels in adjacent cells (see Figure 3-7).

Figure 3-7   *5-GHz 802.11a Channel Reuse*

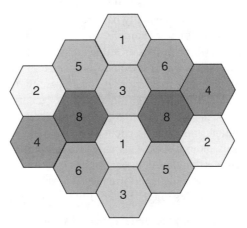

Dynamic Frequency Selection and Transmitter Power Control with 801.11h

The ETSI 5-GHz band is a very wide one, stretching from 5.15 GHz all the way to 5.7 GHz, and is far more than what was defined by the initial UNII definitions in the North American regulatory domain. Because much of this area is in use by other radios services, the ETSI regulatory domain required the inclusion of two features not found in the initial 802.11a products brought to market. These two features are *Dynamic Frequency Selection* (DFS) and *Transmit Power Control* (TPC) and are the primary features of the IEEE 802.11h specification. Both were handled quite well by the HiperLAN 2 specification, a technology that was in competition with 802.11a and supported by Europe-based companies such as Nokia, Ericsson, and Siemens.

With DFS, the concept is that an 802.11 infrastructure device first listens to the whole of the frequency band available to it and then automatically picks the least-congested channel available. Again, the rationale behind this is that portions of the 5-GHz band are assigned for military use and for radar systems. The idea here is that by listening first before determining a channel to operate on, the WLAN will not interfere with incumbent users of the band in situations where they are collocated. Second, the availability of such a feature simplifies enterprise installations because the devices themselves can (theoretically) automatically optimize their channel reuse pattern.

TPC is a technology that has been used in the cellular telephone industry for many years. By setting the transmit power of the AP and the client adapter, you can allow for different coverage area sizes and, in the case of the client, conserve battery life. Devices that do not enable you to set power levels usually have static settings and are totally independent of each other (AP and clients). For example, an AP can be set to a low 5-mW transmit power to minimize cell size, which proves useful in areas with high user density. The clients will, however, be transmitting at their previously assigned transmit power setting, which is likely more transmit power than is required to maintain association with the AP. This results in unnecessary RF energy transmitting from the clients, creating a higher level than necessary of RF energy outside the AP's intended coverage area. With TPC, the client and AP exchange information, and then the client device dynamically adjusts its transmit power such that it uses only enough energy to maintain association with the AP at a given data rate. The end result of this is that the client contributes less to adjacent cell interference, allowing for more densely deployed high-performance WLANs. As a secondary benefit, the lower power on the client provides longer battery life because less power is used by the radio.

In 2004, the FCC opened up the frequencies between 5.470 and 5.725 GHz, provided that DFS and TPS are implemented properly. This now provides up to 23 nonoverlapping channels in the North American regulatory domain, making 5 GHz a much more scalable solution.

Because of the long lead time in development of silicon devices used in WLAN radio devices, DFS and TPC features only started to be incorporated into 802.11a devices in 2004. The Wi-Fi alliance has plans to offer interoperability testing of these two features at some point, but the timeframes have not yet been defined.

Regulatory Channel Selections

The WLAN bands are divided up into channels, with each local regulatory agency defining what is permitted for use in its area. This section defines the major regulatory domain regulations regarding power, antennas, and other compliance requirements.

North American Domain Channel Scheme

In the *North American* (NA) domain, the 2.4-GHz band ranges from 2.400 GHz to 2.4835 GHz; the 5-GHz band ranges from 5.150 to 5.825 GHz. Both bands are divided into channel schemes, which vary by regulatory domain.

2.4 GHz (NA)

In the NA channel scheme for 2.4 GHz, 11 channels are identified. As previously mentioned, these channels are 22 MHz wide, and the center of each channel is separated from the adjacent channel center by only 5 MHz. The lower channel is centered at 2.412 GHz (channel 1) with the upper channel (channel 11) centered at 2.462 GHz. (See Table 3-2.)

Table 3-2   *2.4-GHz Channel Allocations*

Channel Number	Frequency	NA	ETSI	Japan
1	2.412	x	x	x
2	2.417	x	x	x
3	2.422	x	x	x
4	2.427	x	x	x
5	2.432	x	x	x
6	2.437	x	x	x
7	2.442	x	x	x

continues

Table 3-2   *2.4-GHz Channel Allocations (Continued)*

Channel Number	Frequency	NA	ETSI	Japan
8	2.447	x	x	x
9	2.452	x	x	x
10	2.457	x	x	x
11	2.462	x	x	x
12	2.467		x	x
13	2.472		x	x
14	2.484			x

5 GHz (NA)

The 5-GHz band in the NA domain is divided into four segments. The UNII1 band runs from 5.150 GHz to 5.250 GHz and is divided into four channels. The UNII2 band runs from 5.250 GHz to 5.350 GHz and is also divided into four channels. The UNII3 band starts at 5.725 GHz and ends at 5.825 GHz and also has a total of four channels. Between 5.470 and 5.725 GHz lie the newer channels permitted by the inclusion of 8021.11h (an additional 11 channels).

ETSI Domain Channel Scheme

In Europe, the regulations are quite a bit different and hence not just power levels differ from the NA domain, but also some of the permitted frequency usage.

2.4 GHz (ETSI)

In the ETSI channel scheme, 13 channels are identified. The lower 11 channels are identical to the NA channel scheme, with two additional channels. These channels are centered at 2.467 GHz and 2.472 GHz.

5 GHz (ETSI)

With the recent addition channels to the NA domain, the ETSI domain now shares the same frequencies. However, there are some differences in permitted power levels and adherence to DFS and TPC that must followed.

Japan Channel Scheme

In Japan, some changes were made to the 2.4-GHz band permitting more frequency usage; however, the 5-GHz band has some stricter regulations.

2.4 GHz (Japan)

The Japan 2.4-GHz band originally supported only a single channel, centered at 2.484 GHz, and that channel was noninteroperable with any other country. A few years ago, the Japan TELEC opened up the rest of the 2.4-GHz band, permitting operation on the same 13 channels as the ETSI domain, while still keeping the single upper channels as 2.484 GHz, providing for a total of 14 channels.

5 GHz (Japan)

Japan has taken a much more restrictive role in the 5-GHz area than other regulatory domains. They only permit operation from 5.150 GHz to 5.250 GHz with four channels located at 5.170 GHz, 5.190 GHz, 5.210 GHz, and 5.130 GHz. You will notice that these center frequencies differ from those used in ETSI and the NA domains.

Other Regulatory Domain Frequency Limits

Some countries have based their permitted frequency usage on a portion of one of the ETSI or NA domain specifications, resulting in a fewer number of available channels. France and Israel were two such countries; however, they have recently changed and now permit a full range of frequencies based on either the ETSI or NA domain. It is important that the installer check with the local agency to verify what is permitted in the country in which the equipment will be used.

Maximum Transmitter Power Levels

When defining rules and regulations surrounding transmitter power, several methods can be used to define the limits. First, there is straight transmitter output power, which is the amount of RF energy sent from the transmitter power amplifier to the antenna connector. As discussed in Chapter 2, "Understanding RF Fundamentals," these power specifications are typically rated in *decibels per milliwatt* (dBm) for the WLAN industry. Second, various limitations pertain to the antenna gain that may be used.

EIRP

Regulatory requirements for power output levels are sometimes rated in actual transmitter power, or in many cases effective power based on both the transmitter and antennas values. This method is known as the *Effective Isotropic Radiated Power* (EIRP). This value is a calculated value, using not only the transmitter power, but as you might have guessed from the name, the isotropic gain of an antenna (dBi ratings). This value also includes any losses for cable, lightning arrestors, or any other devices placed between the antenna and the transmitter connector. This is the effective power that is radiated from the antenna.

To obtain an EIRP rating, you can just take the transmitter power (in dBm), add the gain of the antenna (in dBi), subtract the losses of the cable or other inserted devices (in dB), and you will end up with an EIRP value. An example follows:

> Transmitter with 100-mW output power (+20 dBm)
> Yagi antenna with a 13.5-dBi gain rating
> 50 foot of cable with a loss of 2.2 dB
> TX power + Antenna gain − Cable loss = EIRP
> +20 dBm + 13.5 dBi − 2.2 dB = 31.3-dBm EIRP

North American Regulatory Power Levels

One parameter that is tightly restricted is the transmitter power that is permitted from a WLAN radio transmitter. Because the frequencies used for WLAN are unlicensed, the regulatory bodies thought it necessary to impose limitations as a way of reducing interference.

2.4-GHz Power Levels for the North American Regulatory Domain

The NA regulatory domain sets limits for both maximum transmitter power and EIRP. The maximum power level for transmitters is regulated to 1 watt, or +30 dBm. This is true for both the 900-MHz and the 2.4-GHz WLAN bands. For the 5-GHz bands, however, these maximum power levels are different.

The NA regulations also specify both a maximum antenna gain and an EIRP limit. The regulations limit the antenna gain to 6 dBi if you are using the full +30-dBm transmitter power. This provides a maximum EIRP value of +36 dBm. The NA regulations do permit high antenna gains, however, if the transmitter power is reduced according to the rules and topology of the radio network. This can be confusing to understand, so the following sidebar explains the topologies available.

Point to Point Versus Point to Multipoint

Point-to-point systems are typically used in bridge applications, where there are just two sites connected over the single RF link. Figure 3-8 shows a point-to-point system wherein each device is communicating to just one other point. More recently, some WLAN APs have been designed to use special antennas with very narrow beam widths that change directions on a packet-by-packet basis and communicate to only one given remote user at any one time. Chapter 14, "Outdoor Bridge Deployments," describes this type of device in more detail.

Figure 3-8   *Point-to-Point Configuration*

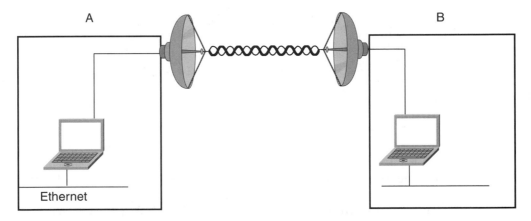

A *point-to-multipoint* (PTMP) system is the way most WLANs are used, and many bridge systems as well. In a PTMP system, a single station communicates to multiple other stations. This can be compared to a WLAN in which an AP, operating on a single channel (that is, one radio) is communicating to multiple client devices at the same time over the one channel (such as happens when a multicast or broadcast message comes out of the AP).

In a bridge system, a PTMP system typically has a single central site communicating to more than one remote site over the same channel. Figure 3-9 shows a typical PMTP system.

Figure 3-9   *Point-to-Multipoint Configuration*

Point-to-Multipoint (PTMP)

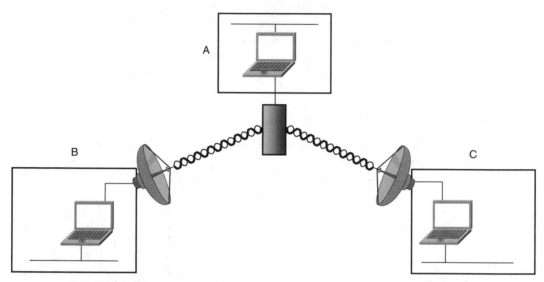

The FCC has different regulations for these two topologies. In PTMP systems, the FCC has limited the maximum EIRP to 36 dBm (EIRP = TX power + Antenna gain). For every decibel that the transmitter power is reduced below the maximum of 30 dBm, the antenna gain may be increased over 6 dBi by 1 dB. (29 dBm TX + 7 dB antenna = 36 dBm EIRP; 28 dBm TX + 8 dB antenna = 36 dBm EIRP.) In many cases, WLAN transmitters are on the order of +20 dBm or even as low as 13 dBm. For a 20-dBm transmitter, which is 10 dB below the maximum of 30 dBm, you can use an antenna that is 10 dB higher than the 6-dBi limit, resulting in a 16-dBi permitted antenna gain. Of course, the antenna must be certified with the device.

In point-to-point systems using directional antennas, the rules have changed. The rule change is because a high-gain antenna has a narrow beam width and therefore the likelihood of causing interference to other users in the area is greatly reduced. Under the rule change, for every decibel the transmitter is reduced below 30 dBm, the antenna may be increased (from the initial 6 dBi) by 3 dB. For example, a 29-dBm transmitter is 1 dB below the 30-dBm maximum transmitter limit. This then allows an antenna that is 1 to 3 dB higher than the initial 6-dBi antenna permitted, or a 9-dBi antenna. Similarly, a 28-dBm transmitter is 2 dB below the 30-dBm limit, and the resulting antenna gain could be 12 dBi (2 * 3 = 6, in addition to the initial 6-dBi antenna). If you look at a 20-dBm transmitter in this case, which is 10 dB below the 30-dBm level, you can increase the antenna gain (again over the initial 6 dBi) by 30 dB, to a theoretical 36-dBi antenna. However, most WLAN and bridge radios have never tested, and therefore are not certified, with any antennas this large, making it illegal to use such a high-gain antenna. (Remember, an antenna must be certified with the transmitter.)

Now for the main question here: What constitutes a point-to-point and what constitutes a multipoint system?

In Figure 3-8, Point A communicates to a single point, B, and Point B communicates to a single point, A. Therefore, both locations see this as a point-to-point installation.

In Figure 3-9, Point A communicates to more than one point, or multiple points. Therefore, Point A is operating in a multipoint configuration. And the largest antenna permitted is 16 dBi. However, how many locations does Point B or Point C communicate to? Only Point A. This then argues that Point B or Point C is actually operating in a single-point or point-to-point operation, and a larger antenna may be used.

5-GHz Power Levels (NA)

The NA regulatory domain identifies the power levels for 5 GHz based on the three different UNII bands. UNII1 band was intended for indoor use, and provides only 50-mW transmitter power. The UNII2 band is intended for both indoor and outdoor usage, and the maximum power is increased to 250 mW. The UNII3 band is intended for use in outdoor systems and has a power limit of 1 W.

NOTE   In the 5-GHz band in the NA regulatory domain, power may not exceed the lesser of the following:

- **UNII1**—50 mW or 4 dBm + 10logB, where B is the 26-dB emission bandwidth in MHz.

- **UNII2**—250 mW or 11 dBm + 10logB, where B is the 26-dB emission bandwidth in MHz.

- **UNII3**—1 watt or 17 dBm + 10logB, where B is the 26-dB emission bandwidth in MHz.

Antenna gain is again limited, as with the 2.4-GHz band for NA. It is 6 dBi maximum in a PTMP mode. To increase the antenna gain, the transmitter must be reduced by the same amount.

In the UNII3 band, however, fixed point-to-point application antennas of up to 23-dBi gain may be used, without reductions in power. For antennas with higher gain than 23 dBi, a reduction of 1-dB transmitter power is required for every 1-dB increase the antenna has above 23 dBi.

For the UNII1 band, a major restriction that applied in the NA domain has been recently removed. The regulations had required that an antenna must be permanently attached to the radio device. External or removable antennas were not permitted. This caused many issues when trying locate an AP in a secure location, such as above the ceiling or in a wiring closet or a NEMA enclosure. Because you could not separate the antenna from the radio device, you had to mount the AP where you need the antenna. UNII2 and UNII3 bands permitted external antennas, with a maximum EIRP limit of 250 mW for UNII2 and 1 W for UNII3.

This restriction has been removed for UNII1, and products may now use external antennas for all channels within the 5-GHz band.

If a device combines operation of the UNII1 band with other bands, the device must comply with the UNII1 regulation requiring a permanently attached antenna.

ETSI Regulatory Power Levels

Similar to the NA domain regulations, the 2.4-GHz and 5-GHz bands have varying power limitations. For the 2.4-GHz band, ETSI regulations are quite a bit more restrictive than the corresponding NA regulations.

2.4-GHz Power Levels (ETSI)

Under the ETSI regulations, the power output and EIRP regulations are much different from what they are in the NA regulatory domain. The ETSI regulations specify maximum EIRP as +20 dBm. Because this includes antenna gain, this limits the antennas that can be used with a transmitter. To use a larger antenna, the transmitter power must be reduced, so the overall gain of the transmitter plus the antenna gain (less any losses in coax) are equal to or less than +20 dBm EIRP. This drastically reduces the overall distance an outdoor link can operate when compared to an NA type system. It also reduces the gain of the antennas that can be used with many indoor WLAN systems, unless they can reduce transmitter power. (Many APs do not have that option.)

ETSI has developed standards that have been adopted by many European countries as well as many others outside of Europe. In some cases, the standards limit the power to +20-dBm EIRP limits, and in others they may set different transmit power, antenna gain, or EIRP limits.

5-GHz Power Levels (ETSI)

The power levels for some countries using the ETSI regulatory domain vary quite widely. Table 3-3 depicts some of the power levels.

Table 3-3   *ETSI Power-Level Variations*

Country	Frequency Band (GHz)	Maximum Transmit Power EIRP with TPC (mW)	Maximum Transmit Power Without TPC (mW)
Austria	5.15–5.25	200	200
Belgium	5.15–5.35	120	60
Denmark	5.15–5.25	50	50
France	5.15–5.25	200	200
Germany	5.15–5.25	50	50
Ireland	5.15–5.35	120	60
Netherlands	5.15–5.25	200	200
Sweden	5.15–5.25	200	200
Switzerland	5.15–5.25	200	200
United Kingdom	5.15–5.35	120	60

Japan Domain Power Levels

Japan uses a different method for specifying power. Instead of using a peak power method, they measure power in relationship to bandwidth. The measured value is rated in megawatts/megahertz.

2.4 GHz (Japan)

The power level for the Japanese 2.4-GHz band is rated at 10 mW/MHz. This is also an EIRP rating, which as you know by now requires the gain of the antenna to be added into the equation. This compares to approximately 19 dBm on a typical 802.11b transmitter.

Japan also requires that any antenna gain be offset by a reduction in transmitter power, keeping the EIRP level equal to or below 10 mW/MHz.

Also note that you can only use antennas that have been certified by the TELEC with the transmitter.

5 GHz (Japan)

The use of 5-GHz WLAN in Japan today is limited to indoor use only. As for power limits, it also has a maximum of 10 mW/MHz EIRP, as well as the requirement to reduce transmitter power to offset antenna gain, keeping the EIRP under 10 mW/MHz.

World Mode (802.11d)

Because of the various regulations around the globe that vary based on power levels and channel use, it becomes difficult to provide a single product that can be used in all locations of the world. Therefore, a device that is set up for use in the United States (using the NA regulatory domain) may not be permitted in the United Kingdom (where ETSI regulations are in place) because of the power-level differences. A U.K. device may not be used in the United States because of the extra two channels that are available in the product (but that are prohibited by the NA regulatory domain). This fact hinders mobility and portability (two key benefits of WLANs). Globetrotters moving from country to country need to carry various cards based on the specific regulatory domains. Even more problematic, a global company has to order, stock, and ship to its users different products based on the locations in which they will be working.

But what happens when the radio device is embedded *inside* your computer? How do you physically change the radio from one domain to another? One option is to require users to set the frequency and power parameters for the location where they are working. Unfortunately, most regulatory agencies fear that users would not do this properly, and therefore this is not permitted in most locations.

A second choice is to set the radio parameters to the lowest common denominator for the majority of the regulatory domains. Consider, for example, a 2.4-GHz implementation. You could set the maximum power to 30 mW (15 dBm). With a 2.2-dBi dipole, this keeps the EIRP to less than 20 dBm, the EIRP limit of ETSI, and meets the 10-mW/MHz Japanese limit; it is also well below the NA limits. For the channel selection, permit only the U.S. channels where all 11 are usable (which is most ETSI countries and Japan). This then excludes only a few select countries that have limited channel operation. However, it also limits the flexibility of the WLAN systems, reducing channel capabilities in ETSI and Japan countries, as well as range (because of lower power) in NA domains.

There is still a third choice. Have the WLAN devices select the domains automatically. But how do the devices know what domain they are in? Because APs are typically installed in a single location and not moved from one location to another, they can be set to the proper domain. In most cases, this means ordering the proper domain from the manufacturer. Then the AP could send out information as to what domain it is set for, and the roaming client devices could listen and adjust accordingly, all with no user interaction.

Permitting world-mode roaming with a single device is exactly what the IEEE 802.11d specification set out to define. However, not all devices today support world-mode roaming. If this is something you are interested in, you need to be certain that the AP as well as the intended clients provide this support.

Figure 3-10 shows one example of the ability to select 802.1d world roaming.

Figure 3-10 *World-Mode Configuration Example*

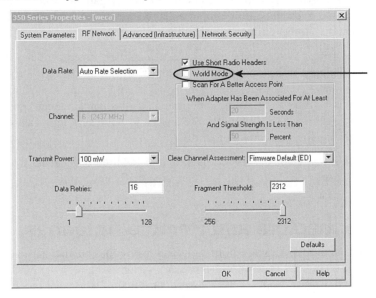

Amplifiers

So you have installed some type of RF system, and you are not getting the range you wanted. How do you increase range? One common thought is just to add an amplifier, which would increase the transmitter power to a level high enough to enable communication at the desired range. In many cases, however, that is not legal for 802.11 devices.

As you have learned, certain rules limit EIRP power. In a good portion of the world, this limit is either 20 dBm or 10 mW/MHz, and that includes the antenna gain. So adding an amplifier is not typically legal in those locations. In an NA domain location, however, you are allowed to have 1 watt of transmitter power and a 6-dBi antenna.

As mentioned earlier in this chapter in the section "Early Spread Spectrum," one of the reasons for the rules and restrictions is to provide coexistence among WLAN users located in the same vicinity. This is the exact reason for establishing antenna and transmitter power limits. The FCC has a specific clause for amplifiers.

The Code of Federal Regulations (the source of the FCC rules) Section 15.204 provides the requirements for amplifiers in the ISM bands. An amplifier may only be marketed with the system configuration in which it was approved, and not separately. It must also be designed using nonstandard connectors or a method of identifying that the amplifier is attached to a qualified transmitter. This is to prevent improper or illegal installation with unapproved transmitters. In plain English, unless the amplifier manufacturer submits the amplifier for testing *with* a given transmitter, the amplifier cannot legally be sold in the U.S. for use with that particular transmitter. If the amplifier has been certified, it must be labeled with an FCC identification number citing its certification testing.

If you are using a system that includes a legal amplifier, remember that the rules concerning power still apply. If the amplifier is 1/2 watt (27 dBm), this means in a multipoint system the maximum antenna gain is only 9 dBi, and in a point-to-point system it is only 15 dBi. (27 dBm is 3 dB below 30 dBm, so the gain of a multipoint antenna can be increased from 6 dBi, by 3 dB, for a total of 9 dBi. For a point-to-point system, it can be increased by a total of 9 dBi, for a maximum of 15 dBi.)

In the ETSI regulations, there is a maximum EIRP limit of 20 dBm. Because most amplifiers start off well above this level, they are usually not permitted.

Antenna Connectors and Remote Antennas

The FCC regulations impose limitations and restrictions on antennas and connectors that may be used in a 2.4-GHz or 5-GHz WLAN system. Although the FCC wrote these regulations, a few other countries have also adopted them. Because of increased popularity of WLAN in the United States, and the desire to build units as a single model, many vendors just follow the same rules for connectors for all the products shipped worldwide.

The Code of Federal Regulations, Part 15.203, states that an intentional radiator (transmitter) must be designed so the user cannot use an antenna that was not provided for the transmitter. The rationale behind this is to prevent the use of improper antennas, which can cause improper action of the transmitter, and to prevent the use of antennas that exceed the maximum permitted gain.

To comply, the regulations suggest that the antenna be permanently attached, or that a unique connector be used. The regulations state that a standard antenna connector is prohibited. The FCC has unofficially stated that their interpretation of a unique connector implies that the connector cannot be readily available to the general public. This antenna and connector requirement does not apply to certain carrier current devices or to devices operated under the provisions of Parts 15.211, 15.213, 15.217, 15.219, or 15.221.

One area of confusion regarding the regulations is this statement: "This requirement does not apply to intentional radiators that must be professionally installed or to other intentional radiators, which, in accordance with §15.31(d), must be measured at the installation site."

However, the regulations go on to state, "The installer shall be responsible for ensuring that the proper antenna is employed so that the limits in this part are not exceeded."

The statement was intended to provide those who install more complicated wireless systems, such as long-range broadband fixed wireless systems or wireless perimeter security systems, with the flexibility they need. The meaning of *professionally installed* is a subjective one, and the definition is not provided in the regulations. Using a definition straight out of a dictionary, a professional is anyone who receives any compensation for services or work, and there are no ties to licensing or certification. However, if an installer claims that he is a professional installer, and exercises this exemption, he becomes the responsible party. As the responsible party, noncompliance with FCC regulations makes the installer subject to fines and even imprisonment.

This exemption afforded professional installers is intended to allow them the design flexibility to shape antenna coverage patterns that allow for maximum power density and, of course, do so in a manner that will not violate any part of the regulations. Professional installers must consider two factors as part of their customer installations. First, applying maximum power to a specific antenna or area is far from the accepted normal practice. A considerable amount of radio interference comes from existing radio systems already installed and operating. Frequency planning mitigates this to a large extent, but the experienced professional installer will typically use the minimum power necessary to provide suitable link margins and performance. Second, the professional installer tends to use antennas that shape the RF beams no wider than absolutely necessary to provide suitable link margins. This in turn helps provide suitable reliability and performance, with minimum interference offered or received from adjacent radios systems.

In legal terms, this statement requires the installer to test the system, once installed, to verify it complies with all regulations, including transmitted emissions that are generated outside of the legal band, noise generated by the receiver, and overall EIRP ratings. In most cases, these types of measurements are well beyond the scope of most WLAN installers.

In mid-2004, the FCC made some changes to Part 15.204 regarding the use of antennas that were not certified by the manufacturer of the transmitter. Basically it states that any antenna may use the transmitter, as long as it is of a similar type (omni-directional, patch, Yagi, dish, and so on) and that it is of equal or lesser gain. It also cites the manufacturer of the WLAN gear with the responsibility of providing users a list of antennas that have been certified.

Health and Safety

You might have heard the claim that cell phone use can lead to cancer or other illnesses. This claim has caused many users to be leery of using any radio devices, including WLAN systems. Because RF can be hazardous to the human body, there have been studies to try to analyze exactly what levels of RF are safe and acceptable. The FCC and other regulatory bodies around the world have done studies on this and provide some guidelines on the subject. In the U.S., the *American National Standards Institute* (ANSI), the *Institute of Institute of Electrical and Electronics Engineers* (IEEE), and the *National Council on Radiation Protection and Measurements* (NCRPM) offer guidelines on *specific absorption rate* (SAR), which is the rate at which a body absorbs RF energy. Based on the input from these organizations, the FCC has identified what is the maximum SAR for portable RF devices, including 802.11 radio transmitters.

This limit for the workplace is 400 mW/kg when the entire body is exposed, and 1.6 W/kg for partial exposure. Devices such as cell phones, cordless phones, two-way pagers, and 802.11 devices fall into the partial-exposure category.

Because of the limited transmitter power of a typical 802.11 transmitter, the levels are well below those of either limitation. Add to this the fact that the transmitter of an 802.11 device is typically in transmit mode a very limited amount of time (it is normally in receive mode), and the overall exposure is even less.

The bottom line is that although users should be concerned about the health and safety considerations of any radio device, they should also be aware that years of research has been conducted in this area and the findings of this research have been incorporated into the applicable regulations. Everyone is familiar with a cellular phone, and when comparing them to an 802.11 device, the 802.11 device delivers a fraction of the transmit power of a typical cellular telephone. The energy exposure of the body is also a fraction of that delivered by the cellular device, and the differing usage patterns of a 802.11 device leads to far less exposure time than would be typical for a cellular telephone.

Even with the preceding health and safety information, keep in mind that high-gain antennas do intensify the energy levels to a very narrow beam. Therefore, it is always wise to not stand in front of, or near, high-gain antennas any longer than absolutely necessary if you are not fully cognizant of the operational parameters of the antenna.

Health Insurance Portability and Accountability Act (HIPAA)

While on the subject of health and WLANs, it is important to point out that a new law called the *Health Insurance Portability and Accountability Act* (HIPAA) was enacted in the U.S. in 2003. Among the provisions of this law are regulations regarding privacy of patient information. Although this is really a security issue, I think it is necessary to include here as part of the regulation chapter.

Because WLANs use the airwaves to transmit signals, there is the possibility of these signals, and the information contained in them, being received by an unwanted party. As you may have heard, various security breaches of WLAN systems have occurred. Many of these resulted from users not implementing any type of security, at most, or a minimal security scheme.

If the system you are installing is going to be used for any type of patient information, you need to be sure the security scheme selected provides adequate measures to protect the data. Many papers and books cover security for wired and wireless LANs, and it is beyond the scope of this book to discuss WLAN security in detail. At a minimum, any system used for sensitive data, including those that need to meet HIPAA regulations, should use some type of authentication and encryption scheme. Several are currently available, such as *Extensible Authentication Protocol-Transport Layer Security* (EAP-TLS), *Lightweight EAP* (LEAP), *Protected EAP* (PEAP), and *Wi-Fi Protected Access* (WPA), with better and tighter security and encryption schemes in development all the time.

Plenum Locations

Because wireless systems need to be placed where the users are, and not necessarily in some wiring or computer closet (like routers and switches), mounting becomes an issue. You will learn about different mounting and locations in Chapter 12, "Installing WLAN Products," but this section briefly discusses some special regulations that can affect locations of devices.

Many areas in buildings are considered *plenum locations*, which means these areas are used for air handling. In many buildings, areas such as those above ceiling panels, below raised floors, or in wiring risers between floors are used as part of the air system and require products to be plenum rated. In the United States, the UL2043 certification provides for testing that is similar to most local fire-code requirements.

Although many APs are designed to be placed in plenum areas, many are not. Make sure you select a product that meets the location needs of your installation. Also keep in mind that any cables and antennas that are placed or run through these areas must meet the local plenum codes.

Summary

It is imperative to have a good understanding of the rules and regulations for the locations where a WLAN will be installed. Failure to comply with the local regulations can result in a requirement to cease operation of the WLAN, or in some cases, penalties of fines and even imprisonment.

Because a WLAN is designed for a particular user, the determination needs to be made as to what regulatory domains the product will be used in, today and in the future. Most companies want to have the same network products and architectures throughout the corporate infrastructure, and if the company has a global presence, this can mean meeting multiple regulatory domain requirements.

When selecting a technology and product to meet the application needs, confirm that they also meet the necessary regulatory domain requirements.

Recommended Reading

During the development of this book, a lot of changes to regulations have been proposed. Some have even likely been implemented, resulting in a changing environment for frequency availability, power-level requirements, and antenna for use with WLANs. It is strongly recommended that you review the requirements of the countries where the equipment will be installed. You can locate regulations information at the following sites:

- **The U.S. FCC**—http://www.fcc.gov/

- **European Telecommunication Standard Institute**—http://www.etsi.org
- **Industry Canada**—http://strategis.ic.gc.ca/epic/internet/insmt-gst.nsf/vwGeneratedInterE/h_sf06165e.html

Another location for FCC technical information is http://www.access.gpo.gov/nara/cfr/waisidx_00/47cfr15_00.html. This site covers Code of Federal Regulations (CFR) Parts 15.245, 15.247, 15.249, and 15.407, which are mostly technical in nature, specifying maximum power outputs and so on.

This chapter covers the following topics:

- Typical WLAN Environments
- Defining WLAN Requirements
- Defining Your Technology Requirements
- Selecting Necessary WLAN Services
- Building-to-Building Connectivity

CHAPTER 4

WLAN Applications and Services

Because you are planning on installing a WLAN, you no doubt realize that a WLAN can provide your business with overall productivity improvements, based on user mobility and resulting improvements in organizational and individual efficiency. Accomplishing an improvement in productivity, however, is based on selecting the proper architecture and hardware to support the desired and needed applications and provide the mobility ranges, level of security, and other features you need for your network. As IT managers rush to integrate WLANs across their networks, they often underestimate and oversimplify the technology.

This chapter first discusses the various common WLAN applications and then details the issues surrounding these applications that you need to consider when selecting and installing a WLAN. You may not require many of these features and functions today, but you should consider future expansion so that you are able to build and scale the network and accommodate technological migrations such as 802.11i and 802.11e, voice, video, and other emerging applications. You have to be prepared for expansion and continued growth, because after users experience a well-deployed WLAN, they will demand nothing less and want it for *all* applications they use.

Finally, the chapter discusses selecting the proper technology for the application and determining what WLAN services will fit the needs of the users.

Typical WLAN Environments

WLANs have been around for more than a decade now, but their use in many different environments is just beginning to take off. As mentioned in Chapter 1, "Defining a Wireless Network's Protocols and Components," the initial widespread use of wireless was for bar coding and data acquisition. However, with the diverse universe where WLANs are now being deployed, many different factors need to be identified. The following lists some of the unique requirements of the most common environments:

- High bandwidth per user (office application, engineering departments)
- Maximum range (retail, warehousing)

- Extremely fast roaming times between access points (voice, video, time-sensitive applications)
- High level of security (health care, government, finance)
- Easily accessible by anyone (public WLANs)

Before you can determine the technology that will work for your system, review the requirements for your particular environment and application. Following that, a preliminary network design and site survey will help to determine whether that technology is right for your site.

For every type of installation, you need to analyze several key items. The topic of bandwidth has been discussed many times already in this book, and this is not the last time it will be mentioned. Adequate bandwidth per user is critical to a successful WLAN. This means making some decisions about the density of users per *access point* (AP) and the 802.11 technology used.

Determining what level of roaming is required for the applications can also be critical to a successful WLAN deployment. Now is the time to determine whether a fast roaming scheme (an extremely fast handoff when moving from one AP to another) is required to prevent problems in the applications. It is also critical to understand at what layer the roams will be occurring (Layer 2 or Layer 3 MAC and transport layers of the OSI model). This will be based upon the necessity of the users to access the network while they are in motion, and at what network layer the application is running. This requirement for voice over the wireless, which requires a very fast handoff, may impact the roaming requirement as well.

The next sections outline WLAN considerations in many common WLAN markets, including retail, enterprise, health care, education, manufacturing, hospitality, public, and *small office/home office* (SOHO) locations.

Retail/Bar Coding

Because the bar coding arena was the first widespread application for wireless, this discussion starts with traditional requirements for retail and warehousing, and includes what some users are doing with wireless today. Typically, in both retail and warehousing, there are a limited number of users, with limited requirements for bandwidth. In these environments, however, there tends to be a need to cover a large amount of area and to keep the cost per square foot of coverage to a minimum. These basic requirements are changing at some retail and warehouse facilities.

Retail

There are several types of retail applications and environments. This section starts by discussing the applications used in the typical retail, large-scale store (that is, a superstore). In the superstore, applications will undoubtedly include inventory control, price shelf auditing, and printing. These applications generally use short packets and require minimum bandwidth. Running at even the lowest 802.11b setting of 1 Mbps provides more than enough speed for the typical number of users on the system.

Figure 4-1 shows several popular bar code scanner styles used in a wide variety of applications. Hundreds of different models and types are available today, with many of them supporting WLAN systems.

Figure 4-1   *Typical Portable Bar Code Scanning Devices*

Along with portable bar code scanners, many large retail outfits provide a "price-verifier" scanning device for customers to check and verify the price of products. These devices are located around the facility, and can be found in standalone kiosks or mounted to the end of a shelf or even to building pillars and walls. Again, these devices require minimum bandwidth; however, their placement is sometimes not optimum. Although mounting the device to a shelf or a building support pillar is easy from the mounting aspect, because these mounting structures are typically steel construction, they tend to block the RF coverage to some degree.

A third application where wireless is used in many retail locations is the *point-of-sale* (POS) device, or cash register. In some cases, the POS devices may be a self-checkout scanner, as shown in Figure 4-2, or even a customer kiosk where coupons are printed. By having the POS device wireless, it enables the placement of the devices at any location in the store where AC power is located, eliminating the need to pull new network cable. This makes rearrangements of a store easy, and proves especially helpful in times of heavy traffic such as the holidays and special store sales. Although the POS device is transacting bar code data, it also must be able to handle transactions for the final sale. Most POS devices will actually download a new product file at given times (usually when the location is closed for business), keeping the pricing and inventory data local. This particular download can be a very large file, and therefore requires a fair amount of bandwidth to complete in a reasonable time. 802.11b tends to provide more than enough bandwidth for such applications.

Figure 4-2 *Typical POS Terminal*

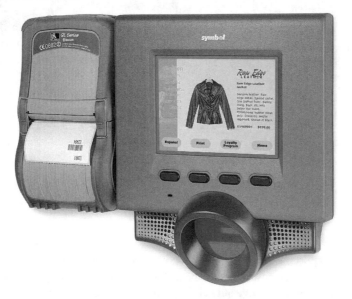

Another application that is becoming popular in many large retail stores is portable *voice over IP* (VoIP) phones. These enable key employees to stay in contact with other stores and even outside parties. VoIP applications, individually, do not require a high level of bandwidth; when several voice streams are running simultaneously, however, bandwidth requirement becomes very important. Voice over wireless also requires time-sensitive access to the network. Therefore, if many VoIP devices are going to be deployed in a retail environment, consideration must be made to providing more AP availability for the required distributed access. This will require reducing the range of each AP (using lower-gain antennas, or lowering the power levels of the radio devices) and thus provide for fewer users per cell.

To assist in voice deployments, it is recommended to implement VLANs over wireless (if supported by the APs). This helps to separate the voice traffic and data traffic and enables you to give priority to voice packets (accomplished by using QoS).

Dead spots in coverage represent another critical issue for voice over wireless applications. With data applications, if the user moves through a small dead spot, the application usually slows down, with the 802.11 protocol just picking up when connectivity is restored, while the data application continues. This is especially true for most IP applications, which are forgiving of missed packets. However, voice applications will show such a drop of communication with dropouts of the audio or by dropping of the call altogether.

Although most of the bar code scanning applications being used in retail facilities have no need for fast roaming capabilities, the use of voice will force this to become a requirement.

But do not forget about future applications that will be used in retail locations. Some stores have already experimented with providing terminals mounted on shopping carts that enable shoppers to browse the Internet while cruising the store. This Internet access will require another piece of that same bandwidth as the store, but will also need to be segmented from the store traffic (another use for VLANs).

In summary, remember the following considerations regarding WLAN usage in retail environments:

- **Bar coding**—Typically, applications using bar code scanners have a very minimal set of requirements, with range and coverage being the most often sought-after feature of the wireless.
    - Low bandwidth
    - Low user density
    - Maximum coverage for lowest implementation cost
- **Voice**—Minimum number of users, but requires minimal dead spots in facility.
- **Roaming**—Usually a single network segment of Layer 2 roaming is adequate. If voice is used, fast roaming is recommended.
- **Security**—Depends on data being passed over WLAN devices. If POS devices are used on the WLAN, a high level of security is recommended, such as *Wi-Fi Protected Access* (WPA).

Warehousing

Although bar coding is a primary application in warehousing as well, warehousing lends itself to other applications and a slightly different implementation of the bar code scanner. Most warehouses use lift trucks or tow motor vehicles, which move around the facility at a much higher pace than people on foot. This requires quick handoff between APs, but nowhere near the handoff requirement for voice roaming (150 ms). It also means the scanner device must be mounted to the vehicle. This can create some obstacles for the antennas.

You must also consider the composition of the items being warehoused. For example, liquid items can be very radio opaque, and metal items can significantly affect the propagation of signals. These items may change in a warehouse as inventory levels change, or worse, not be present at the time of initial survey.

Figure 4-3 shows one typical lift-truck terminal. This style of device is typically ruggedized, with large screens and large keys for easy accessibility while operating the vehicle.

Figure 4-3 also shows a typical mounting of a lift-truck terminal. The antenna is most often located up high for maximum coverage. In some cases, this is accomplished by mounting the entire device high (as shown in this figure) or by running coax cable to a remote antenna.

Figure 4-3   *Typical Lift-Truck Mounting*

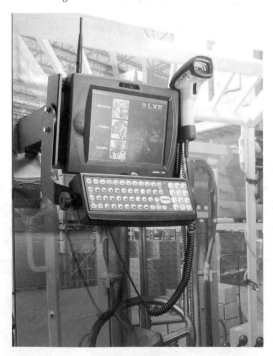

Because of the nature of vehicle mobility, many users think fast roaming is required when using bar code scanners onboard a lift truck. However, as with simple bar code scanners and IP applications, this is not a necessity for most systems. It is, however, still a requirement for voice systems to have fast roaming implemented.

In summary, remember the following considerations for typical WLAN usage in warehouse environments:

- **Bar coding**—Similar to handheld bar code scanners, the lift-truck bar code scanners have similar requirements.
    - Low bandwidth
    - Low user density
    - Maximum coverage for lowest implementation cost
- **Voice**—Minimum number of users, but requires minimal dead spots in facility.
- **Roaming**—Usually single network segment, of Layer 2 roaming is adequate. Tow roaming (even if vehicle is in motion. However, if voice is used, fast roaming is recommended.
- **Security**—Depends on data being passed over WLAN devices and how critical its overall nature is. If the warehouse stores fresh foods, it may not be necessary at all. If the warehouse processes military materials, however, it may be a high-priority requirement.

Enterprise Offices

The enterprise office is one the most recent places were wireless is starting to take a strong foothold. Although many people use wireless networks in offices, many others do not see the benefit of it and view wireless as just a workplace toy. This is especially true of users who are accustomed to a desktop PC and for whom mobility is not a possibility. As more users move to laptops, and portability is available, however, the use of wireless will take off. The ability to have information at your fingertips anywhere in the facility is extremely beneficial to both the user and the company.

Typical applications for enterprise offices include general network use such as e-mail, Internet browsing, and file transfers. However, many applications such as intercompany instant messaging applications are starting to be used in the enterprise and require network connections throughout office.

A well-disciplined and well-used instant messaging program can be an extremely useful tool. Consider this: You are attending a meeting and you need some bit of information that you do not have, but you know someone in your organization does have the information. You have three choices:

- Leave the meeting and go find that person. But this requires that you know precisely where that person is.

- Call the person, hoping he has his cellular phone turned on and he is not in a meeting that precludes him from answering the phone.

- Use an instant messaging application. You can ask the question and get the information without ever leaving the meeting room or disturbing anyone else in the meeting. Think about how much time that saved for everyone in the meeting!

A second application is 802.11 phones (see Figure 4-4). We all understand that the use of a cell phone, which is with you all the time, also dramatically increases your availability to coworkers. But the use of an 802.11 VoIP phone means you do not need to spend the extra expense of cellular airtime when inside your facility.

Figure 4-4   *Typical 802.11 Wireless Phones*

Both the instant messaging and 802.11 applications require connection at all times to the network; otherwise, they are not effective. Although instant messaging can withstand some interruptions (you normally will not be using your computer while walking from one location to another), a wireless VoIP phone requires not only constant connections, but also the ability to roam from one AP to another very fast (under 150 ms). That may mean maintaining the same subnet connection, which can have a huge effect on your network's design because it requires a large "flat" network, with many users on the same subnet. Although some Layer 3 roaming products are available, many are not fast enough to meet the necessary 150-ms roaming requirements needed for VoIP. They are, however, getting faster all the time. Be sure to specify fast roaming as a necessity if you require it for your design.

Wireless VoIP also requires a bit more bandwidth, and has less tolerance to bandwidth congestion than regular data applications. For this reason, it may be necessary to limit the minimum data rate. Also most of the wireless VoIP products available at the time of writing are limited to 802.11b, with several companies' road maps including 802.11g and 802.1a products sometime in 2004 or 2005.

In summary, remember the following considerations regarding WLAN usage in enterprise environments:

- **Bandwidth**—Medium to high.
- **User density**—High.
- **Cell sizes**—Typically small for maximum per-user bandwidth.
- **Voice**—Simultaneous calls can create a large bandwidth requirement. As mentioned previously, separate VLANs are recommended here, and care should be taken to keep dead spots in the facility to a minimum.
- **Roaming**—Layer 2 roaming may be adequate, but Layer 3 roaming is often necessary. Fast roaming is required in most cases.
- **Security**—A high level of security is recommended (WPA).

Health Care

The health-care industry has experienced a surge of wireless usage over the past few years. Although several leading-edge health-care providers were actually using wireless many years ago, wireless has become mainstream only in the past few years.

The scope of applications in health care is as wide as in any segment of the wireless industry. The initial usage of wireless was for medication distribution. The ability to have instant access to a patient's records enabled clinicians to view the last dosage and time, and to immediately update the patient's records when meds were administered, providing up-to-the-minute record keeping. This has been instrumental in reducing medication errors. This application requires minimal bandwidth because it is a simple database update, but it requires coverage in all areas where patients will be administered medication.

Another early application was the use of wireless to connect patient monitors (devices that electronically monitor respiratory, heart, and vital statistics) to monitors at a centralized station such as ward or wing desk. This permits one health-care professional to monitor many patients simultaneously. This also enables health-care workers to monitor patient vitals not only while in the room but also as patients are moved to another location for testing, while in transit between departments, and so on. Once again, this requires only a minimum amount of bandwidth, but does require wireless connection access anywhere that a patient may be located.

As you may have experienced, cell phones are not permitted in most hospitals. Although pagers are used extensively in hospitals, they are usually a one-way communication. The sender has no idea whether the intended person ever received the page. For this reason, wireless VoIP phones are becoming popular in health-care facilities. The phones provide access to doctors and other professionals who require full-time availability.

One major stumbling block for wireless deployment in health care is security. As mentioned in Chapter 3, "Regulating the Use of 802.11 WLANs," *Health Insurance Portability and Accountability Act* (HIPAA) regulations require all patient data to remain strictly confidential. So if there is any possibility that the data over the RF may be intercepted and decoded, the system cannot be used for patient data.

Several other new wireless VoIP applications are entering the market today. One of the forerunners in these applications is Vocera (see Figure 4-5). The Vocera Communications Badge is reminiscent of the Star Trek communicator. It is a wearable device that weighs less than 2 ounces and can easily be clipped to a shirt pocket or worn on a lanyard. It enables instant two-way voice conversation without the need to remember a phone number or manipulate a handset. The communicator is controlled using natural spoken language. To initiate a conversation with Dr. John and LPN McMannon, for example, the user would simply say, "Get me Dr. John and Nurse McMannon." In addition, when a live conversation is not necessary, text messages and alerts can be sent to the LCD screen on the Communications Badge.

Figure 4-5   *Vocera Communicator*

Systems such as the Vocera Communications Badge require some back-end network support. A network server usually houses the centralized system intelligence, such as a call manager application, user manager program, and some type of connection manager program. In the case of Vocera, a speech-recognition program is also incorporated to provide security via speech-pattern sign on.

The same issues apply to voice applications in health-care environments as in other industries; these are bandwidth and roaming issues and product/technology availability.

In summary, remember the following considerations for typical WLAN usage in health-care environments:

- **Bandwidth**—Low-to-medium bandwidth for data applications.
- **User density**—Low, but coverage in rooms is necessary in most cases.
- **Voice**—Can create large bandwidth requirements. Separate VLANs are usually used here. Requires minimal dead spots in facility.
- **Roaming**—Layer 2 roaming may be adequate, but Layer 3 roaming is often necessary. Fast roaming is required in most cases due to requirement of voice application in most sites.
- **Security**—A high level of security is required (802.1a/*Extensible Authentication Protocol* [EAP]).

Education

Education facilities vary in size and format. Today's colleges are reacting fast to the demand for wireless networks. Just like every other industry, secondary education is a competitive business. The ability to provide students with learning and teaching aids is an advantage.

Wireless on the campus provides network connectivity in most locations to students and provides teaching professionals with yet another tool to disseminate information, including class updates and assignments. A fast-growing technology moving across colleges is the virtual class, or online class. Many universities are using online classes to provide lower-level classes or optional classes, and the ability to do it wirelessly means students can have access to these classes from locations outside the traditional classroom or computer lab, providing yet another competitive edge for the university and another advantage for the student.

Many classes today can be quite large, with sometimes as many as 300 students in a basic English or history class. Trying to provide enough bandwidth in such a classroom can be a challenge. The requirements of the students in the classroom need to be analyzed. They can be much different from perhaps a class specializing in video editing, in which video files are being transferred up and down the network.

Also the outdoor areas of the campus, or *green spaces* as they are called, are areas most students want to have wireless coverage (see Figure 4-6). Such coverage enables students to sit on campus lawns and in parks and access the network for work and research, or just to browse the Internet. However, covering these outdoor areas can be difficult, as well as expensive. The cost versus advantage should be analyzed here. Also when covering outdoor areas, you need to be certain coverage in the building structures isn't interfered with. Outdoor coverage should be thought of as part of the indoor system, not as just an "add-on" network.

Figure 4-6 *College Green Spaces*

Another issue that affects education (as well as other public systems) is the content being downloaded from the Internet. When a large number of users are downloading MP3 or video files, or using the Internet to receive radio and TV broadcasts, the network can easily become saturated. Certain protocols may need to be filtered at the router, or at the very least, the AP.

The final major hurdle from an education-use perspective is the hardware. The main staple for wireless today is 802.11b. And it comes in many flavors from many vendors. Whatever radio is in the computer the student got for Christmas, or whatever 802.11b card that is the cheapest at the book store, is what will be used. This means any requirements for proprietary systems (such as security) are simply not feasible. You might need to specify certain requirements for the students who want to access the wireless network. The first and most common requirement is the use of Wi-Fi certified devices only. You also want to specify what technology is to be used. Likely, you will require 802.11b or 802.11g devices, because either type can communicate in an 802.11b or 802.11g infrastructure. The infrastructure, however, will most likely need to support 802.11b devices (meaning it could be either b or g).

The use of 802.11a systems could be an advantage; however, using 802.11a exclusively on a campus severely restricts students today from using most of what is on the market for WLAN devices.

VLANs are another feature often implemented in educational environments. Many facilities use VLAN technology to separate students from faculty and staff. This helps to protect the facility's internal administrative systems from mischievous students and possibly from any viruses or worms students might introduce into the system.

In summary, remember the following considerations regarding WLAN usage in education environments:

- **Bandwidth**—High.
- **User density**—High.
- **Cell sizes**—Typically small for maximum per-user bandwidth.
- **Voice**—Usually limited applications, possible for faculty use only.
- **Roaming**—Layer 2 roaming may be adequate, but Layer 3 roaming is often necessary.
- **Security**—Over-the-air security is optional. You might want network authentication to prevent nonstudents from accessing the network.
- **VLANs**—Virtual LANs should be used to separate and protect the facility's internal networks from the student population and outsiders.

Manufacturing

Manufacturing facilities have very unique requirements that vary quite widely. A critical look at the application is required to understand the bandwidth required and the user density. In most manufacturing environments, user density is not a big issue; however, bandwidth can vary. In some cases, wireless networks are used more for tracking products through manufacturing (using bar code applications) and require minimal bandwidth. In other cases, however, there may be a need to download inspection documents, specifications, and other large files; such downloading requires maximum bandwidth capability.

Another common application in manufacturing and in industrial warehousing is machine automation. WLANs are used to feed control information to an automated crane, railcar, or any other remote-control device. With such, the device can move under remote control, without the need for wiring between the operator and vehicle or device (see Figure 4-7). Of course, the concern here is loss of communication. What happens when that crane is moving with 20 tons of steel and it loses its network connection? (And do not think it has not happened!)

Figure 4-7   *Remote Steel Crane*

For industrial and manufacturing, it is very critical to review the requirements of connectivity, roaming (and roaming times), and bandwidth because applications vary widely.

In summary, remember the following considerations regarding WLAN usage in manufacturing environments:

- **Bandwidth**—Low to medium.
- **User density**—Low user density, maximum coverage.
- **Voice**—Usually limited applications.
- **Roaming**—Layer 2 roaming generally suffices.
- **Security**—Depends on data being passed over WLAN devices.

Hotel, Conventions, and Hospitality

Hotels, convention centers, and hospitability systems are typically discussed as a single entity, but they can be very different. Consider a hotel. Many think of Internet access in a hotel as connectivity in the room. That is true, but is wireless really needed for this application? It is great to have, but is it necessary? If cabling is not yet pulled to each room, wireless may be the single item that makes Internet access affordable for the hotel.

Instead of providing every room with wireless coverage, many hotels only provide coverage for rooms on certain floors. Of course, as more and more travelers demand broadband access, coverage in every room will become a reality at some point in the future.

But what bandwidth is needed? That is the 10-Mb question. Most users would be happy with several hundred kilobits. However, supplying several hundred kilobits to every room requires a big pipe to the Internet. Or does it? Consider how many users will be accessing it at any one time. Most users in hotels use the Internet for e-mail, which has a limited bandwidth requirement. Also there is the question of just how big the connection to the Internet actually is. Having 500 Mb of total WLAN bandwidth available for users, while connecting the same network through a T1 to the Internet, makes no sense. Some balance is needed here.

Typically, the main concerns regarding hotel room access are range and coverage area. This means using the best antennas possible, and finding the best placement for maximum room coverage.

Similarly, the public locations in a hotel, such as the pool, reception, and lounges, do not usually have a high-bandwidth requirement. Although a large number of guests may frequent these areas, the number actually using the WLAN and requiring any volume of bandwidth remains low.

However, the same cannot be said for meeting rooms and convention areas. Here you may have a large number of users, all of whom are using the Internet simultaneously, for e-mail or possibly even connecting as part of the meeting they are attending. A typical Wi-Fi meeting will have as many as 150 to 200 users all online at the same time, from the same room! For example, IEEE meetings, which are held at various hotels and convention areas, are even larger, and virtually everyone has wireless capability.

In some cases, hotels may want meeting room coverage and guest room coverage to be distinct and separate. Some venues may charge large fees for high-speed Internet in a conference room, and they don't want guests with laptops to be able to use the low-priced room systems in these areas. This dual requirement can have deployment implications for power, antenna selection, and antenna placement. This is another area where VLANs can play a role in separating traffic and users.

Just as in an educational environment, the issue of various vendors and technologies applies to hotels, convention centers, and hospitality environments. Traditionally, public-access locations such as hotels and convention centers have been 802.11b. However, if this is a new installation, 802.1g should be considered because it supports all 802.11b devices also. Some large-scale meeting locations are moving to dual band to provide users who have 802.11a with access as well, freeing up some of the 2.4-GHz bandwidth.

Normally, small cells and a higher number of APs are required for convention and meeting room areas. In summary, remember the following considerations regarding typical WLAN usage in hotels, convention centers, and hospitality areas:

- **Bandwidth**—Low for guest rooms and general public areas (maximum coverage). High for convention centers and meeting rooms.

- **User density**—Low for guest rooms and public gathering areas, high for meeting rooms.

- **Voice**—Typically not used.

- **Roaming**—Layer 2 roaming in convention areas. Guest rooms require no roaming.

- **Security**—Typically, no WLAN security is set up. A network authentication server may be used to limit access to approved guests. (Guests are urged to use *virtual private networks* [VPNs] over wireless.)

Public Hotspots

Sipping coffee, waiting for your flight, or having fries with a Quarter Pounder now means having access to the Internet. As more and more people depend on staying connected, and staying connected means keeping people longer in your establishment, wireless Internet access becomes a requirement. There are two main types of installation for such:

- The very local coverage area, such as a coffee shop or fast-food chain restaurant, where typically one or (at most) two APs are needed to provide coverage.

- A widespread coverage area such as an airport or park, where 10 or even hundreds of APs are necessary to provide full coverage.

Generally, these systems are used for one purpose: connecting to the Internet, with limited expectations for high bandwidth. The overall number of users who use these networks, while growing quickly, is still a small number of the total number of people at these locations.

These public systems must follow the same rules as other locations where there is no control over the client device. A public system must allow almost any WLAN vendor's device to communicate, and installers should consider using an 802.11g or even a dual-band AP to provide the widest range of support for the users.

Many public WLAN systems also "regulate" who can use the system. Usually this is not done at the wireless side, but rather through an authentication server on the network. This type of server will usually redirect any new user to a greeting page and sign-on page. Such a feature enables the system to regulate and even charge users who are trying to access the Internet.

In summary, remember the following considerations regarding typical WLAN usage in public hotspots:

* **Bandwidth**—Low to medium for most sites.
* **User density**—Low for most sites, with expectations to grow.
* **Voice**—Typically not used.
* **Roaming**—Small sites require no roaming. Larger sites may require minimal roaming support.
* **Security**—Typically no WLAN security is set up. A network authentication server may be used to limit access to approved guests or to charge guests for access.
* **VLANs**—Virtual LANs should be used to separate internal networks, conference networks, and guest networks.

SOHO

Small office/home office (SOHO) environments do not usually require a site survey (unless, of course, your home is the size of a palace). SOHO sites usually require only a single AP and have a limited number of users accessing the network. Overall throughput is normally limited by the Internet connection. The choice of wireless vendors is usually controlled, and so technology choice is not a problem and any 802.11 scheme will work.

Many SOHO users think security is not a problem. This, however, is probably the single biggest misconception regarding SOHO implementations. These environments should have at least minimal security, and it is recommended to at least use WPA with *Pre-Shared Keys* (PSK) and to require users to change passwords at periodic intervals (every month, every week, and so on).

Another problem that occurs with SOHO installation is interference. Although most education and enterprise offices use 802.11 VoIP phones for wireless phones, or use proprietary 900-MHz wireless corporate phone systems, in the SOHO, it is common to use a standard home-style 2.4-GHz or 5-GHz wireless phone. These phones will cause interference if installed improperly.

In addition to phones, many types of wireless devices can be sources of interference. For example, wireless baby monitors, cordless speakers, and wireless cameras are common users of the 2.4-GHz band. Almost any device that is "cordless" is a potential source of interference, and such devices should be reviewed to determine whether they operate in the same frequency band as the intended WLAN system.

Even the standard microwave oven operates at the 2.4-GHz frequency and will cause interference to most 802.11b and 802.11g WLAN systems.

In general, a minimum of 10 feet should separate the WLAN and the potentially interfering device. However, the best solution is to choose a phone, camera, and so on that uses a different frequency band than the WLAN and to keep any WLAN device at least 10 feet away from any microwave oven.

In summary, remember the following considerations regarding typical WLAN usage in SOHO environments:

- **Bandwidth**—Low (limited by incoming network pipe).
- **User density**—Low.
- **Voice**—Not used.
- **Roaming**—No roaming required.
- **Security**—At least minimal WLAN security is set up (WPA). Suggest a firewall if using public Internet access.

Defining the WLAN Requirements

When designing any network, the first step is to determine user needs. For a WLAN, this includes defining the coverage area. Before you can determine *what* you need, you have to decide *why* you need it. Mobility is most often the reason for implementing a wireless network, although mobility should not be confused with providing uninterrupted connectivity with the LAN. So, early in the planning stage, you must determine the key points at which users will reside, as well as the most common paths between the primary gathering locations, such as conference rooms, the offices of key personnel, development labs, and so forth. Critical to this process is a good diagram of the facility showing what the WLAN needs to cover.

You also need to determine the minimum speeds users require. Toward this end, you must have a description of the applications that the users run. Of course, every network engineer will say that each user needs 100 Mbps, just as in a wired switched network. However, wireless is not a switched medium. It is a shared medium. Therefore, not all applications will truly fit well into a WLAN system. Based on most networks analyzed, network use is in fact very "peaky"—a user requests a download (low speed required), followed by the actual download (greater speed required). The opposite can be true when uploading documents. Because traffic loads tend to vary to a great extent, most network designs require a fraction of the available bandwidth thought of as mission critical. This does not mean that high-speed networks of 100 Mbps and even gigabit rates are never needed; after all, the minimum amount of speed required generally increases over time as more users access a LAN.

It is unlikely that all users in a LAN will use the same client device. Therefore, you need to determine whether users need specialty devices on the wireless system, such as bar code readers, PCI cards, PCMCIA cards, wireless IP phones, or perhaps even wireless print servers. If so, you need to decide whether it is possible to procure all the end devices from the same vendor or whether there will be different-vendor products in the mix. This decision could be very important because of some vendor-interoperability issues with proprietary features.

Defining Your Technology Requirements

As you learned in Chapter 1, the three primary technologies available today are 802.11a, 802.11b, and 802.11g. Now it is time to decide which one fits your needs (or at least try). Before you can decide which technology to use, you first must answer more questions. As mentioned previously, there are many different types of WLAN uses and applications. These variations can cause major differences in WLAN designs.

One thing that is important to discuss here is the difference between 802.11b and 8702.11g, from the AP perspective. If the system being installed is a new purchase, you should use 802.11g APs. These support both 802.11b and 802.11g clients and are typically priced at the same level. In fact, the availability of 802.11b APs will start to diminish. However, 802.11b clients will be around for several years still because of the current ubiquity of laptops with embedded 802.11b radios.

As you move forward toward a decision regarding technology, answer the following questions:

- What present applications will be used and what is their bandwidth requirement per user?

  This question is vital. If you plan to use the network for simple network connection and average office-type applications (MS Office, e-mail, web browsing, database access, and so forth), the bandwidth of a normal 802.11b/g system will probably suffice (depending on the answer to the following question).

- What is the average and maximum density of WLAN users in any given coverage area, and will this density increase over time?

  You need to determine how many users will be in a given area, both on a routine basis and on a maximum-user basis. For the average office application (as defined by your answer to the first question in this list), you can get reasonable performance with 10 to 20 users per AP when using 802.11b data rates. For small-transaction applications with a low-bandwidth requirement, such as a stock trading floor or bar coding, the number of users per AP can increase dramatically. Remember that the aggregate throughput (not data rate) of an 11-Mbps 802.11b system is about 5.5- to 6-Mbps aggregate per AP (and the average throughput of a 802.11b and 802.11g mixed system, with an 802.11g AP, is about 8 Mbps).

- What future applications are being considered, and what are their expected bandwidth requirements?

  The answer to this may determine whether you need to move today to a higher-speed broadband wireless system or may wait to upgrade in the future. If you decide that an 802.11b data rate is adequate (based on answers to these questions), you may elect to install 802.11g APs (which support both 802.11b and 802.11g clients) and use the available 802.11b clients. However, you may need to migrate to higher bandwidth at a later date, and adding 5 GHz is one possibility (again depending on your answers). Either solution permits slow migration and investment protection, because you can continue to use your existing 802.11b clients for the lower-bandwidth applications. Looking forward approximately 12 to 18 months will help guide you in this part of the preplanning process.

- To which physical areas do you plan to provide WLAN access?

  If you are looking for maximum coverage, 802.11b systems will provide the best solution. If you are looking to cover both indoor and outdoor areas, you must use 802.11b or 802.11g, or limit the use of 802.11a systems (restricting use of the lower four channels [UNII1] for outdoor usage because the lower channels of the 802.11a [UNII1 channels] are for indoor use only).

- Do you plan to use the WLAN for portable VoIP connections, and if so, how many concurrent VoIP connections will be used in any given AP coverage area?

  This could also be a stumbling block if you are trying to install 802.11a today. Most 802.11-based phones are limited to 802.11b systems, with 802.11g and 802.11a phones due to hit the market in late 2004 or 2005. If you need the bandwidth of 802.11a for other applications, and still want to install VoIP wireless phones, your best solution is a dual-band AP, which provides an excellent way to separate VoIP and data traffic (aside from using VLANs); another satisfactory architectural approach is to use separate virtual collision domains or VLANs. Present 802.11b APs and 802.11b phone systems can carry, at a maximum, four to seven concurrent calls. Add data to this and the number of calls decreases. The 802.11b phone vendors are making major improvements to their products, so ask the vendor for guidance on the number of calls, the overall bandwidth, and so forth that you need.

- Do the APs need to be placed in the ceiling or in secure, out-of-sight locations?

  This is a critical issue, and you will learn more about it Chapter 12, "Installing WLAN Products." Remember, however, that some 5-GHz AP antennas have limitations. In public-access sites, schools, health-care facilities, and other public places, the APs are usually kept out of sight, and external antennas are used both for aesthetic reasons and to protect the equipment from vandalism and theft. If this describes your situation, you need to determine whether you somehow can mount them in an area that will not hinder the antenna performance or require the use of external antennas. In some cases, mounting above the ceiling tile *might* work, but you need to ensure that air-conditioning ducts, electrical conduit and other cable trays, and lighting fixtures will not hinder the antenna performance. In most cases, this is not an acceptable location to put the antenna, and hence these types of 802.11a APs are probably not a good solution.

Another issue with placing APs in the ceiling may be plenum ratings. The *plenum* is the area above a room where heating and air conditioning run. Fire regulations require that the materials used in that area not contribute poisonous gases or excessive flammability in the event of extreme heat or fire. Many local regulations require that the equipment placed above ceilings meet certain fire and smoke regulations. Check with the local authorities to determine what these regulations are, and verify that at a minimum the device meets the UL2043 standard.

- Who will determine the client radio vendor: users or administrators?

  If the WLAN client devices will be determined by the IT staff, this is not an issue (in most cases). However, if the users decide which client device they will use, this can complicate the product decision. Consider an educational facility in which both students and faculty will be using the WLAN. The faculty members will likely get their devices via the network administrator; however, the students will be bringing in their Linksys, D-link, Microsoft, or other WLAN card that they bought at the local store. With the abundance of available 802.11b cards, this makes the decision easier. In addition, many computers today come with built-in 802.11b radios and integrated antennas. As of this writing, most PCs are being delivered with 802.11b radio devices, and because the antenna is integrated into the computer (and antennas are frequency sensitive), you cannot exchange the 802.11b radio for an 802.11a radio. The road maps of most PC vendors do include a combo 802.11a/802.11g radio card and antenna, so this issue will diminish over time, but it will linger for quite a while still. One other item to consider is this: As dual-band clients come on the market and become more common, users will demand dual-band support as well. For this reason, a dual-band AP may be the best strategy for future growth (or an AP that can be upgraded to a dual-band AP).

- Which types of client devices will be used on the WLAN? Do you need specialty devices, such as bar code scanners, wearable computers, PDAs, cash registers, location-finding devices, and so forth?

If so, you need to determine, with the help of the device vendor, whether these devices can support 802.11a and either Cardbus interfaces or mini-PCI interfaces. Because 802.11b is only 11 Mbps, a PCMCIA interface to the radio is perfectly acceptable. If you are moving to 802.11a (or 802.11g), however, you need Cardbus support or mini-PCI support, because a PCMCIA interface is not fast enough to provide a 54-Mbps data rate. If there will be an array of various client devices, interoperability will be a greater issue, which means you need to select an AP with the greatest degree of proven interoperability, from a company that has been deploying WLANs for a considerable amount of time.

- What regulations govern the use of IEEE 802.11 in this region?

  As explained Chapter 3, some countries still do not permit 802.11a systems. Other countries require the use of dynamic frequency selection and automatic power control (both of which are part of 802.11h) for 802.11a or other 5-GHz radio systems.

  Other regulatory issues, such as *Effective Isotropic Radiated Power* (EIRP) limits, frequency allocation, and antenna limitations, can come into play as well. Even 2.4 GHz has many different regulations from country to country. You need to check the local regulations for the countries in which you will be using the systems. The last thing you want to do is choose a technology or product line, install it in half of your facilities, and then find out you have to use a different system in the remaining facilities because what you selected is not permitted in certain countries. You can avoid much of this problem by selecting a vendor that provides this technology on the open world market, as opposed to a vendor that does not export any of this technology. Also ensure that the security assets you purchase are appropriately configured, and legal, to export; again, this issue will be greatly alleviated if you select a vendor that routinely ships this technology to many countries around the world.

- Will anything in the building construction interfere with the RF signal?

  You need to determine whether the facility is built such that RF will penetrate into the necessary areas or whether you require special antennas to get coverage in certain areas. Remember that 2.4-GHz signals will penetrate standard construction easier than 5-GHz signals. A good practice is to actually do some on-site testing with both technologies to verify performance in your typical environment.

- Does the facility use any other 2.4- or 5-GHz equipment, such as Bluetooth systems, cordless phones, microwaves, wireless security cameras and alarms, and so on?

  If other systems are installed and actively used, this may be a reason to choose one technology over another. However, it may also just require your attention during the site survey and installation to be certain the interference is kept to a minimum. Many times this can be achieved by proper placement of APs and antennas.

Selecting Necessary WLAN Services

Now that you have considered the preceding questions and determined the technology you want to use (or at least have a good idea), you need to determine what other functions are important to your installation. Previous chapters have discussed VLANs, QoS, roaming, security, load balancing, and interoperability, and it is important that you understand the issues that some of these services and their support (or, in some cases, lack of support) will cause. This will also be an important part of choosing the proper WLAN products.

VLANs

VLANs are a relatively new feature in many of the WLAN products on the market. A VLAN enables you to separate traffic into separate virtual LANs over the RF. In the past, this had to be done at the switch, and for every VLAN, you needed a separate WLAN system (separate APs).

Why would you want VLANs over the wireless? One reason is for guest traffic in an enterprise system. Typically, a security system is set up on the WLAN for the "normal" users. When guests arrive, giving them access to the network is not necessarily easy (or even desired), because passwords and accounts need to be set up, and these visitors may change on a day-to-day basis. By using VLANs, you can provide one internal-user VLAN that incorporates certain security modes (PEAP, LEAP, EAP-TLS, WPA, and so forth) and permits access to the corporate network, and you can provide a separate VLAN for guest users with static wired equivalent privacy (WEP), or perhaps no WEP at all. The latter VLAN would funnel the guest user only to certain network areas or perhaps even just the "dirtynet" for Internet access only. With the use of VLANs, both types of users can share the same AP.

If you plan to carry voice traffic over your WLAN equipment, you probably also want to configure your WLAN equipment such that all the voice traffic is carried over dedicated VLANs to ensure that the low-latency traffic (voice in this case) is not competing with data that has lower latency after it hits the wireless network.

See Chapter 10, "Using Site Surveying Tools," for more on VLANs.

Quality of Service

QoS is necessary if you intend to support VoIP, and if you want to differentiate traffic by port, application, or user. Various QoS schemes are on the market today, with most being proprietary. Most vendors comply with the IEEE 802.11e standard for QoS. Chapter 10 provides more detail on QoS as well.

IP Subnet Roaming

IP subnet roaming (Layer 3 roaming) is an issue that also requires some planning. Although the intention of wireless is to be portable and mobile, you need to realize that it is *part* of the wired network. In fact, the AP is really at the edge of the network. The switch (or hubs in older days) used to be considered the edge of the network, but now it has been moved out to the AP. If you plan to install five APs, keeping them all on the same subnet is not a problem. However, if you are installing 2000 APs across many campus buildings, it might be very difficult (and very undesirable) to keep them all on the same subnet, especially if you include low-latency-sensitive traffic over the same subnet.

If you move from one subnet to another, you will drop any IP connections that are presently running, and unless there is some method for a release-and-renew function for IP addresses, you will not have IP connectivity. Mobile IP was developed several years ago to handle these issues. Through the use of home and foreign agents on the infrastructure, and a special IP stack on the client, a client can move across subnets without ever changing the client IP address. (A detailed description of mobile IP is beyond the scope of this book, but more details are included in Chapter 10.)

Security

Security is a major concern. This book does not go into detail on security because there are numerous books dedicated to that topic. Aside from brief introductory comments, security is not possible to cover in detail here. You need to verify that the security solution you select and the products you select are compatible, keeping in mind again that you will have no higher level of security than the least-sophisticated device on your network. An example is a health-care facility in which the patient-records application runs on standard laptop computers that support many different versions of security (PEAP, LEAP, EAP-TLS, WPA, and so forth), but the pharmaceutical application requires bar coding, and the bar code scanners may or may not support the same security solution.

To resolve this issue, you can use VLANs to separate the devices (and their security types). Devices with lower-level security may have a VLAN that accesses only network systems with minimally sensitive data. At the same time, network systems that have highly sensitive data may be on a separate VLAN and accessed only by devices that can use higher levels of security. So take care to select products that support the security method that you have chosen.

Load Balancing

Load balancing and hot standby in APs are also things to consider. Most of the higher-end enterprise-type APs support these functions, but in some cases may require your attention to how they are configured. However, many of the lower-end products (products targeted for the SOHO markets) that IT professionals may be inclined to evaluate (based on pressure from upper-level management to lower costs) do not support most of these advanced types of WLAN services.

Interoperability

Interoperability is also a concern when you are selecting products. Make sure that any product you select is Wi-Fi certified (and not just that they use the term *Wi-Fi* in their literature). Go to the Wi-Fi Alliance website (www.wi-fi.com) and view the list of certified devices. This at least provides some basic level of interoperability testing and certification. Also be aware that there are several different Wi-Fi certifications, such as 802.11a, 802.11b, 802.11g, security, quality of service, and so on. The packages of newer Wi-Fi certified products include a certification compliance label that lists the features supported by the product (802.11a, 802.1b, WPA, QoS, and so forth).

Building-to-Building Connectivity

You need to review several key issues when selecting a bridge technology for building-to-building connectivity. As with WLANs, the first requirement is bandwidth. You must determine what overall bandwidth will be required between sites. If the bridges will be used for both wireless bridges and for WLAN access, the bridges must follow the appropriate technology for the client devices. If the bridge will be strictly for site-to-site connectivity, however, any bridge technology can be used, including proprietary systems.

Bridge systems come in many flavors and sizes, with various throughputs available. 802.11b systems can provide throughputs of up to 6 Mbps per system, and ranges up to 20 miles (at 6 Mbps) in locations where high-gain antennas are permitted. Bridges based on 802.11g and 8021.11a technologies typically provide throughputs in the mid-20-Mbps range, but with reduced range. Some 802.11a-based or 802.11g-based bridges can provide maximum throughput at about 12 or 15 miles.

For much higher throughput, you need to review some proprietary systems. Many different systems are available, including free-space optical bridges, through which data rates can reach 155 Mbps or higher but with very limited range.

In all cases, line of sight is required for the longer distances, and usually for even short links.

Most bridges will provide a link joining the two networks to the same subnet. If the sites are on separate subnets (typical), the bridges should be attached to a router port for proper segmentation between networks.

Even proprietary systems are not secure (many think that you can have "security be obscurity") because traffic can be "received" by anyone owning a device from the same company. Security needs to be reviewed carefully and should be used if any type of sensitive data is to be sent over the link. Some bridges support EAP-type authentication, whereas others may only support the easily compromised WEP. An alternative is to use a VPN tunnel between the routers on each side of the link and have the bridges attached to these routers. This provides all bridge traffic a VPN security tunnel.

Summary

When selecting the appropriate technology for your system, in the initial discussions you must review the applications intended to be included. Which features are required, what bandwidth is needed, and what future applications may be used over the WLAN. These key issues will assist in determining whether 802.11a, 8092.11b, 802.11g, or dual-band systems will provide the necessary support. Also you should review features such as VLANs, security, QoS, load balancing, interoperability, voice support, fast roaming, and Layer 2 or Layer 3 roaming to understand whether they are required today, or whether they will be required in the near future. Based on these facts, you can make a preliminary decision on the technology. Notice the use of the word *preliminary* here. Why preliminary? Because until a full survey is completed, you many not be able to make a certain decision, and there is always a chance that the site itself may have issues that cause you to change your plans.

This chapter covers the following topics:

- Key Features of a WLAN
- Various WLAN Architectures
- Selecting the Access Point
- Selecting the Client Products

CHAPTER **5**

Selecting the WLAN Architecture and Hardware

As you no doubt understand by now, a properly selected and installed WLAN can provide a dramatic increase in productivity at the individual level, which in the end affects the bottom line for the company. However, selecting the wrong WLAN architecture or hardware can just as easily result in a system that causes the network to become unbearably slow, insecure, extremely unstable, or worse, a system that the users hate because of its archaic access and use rules.

Over the past couple of years, WLAN architectures have undergone many changes, with some claiming that a particular system is a totally new leading-edge design that solves all the WLAN problems for everyone. Well, unfortunately, no single system solves every problem.

This chapter discusses the various architectures, features, and functions available in WLAN products. It also explains what to consider so that you can build and scale the network in the future and accommodate technological migrations such as new security and data-rate advancements. You have to be prepared for expansion and continued growth; after all, when users start to see the benefits that a WLAN provides, they will start to consider it a necessity for daily work habits.

Key Features of a WLAN

Users believe that many features are critical to selecting the architecture and components that comprise a WLAN. In the past, range and throughput were the primary factors used to evaluate WLANs. Although these can be two important items, they are, by far, not the only or the most important in many systems. With the wide range of applications and devices used in conjunction with a WLAN, it is vital to evaluate the various features and architectures used in WLANs today.

NOTE   Although every design and application will vary as to what the most important features of the WLAN are, several features are usually critical to WLAN systems for growth, performance, and versatility. Some of today's WLAN architectures include many or all of these items, and many do not. It is critical to verify what is appropriate for your system.

Aside from the features discussed earlier in the book, such as *virtual local-area networks* (VLANs), *quality of service* (QoS), roaming, and security, consider several other features when selecting a WLAN infrastructure. Many of these features are not in just the *access point* (AP), but actually reside either in the management station or as a combination of operation between the AP and the management station. Be certain to analyze the systems you are considering to see which system can meet your needs. The following sections discuss some of the additional features to look for in an AP.

Software Upgrade Capabilities

Although many of us do not like to think about upgrading software in our systems, it is a way of life in networking. New features, patches, and performance improvements are continually being made in firmware. Therefore, you must have a method of upgrading your systems. In the case of a single, or even a few APs on the system, upgrading can be done on a "one-at-a-time" basis. As the number of APs on your network increases, however, upgrading becomes much more of a resource (and time) issue. A good system should have multiple methods for upgrading firmware.

Some of the more common upgrade methods include uploading from a web browser, SNMP, FTP, and TFTP, or custom applications. In some cases, you can even distribute from one AP to all others on your system. Regardless which system you choose, consider the length of time it takes and ease of which upgrades can be accommodated, because upgrades will be required if you have a WLAN system installed for more than a few months.

Most APs on the market today permit upgrading of the firmware, but it is important to select a product that can be upgraded with not only firmware, but radio hardware as well. Many APs contain a radio that is embedded into the device and cannot be changed. This means if a new technology comes to market (as happened when 802.11g technology superceded 802.11b technology) there may be a need for a complete AP replacement. Being able to replace just the RF section provides a much lower cost of upgrading. As you will learn in the section "Various WLAN Architectures" later in this chapter, some APs have removed much of the intelligence and hardware from the AP and placed it in a centrally located device. However, the AP must still contain the actual RF transceiver. The ability to upgrade the RF section of the AP can be extremely cost effective when upgrading is required.

Rogue AP Detection

Far too often, managers and IT folks, who have not yet installed a WLAN, believe they do not have a WLAN on their network. Or that with an IT-installed WLAN, that these corporate APs are the only ones on the network. It is very common to find rogue APs (APs that have been placed on the networks without the permission of the network administrator) on networks, both in locations that already have IT-installed WLANs, but particularly in those that do not. The WLAN installed should include APs that are part of a system that can assist in detecting *and locating* rogue APs. Many WLAN products just detect interfering APs and market this as something important, but there should be some features that assist in locating where the device is in your facility.

Flexible and Secure Mobility

Enabling users to roam between different APs, subnets, buildings, and WLAN systems is vital to WLANs. A WLAN should be able to marry each user's security profile with the required mobility. A good WLAN system enables you to define per-user security policies that follow the user. In wireless environments, enterprises may choose to use encryption mechanisms that operate at Layer 2, Layer 3, or both. Such security should be applicable to different users or communities, simultaneously. Remember, existing VPN technology cannot scale to WLAN performance levels, so the WLAN system must provide this capability. Perhaps most important, for encryption to be robust and flexible, it requires more than a single point of processing (such as a core security processor). If encryption is done at the radio device itself, it usually results in faster processing and improved throughput performance. In addition, you typically have a more secure system if authentication is handled at the AP, preventing unauthenticated packets from ever entering any portion of the wired network. For more on security, refer to one of the many books that have been written dedicated to WLAN security, such as the Cisco Press title *Cisco Wireless LAN Security*, by Krishna Sankar and Sri Sundaralingam (October 2004), as well as the Wi-Fi Alliance website (www.wi-fi.com).

Assisted Survey and Installation Tools

Many systems rely on experienced personnel to do the site survey, installation, and con-figuration of a WLAN. This is one side of the measuring stick. On the opposite end of that stick, some products claim there is no need for a site survey at all. The vendors claim their products have software that can automatically adjust and configure all necessary parameters on the AP, so no survey is necessary. But reality resides somewhere in the middle of that stick.

WARNING   Be aware of automatic site survey claims from vendors. In almost every case, there will be a need for some site survey work, including some range, throughput, and interference testing of a manual type.

Self-Healing Systems

Some APs require configurations that must be set and tuned manually. In the case of a small system, this is fine. As the number of APs on your system grows, however, manual configuration becomes a challenge. Many systems out there permit automatic adjustment of certain RF parameters. The most common of these are power levels, and channel or frequency selection. Some features can also be used to automatically maintain coverage in the event of AP failure (by power-level adjustments); other features enable you to adjust frequency selection to compensate for interference. WLAN systems should not only have the capability to measure the RF characteristics of a facility on a continuous basis, they should also be capable of recalibrating RF settings on APs to accommodate for these type of changes, thereby reducing the possibility for repetitive site surveys, unless there is a major change in the physical environment.

Remote Debugging

Some very useful features for your WLAN fall under what is commonly known as *radio management*. These are features that enable you to manage the RF portion of the WLAN and to perform tasks such as remotely capture wireless traffic, identify and display interference signal levels, and gather WLAN client information, all from a central point of management. Although most IT troubleshooters are familiar with wired tools for performing these troubleshooting tasks, radio management is a new world, and the point of capture changes. You cannot troubleshoot what you cannot see. Other tools are also available, and you will learn about them in Chapter 10, "Using Site Surveying Tools."

Various WLAN Architectures

Quite a few WLANs introduced to the market have a central management device, which in many cases is dubbed a *wireless switch*. Before engaging in a discussion about wireless switches, first familiarize yourself with the definition of a network switch. One definition of a network switch is written as follows (http://wi-fiplanet.webopedia.com):

> Short for *port-switching hub,* a special type of hub that forwards packets to the appropriate port based on the packet's address. Conventional hubs just rebroadcast every packet to every port. Because switching hubs forward each packet only to the required port, they provide much better performance.

In simple terms, "independent collision domain" identifies the key element that most network engineers perceive as a network switch. In the wired world, this means that only traffic destined for or leaving from a given station is on the local leg or wired segment of that station's network. To accomplish this in an 802.11 wireless network, you need to have every station on its own independent, nonoverlapping, noninterfering RF channel. If you were using a 2.4-GHz network, which has a total of three nonoverlapping channels, this means you can have up to three users. This does not make for a real scalable network!

In some definitions, the use of the term *switched wireless* may in fact be a true statement for 802.11. In either case, it has caused much confusion in the marketplace today, and many vendors have used the term *switched wireless* in such a way that it confuses many new-comers to the WLAN wireless world. WLAN technology is not a system that can be truly switched as defined and understood by most network engineers. WLAN devices operate in a shared medium, and the design of WLAN networks needs to reflect that fact.

This section covers five of the most popular wireless architectures and identifies some of their strengths and weaknesses (to the extent possible in this chapter). After you understand the differences, you should be able to make a decision on the architecture that best suits the needs of your network and applications.

The five primary architectures are as follows:

- Distributed intelligence
- Centralized intelligence
- Core device architecture
- Edge device architecture
- Switched antenna systems

Two other architectures that are not commonly used today, but that are gaining popularity, are mesh networks and free-space optics networks.

By deciding on an architecture and defining technology requirements, as discussed earlier in Chapter 4, "WLAN Applications and Services," you should be ready to select the necessary devices, and possibly even the actual vendor and product models for your WLAN.

Distributed Intelligence

As has been the case because the inception of wireless, an AP has contained a fair amount of processing power and maintained most of the RF intelligence at the edge of the network. The AP then ties directly into the network, usually at a network switch, and is an inde-pendent AP, which means it is not reliant on any other server or controller on the network (other than Ethernet connectivity) to maintain 802.11 communications to the wireless clients.

The intelligent AP is often called a fat AP because it contains such components as a powerful processor and significant RAM and ROM. By containing these components, the AP can do more than just bridge Ethernet to 802.11 wireless.

Figure 5-1 illustrates a distributed intelligence system, where the AP is connected to a standard Ethernet switch and operates as a standalone device, without requiring a device on the network to provide overall operation of the AP.

Figure 5-1 *Distributed Intelligence System*

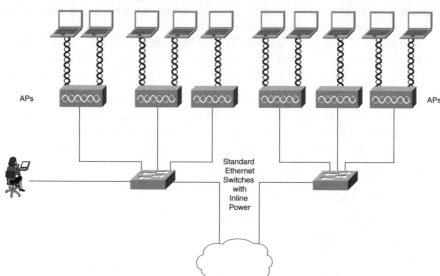

One key feature of an intelligent AP is that it can be used as a port-based authenticator. When used as such, the AP actually blocks traffic inbound from the RF and destined for the Ethernet from passing beyond the Ethernet port, keeping it off of the wired network unless the traffic is authen-ticated. If a packet is received from the RF and is not from an authenticated station, it is redirected to the authenticated server only. In this manner, only secure, authenticated traffic is permitted on the wired network.

Local encryption and decryption is also another key advantage of intelligent APs. The AP is the point at which the RF traffic gets encrypted on the transmit side and decrypted on the receive side. Although some may not see this as an advantage, a high-performance AP will use hardware acceleration in the AP, performing the encryption with very little overhead to the throughput of the WLAN data traffic. By distributing this task to every AP, the proba-bility of overburdening some processor that handles all RF traffic encryption from several to perhaps hundreds of APs is nonexistent.

Another often-overlooked feature of an intelligent AP is one of system resilience to failure. If one AP fails, only that one AP is affected, and all other devices continue to operate normally. It is not dependent on code running in some other device to operate.

In small installations, where you need perhaps only a very small number of APs, such as a small retail store or branch office, you have no need for an expensive controller or propri-etary switch. You can manage the APs using their internal software and a simple web browser, or small management program that resides on one of the networked servers.

For optimum management, an intelligent AP approach, at least in large installations, usually requires a management server (for example, SNMP Manager) to provide adequate support, configuration, and management of the numerous APs. If the product is chosen so that its management requirements can be incorporated into the wired network management system already in use, however, integration of management is very easy and efficient.

The ultimate downside to an intelligent AP is that because of the extra components in the AP, it typically comes with a higher price tag. However, before deciding that price of the AP is the determining factor, make sure you put together a spreadsheet of overall costs, including management stations and controllers or proprietary switches. In many cases, the higher cost of the intelligent AP does not outweigh the high cost of other components needed in the following architectures.

Centralized Intelligence

In 1999, Proxim Corporation came out with the Harmony product line, consisting of a centralized controller and of access points that relied on the controller for proper operation. Enter wireless switched networks. In 2002, Symbol Technologies followed suit with a similar centralized WLAN system, which it called a *switched wireless system*. Known as the *Mobius product line*, this system uses a controller and associated "slimmed-down" APs. In contrast to an intelligent AP, most centralized intelligence systems remove most of the tasks and processing from the AP and place the processing of these tasks in a switch or master WLAN controller located in a central point of the wired network. These types of APs are often referred to as thin APs. The two types of centralized intelligence architectures are as follows:

- A system that uses core devices (residing in the core of the network) for maintaining the intelligence
- A system that uses edge devices (edge of the wired network, such as an Ethernet switch) for maintaining the intelligence of the WLAN

In the case of wireless switching, APs are simplified and perform only transceiver and, in some cases, air-monitoring functions. In some systems, these APs are connected to the WLAN switch directly or over a Layer 2/3 network, or to their controller (as in the core device systems). The APs become extended access ports on the WLAN switch, directing user traffic to the switch or controller for processing.

Security functions used in the WLAN switch systems, such as encryption, authentication, and access control, are adapted to follow users as they move. Most wireless switch systems provide extended Layer 2/3 switching, enabling mobile users to roam between APs, switches, VLANs, and subnets without losing connectivity.

WLAN switching also provides a different approach to the operational management of 802.11 networks. AP configurations are stored on the controller or WLAN switch rather than on the AP itself. With the ability to control individual AP power and channel settings, some WLAN switches can automatically detect failed APs and can instruct nearby APs to adjust their power and channel settings to compensate accordingly. When the failed AP is replaced by a working AP, the WLAN switch automatically notes the event and configures the new AP.

The more sophisticated WLAN switches constantly monitor the air space to observe network and user load. They may even dynamically adjust bandwidth, access control, QoS, and other parameters as mobile users roam throughout the enterprise.

Core Device Architecture

In a core device architecture, the intelligence resides anywhere on the network, usually inside the *network operations center* (NOC), or at the very least a remote computer or network room. Oddly, several of these systems use the term *wireless switch* to describe their centralized controller, even though it has no network switching capability at all (as defined in the beginning of this chapter) and provides only one ingress and one egress port on the device.

In these systems, an AP is usually stripped of both intelligence and many of the responsibilities associated with an edge device. It performs only the radio function and passes all traffic back to a centrally located controller (often referred to as the *switch*). This controller device is responsible for all packet-handling functions, including security, QoS classification and tagging, and packet filtering, for all associated APs.

The intended primary benefit of such a system is lower cost. By lowering equipment, deployment, and maintenance costs, the intended result is a lower total cost of ownership. Intelligence (and, therefore, cost) has been removed from the APs and has been moved into the network to the switch. However, the cost is really transferred to the switch as well. In the long run, there is minimal if any cost benefit over distributed intelligence systems.

Deployment of a core device may be accomplished in either of two ways. Figure 5-2 illustrates the deployment method suggested by most vendor literature. At the center of the Figure 5-2 is an Ethernet switch (for example, Cisco Catalyst WS-C3560-24PS) that serves dual purposes: to provide inline power to the APs (commonly the only power option, helping keep the hardware cost down) and to provide a point of aggregation for multiple APs. The controller in this scenario functions similarly to a one-armed router in that it is inline to all traffic to provide some higher-layer function (for example, security, QoS, filtering). In this case, all traffic would have to flow into and out of the switch on the same Ethernet interfaces.

Figure 5-2   *Centralized, Core Intelligence System*

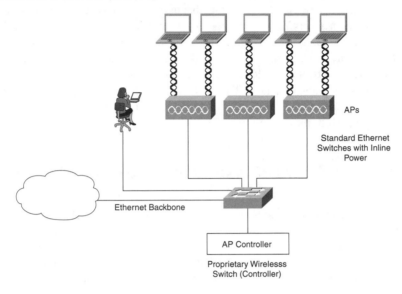

Figure 5-3 shows another deployment scenario with a centralized, core device architecture. In this diagram, the controller interfaces to a northbound switch that aggregates APs, and a southbound switch that provides access to the backbone. Each link is 100 Mbps, full duplex.

Figure 5-3   *Alternative Centralized, Core Intelligence Architecture*

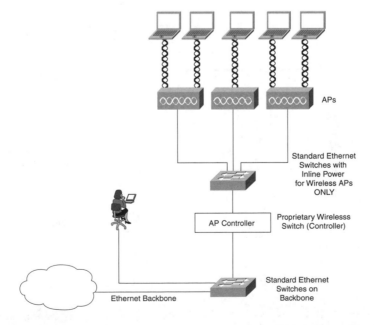

Security is an issue in any wireless network. Even though strong authentication and encryption might be deployed, the fact that intelligence has been removed from the APs and placed in the network's controller means that traffic must flow to the controller before it is secured. With this system architecture, unauthenticated traffic is traveling across the Ethernet switch, which has connection directly to the backbone. To make the network secure, wireless traffic should be placed on a "dirty" segment, or *demilitarized zone* (DMZ), until it has been authenticated. The only way to accomplish this is to pass through the controller to a separate switch that then passes traffic to the backbone. Each link is 100 Mbps, full duplex.

Comparing Packet Flows of Distributed and Centralized Intelligence Systems

In fact, basic network speeds and feeds bores a hole in this architecture in more than one way. To illustrate, look at a simple packet flow through the network, from a wireless client to a wired client. Figure 5-4 shows a day in the life of a packet in a centralized intelligence core system environment. Keep in mind that the APs have been effectively "lobotomized," forcing each and every packet back to the controller for inspection.

Figure 5-4 *Life of a Packet in a Centralized Core Intelligence System*

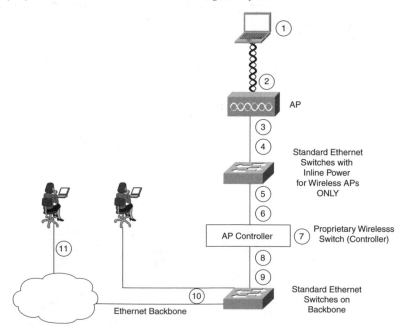

The following traffic flow (typical packet sequence) describes Figure 5-4:

1 A ping packet (ICMP Echo Request) is generated by the client workstation.

2 The packet contends for air space over the 802.11b wireless network and arrives at the AP.

3 The packet is bridged to the Ethernet LAN and directed toward the controller.

4 The Ethernet switch receives the packet.

5 The packet leaves the Ethernet switch on the controller's port.

6 The controller receives the packet.

7 The controller processes the packet (classifies, filters, tags, and so on).

8 The packet is directed toward the backbone network via the egress port.

9 The backbone switch receives the packet.

10 The packet is sent to the IP address to which it was intended.

11 The target PC receives the packet.

Now the packet must traverse back through the same steps in reverse order to the appropriate AP and client, for a total of 22 steps to move from one wireless client to another (even if these clients are on the same AP)!

A simple ping travels across 22 interfaces. If the source and destination IP devices are on different subnets, add a Layer 3 hop in the controller to that total.

Contrast the centralized intelligence system to a distributed intelligence system where the AP provides port-blocking authentication services, as well as local encryption.

Figure 5-5 shows the life of a packet in a fat AP.

Figure 5-5   *Life of a Packet in a Distributed Intelligence System*

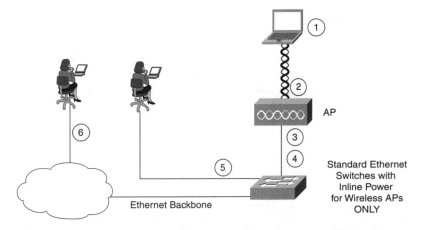

The following traffic flows describes Figure 5-5:

1 The packet contends for air space over the 802.11b wireless network and arrives at the AP.

2 The packet is received on the AP, the AP's internal CPU processes the packet (classifies, filters, tags), and then the packet is bridged to the Ethernet LAN.

3 The Ethernet switch sends the packet.

4 The Ethernet switch receives the packet.

5 The packet leaves the Ethernet switch toward the client PC.

6 The target PC receives the packet.

If the packet is destined for another wireless device (on a different AP), it simply travels from step 5 to the other AP and then to the client. If the traffic is between two clients on the same AP, it travels from the client to the AP and then to the next client. In both cases, a distributed intelligence WLAN network results in much less overall traffic than a centralized intelligence system.

The centralized controller solution hits nearly twice the number of interfaces per packet as the distributed solution. The implication for traffic is profound. Delays can occur in numerous areas, including the following:

- RF port on the AP
- Egress port on the AP
- Ingress port on Ethernet switch
- Egress port on Ethernet switch
- Ingress port on controller
- The controller itself
- Egress port on controller
- Ingress port on the second Ethernet switch
- Egress port on the second Ethernet switch

Any given packet can be subject to propagation delay and processing delay, both of which effect the variation of delay, also known as *jitter*. The net effect is a slower, less-predictable network. This is particularly a concern with applications such as *voice over IP* (VoIP) that are very sensitive to jitter.

Edge Device Architecture

Starting in 2002, several new start-up companies such as Airespace and Aruba, as well as several established networking companies such as Extreme and Nortel, came out with their versions of switched wireless architecture. In these cases, the term *switched wireless* is a bit closer to what you know and understand as network switching. Here an Ethernet switch houses the intelligence for the APs.

By centralizing some of the wireless services and troubleshooting tools into a structured WLAN switching system, systems engineers can build, manage, and operate large-scale 802.11 infrastructures with improved performance and management capabilities. However, pulling in too much intelligence and processing into a central point can produce many of the same issues as a centralized core controller.

WLAN switching is based on bringing a system's approach to 802.11 wireless network infrastructures. Most of the WLAN switch systems today move intensive-processing functions such as encryption, authentication, and mobility management that are found in today's intelligent APs into a centralized WLAN switch; they do this while also adding important new wireless features, such as air monitoring and automated site surveys, that give network managers more visibility, security, and control. With WLAN switching, a multilayered approach is necessary for security protecting the air space, the network, and the user.

The use of actual Ethernet-type switches as the controller for APs is a better approach than a centralized controller, in that it actually improves security by having the switch become the port authenticator. In this manner, unauthenticated traffic will not pass beyond the switch port. However, this depends on whether the AP is connected directly to the switch providing the control for this particular AP. In most edge wireless switch systems, you can use one switch to control many APs, including those that are located at another switch (see Figure 5-6). In this case, you still have unauthenticated packets on the network.

Another downside to edge switch device systems is the use of a proprietary switch. Most networks already have a network installed, and the wireless is an additional system, to be incorporated as part of the network. Requiring a separate, proprietary switch just for wireless can be a management challenge (and can increase the overall cost significantly).

The one key item that both core and edge device and centralized intelligence systems promote is ease of management. In most cases, however, the switches or controllers have a maximum number of APs that they can support and manage. In a large enterprise system, this requires that you add yet another component, a sort of manager of managers, required to manage these WLAN switches or controllers. In an ideal system, the same manager that is used to manage your wired routers and switches would be used to manage your wireless network.

Figure 5-6   *Centralized Edge Intelligence System*

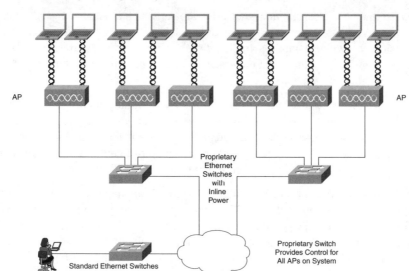

Switched Antenna Systems

Switched antenna systems are new systems that have come to the 802.11 market over the past year or so, and again use the term *switched wireless*. These systems are probably the closest thing to meeting the understanding of switching, but still do not completely fit the idea of independent collision domains. Switched antenna systems use a phased array antenna and perform *beam steering* for the RF radiation. Beam steering refers to the capability to focus the RF energy in a narrow beam of energy and steer or change the beam's primary point of focus from one direction to another. Beam steering is not a new technology to RF in general; it has been used in the military for some time.

The two advantages to this architecture are range and ease of installation. Most WLAN models require hard wiring dozens of APs to cover the large areas where users are located. This wiring and installation can represent a large portion of the cost in many sites. Systems with large numbers of APs rely on what is known as a *microcellular architecture*, where a network of APs covering small areas (or microcells) are connected and the wireless client can move from one microcell to another, much like a cellular telephone system operates (see Figure 5-7). This type of microcellular system requires maintaining and managing a large number of APs on the network. Some view this as a strain on network management resources.

These issues have posed unique problems for the traditional design of the 802.11 solutions, and deploying dozens of APs raises the issues of installation, network management, security, and QoS. The switched antenna system is an attempt to improve these areas for WLANs.

Figure 5-7   *Microcellular Architecture*

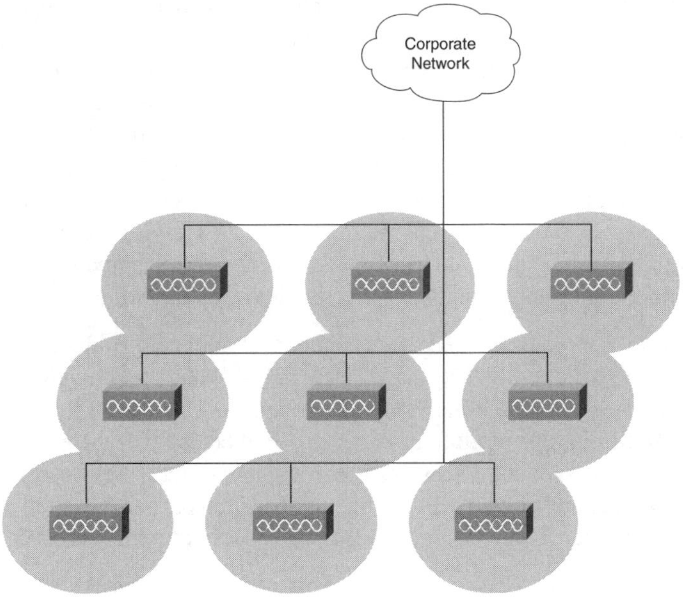

Phased Array Antenna Technology

Using phased array antenna technology is new to the wireless LAN industry, but it is not new in the communications domain. The principle of phased array antennas has been applied in radar since World War II.

Phased array antennas are capable of redirecting antenna beam position in space by the electronic movement of the entire array structure without any physical movement. The term *phased array* originated from sinusoidal signals such as electromagnetic waves and the time delay that can be translated as a shift of the phase of the signal.

The characteristics of a phased array antenna allow the signal to be directional and less sensitive to radiating interference (the technical rationale for why it was used for radar). In the world of WLANs, using a phased array antenna system equates to less interference from other devices because of the narrow directional beams. This is particularly important because of the unlicensed and free spectrum in which it operates. The Vivato switch uses a phased array antenna (sometimes called *panels* because of their physical size and shape) as part of their AP. This antenna is composed of 128 array elements that work in unison to transmit the 802.11 signal. The beamed power is provided only in the locations where there are users; consequently, there is a significant reduction in possible interference. As a result of the narrow beam widths, users enjoy a considerable increase in antenna gain. This increase in gain provides a significant improvement in range. Therefore, the range of a phased antenna system can be measured in kilometers.

Although this all seems great, remember what your dad used to tell you, "If it seems too good to be true, it probably is." The same holds true here. When using a beam-steering technology such as this, utilizing very high-gain, narrow-radiation beams, RF-reflective surfaces can become a major hurdle. In most cases, if there is any type of metal or other RF-reflective surface in the first 20 to 50 feet or so of the antenna's radiation path, the beam steering becomes distorted, and the overall performance of that beam is dramatically reduced, usually to the point of a normal dipole antenna. This severely limits the use of the system in an indoor environment. This is also the reason a vendor that sells this type of device also sells a single, typical intelligent AP. This AP is used for "filling in holes" of RF coverage, caused by items such as bookshelves, storage cabinets, stairwells, elevators, and many other commonly found RF-reflective items in a building.

The second drawback has to do with capacity. If, in fact, the AP can support an entire floor of 250 people as a result of its increase coverage, what about bandwidth? The AP provides coverage using all three nonoverlapping channels. This means that when optimized, the maximum throughput of all three combined will be about 16 Mbps, and this will be shared among all 250 users! As discussed in later chapters, many industries, including enterprise, are looking at smaller-size cells, so the number of users per AP is lower and the bandwidth per user is higher. Using a switched antenna system eliminates this capability.

Because of the gain of the antennas in most phased array antenna systems, the use of this technology device is limited to regions that permit high gain. The devices actually communicate over one antenna beam to one device at a time; therefore, they fall into the point-to-point regulations under FCC rules. Because each user may have its own beam pattern, and because it operates on a point-to-point protocol, range is increased. As a result, broadcast and multicast packets must be converted to unicast packets and sent to every user individually. This reduces efficiency drastically in systems that have a fair amount of multicast packets.

Two of the biggest drawbacks to this technology are size and cost. A typically indoor AP has a list price of more than $8000 and requires wall space of 2 feet by 4 feet.

In outdoor systems, the switched antenna array may have more usefulness. It can provide distances of up to 1 kilometer for non-line-of-sight links, which can help with last-mile solutions for hard-to-reach areas. Campus green spaces are another area for which this system has been positioned, and it may have valid usage there, provided the following:

- The number of users (and their required aggregate bandwidth) in the green space is within the capable bandwidth of the AP.
- The strong signals do not interfere with the in-building wireless systems.

Phased Array Antenna Extends Range

Companies such as Vivato and Bandspeed have taken a new systems approach for the design and integration of WLAN. This type of system uses a unique phased array antenna panel that can significantly extend the range of transmissions. This powerful antenna is combined with a centralized intelligent controller (called a *switch* by Vivato) that mirrors a similar management model as an Ethernet switch, but takes into account the specialized aspects of the management of WLANS. The intent here is that the long-range capabilities of this device will solve the issues of installing dozens of APs for providing coverage to a large area.

Instead of emitting a 360-degree coverage pattern like most APs, the phased array antenna has a radiation pattern of 100 degrees and will associate with any client within this field of view (see Figure 5-8). It transmits on a particular beam only when a client is active, by sending a narrow beam of energy directly to the client. The powerful antenna is used to send and receive on a packet-by-packet basis, enabling seemingly multiple conversations at the same time. Notice the use of the word *seemingly*. In reality, it provides a platform that three users can communicate with at any one time (based in 802.11b or 802.11g having only three nonoverlapping channels). The Vivato AP uses several (as many as 13) radios in each AP to provide the three-channel coverage and to power the antenna array structure.

Figure 5-8   *Phased Array Antenna Radiation Pattern*

100 1° Beams

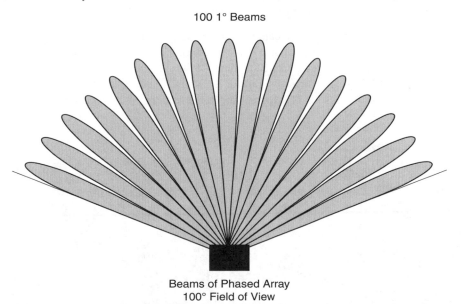

Beams of Phased Array
100° Field of View

These phased array antennas are intended to be used both indoors and outdoors. Indoor panels are designed to be mounted flat on a wall or in a corner that can provide coverage for an entire floor in the 100-degree horizontal beam width with a range of up to 300 meters (see Figure 5-9). The idea here is that this eliminates the need to install and maintain multiple APs.

Figure 5-9 *Phased Array Antenna Implementations*

Indoor Deployment
Corner Mount

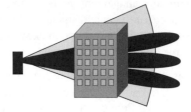

Outside to Inside Deployment

Because an outdoor switch is exposed to the elements of nature, it must be enclosed in a dust- and moisture-proof, temperature-controlled environment. This is accomplished by incorporating the device in a NEMA 4-rated enclosure to withstand severe weather conditions. The weather-proof enclosure is a complete package that can easily be mounted on the outside of a building or on a tower (see Figure 5-10).

An outdoor wireless switch can provide coverage for an entire building from the outside. In some cases, the ranges of an AP using a phased array antenna in an outdoor environment can be much farther than with a standard AP implementation. For example, the range can be up to 4 kilometers (line of sight) for the Vivato Outdoor Switch AP, and it can penetrate into some buildings for 11-Mbps connections from up to 1 kilometer away.

Figure 5-10 *Phased Array Products*

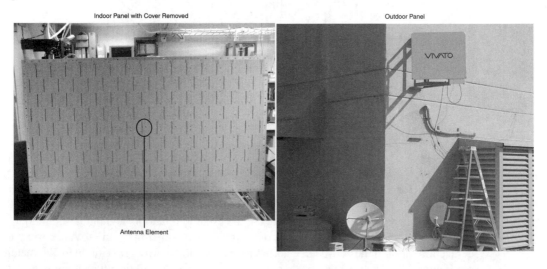

Mesh Networking

Mesh networking is an ad hoc peer-to-peer routing technology that leverages routing techniques originally developed for battlefield and other temporary communications systems. By pushing intelligence and decision making to the edge of the network, you can build highly mobile and scalable broadband networks at very low cost.

Some systems, such as the MeshNetworks system, support both infrastructure meshing and client meshing. Infrastructure meshing creates a scalable network, whereas client meshing enables clients to instantly form a broadband wireless network among themselves, with or without network infrastructure. Using the MeshNetworks multihopping routing technology, you can use every client device as a router/repeater, so every user on the system plays a part in network coverage and network throughput for other users. Figure 5-11 illustrates a mesh network topology and the RF traffic patterns.

Figure 5-11 *Mesh Network Architecture*

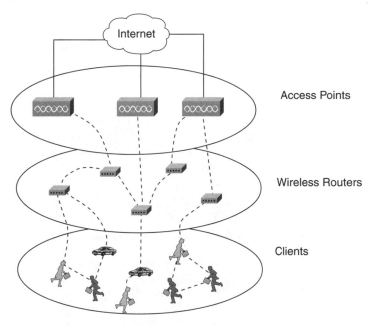

One issue with a mesh network approach is security. The fact that every client can become a repeater for other devices means that other clients' traffic is traversing systems that may or may not be totally secure. Add to this the fact that some clients may be turned off or moved, and the overall stability and performance of such a network can be questionable. Typically, mesh networking is done for only temporary and unsecured systems.

Free-Space Optics (Laser)

Free-space optics (FSO) is a line-of-sight technology that uses lasers to provide optical bandwidth connections. Currently, FSO is capable of up to 2.5 Gbps of data, voice, and video communications through the air, allowing optical connectivity without requiring fiber-optic cable or securing spectrum licenses. FSO requires light, which can be focused by using either *light emitting diodes* (LEDs) or lasers (light amplification by stimulated emission of radiation). The use of lasers is a simple concept similar to optical transmissions using fiber-optic cables; the only difference is the medium. Light travels through air faster than it does through glass, so it is fair to classify FSO as optical communications at the speed of light.

FSO technology is relatively simple (see Figure 5-12). It is based on connectivity between FSO units, each consisting of an optical transceiver with a laser transmitter and a receiver to provide full-duplex (bidirectional) capability. Each FSO unit uses a high-power optical source (that is, laser), plus a lens that transmits light through the atmosphere to another lens receiving the information. The receiving lens connects to a high-sensitivity receiver via optical fiber. FSO is easily upgradeable, and its open interfaces support equipment from a variety of vendors, which helps service providers protect their investment in embedded telecommunications infrastructures.

Figure 5-12 *FSO*

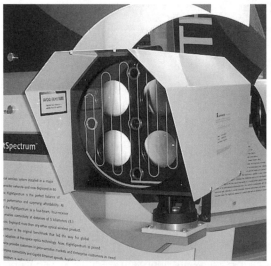

FSO systems are usually used in point-to-point systems that are fixed mounted. They have a very narrow beam focus, and therefore need to be mounted to a sturdy fixture that has minimal movement (due to wind or other vibration problems). Although they can provide very high bandwidths, FSO systems are relatively short-range devices (1000 feet to a few miles).

Most FSO systems are installed with a backup RF system in the event that some environmental conditions, such as fog, heavy snow, or heavy storms, interfere with the light signal.

Selecting the Access Point

As you have learned up to this point, there are several different architecture designs of WLAN out there. You have intelligent or fat APs, and lightweight or thin APs with limited intelligence and dependence on some controller. Just as selecting the proper architecture is important to your system design, so is selecting the proper AP. There are several different issues to review on the AP side as well. This section looks at the two major different AP implementations: single- or dual-radio architecture and AP radio styles.

Single- or Dual-Radio Architecture

Most APs were designed to support a single-radio platform, having one radio per AP (see Figure 5-13). This has been the most common AP design to date. Some APs were provided with dual PCMCIA slots so that a second radio could also be operated (see Figure 5-14). At the time of introduction, dual-radio platforms were actually intended to provide a migration path from 900 MHz to 2.4 GHz. You could put one of each radio into the AP and have support for both bands as you migrated away from 900 MHz. However, some vendors promised double the bandwidth with the architecture by using two of the same radios in the AP. This actually introduces a problem called *receiver desensitization*, which causes poor performance of both radios.

Figure 5-13 *Single-Band AP*

Figure 5-14 *Dual-Radio AP*

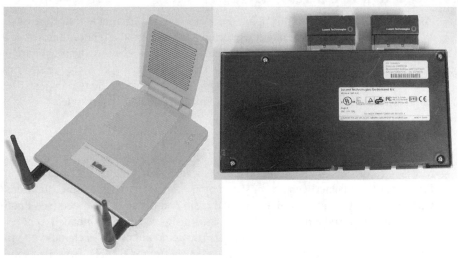

Receiver Desensitization

Every radio receiver has a specification that defines the capability of the receiver to "hear and understand" some minimal signal strength. This is called *receiver sensitivity* or *receiver threshold* (see Figure 5-15). This value represents the lowest signal that a radio can receive and still recover the information or data from the signal. In the case of most 802.11b WLAN radios, this is on the order of –80 dBm to –85 dBm. (The more negative the number, the smaller the signal.) The typical 802.11b transmitter has a transmit power of +15 dBm to +20 dBm (or 100 dB stronger than the receive threshold).

Because some cross talk may occur between the different channels in the 802.11 band, the receiver incorporates filters and circuitry to reduce interference from other channels in the same band. With the available 802.11 chipsets (components that are used in the radio portion of the devices), the best RF filtering (the capability to reject certain RF energy) that you can obtain, even at opposite ends of the band, is perhaps 65 to 75 dB. Most receivers have a sensitivity in the –80- to –90-dBm range, and with the signal level coming out of a transmitter set to channel 1 at 15 to 20 dBm (depending on transmitter power capabilities). The signal level measured at the radio adjacent to it on channel 11 is 65 to 75 dB lower. This places the received signal from the unwanted channel 1 at 50 dBm to –60 dBm. This value is stronger than the minimal signal level of the receiver by a large margin. If the AP radio on channel 11 is trying to receive a signal from a distant client, and the signal level is near the minimal receiver threshold, the energy present in the channel 11 area transmitted from the channel 1 transmitter only a few inches away will have a stronger signal level and mask out the desired signal from the desired channel 11 client. This effectively reduces the coverage area any time the adjacent radio is transmitting.

Figure 5-15 *Receiver Desensitization*

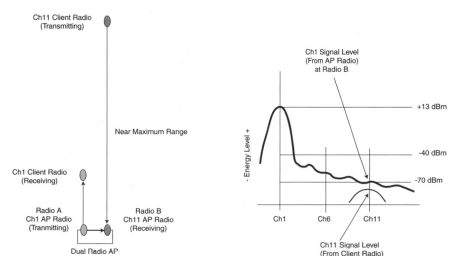

This issue can also result from placing two single-band APs in close proximity. There should be, at minimum, approximately 5 feet between any two antennas attached to different 802.11 radios to provide adequate separation and receiver performance.

You can use a true dual-radio architecture to migrate from one technology to another or to just add bandwidth by permitting some users on one technology and other users on another technology. However, because these architectures have different specifications and ranges, you must consider a few items during the network design stages. If you want the cell sizes the same for both technologies, you have to adjust power levels or antenna selections appropriately.

A number of dual-band APs have come on the market over the past year. These were designed with the intention of providing support for both 2.4 GHz and 5 GHz. Some of these devices use two separate radios offering simultaneous support for both bands, whereas others use a single radio that can be set up to operate in either band, in which case it supports only one band at a time. It is imperative to understand the difference between the two types of systems. An AP with the single radio, although supporting both bands, does not lend itself to migrating easily from one technology to another and does not permit scaling by adding clients on both bands.

AP Radio Styles

All APs contain some type of radio. The form factor for these radios varies widely. In some cases, they are internal and not accessible to the outside. In the case of many low-end products, this means the antenna is also internal, providing minimal possible antenna configurations. This can limit performance, AP placement, and versatility. For most sites, it is desirable to have the option to use external antennas when the regulations permit it.

There are also some AP devices in which the radios can be plugged in to the AP, providing upgradability. However, the style of radio interface may present two issues. First, the radio card must enable you to secure it to the AP, otherwise it stands the chance of "walking away" (see Figure 5-16). Second, the antenna selection may be limited. (Remember, some antennas may be part of the radio itself, with no possibility to change antennas.) For 2.4 GHz, if the form factor is a PCMCIA card, this means external antennas will have to use a very small cable and connector, resulting in an easy failure point. If external antennas are required, consider an AP that uses antenna connectors such as a TNC, SMA, or N connector (or some variation of one of these).

Figure 5-16   *Physical Security of an AP Radio*

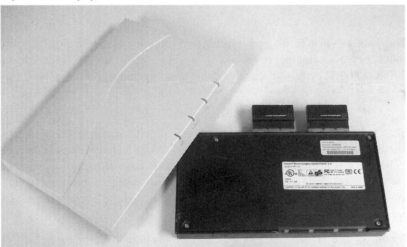

One other, often overlooked item has to do with diversity antennas. Several such products are on the market. Be aware, however, that although they support diversity antennas in their radio cards, when using external antennas the feature is no longer functional, or its functionality is severely degraded because there is only a single external antenna connection.

Upgradability of the radio section of the AP is another issue. Your plan should always include upgradability, to move to a newer RF technology (much like the upgrading from 802.11b to 802.11g) if and when it becomes available. Because most RF technology upgrades require a hardware change, consider an AP that not only supports both of the present RF bands simultaneously, but one that also enables you to change the RF interface easily. This helps to keep down installation and upgrade costs, as well as wired infrastructure costs. (Every extra AP costs an extra wired switch port and cabling.) If you start with 802.11b and move to either 802.11a or 802.11g, for example, you want to make sure the AP uses a cardbus or mini-PCI interface, rather than a PCMCIA interface for the radio, and that it supports upgrades to the desired path (because of the lack of support for 54 Mbps on a PCMCIA interface).

Inline power is a feature supported by many vendors today, and can significantly lower installation cost. Inline power comes in several flavors and architectures also. Although there is an IEEE standard (802.3af) for *Power over Ethernet* (PoE), there are several common ways to implement PoE (see Figure 5-17). To apply power to the Category 5 cable, you can use an Ethernet switch to provide this power, or you can use some power injector, which is inserted into the Category 5 cables between the network and the AP. Some APs have an internal circuit to separate the power and Ethernet signals. Other vendors provide a power injector and a power splitter. The splitter goes at the AP end, and has the circuitry to separate the Ethernet from the power. The splitter then has two output cables, one for Ethernet and one for power.

Figure 5-17 *PoE Examples*

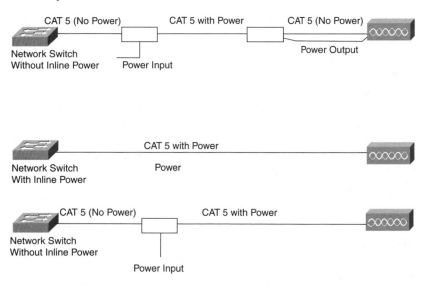

If you plan to power your AP from your network switches, investigate the power options of the switch (does it support 802.3af, or some other vendor's specific scheme?) and the AP to confirm compatibility. Also be aware that some switches might not have enough power to support dual-band APs, resulting in the need to use a power injector or a third-party power module.

Selecting the Client Products

Before discussing what you need to consider when making client product selections, this section first examines a new initiative in client cards. In the past, client cards supported a single RF technology. If you moved from 802.11b to 802.11a, you had to change radio cards in your client device. In 2003, the introduction of dual-band client cards changed how to migrate from one technology to another. Several of the newly introduced cards support 802.11b or 802.11a. (Notice the *or*; one band operates at a time!) So, a single card can be used to operate on either system.

Shortly after that, cards started to appear that support 802.11g (and hence 802.11b by definition) and 802.11a. Many of these cards enable you to actually roam from one technology to another, and thus promote greater scalability. If you have a dual-band AP installed, the client treats them like two different APs and selects the AP (in this case, the same AP but different radios) with the best performance. Virtually all new cards are now dual-band (tri mode: a, b, and g) radios. This is the industry trend today.

Because most of the network features reside in the AP (at the edge of the network) or in the controller, you have to consider significantly fewer items on the client side. The biggest question is what type of clients will be required, and who controls the client selection.

First, look at issues regarding the type of client. Not all devices have been migrated to support 802.11a or 802.11g. This can be one crucial factor in the technology decision. You must also consider interoperability (not only for the basic 802.11 side, but also for things such as security and QoS). Many of the specialty client devices on the market today do not support the wide range of features that are supported by the standard WLAN *network interface card* (NIC)-type devices. Some devices even still operate under DOS environments, severely limiting their feature support. For this reason, first select the features your system needs and then search for the client devices. Sometimes you may have no choice but to use some of these "featureless" client devices; in such cases, you might want to use VLANs to segregate traffic and help keep the main network secure.

Then you must look at who determines which clients are used on the network. If this is an education or public network, the network administrator typically has minimal input on the client-side decision and is limited to a statement similar to "802.11b Wi-Fi compliance is required." Although this seems fine at first, it has a major effect on the design of the network, because not all clients' radios are created equal.

Some radio vendors provide a very typical transmitter power of 15 dBm (30 mW), whereas others provide a slightly higher transmitter power of up to 20 dBm (100 mW) or even more, and yet a few have very low power levels (such as an SDIO radio). Using a 100-mW AP with a 30-mW client card results in asymmetrical performance. (Remember, this is a two-way communication path.) The client can hear the AP, but the AP cannot hear the client. As a result, the lower-power client limits the performance and the range of the system. If you plan to permit such lower-powered clients on your network, perform survey testing with a device set to the minimum power you anticipate being used by a client. If you are installing a 100-mW, higher-end AP into the system, set the power levels of the AP to be comparable to the lowest-power client card. This provides the best overall performance from *all* client devices, and minimal interference between APs.

Some client-end, wireless devices support several wired devices over a single radio connection (see Figure 5-18). This is known as an *Ethernet client*, *bridge*, *minibridge*, or *workgroup bridge*. The idea behind this device is to provide RF connectivity for some small number of wired devices. Consider, for example, a hospital nursing station that has three or four wired computers at the desk. Instead of pulling three or four cables (or even a single cable) to the desk, you can install one of these Ethernet clients, add an inexpensive hub, and attach all the devices to the hub. The devices will all access the network via the single radio device.

Figure 5-18 *Ethernet Client*

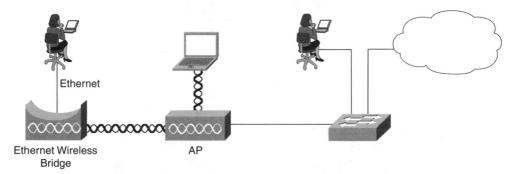

Ethernet Wireless
Bridge

AP

Another example is a mobile crane in a shipping port. Such a crane likely has more than one computer device, and therefore requires more than one radio device and corresponding antennas. (Because the crane is made almost entirely of metal, the antenna has to be remote and placed outside the crane operator's suite or computer closet.) By using the Ethernet client, you can funnel all the network devices in the crane to a single radio and one antenna.

Be aware, however, that some of the Ethernet clients on the market are designed for only a single connection. The rationale behind such a device is to connect systems that have only an Ethernet connection for networking. Because the Ethernet clients run their own driver and firmware, there is usually no need for a driver. Some similar devices have USB connections, but these typically have the limitation of a single device connection as well.

For desktop-style computers, or other devices that require PCI cards, two main styles of devices are offered today, the main difference being their antenna options. Figure 5-19 shows both styles of PCI cards. In one case, the PCI card is really a PC card-to-PCI converter, and a standard PC or cardbus is used. This means that the antennas are typically attached and remote antennas are not available. The second style of PCI card is one that offers an external antenna (one that you can mount remotely). So why the two different styles? Suppose that your computer is one that you put on the floor under your desk, and that your desk is made of steel. Or perhaps your computer is in a point-of-sale device, such as a portable cash register, that you mount under the mobile cart. These typical installations can affect the antenna's capability to transmit or receive properly, unless you can position the antenna in an open area.

Figure 5-19 *PCI Client Examples*

The most common client by far today is the embedded radio card. PC manufacturers are now putting WLAN cards into a wide range of laptops as standard or optional features. Included with such a system is an embedded antenna. However, different PCs perform at different levels. Although most vendors have tested and found optimum locations for the antennas, some devices have antennas placed in less-than-optimum locations (such as under where your hands rest when typing on the keyboard). You may find varying performance between different versions of laptops, and you need to maintain some margin to compensate for these differences.

Summary

As this chapter makes clear, you must consider many factors when selecting WLAN architecture and products. It is not as simple as picking a Wi-Fi–certified AP, or choosing one based solely on cost. Doing so will probably result in a system that is far less productive and useful than desired. Take special care in this selection process to ensure you can support all the users, applications, and features, as well as future growth.

Here are several key hints for a successful selection:

- Treat WLANs as building blocks. From an architectural perspective, WLANs must be thought of as another enterprise building block, not as yet another remote-access technology that can be DMZed. This does not mean that proven components of the DMZ building block, such as VPNs and firewalls, must be eliminated. Instead, they need to be rearchitected for the mobility and scaling requirements of WLANs.

- Understand how the WLANs will connect to the existing wired network. Interworking issues between wired and wireless networks must be minimized with few changes to the production wired network. This will make the addition much easier for the support staff.

- Realize that security is a process with dynamic requirements. Security in WLAN systems is no exception to this rule. Today's best practice (TKIP/WPA) is tomorrow's security history. Review and revise deployment decisions often.

- Centralize upgrades and manageability. The life cycle and the operational costs of keeping a WLAN system primed for security and technology upgrades must be considered. Upgrades are ongoing, and IT staff must consciously avoid devoting their capital dollars to approaches that do not allow for simple scalability or permit ongoing change. Leveraging best of breed in upgrades for both software and hardware is vital for future growth and scalability.

- Strive for minimal client configuration. Consider standards-based and nonproprietary authentication types that are part of the client operating system. Trying to fix interoperability issues across PDAs, notebooks, and other clients with different proprietary features might prove a big challenge.

- Look for comprehensive WLAN debugging capabilities. Wireless users often have problems troubleshooting at multiple levels, from the RF layer through to 802.1x or IPSec-based VPNs. To improve troubleshooting for the WLAN, pay special attention to capabilities that can quickly help identify and pinpoint issues in the different WLAN building blocks.

- Do not forget RF tools to control air space and maintain WLAN health. WLAN security depends on wireless tools that not only lock out and identify locations of rogue APs but also permit ongoing audits of air space. Also use site survey tools to better anticipate WLAN installations and thus avoid overengineering the WLAN network (that is, avoid overspending).

PART II

The Site Survey

Chapter 6   Preparing for a Site Survey

Chapter 7   Site Surveying Equipment

Chapter 8   Discovering Site-Specific Requirements

Chapter 9   Discovering Wired Network Requirements

Chapter 10   Using Site Surveying Tools

Chapter 11   Performing a WLAN Site Survey

This chapter includes the following topics:

- Pre-Site Survey Form Information
- User Input
- Balancing Wants, Needs, and Capabilities

CHAPTER 6

Preparing for a Site Survey

This chapter helps you determine basic site survey requirements before deploying an engineer to the network site. You should always collect as much information as possible about the site to be surveyed before sending someone on site so that he or she can be prepared for the required work with the appropriate types of equipment and knowledge. Industry practice has honed this process so that now most good engineers start with a document referred to as a *pre-site survey form*. This form is a living document that covers all aspects of pre-survey discovery. It is a living document because it can and should be adjusted based on the type of site that will be surveyed. The pre-site survey form is designed to be filled out in partnership by the customer and the survey team. It enables the engineer to get all the discovery questions covered without forgetting or omitting things by accident.

In this chapter, you are going to look at the basic components of the pre-site survey form, compile those components at the end, and then learn about some of the discussions that are common prior to the site survey.

Pre-Site Survey Form Information

Most work orders or job assignments begin with a pre-site survey form being filled out by one or more individuals, including the customer, IT staff, facilities personnel, and application specialists. One benefit of using this form is that it prompts those involved in completing the form to consider all their potential WLAN needs and discover other potential networking needs. This form also gives the WLAN engineers a chance to converse with the customer to explore other potential issues, such as additional bridging requirements that were not originally considered or aging, incompatible network components. This information is then used to manage the project by scheduling an appropriate amount of time for the engineer to complete the work and providing for any special considerations such as a high-lift rental or security escorts.

In addition, these forms ask important questions that might save days or weeks of extra, unbudgeted effort once the engineer is on site. Those involved in completing this form need to understand that minimal time required to fill out this form will save money and time in the long run. For example, performing a survey at an aluminum smelting plant or oil refinery will require that all engineers take the required Occupation Safety and Health Administration (OSHA) safety courses offered by the plant. This can add several days per person to the survey process. It is better to know this prior to development of the work schedule.

The following basic sequence of events helps facilitate the flow of work at both your company and the survey at the client's site:

1 The survey engineer or WLAN project manager sends the pre-site survey form to the IT staff responsible for the facility where the WLAN will be installed. In addition, this form is routed to those individuals responsible for implementing the new applications on the WLAN as well as to a few key WLAN users.

2 Data is collected and entered on the pre-site survey form, which is then returned to the survey engineer or WLAN project manager.

3 The survey engineer or the project manager then sets up a series of interviews with key IT personnel, WLAN end users, and facility personnel as necessary, based on the returned pre-site survey. The interview is intended to ask the questions that may have been overlooked or that the responses on the pre-site survey form generated. Issues such as hazardous materials, explosive gases, or imaging equipment such as x-ray machines or MRIs need to be discussed.

4 The survey engineer or the project manager then determines the resource requirements and schedules the work to be done.

5 The site walkthrough occurs. If possible and within the time and budget constraints, a pre-site survey walkthrough can provide a large volume of information. This can assist in completing the pre-site survey form and prepare you much better for the actual survey.

The information that you should collect can be broken into the following parts:

- Customer information
- Site survey location
- Current network and communications information
- WLAN equipment requirements
- Site information
- Survey personnel requirements
- Scope of work
- Coverage map
- Outdoor bridge link

The engineer who deploys to the site should have a copy of the completed pre-site survey form along with the other materials such as a set of blueprints or floor plans and survey equipment. If possible, have both a hard copy (for making fast notes) and an electronic copy (for documenting and saving the work).

You can find two samples of a pre-site survey forms in Appendix D, "Sample Forms."

Customer Information

The first part of the pre-site survey form contains all the relative information about the customer and the site as well as administrative information such as the job or work-order number (if your company uses this method to track projects).

- **Work-order number**—This is an administrative tracking number for your own use depending on how your company assigns or tracks project engagements. Many companies use sequential numbers for every quote, site survey, and then installation performed. This work-order number might include a customer identification number, too.

- **Date**—This is your company's administrative date for the delivery of the form to the customer.

- **Purchase order (PO) number**—The person contracting the work may not be the person responsible for paying for the work. In fact, larger, more complex companies may have several departments with this responsibility. You will find it very helpful to have the customer's PO number for the purpose of tracking payments with an *Accounts Payable* (AP) department.

- **PO date**—Knowing the PO date can be very helpful when tracking payments with the customer's AP department.

- **Company name**—Your customer's company name might not be the name of the company you are doing the site survey for. As a consultant or contractor, you might do this work at many different companies for your customer.

- **Address, city, state, zip code**—Many larger companies have several national and international offices; this can make it difficult to track the customer responsible for contracting the site survey, so it is important to have the actual office address of that person or group of persons.

- **Point of contact (POC) name**—In most cases, you will interface with one primary person for the overall WLAN project, as well as an individual responsible for the activities that occur at any particular site. They might be one and the same, so it is best to identify that person for informational purposes.

- **Phone, fax**—These entries should have the relative business telephone and fax numbers of the contracting person.

- **E-mail**—Much of today's communication is via e-mail for reasons such as the ease of retransmitting a conveyed message to many or being able to track conversations and their progression. E-mail communication about any project can be of great benefit for a number of reasons; therefore, I highly advise using this as a means of communication over the span of any project or relationship.

- **Mobile phone**—Many people travel or work remotely in today's world of telecommuting. Because of that, it is always handy to have a person's mobile telephone number.

Site Survey Location

Many times, the site survey will not be at the location of the corporate office. Many companies today are located across multiple buildings, campuses, cities, or even countries; and when one project is started for one facility, it will be implemented company-wide. For this reason, the location where the actual work will be completed needs to be identified for each individual facility. Fill out a separate pre-site survey form for each facility or building. Much of the information might be similar, but there may be distinct differences between them as well.

Be sure to note the following:

- **Total number of sites**—Determine how many sites overall require a site survey. Also identify which site this form is dedicated to (site x of x).

- **Site name**—The site name will continuously be referred to in documentation, such as the survey report and installation reports. It is important to define what the name is in the event of multiple sites or multiple buildings in a campus environment so that the technician can go to the proper location.

- **Working hours**—After the customer determines the working hours that the surveying technician can work, the sales or project management staff can derive information such as special considerations for day or night work and the total number of work days that a project may take if the available working hours are less than a standard business day of eight or nine hours.

- **Point of contact (POC) information**—In most cases, there is one primary person who interfaces with you at the specific site. This person might not be the same person who is your overall project point of contact identified at the top of the form. This person might also be responsible for your access to a particular facility. You might find it helpful to touch base with this person prior to arriving at the work site.

Current Network and Communications Information

As you will learn in detail in Chapter 9, "Discovering Wired Network Requirements," information about the existing wired network is essential to completing a site survey. Details of the type of network and the topology, as well as a location of the network components, should be included in the pre-site survey form, as follows:

- **Type of wired network installed**—It is important to understand the wiring presently installed so that the proper topology can be maintained. Although Token Ring might be a fading technology, many sites still have Token Ring installed. This can lead to issues related to the lack of WLAN products available for Token Ring connectivity.

- **WAN connectivity**—Define the overall network, indicating whether and how multiple sites are connected together via any type of wide-area network.

- **LAN connectivity**—Define the protocols and wiring used in the facility for the existing network.

- **List any current WLAN or RF equipment installed**—This information can significantly impact both the site survey and the installed network. If this part of your form is not large enough to list all the devices, just expand the table or input area or have the customer send an additional list in this format. Knowing what other RF is in use at the site will impact how the survey is performed.

  If another source of RF at the same frequency is revealed, you might need to work with the customer to determine a better networking solution. If you are going to perform a site survey for a new 802.11g network and the customer has revealed that they use a very high-power and high-density 2.4-GHz *frequency-hopping* (FH) network that will remain in place for other proprietary applications, it is appropriate to assume potential interference issues. At this point, you might need to discuss the alternative solution of 802.11a for the WLAN networking needs.

  This information might also help to determine whether a spectrum analyzer is needed to analyze the overall RF noise floor or radiated signal strength from the identified sources.

  When possible, identify as much information about the existing RF equipment as possible. Devices sold in the United States contain an FCC ID number on the outside of the device. A search of the FCC.gov website will reveal the details about the RF capability of the device (power, frequency, modulation).

- **Network security**—The customer should tell you what type of network security is either in place or going to be in place. This can be an important factor in the survey process because different types of security impact on performance in different ways. Consult with the customer to discuss the performance impact.

If no network security is identified, you have an opportunity to work with the customer to implement a solution that will best fit its needs. At a minimum, design a solution that uses all the available built-in security, such as *Wired Equivalent Privacy* (WEP) or *Wi-Fi Protected Access* (WPA), and discuss other solutions that work in conjunction with the build-in security, such as a *virtual private network* (VPN), Cisco Secure *Access Control Server* (ACS), or other authentication and encryption systems. Cisco has produced several white paper documents regarding WLAN security that will help you understand this issue. One of the documents is titled "SAFE: Wireless LAN Security in Depth."

WLAN Equipment Requirements

Understanding what is expected of the WLAN is vital to a proper site survey. Although coverage area is obvious, many other WLAN parameters are needed to perform a thorough and complete site survey. Coverage, data rate, rate shifting redundancy, and packet size all affect the method used to perform a survey.

Note the following when determining WLAN equipment requirements:

- **Access point manufacturer**—The customer may have a preference as to the equipment manufacturer to be used for their WLAN, such as Cisco.

- **Access point model number**—Each manufacturer follows their own model numbering scheme to indicate various features. For the surveying technician to complete an accurate site survey, this information must be clearly identified. For example, if the model number weren't clearly identified, a technician could be improperly surveying with a Cisco model 1100 series *access point* (AP) with integrated antennas rather than a model 1200 series with external connections and an upgrade path to 802.11a.

- **WLAN end-user devices**—Knowledge of the end-user devices that will be used is critical for selecting the proper survey test tools and parameters. Chapters 7, "Site Surveying Equipment," 10, "Using Site Surveying Tools," and 11, "Performing a WLAN Site Survey," discuss this topic in more detail.

- **Minimum data rates**—The customer's application might require a specific minimum data rate to properly function; in that case, your site survey must make that data rate the minimum level of coverage and connectivity. If the customer requires a low data rate, but high data rates are preferred, the survey should be based on the higher data rates with the lower rates denied to have better isolation of the coverage cells.

  Minimum data rates become a primary topic during a discussion of wants versus needs versus capabilities because this information can have the greatest impact on coverage area and amount of equipment required to fulfill the coverage needs. (See the "Balancing Wants, Needs, and Capabilities" section later in this chapter.)

- **Rate shifting**—In some cases, rate shifting might be desired to provide maximum performance and yet maintain maximum coverage.

- **Redundancy**—Redundancy might be required for certain applications, such as critical care units in a hospital.

- **Total number of users**—To determine the proper number of WLAN APs, you need to know the average and maximum number of WLAN users. Chapter 5, "Selecting the WLAN Architecture and Hardware," discusses this in detail.

- **Packet size**—As packet size increases, the likelihood of interference on that packet increases. This in turn reduces the overall range of the system. Maximum packet size should be identified because this is a parameter used during the actual survey process.

- **Coverage areas**—Using the floor plan or building blueprint, identify the desired coverage areas. Note whether this is indoor or outdoor coverage as well.

- **Applications that will use the installed equipment**—If the WLAN is proposed for a specific purpose, every detail must be explored, including the applications that will require the use of a WLAN.

- **Special needs**—This section gives the customer an opportunity to specify a level of protection or insurance that must be built in to their WLAN. You know, for example, that a high-availability WLAN supporting medical applications is important to medical professionals. Now compare that need with a WLAN used to support point-of-sale transactions in a retail environment. If that network has a problem, the retail store cannot do business. In a medical environment, however, the network might provide a link for life-support monitoring.

Site Information

Each site will likely have different physical characteristics and requirements. Therefore, you might need to perform surveys differently. If the site includes indoor and outdoor areas, antennas that are capable of outdoor installations might be necessary. If the site has extremely high ceilings or very low ceilings, you need to use the appropriate antennas for the survey. Other characteristics such as temperatures, hazardous environments, and public areas can also affect what equipment is needed for the survey.

Note the following site information:

- **Number of floors**—If this is a multiple-floor facility, discuss with the customer the coverage expectations for isolated areas, such as stairwells or elevator shafts. Also, the technician should be ready to consider extra time required for a 3D site survey, as discussed in Chapter 11.

- **Floor construction**—Floor construction impacts the propagation between floors of a multiple-floor building. This issue is especially significant with regard to construction techniques today that use a metal underpanning that is installed to allow concrete to be poured on top of it. This underpanning isolates RF coverage cells to a single floor in most cases.

- **Ceiling height**—Ceiling heights in any environment impact propagation patterns and work areas. A surveying technician can normally use a stepladder to reach shorter ceilings (such as in an office); however, you must then consider whether to survey with low-profile antennas that are not intrusive in the environment. In contrast, a 35-foot-high warehouse ceiling might require you to use a lift to reach the top to mount equipment for the site survey.

- **Ceiling construction**—The ceiling construction factors into consideration the type of antenna to use at a facility (and, therefore, what type of antenna the surveying technician needs to use). For example, low-profile diversity ceiling-mount omni-directional antennas are appropriate in drop-tile ceiling areas, and medium-gain omni-directional antennas are typically appropriate for a warehouse ceiling. Protruding medium-gain antennas in environments with low-height, drop-tile ceilings are at risk of being struck or even damaged.

- **Lift availability**—If a lift is not on site for high-ceiling work, you must rent one prior to the survey date to ensure its on-time delivery. Remember, safety first! The person using the lift should be both comfortable and trained with the type of lift and use applicable safety equipment. Some locations require a union worker to operate lifts.

- **Plenum ceiling**—If the ceiling is plenum rated, you might have to take extra steps during the site survey process to find alternative equipment-mounting locations. The AP as well as cables and antennas might need a plenum rating, too.

- **Wall construction**—Propagation is affected by the obstacles in the path between the client device and the AP, so it is helpful to know whether the wall construction is simple sheetrock or whether it is of a material that makes propagation difficult (such as plaster over metal lathe). If the latter, set expectations with the customer regarding propagation and a plan for higher number of potential APs (before the technician deploys to the site).

- **Current percentage of stock level**—Stock levels vary in warehouse environments, and so networks are designed to incorporate this as much as possible; however, the ever-changing environment can cause "dead" spots of no coverage. If stock levels are far below usual, a conservative survey should be done to anticipate coverage for a full warehouse by reducing power of an AP and raising acceptable thresholds of the diagnostic tests.

- **Temperature ranges**—Temperatures at a site might vary from extremely hot to extremely cold. Exposure to temperature extremes is a factor to consider (with regard to the survey engineer and the survey gear). Again, remember, safety first. Prepare for extreme exposure, no matter whether it is a cold freezer or ceiling work in a hot warehouse during summer months.

- **Hazardous areas**—Identify any areas that might be hazardous. Certain areas such as painting facilities or chemical factories might require special equipment to prevent fires or explosions. Once more, safety is a primary concern.

  If the facility has hazardous areas, brush up on your *material safety data sheets* (MSDS) regarding the hazardous materials. Also have other safety equipment prepared for physical hazards, such as electrical shock or falling objects. You might require additional safety equipment, such as grounding straps or electrical insulators, safety harnesses, and even biological suits with respirators. Before working in a hazardous environment, be sure to take time to understand the hazards and preventive measures as well as the emergency-response conditions.

Working in a Hazardous Area

One customer story involves a site where the customer needed assistance getting the WLAN running properly. No site survey was completed, and the customer was having problems. After some investigation, a third-party contractor was called in to assist with the troubleshooting and some site survey work. Unfortunately, little discussion took place concerning the site other than that the WLAN was used to control machinery running in a large field.

Upon arriving at the site, the engineer received an emergency respirator pack for use in the field in the event of an emergency. The engineer recalled smelling the faint scent of mustard gas in the air as he was moving around the field. Later that evening, he was quarantined because it was suspected that the crew had been exposed to a neurotoxin that had been detected in their vicinity.

The site was a five-acre toxic-waste site full of exposed and buried chemical and biological weapons that were collected for disposal from the early 1900s to the later part of the century.

This story highlights the importance of correct safety measures. Although the contractor was delighted that the customer solved the problems, the contractor informed the customer that they could not provide assistance for this site in the future and would instead train the customer's own personnel on WLAN topics.

Survey Personnel Requirements

The customer might place certain requirements on you before you are permitted to enter or work in a given facility. In some cases, you might need protective clothing such as steel-toed shoes, hardhats, or hairnets. You might need to meet prerequisites such as drug testing, background checks, or security clearances. Be certain to verify any such issues with the point of contact at the facility before scheduling any work.

Scope of Work

The scope of work section details exactly what the survey engineer will do and what he will need to complete a proper job. This section of the pre-site survey form includes information such how the survey will be completed, how the engineer will mount antennas and APs, whether ceiling tiles will be moved, and so on. Anything that might cause disruptions to the production environment is vital and should be spelled out in detail. In addition to the details contained in the sample survey and scope of work, there should be a description of applications and the client devices that will be used with the WLAN. This section is one portion of the pre-site survey form in which you, as the survey engineer, provide feedback to the customer.

Coverage Map

As part of the pre-site survey form, develop a floor plan showing coverage areas and areas that the customer has defined as no-coverage areas. The coverage map indicates to the customer, the installer, and a troubleshooter the areas the system is designed to cover. Figure 6-1 shows a simple coverage map.

Figure 6-1 *Sample Coverage Map*

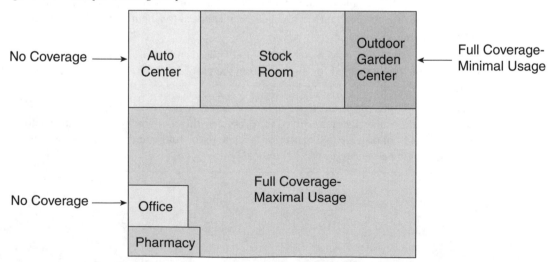

Outdoor Bridge Links

Although this book is principally for wireless network site surveying and installation, it is likely that you might also become involved with wireless network bridging at some point to extend networks or to help reduce recurring costs for leased telco lines. Therefore, you might want to consider adding a section on bridging information to the pre-site survey. Even if the customer envisions only a WLAN, such information might stimulate the thought of other uses for wireless.

Much of the information that you collect for a pre-site survey for an outdoor bridge link is quite a bit different from that for a WLAN system. Key items are discussed in the following list, with a more in-depth discussion of wireless bridging in Chapter 14, "Outdoor Bridge Deployments":

- **Site-specific information**—Site name, *Global Positioning System* (GPS) information, main address, and POC contact information are needed just as at the beginning of the pre-site survey form and for the same reasons.

- **Line of sight (LoS)**—For the best signal quality and performance, you should have *line of sight* (LoS) between the main sight and the remote end. This is somewhat misleading because optical LoS differs from RF LoS; however, filling out the form does help the customer to determine link feasibility prior to a survey engineer arriving on site.

- **Existing tower use**—When elevation is needed, so are communication towers. If there is access to an existing tower, the customers might save the expense of installing one themselves; however, consider that there might be a lease fee for that tower space. If constructing a tower is required, be prepared for additional costs in the project ranging from $2000 to more than $200,000 depending on the type of tower and construction requirements. Also seek professional assistance with this structure from those who specialize in this work; the consequences of this structure failing while it is near a populated area could be terrible (and costly). State and local codes often apply to tower use in populated areas. Such regulations might specify that a tower be constructed with enough free space around it so that nothing would be damaged (or anyone injured) if the structure were to fail.

- **Building rights and mounting height for antennas**—If the proposed bridge antenna will mount to the exterior of a building, try to determine the customer's preference for mounting the antenna and the maximum elevation to be achieved with this structure. If the customer solely owns the building, elevating the bridge above ground obstructions is usually the best option. If the customer does not have roof rights in a building where space is rented, a suitable wall or inside window mount might be required.

- **Building exterior construction**—Some buildings are constructed in such a way that the construction actually limits how a technician can install equipment. To protect certain décors, a technician might have to find a nonintrusive way to install equipment. If the exterior is corrugated metal or highly reflective metal-oxide tinted glass, the bridge might suffer from reflection and multipath mitigation issues. A technician must install the bridge in such a way that this is not an issue for LoS bridging. *Non-LoS* (NLoS) bridging uses the multipath and reflection in an urban environment as part of the functionality.

- **Roof access**—Because basic short-range bridging is best done from the highest elevation possible, roof access to a building that is to be part of the bridge is desirable. Also determine whether roof penetration (the ability to pass the necessary cable through the roof) is already in place. Otherwise, the roof will need to have appropriate passages cut.

User Input

No site survey can be completed without the input from the persons who will be using and administering the network after it has been installed. It is very important to have the input from both groups because the actual users of devices on the network might have different concerns from those of the network administrators. For example, warehouse stockers using WLAN voice technology for their instructions might want 100 percent network connectivity RF coverage so that they can transmit and receive data even while reaching into the shelving. However, a network administrator who does not interface with this part of the company might not have relevant knowledge of day-to-day operations. The pre-site survey form is the foundation for all of this input; it provides the foundational information from which to extrapolate ideas and contribute solutions.

Experienced survey technicians should look for additional network needs and survey issues during the pre-survey walkthrough so that these issues can be discussed prior to the site survey being performed. Such observations include identifying all aspects of the proposed WLAN use and implementation restrictions.

Balancing Wants, Needs, and Capabilities

As a knowledgeable consultant or network administrator, you must understand the nature of the LAN that is in place at the facility and the propose the right WLAN to best suit the needs of those using it. I have had to introduce people to the realities of WLAN many times in the past and will likely have to do so countless times to come. In so doing, I keep expectations at a realistic level, and then I design the best possible WLAN based on the information I have collected.

Based on the information from the completed pre-site survey form, you will know the wants of the customer and be able to determine whether the equipment they have chosen is capable of such wants or needs. Any decision on equipment and implementation should begin with *needs*, to establish a baseline of performance that is absolutely required.

Suppose, for example, that a small doctor's office wants your assistance with WLAN connectivity throughout the office. The office has already purchased an 802.11b AP for this purpose. You must first determine what applications and devices will be using the WLAN, and then how many users and where will they be using WLAN devices. If several high-bandwidth applications are identified, including some that would be life threatening if not available, you must consider the actual capabilities of 802.11b devices as insufficient for this purpose because of their low data rates and an identified need for redundancy or fallback protection. You should then recommend more than one AP capable of higher data rates, such as 802.11a/g devices.

Continuing with this example, if the area is small enough to be covered by one AP, but the application bandwidth requirements and number of users are so great that they would overload the AP capabilities, you must survey to implement more APs to increase the load-carrying capabilities of the WLAN in that area. Although this is logical to those who understand the realistic capabilities of WLAN devices, be sure to explain your reasoning to the customer, who is now required to purchase additional equipment that perhaps was not previously accounted for in the budget.

In this example, the customer's desire (want) to have one AP did not match (capability-wise) the needs identified. Be sure to assess all aspects of the customer wants, needs, and capabilities for every facility or application, even though many might be similar.

Summary

When surveying for a WLAN, technicians must account for all information and then design a network for the worst-case scenario to ensure the WLAN will function under the most difficult circumstances. The first step in your assessment is the pre-site survey form to begin gathering this information.

Completing the pre-site survey form enables you to prepare for the actual site survey and budget the appropriate costs, equipment, time, and resources. The pre-site survey documentation is a key step in a thorough and efficient site survey.

This chapter covers the following topics:

- WLAN Equipment
- A Site Survey Kit

CHAPTER 7

Site Surveying Equipment

Several different styles of site survey methods are in use today. Some techniques purport to be automatic—implying that no actual "site" work has to be done and everything is fully automatic, being handled by a system that resides somewhere on the network. Other techniques are totally manual, meaning you need to walk the entire facility to gather the necessary information required for installation. Somewhere in between is the assisted site survey, which means you use a system on the network to augment a manual survey.

In reality, there is almost no site in the world that does not require some amount of manual site surveying work to install an efficient, properly working WLAN. Chapter 10, "Using Site Surveying Tools," discusses in detail the different survey techniques. In this chapter, you learn about the tools needed for the manual site survey process.

WLAN Equipment

This section describes various tools needed in a WLAN, including the following:

- Access points
- Client devices
- Connectors
- Antennas
- Cables
- Attenuators
- Physical measuring devices
- RF analyzers
- Two-way radios
- Outdoor tools
- Battery packs
- Digital camera
- Mounting hardware

| NOTE | Before surveying, it is important to understand what the customer applications will require for bandwidth and range. This may make a difference in what technology will work best for the site. |

Before surveying, it is important to understand what the customer applications will require for bandwidth and range. This may make a difference in what technology will work best for the site.

You have a wide variety of WLAN products from which to choose. The customer's network design should have the technology defined (or recommended) as well as the product models. The survey engineer must verify that these will, in fact, work for this site. The survey should not only provide the location, antenna style, configuration, and so on, it should also actually verify that the customer's design will result in adequate performance. If you have any doubts, raise them with your customer (and document them in the site survey report).

Access Points

Many users believe that for a survey, any *access point* (AP) will work and that they all work similarly. Such a belief strays very far from the truth. As you learned in Chapter 5, "Selecting the WLAN Architecture and Hardware," APs vary drastically with regard to technology, style, capability, and performance. To complete a successful survey and installation, you must use the AP that is intended to be installed. As with any radio technology, the performance from one radio device to another can have drastic differences. This is even true of different radio models from the same manufacturer.

A comparison of two of the more popular APs in the enterprise industry today—the Oronoco AP2500 with an 802.11b radio and a Cisco AP1100 with an 802.11b radio— shows the variations that can occur between different products. The Oronoco has a transmitter power of +15 dbm (30 mW), whereas the Cisco AP1100 has +20 dbm (100 mW). That is a 5-dB difference. The difference of transmitter power between these two devices can make as much as a 30-percent variation in cell coverage.

Another difference that occurs quite often is variation in receiver performance. The Cisco AP1100 has a receiver sensitivity of –85 dBm when operating at 11 Mbps. Yet the 802.11b radio in the Oronoco AP has a receiver sensitivity of only –82 dBm. Although 3 dB may not seem like much, it can have a dramatic effect on the fringe areas.

Figure 7-1 shows various APs that you can use for site surveys. Notice the variations between antenna styles, capabilities (attached versus remote), and physical size.

Figure 7-1   *Various Access Points*

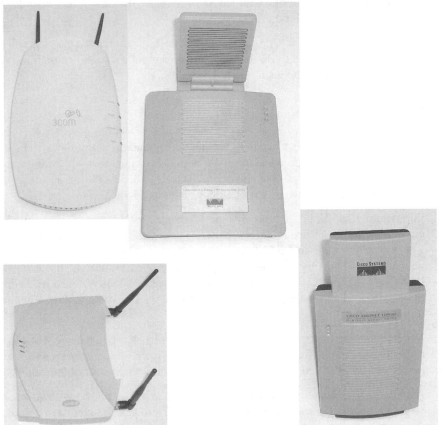

Looking at two APs from the same company, the Cisco AP1100 and AP1200 both have the same radio and the same radio specifications. Because of the antenna variations, however, they are miles apart (figuratively speaking) on coverage performance. The AP1100 has an internal dipole antenna, and unlike the AP1200 it has no options of adding external antennas and no way to improve coverage performance by changing antennas. The same drawback is true of the Avaya AP5 AP.

Another common issue that comes up when trying to select an AP for a survey is the ability to use various antennas. Antennas must be certified with the radio in many regulatory domains. Some vendors have a limited number of available antennas. The Enterasys Roamabout R2 with an 802.11b radio, for example, offers an external antenna capability, but does not enable you to use external diversity antennas. In addition, the selection of certified antennas is very limited.

Be aware that some of the centralized intelligence architecture products require you to have the controller or switch along with the AP; otherwise, the AP will not operate. This can be quite a cumbersome solution for surveying.

Surveying with one model AP and installing another can create a major problem in the system when it is installed. Bottom line, and it cannot be stressed enough, survey with the same product that will be installed!

Client Devices

It is also of utmost importance to know and understand the client that will be used in the site. Although it is not practical to survey with every client that will be used, it should be noted in the survey report what clients will be used, what the radio transmitter and receiver specifications are, and what type of antenna is used on the device.

For example, on the pre-site survey report, you see that a warehouse may use various clients, including a standard laptop, bar code scanners, and *Voice over IP* (VoIP) phones. The warehouse manager and a few of the employees who need network access in both the warehouse and the office will use the laptop. The radio card used in this device is the Cisco PCM350. These radios provide a transmitter power of 100 mW, and a receiver sensitivity of –85 dBm when running 11 Mbps (802.11b). They also use a built-in antenna that has a unity gain (0 dBm).

The bar code scanners may be mounted to the lift trucks. These devices use the Symbol radio that has a receiver sensitivity of –84 dBm. Again, the scanners have a transmitter power of 100 mW, and use a 5-dBi antenna mounted to the roof of the vehicle.

Also in the warehouse is a Symbol Netvision 802.11b VoIP phone, with an output power of 60 mW, a receiver sensitivity of –82 dBm, and an embedded antenna that, as a best guess (it is not documented), has a gain of 2 dB or less (based on size).

So which client do you choose to survey with? Unfortunately there is no simple answer. However, you can make certain assumptions. First, the device that has the minimum receiver sensitivity should be viewed. From this list, the phone, with a sensitivity of –82 dBm, probably has the worst-case receiver. It is down 3 dB from the Cisco client card. Because the phone antenna is not exactly known, assume it is no more than 1 dB, giving the receiver a total receive performance of –83 dBm. Still, it has the lowest performance of the three devices cited on the presurvey report.

For the transmitter side of the clients, you also need to consider the antenna as well as transmitter power. In this case, the lift-truck system has a 5-dBi gain antenna, so it will by far have the best performance. The PCMCIA card in the laptop has 100 mW with a 0-dBi antenna, and the phone has a 60-mW radio with a minimal-gain antenna. So again, the phone has the worst-case specifications.

The dilemma is that the phone may not have a good site survey tool. Certain client devices can adjust transmitter power, so as a solution you can set this to an appropriate setting, comparable to the lowest-performing transmitter device.

Although it is easy to compensate for transmitter power differences, simulating receiver sensitivity is not quite as easy. To compensate for the difference in the client receiver, you can usually adjust the AP transmitter power (assuming the transmitter power is programmable) to effectively reduce the signal to the receiver, emulating a lower receiver performance.

Figure 7-2 shows several different devices that you might use in any given site and will have to evaluate for overall RF performances. Included in these may be bar code scanners, VoIP phones, PCI cards, laptops with built-in radio devices, or specialty RF devices.

Figure 7-2   *Various Client Devices for Surveying*

To summarize, follow these steps when selecting client survey devices:

Step 1. Analyze the client devices intended to be used in the site.

Step 2. Select devices that support the defined minimum data rates and technologies (802.11a, b, g).

Step 3. Select a device that has programmable client power settings.

Step 4. Take into account device antenna gains.

Step 5. Set the power to simulate that of the lowest power device to be used in the site.

NOTE	Many 802.11b and 802.11g devices on the market only offer 15 dBm (30 mW) of power, whereas others offer 200 mW. The 802.11a product lines vary even more widely. Be certain to do the proper research before going on site to perform a survey.

Connectors

Most of the connectorized APs use unique connectors and vary from vendor to vendor. As a survey engineer, it might prove helpful to build some very short adaptor cables, allowing the use of one style coax and antenna connector with any of the APs you might encounter for surveys. In this manner, you can carry a single set of antennas and accessories but still connect to any of the various APs that the customer may specify. Figure 7-3 shows connector and adaptor cable examples you might use in site surveying.

Figure 7-3 *Various Connectors Used in Surveying*

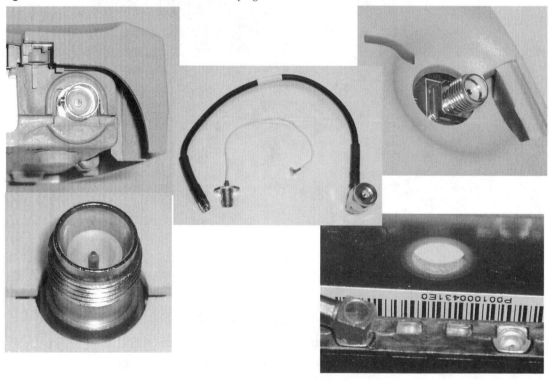

Antennas

Maintain a wide selection of antennas in any survey kit. Although there are certain standard antennas, the ability to use different antennas to cover different situations makes the difference between a professional site survey and a survey that has been forced to work using compromises (and sometimes performance or cost trade-offs).

Omnidirectional antennas are, by far, the most common, and every kit should contain a typical omnidirectional dipole antenna. This is like a universal soldier, and can be used in many different locations. In many cases, you will need a pair of these for supporting the diversity capabilities of the AP. Appendix B, "Antenna Radiation Patterns," shows examples of different antennas.

A good understanding of these antennas and their particular type of radiation patterns will help in selecting the proper antennas.

Another very common and useful antenna is the diverse ceiling-mountable omnidirectional antenna. You can attach this antenna below the ceiling and locate the cable routed to the AP above the ceiling. This setup enables you to hide the AP, enables coverage similar to a dipole antenna, and supports diversity. An added advantage of this antenna is its ease of deployment. Installation takes about 30 seconds; you snap the antenna onto the ceiling crossbar.

For some applications, you might have to use a slightly higher-gain omnidirectional antenna. For this, you have several choices. When selecting which omni to use, remember the issue of radiation pattern. When mounting one omni in the ceiling in an inverted fashion (like a mast-mount antenna, hanging down from the building truss), it may have a different vertical pattern than an antenna that is designed to be mounted in that fashion. Such an antenna is designed to be mounted to a mast, with the feed line at the bottom. The radiation pattern has more energy below the horizontal line than above it; and if you invert this antenna, you will have more energy radiating into the ceiling than at the floor. An omni antenna designed for ceiling mountings is virtually the same antenna with a different mounting design, and it does have the same radiation pattern. When mounted to the ceiling, however, it radiates more energy downward, as designed.

An omni antenna is almost never intended to be mounted in a horizontal (sideways) position because the radiation pattern would radiate in a vertical pattern rather than a horizontal pattern.

Sometimes a higher-gain omni is needed, such as the 5-dBi antennas, but the environment will not permit (because of aesthetics) the ceiling-mount or mast-mount antennas. A few antennas are available that offer a "stealthy" look. The pillar-mount antenna provides a diversity antenna with a look that blends into the surrounding walls.

Directional antennas are often used for coverage of outdoor sites, but they can also prove very useful in covering indoor areas. One of the most useful is a lower-gain patch or panel antenna. There are quite a few different versions out there, but they are all similar in performance if the gain is similar.

One advantage of a panel or patch antenna is that they can be mounted to a wall, with the cables exiting through the wall, or up behind the ceiling. And the antenna itself can be painted the same color as the wall. (Just be certain the paint has no metallic properties.)

For certain applications, such as a very long corridor, a warehouse with long narrow racks, or even certain manufacturing areas, a Yagi can be used. It is not uncommon to use directional antennas to "fill" a particular area with RF. An airplane hangar is one site where this has been done. The hangar ceiling is extremely high, and the antennas must be placed above the planes. The Yagis are mounted in the ceiling and pointed down to provide coverage of the area below it.

No single antenna is perfect for all applications. A variety of antennas are included in most site survey kits because they are needed at certain times. (See Figure 7-4.) The customer in many cases dictates antenna choice and placement. A customer might not want the antenna to be visible or to be located in a high-traffic area. By carrying a variety of antennas, you will be prepared for any situation. To summarize, the recommended minimum collection of antennas should include (but is not limited to) antennas similar to the following:

- 2.2-dBi dipole antenna rubber duck
- 2.2-dBi diversity omni ceiling-mount antenna
- 2.0-dBi ceiling-tile antenna
- 5.2-dBi mast-mount antenna
- 5.2-dBi omni ceiling mount
- 5.2-dBi pillar-mount diversity omni antenna
- 6.0-dBi diversity patch wall-mount antenna
- 8.5-dBi hemispherical patch antenna
- 10.0-dBi Yagi mast-mount antenna
- 13.5-dBi Yagi mast-mount antenna

If you plan on using diversity antennas, you need to carry two of every antenna unless the antenna is especially made to support diversity and contains two antennas.

Do not use a different antenna and attempt to "guesstimate" the coverage. You are performing the site survey *to take the guesswork out* of the installation.

Figure 7-4   *Antennas for Site Surveys*

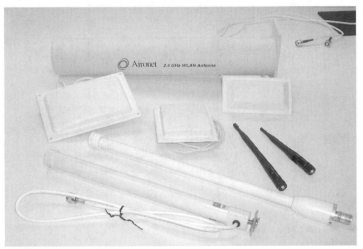

Cables

Additional antenna cable introduces loss, and therefore should be avoided whenever possible. In some situations, however, it is not possible to locate the AP within reach of the antenna's attached cable. In these cases, you can use coax cable to extend the reach.

As RF energy is carried between the antenna and the radio equipment through a coaxial cable, it introduces signal loss for both the transmitter and receiver. To reduce signal loss, minimize the cable length and use only a very low-loss antenna cable to connect radio devices to antennas.

It is not necessary to carry various cables in a survey kit. If you anticipate using a cable for the actual install, the survey should note what cable is to be used (type and length), and the survey engineer will simulate the cable loss by using an attenuator. This enables the engineer to simulate virtually any cable type and length. It is recommended, however, to carry the information for typical coax cables that would be specified. This way the engineer can calculate the losses and program the attenuator with the proper simulation loss.

Figure 7-5 shows the LMR-400 and LMR-600 cables. Table 7-1 describes the features of each.

Figure 7-5 *Cable Examples*

Table 7-1 *Features of the LMR-400 and LMR-600 Cables*

Cable Type	2.4-GHz Loss (dB/100 feet)	5.8-GHz Loss (dB/100 feet)
LMR-400	6.6	10.8
LMR-600	4.4	7.25

It might prove helpful to carry a single 10- or 20-foot (3- or 6-meter) cable in the kit for surveys in locations where the AP cannot be located with the antenna, even for the survey itself. Locations such as extremely wet areas (processing plants) or extremely cold areas (freezers) might require the survey AP be located outside the environment and the antenna located inside the area. In this event, you might need a cable to complete the survey.

Attenuators

Always perform surveys using the equipment that will eventually be installed. This can sometimes be difficult with splitters, lightning arrestors, and extension cables.

Instead of carrying one of every length of cable, lightning arrestors, splitters, and other accessories, some engineers outfit the site survey kit with an attenuator. The attenuator enables you to inject varying amounts of loss without needing the actual accessories.

The attenuator must have the proper RF specifications. Many attenuators are only good up to 1 or 2 GHz, and you must use one that has a specification high enough to cover the band that you will be using. An attenuator good for up to 2.7 GHz is fine for a 2.4-GHz survey, but it will not work in a 5-GHz system. An attenuator with a 6-GHz rating could be used at either 2.4 or 5 GHz. Figure 7-6 shows a variable attenuator that can be used to simulate various losses in the antenna system or cables.

Figure 7-6 *RF Attenuator*

Attenuators are expensive. As frequency of the device goes up, so does the price. This is one area where you cannot cut costs.

Physical Measuring Devices

One tool that is often overlooked is a measuring device—something that can measure long-distance runs of hundreds or even thousands of feet or meters. In many cases, you need to add measurements to your drawings for room size, building size, or even parking lot size. Or you might need to measure the distance a cable will have to run between and AP and a switch (keeping in mind whether that will meet the intended cable-length limitation). If you guess the *Category* (Cat) 5 cable run to be 300 feet (91 meters) and it turns out to be 380 feet (116 meters), the customer will be very dissatisfied. For some measurements, a tape measure might prove impractical and difficult to use (especially for one person). Your kit also should include a measuring wheel similar to the one shown in Figure 7-7.

Figure 7-7   *Measuring Devices*

Many survey engineers find that some of the more advanced equipment, such as laser measuring devices and range finders, can save time and effort. For measuring vertical distances, these can prove extremely helpful, especially when doing a survey alone. An alternative method is to use a rope marked in 10-foot (3-meter) increments so that you can accurately judge distances floor to ceiling.

RF Analyzers

In today's world of communications, RF is everywhere, in every possible environment. Therefore, survey engineers must look at the RF environment for other radio devices and interference. Failure to do so can result in a system that is installed but never works.

Looking at the RF spectrum requires a specialized receiver or a spectrum analyzer. The next section examines different tools for analyzing the RF environment.

Spectrum Analyzer

The spectrum analyzer is the best and most useful tool for RF spectrum analyses. It not only provides a look at the spectrum in which the WLAN system will operate, it can also determine the frequency of other signals, the duration they are transmitting, the strength of the signal, and with some experience the engineer may even be able to determine the type of modulation in use, leading to an understanding of the type of device being used. By using a directional antenna, you can use a spectrum analyzer to locate a signal source.

Spectrum analyzers have several drawbacks as a site survey tool. The first drawback is cost. For an analyzer that supports the 5-GHz band, the cost could reach well above $10,000! Second, most spectrum analyzers require AC power. A few models are offered with battery packs, but the duration of operation is limited based on the battery power.

Portable Analyzer Tools

Portable analyzer tools such as the Berkley Valtronics Grasshopper can prove very useful and cost-effective (see Figure 7-8). The Grasshopper is a handheld, wireless receiver designed specifically for sweeping and optimizing WLANs. It can measure coverage of 802.11b systems, enabling the user to measure and determine the AP and *received signal strength identification* (RSSI) signal levels (which helps the user locate the APs throughout a building). It can also detect and differentiate from narrowband multipath interferences (such as from microwave ovens and frequency-hopping systems) and features a built-in display, keypad, and removable battery pack for true portability.

Figure 7-8   *Portable RF Analyzer for 802.11*

Some WLAN products enable you to sniff, or listen, to the RF, acting like a spectrum sniffer listening to frequencies the gear is designed to operate in. This is a convenient tool, but it is not as effective as a good spectrum analyzer. One such WLAN product is the Cisco Aironet AP1200 AP. It offers a feature called *carrier test*. It provides a dBm level of the highest signal received on any of the available 802.11 channels. The AirMagnet wireless sniffer product also offers a feature to sniff the air for other RF energy. Although these tools are very useful, they do not compare to the versatility of a spectrum analyzer in the hands of an experienced engineer.

Two-Way Radios

In some situations, two engineers will conduct a survey together. In such cases, a communication link between them can help to reduce time. Family Radio Service walkie-talkies are very inexpensive and typically require no license (at least in the U.S.). Before using them in a customer site, however, always inquire as to any company regulations about radios. Some sites may have areas where high-power two-way radios are not permitted.

Outdoor Tools

If the survey is for outdoor links, you might need other equipment. Tools to determine necessary antenna height, waterproof-test enclosures (for the equipment during testing), and *Global Positioning System* (GPS) receivers are just a few tools that can prove very helpful. Chapter 14, "Outdoor Bridge Deployments," covers some of the tools used in outdoor site surveys.

Battery Packs

APs require power to operate. However, power will not always be available nearby while you conduct a site survey. A solution that enables you to power the AP without running long cables is the best method for surveying. A good survey battery pack will last for at least eight hours, enabling the engineer to survey all day without having to recharge.

Because power requirements vary from one vendor AP to another, a single power pack is not something that is universal. Some battery packs are available with various power offerings (such as the TerraWave pack shown in Figure 7-9).

Figure 7-9   *Site Survey Battery Pack and Adaptor*

With this particular site survey battery pack, you can easily survey for up to eight hours without worry about having to pull around a long AC power cable or worry about having anyone trip over your power source. It provides 5V DC and 12V DC outputs for powering Telxon, Aironet, and some Cisco, Lucent, Symbol, Intel, and Proxim APs and bridges. With the in-line power adaptor, you can use that supply to power other APs that utilize the Cisco *Power over Ethernet* (PoE) scheme or 802.3af PoE.

Another way to provide power to APs is to use a UPS type of supply that provides AC power. However, these can become very heavy, and their overall available power is usually fewer than eight hours.

Also recommended is a fast charger for the client site survey tool. If a laptop is used, spare battery packs that can be charged separate from the laptop are always recommended. Wireless PC cards require a constant source of power while surveying and might reduce battery life to fewer than two hours.

Another possibility is a high-capacity battery pack such as the N-Charge power system from Valence Technologies (see Figure 7-10). This type of battery can provide power to a typical laptop for four to five hours. (The specification says up to 10, but that does not factor in running a radio in site survey mode.)

Figure 7-10 *Site Survey Battery for Laptops*

Digital Camera

Another device to consider adding to your site survey kit is a digital camera. Taking a picture of antenna mountings, AP locations, special fixtures, or locations and adding these to the site survey report can save countless hours trying to describe details in words.

Use pictures whenever you have any doubt about how to mount or about where to locate something. Also use pictures to show possible interference (environmental) issues in the survey reports.

Mounting Hardware

Mounting hardware for the site survey can be quite a bit different from what is needed for the actual install. For an install, you are leaving the WLAN components installed permanently. For the site survey, the mounting is just long enough to complete your measurements. However, based on the environment and who is around when you are surveying, mounting options can vary widely. Although the installation might be temporary, it needs to be secure enough so that something does not come loose and fall, creating a hazard for someone who happens to be in the area while you are working. It must also be secure enough that someone does not "walk off" with the test gear while you are making your rounds performing testing.

Always carry an AP mounting bracket (when available). Your kit should also contain various mounting solutions for the bracket (beam clamps and C-clamps, for example) as well as mounting brackets for each antenna (when available). Ladders and a collapsible pole for temporary placement of an AP prove extremely useful as well. Beyond this, you must again be creative. Zip ties, duct tape, bailing wire, electrical tape, two-sided tape, and Velcro are common components in a good engineer's kit (see Figure 7-11).

Figure 7-11 *Site Survey Mounting Examples*

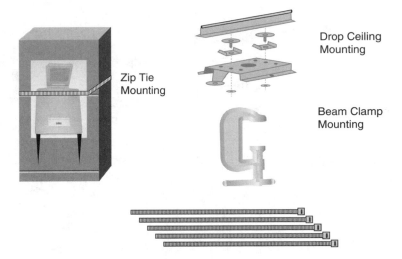

Zip Tie Mounting

Drop Ceiling Mounting

Beam Clamp Mounting

Remember, during a survey there is no bad mounting solution except the solution that does not properly secure the AP, battery pack, and antenna. If these are not properly secured, not only might you damage your equipment, you risk injuring yourself or others when the equipment comes crashing down.

Site Survey Kits

If you plan to perform more than one site survey, it makes sense to assemble all the necessary components needed into a single kit. With this kit, you can keep all your tools together and ensure you have what you need when you get to the site to do your work (and then provide the best possible solution for the site). You have learned the importance of using the proper APs, client cards, antennas, battery packs, and cables. You have also read about the importance of having a variety of mounting solutions, measuring devices, and attenuators for your survey. With all these tools in one place, you can ensure that you have what you need when rolling out to a customer site.

In come cases, you might just want to buy a site survey kit and add equipment to it. Terra-Wave offers one such kit (see Figure 7-12). This kit is built around the Cisco Aironet product line. With some thought and adaptation, however, you can use it for virtually any product line. Just apply a little ingenuity and build adaptor cables to mate to other AP types and to a few other APs, and you can have a complete arsenal for your site surveys.

Figure 7-12 *Complete Site Survey Kit*

The TerraWave product is intended for indoor site surveys and includes the following features (subject to change):

- A durable and transportable carrying case
- 2 * AIR-352E2R-K-9 (11-Mbps APs)
- 2 * AIR-PCM352 (PC cards with fixed antennas)
- 1 * AIR-LMC352 (PC card without antenna)
- 4 * AIR-ANT4941 (2.2-dBi "rubber duck" antennas)
- 2 * AIR-ANT5959 (2.0-dBi ceiling-mount diversity omni)
- 1 * AIR-ANT3213 (5.2-dBi pillar-mount diversity omni)
- 2 * AIR-ANT2506 (5.2-dBi mast-mount omni)
- 2 * AIR-ANT2012 (6.0-dBi diversity patch wall mount)
- 2 * AIR-ANT3549 (8.5-dBi hemispherical patch)
- 2 * AIR-ANT1949 (13.5-dBi Yagi)

- 2 * AIR-ACC55959-072 (serial cables for configuration)
- 2 * AIR-420-1625-0500 (RP-TNC assembly −5")
- 2 * TW-SSBP-001 (site survey battery packs with in-line power)
- 2 * TW-IPMB-001 (industrial-purpose mounting brackets)
- 2 * TW-RSA-3510 (attenuators)
- 1 * TW-AATC-001 (travel case with foam cutout)
- 1 * TW-SSMW-001 (measuring wheel)
- 50 * TW-APMRK-050 (AP marking locators)
- Mounting devices, including duct tape, zip ties, Velcro, and colored-tape rolls
- Custom foam inserts to protect and organize each individual item
- Wheels and handle for easy transport
- Industrial safety lock

The TerraWave kit has the following dimensions:

- Total weight: 67 lbs. (31 kg)
- Inside dimensions: 29" * 17 $^7/_8$" * 10 $^1/_2$" (73.6 cm * 45.4 cm * 26.7 cm)
- Outside dimensions: 32 $^1/_2$" * 20 $^1/_2$" * 11 $^5/_{16}$" (82.5 cm * 52.0 cm * 28.7 cm)

Summary

Site surveys require specific equipment and creative thinking for placement and use. Knowing and understanding the characteristics of the different WLAN equipment, antennas, and accessories can greatly assist in solving simple survey problems.

Having the proper equipment at the site is also vital. Trying to use one device such as an antenna just because you do not have a different, more appropriate style is not acceptable. It is imperative that a survey kit contain a wide variety of equipment so that you can complete the survey properly and efficiently.

Through the use of specialized survey gear and creative thinking (including a willingness to "think outside the box"), you can perform a proper survey and ultimately provide the best possible installation for the customer.

This chapter covers the following topics:

- Recommended Facility Documentation
- Limitations Affecting Equipment Installations
- Using Cookie Cutter Designs

CHAPTER 8

Discovering Site-Specific Requirements

Often when a decision is made to install a WLAN, the decision makers do not realize that WLAN installation sites vary widely. Those who decide to move to wireless networks understand their environment and assume that most other WLAN systems and sites are much the same as theirs, and therefore the WLAN installation should be similar (and easy). Even in something as similar as a chain of retail stores, minor variations such as stock and shelving arrangements can cause coverage to vary. In reality, unless the two sites are built from the same architectural plans and populated with users and contents in a similar way, the two seemingly similar sites can be as different as night and day. Before a survey or installation is scheduled, each site needs to be evaluated separately.

This chapter addresses site-specific issues relevant to WLAN survey and installation tasks. This chapter examines topics such as site layouts, facility contents, building and construction variations, different environmental conditions at the site, and other site-specific requirements. This chapter also discusses the need for accurate floor plans, building and construction specifics, an inventory of building contents, and an awareness of customer issues related to specific installation limitations.

Recommended Facility Documentation

Any engineer surveying and installing a WLAN system needs facility documentation, the collection of which should be part of the initial design stage. Facility documentation enables the engineers defining the WLAN, or trying to survey and install it, to identify areas of concern, areas of coverage, user densities, and even types of antennas to consider, before ever walking onto the site. After the survey has been completed, the facility documentation becomes a critical part of the overall documentation and should be kept current as to any changes and maintained with the rest of the network documentation for future reference. The facility documentation should include (but is not to limited to) the following:

- Site map (or floor plans)
- Building construction details
- Building contents inventory
- User-area and user-density information
- Problem-area (for WLAN) information

Site Map

Before beginning any site survey, obtain a good site map or floor plan of the site. In some cases, the site map might not really be a floor plan, but more of a site layout, including building layout and contents as well any outdoor areas that will be covered.

This site layout document will become part of the final survey and network documentation. As such, having a soft copy of this document is very helpful so that it can be copied and distributed as necessary to the survey engineers, installation team, and network support staff. Extra copies of the site map should be available to make notes on during the actual survey and installation steps, as well as during any presurvey discussions.

Prior to the survey, you can use the site map document to define desired coverage areas; identify where coverage is not needed; and define user locations and densities, problems areas, network closets, cable runs, and plenum areas. Basically, this document becomes the physical schematic of the wireless network (see Figure 8-1).

Figure 8-1 *Typical Site Map*

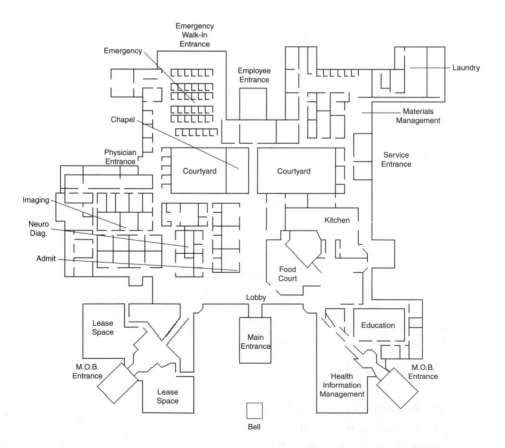

Building Construction

Building construction can vary widely from site to site. Materials and construction techniques in San Francisco differ significantly from those used in New York City, London, or Cairo. Differences in building construction, even though sites might look similar, can cause RF to react in completely different ways. Figure 8-2 shows examples of various building materials.

Figure 8-2   *Building Materials*

A multifloor building might use precast, reinforced concrete for flooring. Although this type of construction might create some attenuation problems for RF, the effect on RF penetration is significantly less than it would be with a floor of poured concrete over a steel pan. Although some RF may get through in this latter example, the steel pan provides a very good RF shield between floors (see Figure 8-3).

Walls can be similarly deceiving. In most industrial buildings, it is common to use steel studs with drywall or plasterboard over them. The drywall and plasterboard cause only a slight attenuation of RF signals, and the placement of the steel studs has little effect at all. Other walls might be concrete block, with or without steel reinforcement, which cause only limited attenuation of RF. However, precast concrete, typically using steel reinforcement, is a different story. The amount of steel used for reinforcement inside the concrete will cause the RF attenuation to vary from one building to another.

Although drywall and plaster usually minimally affect RF, the material behind the wall can pose problems. Consider a real example from a health-care facility. The RF energy was having a hard time getting into several offices. Further questioning of maintenance personnel at the facility and reviewing some older building documents revealed that this area had been remodeled recently. Before the area was used as offices, it was the radiology department. The x-ray room had been turned into offices. And, as typical with x-ray rooms, the walls were shielded to prevent x-ray energy from leaking out of the room. The walls were not removed, just covered over; therefore, the RF could not get into the offices.

Figure 8-3   *Steel-Pan Floor Construction*

In some buildings, the walls might be made from a form of reinforced wire mesh, with a plaster-type material spread across it (often called *stucco*). The mesh can work much like an RF screen, causing a severe level of signal loss or RF attenuation.

Steel outside walls, or steel walls separating parts of a building, can detrimentally affect RF coverage (because the wall might not just restrict RF penetration, it might also create a large number of multipath signals). This is common in industrial facilities, where a building has undergone one or more additions. What was once the outside wall might now be a partition between the old and new sections of the building, causing both multipath signals and an RF shield between building sections.

Be sure to research this information before or during the survey and document your findings on the site map.

Building Contents

One often-overlooked area of concern is the building contents. Those with minimal WLAN and RF experience sometimes underestimate the effect that building contents can have on a WLAN.

Figure 8-4 shows several examples of problems that can occur in a typical office environment. Areas such as file rooms and storage rooms are often filled with steel cabinets, creating a very large RF shield for RF entering that room, or even passing through it to other areas of the facility. Although most would assume an area filled with cubicles should have minimal effect on RF, it might in fact create a challenge for RF coverage. The number of cubical partitions, the amount of steel in the partitions and desks, and the size and make-up of the bookshelves can affect RF range.

Figure 8-4   *Office Issues*

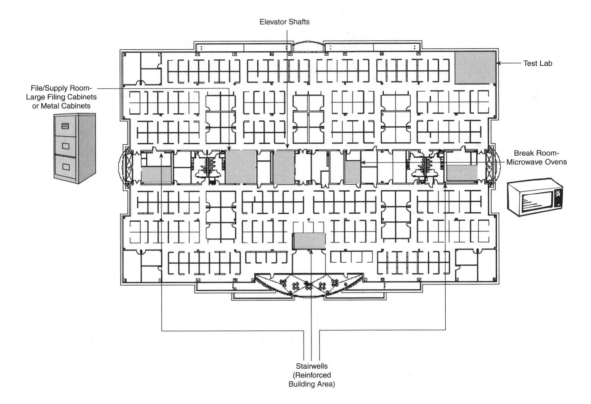

Another area that is very difficult to cover is a library or documentation area. Shelves full of books are shelves full of paper, and most paper has a high level of attenuation to WLAN frequencies. It is very common for WLANs to use directional antennas, focusing the RF energy down the aisles of the books. (See Figure 8-5.) Because of similar shelving, warehouses and even some retail stores also use directional antennas in this way.

Figure 8-5 *Directional Antennas for Library Coverage*

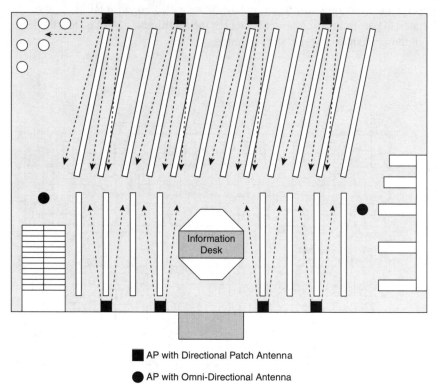

■ AP with Directional Patch Antenna

● AP with Omni-Directional Antenna

Kitchens and break-rooms usually contain microwave ovens. Microwaves are also found around many health-care and industrial facilities for purposes other than heating food. Although microwaves pose no problems for 5-GHz WLANs, they can be problematic for 2.4-GHz WLANs. The typical microwave oven uses the same frequencies as a 2.4-GHz WLAN. (This is because 2.4 GHz is the resonant frequency of water, and when 2.4-GHz energy strikes water molecules, it is absorbs the energy and causes the molecules to vibrate, creating friction and heat.) Locating a 2.4-GHz *access point* (AP) close to a microwave can cause undue interference and result in poor RF communications. Take care to keep these APs (and clients when possible) at least 10 feet away from any standard microwave oven. It is therefore recommended to note the location of any such devices on the site map. Also be aware that industrial microwave ovens sometimes have a much higher power than those found in the home or office, possibly creating even more interference. Testing should include RF coverage verification while any microwaves in the local vicinity are in full operation.

In one case, a health-care facility was having trouble with one particular AP that was dropping all associations intermittently. Close inspection of the facility turned up a microwave oven in an area that was not part of the RF-covered area, but was located in a lab adjacent to the AP-covered area. The problem was that the oven was located on the other side of the wall (made from drywall) from the AP, with a total of about 5 feet (and two pieces of drywall) separation. This is why it is important to understand the entire site, including areas where coverage may not be needed. Figure 8-6 shows a site map with potential problem areas labeled.

Figure 8-6   *Hidden Site Problems*

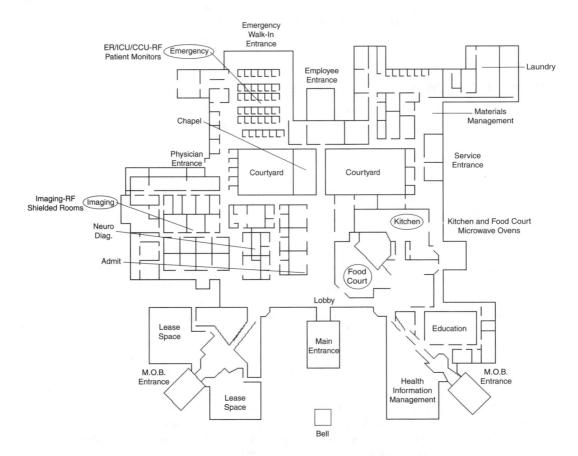

Locations such as emergency rooms and cardiac care in hospitals use sensitive equipment such as *electrocardiographs* (EKGs) and other monitoring systems. Although these devices are not generally a problem with WLANs, take care to locate the radio gear near the devices and to verify that the RF in the area does not cause any interference. One common problem occurs with older plotters and printers. The RF energy can cause slight variations in the print and plotter driver mechanisms, resulting in "glitches" in the patient printouts.

As discussed in Chapter 6, "Preparing for a Site Survey," all cordless and wireless devices should be inventoried. Phones, speaker, cameras, cordless mice, cordless keyboards, baby monitors, and virtually anything that might be RF related should be noted.

In a warehouse, retail environment, or even an office building, a change of contents can greatly affect the coverage of an AP. Inventory levels often change in a warehouse or retail facility. At certain times of the year (such as early November, when stock levels rise for the holiday shopping season), stock levels in some facilities may reach beyond 100 percent, with material placed in any possible free space, such as directly in front of the AP that provides coverage to the area. This poses a real problem for the survey engineer who is trying to survey when the stock level might be at a low level corresponding to the season. (Many installations occur during the off-season, when facilities are not running at peak capacity.)

Defined User Areas and Densities

The topic of user density has been brought up many times in this book. As stressed previously, defining user areas and densities is a crucial part of the design and must be on the minds of design engineers and survey engineers at all times. The overall performance of the WLAN system depends on proper user density.

There have been surveys based on nothing but user density. At one very large software company, the buildings were all built in a very similar manner, and with identical internal design and contents. All cubicles were identical, all office construction was identical, and the number of users in a given area was very similar.

For this customer, it was decided that the applications used by nonengineering employees would permit between 20 and 25 users per AP. This provided adequate performance for normal operational network load. The engineers, however, required a bit more performance, and the user density was lowered to between 10 and 15 users per AP.

Based on information such as this, some of the design can be done up front. You can use the site map to determine how large the cell coverage needs to be. For example, a survey determined that a single AP set to default power levels, with dipole antennas, could provide coverage for many more users (based on their seating locations) than the design calls for. In this particular case, the desired coverage turned out to be a small circle on the site map, and was about the size of a coffee cup. From this point, it was a matter of defining how many "coffee cups" were needed (see Figure 8-7). The engineers then selected the power setting to provide the proper coverage for the user density in the appropriate areas. Finally, testing was completed to prove the guesstimations of the coffee cup survey.

Figure 8-7 *Coffee Cup Layout*

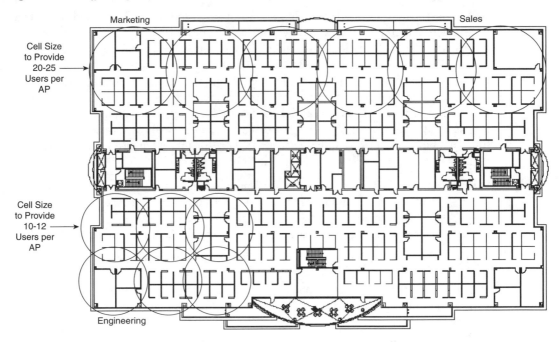

If voice is to be used over the WLAN, it is vital to the design to understand the capacity of the AP versus the number of calls that can be carried by one AP at any given time. Typically, a standard 802.11b AP supports only between six and eight calls with the standard compression used in 802.11 *voice over IP* (VoIP) phones. As compression techniques improve, or as the wireless 802.11 VoIP phones move to support 802.11g or 802.11a, the number of calls per AP will increase.

Limitations Affecting Equipment Installations

As with any installation, when installing a WLAN restrictions are always put into place by one or more of the following:

- Customer requirements
- Regulatory limitations
- Environmental concerns

Take care to note any and all restrictions that might be in place. Also document any restrictions in the final site survey report so that the customer understands why a particular method was used (based on a given restriction).

Customer Restrictions

As you have learned in this chapter, understanding the customer's environment is important. Installation limitations can vary widely from customer to customer. Based on the surroundings, imposed limitations might require a survey engineer to make minor changes to a design. For instance, where a 5.2-dBi 2.4-GHz omni antenna is needed to provide coverage, it might not be possible to use one because of the antenna's physical size. A typical 5.2-dBi omni, which is approximately 10 inches or longer, might be too large to hang from a ceiling in a facility such as a school or hospital, for example. A Yagi antenna might work well in a long hallway, but the owner might require that the antennas remain unobtrusive. At 18 inches long and 3 inches in diameter, the 13.5-dBi Yagi does not meet the customer's unobtrusive requirement. In both cases, you need to use different antennas.

Perhaps the customer has required that the equipment be totally out of sight, as would possibly be the case in a museum or theme park. You could place the APs above the ceiling or in isolated locations, but then the antennas become an issue. You will need to verify that the AP supports external antennas and that the antennas available have plenum-rated cables.

Another such issue generally comes up in all locations where there is public access. Antennas and APs must be totally out of sight, hidden, or disguised. In the case of one theme park, all the APs are located in little cupboards, which have hidden and locked doors. The antennas selected were very slim patch antennas, which were attached to the wall and painted to blend in.

In one college, a WLAN system was installed for student use, and the APs selected used standard PCMCIA-type radio cards that plug into the AP. (This is a common design method for APs, and is popular among customers because of the easy radio upgradability for the AP.) The APs were just mounted in hallways near the ceiling. The IT staff of the school started to notice that some APs were no longer handling traffic. Upon inspection, it was found that the radio cards were being removed from their APs. The students had learned that the same radio card used in the AP could be used in a laptop!

An environment such as this university might require some type of enclosure for the AP that can be locked for the sole purpose of maintaining visibility but ensuring security against tampering hands.

Regulatory Limitations

Although discussed at length in Chapter 3, "Regulating the Use of 802.11 WLANs," limitations based on regulatory domain requirements are worth reiterating here. Be sure to address each of the following questions for the specific site in which you are working:

- Is the RF system that is specified in the design legal in this location?
- Are there limitations on the antenna gain (and style) that can be used at this facility?
- How many channels are available for use in this location?

These questions require some investigation so that the system, once installed, meets the local regulatory specifications.

As a reminder, some countries specify a maximum of 20-dBm *Effective Isotropic Radiated Power* (EIRP), which limits antenna choices. Other countries do not permit 5 GHz, or limit the 5-GHz channels that can be used. Still other locations restrict certain channels for use with indoor applications only.

See Chapter 3 for the details of the various regulatory restrictions.

Environmental Concerns

Many WLAN installation areas require special designs. The most common is the plenum area above a ceiling in a standard office environment. As defined in Chapter 3, a plenum area requires that devices meet certain specifications regarding flame and smoke. Many APs use a plastic housing and, depending on the type of plastic, might meet these requirements. However, many plastic devices have not been tested or do not meet the necessary ratings and are not intended for use in these areas. For this reason, several vendors offer a metal housing for the AP.

Similarly, antennas also have environmental restrictions. Most external WLAN antennas on the market today that have been designed for WLAN usage are not plenum rated. This means they cannot be located above most ceilings. The cables on the antennas may use plenum cable, however, which means you can legally attach them to a plenum-rated AP and run the cable through the ceiling to the open air space (below the ceiling) where the antenna itself is located.

Local regulations also address plenum use. In some municipalities, any work done in plenum areas (such as above the drop ceilings) requires a licensed *heating, ventilation, and air conditioning* (HVAC) technician. If the AP is mounted above the ceiling, a licensed HVAC technician must be on site to supervise the installation. But what happens if an AP fails or needs to be replaced or accessed? Most IT professionals are not HVAC licensed. One possible solution (discussed later in Chapter 12, "Installing WLAN Products") is to place the AP inside some type of enclosure that is located in the ceiling, where the cables enter from above the ceiling. The metal box itself, installed by the HVAC professional, isolates the plenum area from the open air space of the room. The AP is now located outside the plenum area, and therefore plenum-rating requirements do not apply to the AP. This setup also obviates the need for an HVAC technician to be on site during AP servicing. In addition, the locked door provides physical security for the AP.

Most WLAN devices are designed to be located in a "friendly climate," meaning areas where the temperature ranges from 0 and 60 degrees Celsius. In addition, a friendly environment is one in which the AP stays dry and clean and vibrations are minimal. If you are putting an AP into a retail store or office building, a friendly climate might very well exist. In many scenarios, however, such as a food distribution center with a large freezer that might reach temperatures of –20 Celsius, or for outdoor installations in climates with extremely cold or hot weather, you need to design the WLAN based on the worst-case conditions.

WLANs are deployed in a wide range of locations, from climate-controlled offices to truck loading docks, outdoor rental car lots, airport tarmacs, shipyards and railyards, and even on board luxury cruise liners, locomotives, and passenger trains. Each location entails slightly different circumstances and therefore requires different survey tactics and installation techniques.

For applications that require the AP to be mounted outdoors, use an AP that has an appropriate *National Electrical Manufacturer Association* (NEMA) rating, or place the AP inside a NEMA type of enclosure. This provides proper weatherproofing to prevent moisture damage and corrosion. Salt water is extremely damaging to most APs, so consider this fact if your WLAN installation area is anywhere near an ocean or sea.

Some WLANs are even used in hazardous areas, including industrial facilities where chemicals are manufactured or stored, locations where painting is occurring (for example, automotive factories), or sites where explosives might be used (mines, for example). At such a hazardous site, use products that meet the site's intrinsic requirements or find suitable enclosures. Check with the customer to determine the level of safety necessary and the degree of isolation required.

Using Cookie Cutter Designs

Although every site differs and a survey for each site should be considered, you might be able to use a cookie cutter approach in some cases. Consider, for example, a chain of small auto-parts stores (see Figure 8-8). These stores are built in a very similar manner and are all about the same size. They also contain very similar products, arranged in a similar way. A single AP positioned in almost any location provides adequate coverage for a store. After you have determined this fact (by a survey), you can establish specific guidelines regarding AP placement and make deployment much simpler.

Figure 8-8   *Cookie Cutter Design for Auto-Parts Store*

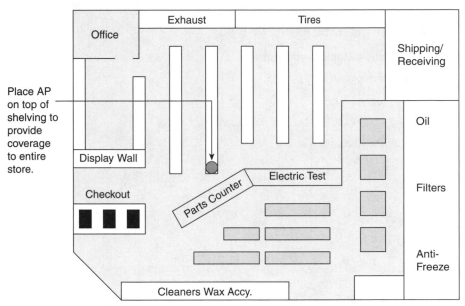

In contrast, consider a WLAN deployment for a department store chain. Although the stores might look similar, they vary in both size and content arrangement. In this case, if you were to follow a cookie cutter approach, you would likely end up with some stores having a poorly working WLAN system (and hence a site visit to redesign and reinstall the WLAN). You can avoid this scenario by conducting a thorough survey up front for every store.

Summary

As WLANs continue to increase in popularity and WLAN applications continue to emerge in every type of business, engineers are deploying APs in more types of locations than ever before. But do not be tempted to force fit a device designed for one environment (perhaps a climate-controlled office) into another, perhaps hostile, type of environment (outdoors, for example). To ensure a properly operating WLAN, you must consider and design around site-specific requirements.

WLAN survey and installation teams need to be aware of all regulations that apply to a site, the various applications planned for the WLAN, and the full customer expectations. Among other things, these factors influence which installation techniques will be used. Other site-specific factors that survey and installation engineers need to consider are outdoor versus indoor installation, plenum ratings, vibration, and hazardous areas.

This chapter covers the following topics:

- Switches, Routers, and Hubs
- Roaming
- Deploying VLANs Over WIreless
- QoS for WLANs
- Cabling Requirements

CHAPTER 9

Discovering Wired Network Requirements

In the early days of WLAN implementations, a WLAN was usually viewed as a standalone network. Although the WLAN might have been "connected" to the wired network, it was typically considered an individual entity, and the standard (that is, wired) network had little or nothing to do with the wireless network.

Now that wireless has become more than just a bar code data-acquisition tool or a networking toy, it is important to consider the wireless as part of the wired network. It must integrate seamlessly into the wired network, and work hand in hand with the features and components on the wired infrastructure.

This chapter covers the wired infrastructure, and how it affects the WLAN. Topics include how the mainstream networking devices such as routers, switches, and hubs can affect the WLAN design, how the subnet architecture affects roaming of wireless clients, and how the *access points* (APs) can be connected to the wireless network. So that you gain a full understanding of these issues, this chapter covers the client association process, Layer 2 and Layer 3 roaming, and different methods for supplying power over the Ethernet to the APs.

Switches, Routers, and Hubs

Most networks today contain a collection of routers, switches and hubs, servers, gateways, and management platforms, populating the core and edge of the network. With the addition of wireless to the network, the infrastructure now moves a bit further out. You should consider the APs as part of the edge of the network, just like the Ethernet switch that a computer's wired *network interface card* (NIC) plugs into.

In addition, most large networks use some type of management platform to configure, monitor, and troubleshoot the network. Because the APs are now part of this infrastructure, they too should be included in the list of managed devices that the management platform can support.

Many of the features that you might want to use on the wireless network will need to be supported on the infrastructure. Features such as roaming, *virtual LAN* (VLAN) tagging, *quality of service* (QoS), Mobile IP, and *Power over Ethernet* (PoE) require support on the wired network. The level of support provided on wired devices can vary, and it is important to study the existing wired network to verify that the wired infrastructure can support the desired wireless services.

Roaming

In the wired world, devices are placed at a given physical location and typically stay there until the network staff moves them. As networks grow and more devices are placed on the networks, features such as *Dynamic Host Configuration Protocol* (DHCP) addressing and user authentication are important to assist the network staff to meet the growing number of users.

Wireless adds yet another requirement into the mix. Because mobility is one of the main advantages to wireless networks, how you move, or *roam*, from one area to another and still maintain connection to the network is important (see Figure 9-1).

Figure 9-1   *Roaming*

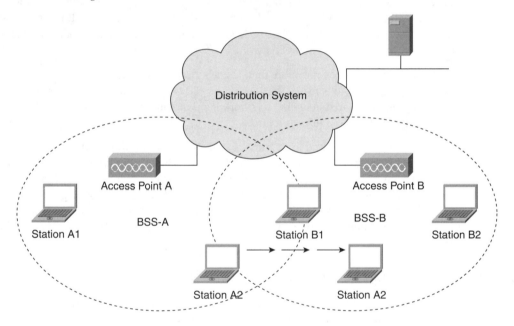

Although roaming (at least for corporate and enterprise WLANs) is something that is thought of as a given feature, it is important to the design to understand exactly how it works and what the implications are for the wired side of the network.

During the roaming discussion here, it is important to remember that the 802.11 specification, to prevent network loops, explicitly states that a client has a single association at a given time, meaning it can communicate to only one AP at any one time.

The 802.11 specification provides details about how a client radio communicates to an AP, but until recently it did not discuss how roaming actually should be handled. All it said was that during a roam, the AP should "notify the infrastructure." In addition, many of the possible implementation approaches involved higher network layers. Although this allowed great flexibility in design, the associated cost was that different vendors' AP devices (on the same network) were unlikely to interoperate efficiently for handoff of roaming clients. This was mainly because most WLAN vendors implemented their own form of roaming, including how APs communicated to each other and how the handoffs of clients occurred from one AP to another.

The Wi-Fi Alliance, during its development of the certification plan, determined that clients should be able to roam across different vendors' APs on the same network. However, the Wi-Fi Alliance did not test the efficiency of how well and how fast clients did actually roam. The client just must associate to a new AP and be able to ping across the network after roaming.

The following sections discuss several area roaming issues, and the methods and concerns related to roaming in a Layer 2 and Layer 3 network. The supporting wired infrastructure devices need to be able to support the necessary services if certain WLAN features are implemented.

Developing a Policy for Device Roaming

Many WLANs are limited in geographic area, such as a single building or facility, or even a single campus. With this type of design, it might be possible to maintain a single Layer 2 subnet for all wireless users and devices. This Layer 2 roaming makes implementation of wireless easier, simpler, and more efficient for roaming between APs. As wireless network usage grows and the number of users and geographic areas grow, however, it becomes necessary to place devices and users on different subnets. This in turn creates the need for Layer 3 roaming capabilities.

Figure 9-2 shows both types of roaming. Client 1 is performing a Layer 2 roam, moving between two APs, which are both located on subnet A. Client 2 is performing a Layer 3 roam, moving from an AP on subnet A to an AP on subnet B.

Figure 9-2   *Layer 2 and Layer 3 Roaming*

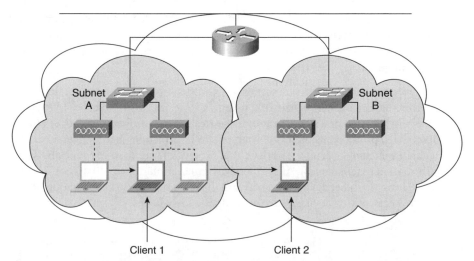

IT managers need to determine whether all devices affiliated with the network should be allowed to roam. An IT manager should consider the following questions when making this decision:

- Are all devices capable of roaming?

- Should devices be allowed to roam through all subnets, including networks that might carry sensitive traffic?

- Can VLANs be used to provide necessary separation between users?

- Are all the roaming devices capable of roaming quickly enough to support the applications of the WLAN users?

The answers to these questions vary according to the type of network:

- If your network is a university campus, roaming might be a requirement for all students. However, you might need to impose certain restrictions to limit student roaming to selected "student" subnets or VLANs in dormitories, lunch areas, classrooms, and open spaces. This will facilitate the separation of sensitive university operations traffic from student traffic.

- If your network is a large corporate campus, mobility might be available only in conference rooms or group work areas.

- A police department might have an arrangement with local hospitals to allow radio clients in the police cruisers to access the hospital's network while parked near the emergency room entrance. The hospital provides the police department with access to a particular subnet or VLAN with only Internet access, segmenting this traffic from its main hospital network.

802.11f IAPP

Recently, the IEEE completed the 802.11f, *Inter-Access Point Protocol* (IAPP), which is a best-practices document. This document specifies the information to be exchanged between APs among themselves and higher-layer management entities to support the 802.11 networks and enable the roaming interoperation of wireless networks containing APs from different vendors.

This recommended practice describes a set of functions and a protocol that allows APs to interoperate on a common network, using TCP/IP or UDP/IP to carry IAPP packets between APs, and describes the use of the *Remote Authentication Dial-In User Service* (RADIUS) protocol, whereby APs can obtain information about one another. A proactive caching mechanism is also described that provides faster roaming times by sending client information to neighboring APs. The devices that primarily would use the IAPP are 802.11 APs. However, other devices in a network that are affected by the operation of the IAPP are Layer 2 networking devices, such as bridges and switches.

802.11f has not gained a lot of traction in the industry, primarily because most installed WLANs use a single vendor's AP. Mixing different vendors' APs on a network means becoming familiar with more than one interface and configuration structure, different mounting methods, different antenna capabilities, and so on. This is just not something that most IT folks want to contend with, and staying with a single vendor makes this part of the network much easier to manage.

In addition, for many years vendors have been working on and improving their own, proprietary roaming capabilities. Typically, enterprise devices now provide roaming times (at Layer 2) under 150 ms, enabling the use of applications such as roaming VoIP and video.

As mentioned in Chapter 5, "Selecting the WLAN Architecture and Hardware," you must consider roaming when deciding which product to choose. Products intended for the small office and home typically do not have an extensive roaming algorithm because these devices are typically used in a single-AP environment. The lack of a high-quality, fast-roaming algorithm could result in poor or failed performance of some applications during a roam.

Association of Clients

Before you can gain a good understanding of roaming, you need to understand how the client-to-AP association process occurs.

While trying to connect to a WLAN, the client adapter card undergoes a two-step process: authentication and association. *Authentication* is the process of verifying the credentials (MAC layer credentials at this point) of a client adapter card desiring to join a WLAN. *Association* is the process of associating a client adapter card with a given AP in the WLAN.

Figure 9-3 illustrates the following process:

1   When a client adapter card comes online, it broadcasts a probe request.

2   An AP that hears this responds with details.

3   The client adapter card makes a decision about which AP to associate with based on the information returned from the AP. In the case of Figure 9-3, AP A has a stronger signal, so AP A is selected as the "desired" AP. Then the client adapter card sends an authentication request to the desired AP.

4   AP A authenticates the client adapter card and sends an acknowledgment back.

5   The client adapter card sends up an association request to that AP.

6   The AP then puts the client adapter card into the table and sends back an association response. From that point forward, the network acts like the client adapter card is located at the AP. The AP acts like an Ethernet hub.

Figure 9-3 *Authentication and Association*

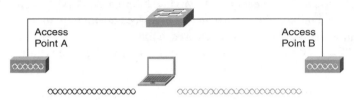

The APs broadcast a beacon at predetermined (and usually programmable) intervals. This broadcast contains information about the AP, such as MAC address and *system set identifier* (SSID), but can also contain some vendor proprietary information such as RF load, number of users, repeater operation, and so on. The client adapter card listens to all APs that it can hear (beacons received) and makes the decision as to which to associate to. Note here that it is the *client* that makes the decision for which AP to associate to, not the AP. However, the decision is based on information it receives from the AP.

Layer 2 Roaming

Although there are many different designs for roaming, this section discusses the general methods of Layer 2 roaming. Two types of roaming—active and passive—can occur. In active roaming, the APs do part of the data message handling. In the passive scheme, the APs do little in the data stream except pass the data to the client or drop the data.

Keep in mind that as a client is moving out of range of its associated AP, the signal strength will start to drop off. At the same time, the strength of another AP will begin to increase. It is important to make sure there is overlap between cells strong enough so that the client has a usable signal at all times.

In some devices, a roam occurs only after the client has lost association (that is, no longer has network connectivity) to the present AP. At that point, the client starts the authentication/association process again, as detailed in the preceding section.

In other devices, the client actively listens to the beacon from all APs that it can hear. As signal strength of the present AP drops below a specified level (which might or might not be a parameter available to the user), the client evaluates other APs' signal strength.

Figure 9-4 corresponds to the following re-association process:

1 The client is currently associated to AP A, but listens for the beacons from all APs. The client evaluates the beacons received from APs A and B and selects the best AP to connect to.

2 The client selects AP B over AP A and sends an association request to the AP B.

3 AP B confirms the client's association and registers the client.

4 AP B sends out a broadcast packet on the Ethernet with the source address of the client. This packet provides update information for the *content-addressable memory* (CAM) tables in the network switches and informs AP A that the client has roamed.

Figure 9-4   *Re-Association*

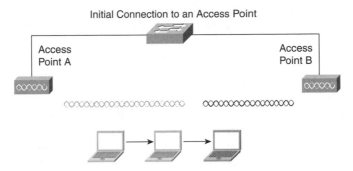

Initial Connection to an Access Point

Access Point A

Access Point B

In this process, the only metric used to determine whether the client should roam is the signal strength received from the available APs. This is the most basic mode of active roaming. Many vendors take roaming well beyond the simplistic approach of using signal strength as the only parameter to determine whether roaming should occur.

Forwarding of packets is one item that can be useful after a roam occurs. If an AP is buffering packets for a client, and the client roams, it might be useful for the AP that buffered the packets to forward them to the new AP, after it receives the notification that the client has roamed. This is a common feature used for clients that support what is known as *Power-Savings Protocol* (PSP). PSP permits the client to go to "sleep," or to a very low power setting through which the radio is turned off. During this time, the AP must buffer packets. When the client "awakens," the buffered packets can be forwarded properly.

Other vender differences include parameters that might be transmitted as part of the beacons. Items such as loading of the AP might indicate to the client that if he roams to another AP, which has similar signal strength, it might have better throughput performance. Or if the client is in range of both a repeater and an AP that is attached directly to the infrastructure, the client would determine that the wired AP would be more efficient. These are just examples of differences in vendor implementations. Not all vendors offer the same features, and most features are not cross-vendor interoperable.

Layer 3 Roaming

As WLANs grow, so does the demand for Layer 3 roaming. Roaming beyond the single building—moving from one building to another, across campus, or even across town—has become a highly desired feature for WLAN users. In many cases, this can be an easy thing with today's client devices. In most environments, users are not actively connected to the network during this roaming time. The computer or device is stowed away during transit and then brought back alive after the roam. In other cases, users might want to use a VoIP phone while walking from one campus building to another.

Various approaches exist to provide network access to devices or nodes that have roamed away from their home network to a foreign network. A *foreign network* might be a Layer 3 subnet at a remote facility of a large enterprise or university campus, or a network owned or administered by an entirely different entity, such as a police or fire department.

The Nomadic-Node Approach

One way to provide network access to devices or nodes that have roamed away from their home network is the nomadic-node approach. A *nomadic node* is a device that moves or roams from one network to another and must renew its IP address and reestablish connectivity to the network applications in progress.

One advantage of nomadic roaming is that it requires nothing special in the client, infrastructure, or APs. It follows the simple Layer 2 roaming and association methods. However, nomadic roaming does not maintain any connection-oriented sessions that are in progress. Nomadic roaming might require user intervention (re-log in, perform a release/renew, or reboot) to continue to work on the network. This is typically how most laptop computers are used with roaming. The user closes the computer, moves to another building or site, and opens the computer, starting a new IP session.

The Mobile-Node Approach

An alternative method to provide network access to roaming devices or nodes is the mobile-node approach. A *mobile node* is a device that moves from one network to another, but keeps its original IP address, allowing for uninterrupted access to connection-oriented applications (assuming the brief delay involved in roaming does not prompt a disconnect). The major advantage of mobile nodes is that they allow devices to cross Layer 3 boundaries and, by means of a tunnel back to a router on their home network, have their network traffic forwarded. This allows a device to keep its original IP address even though its IP address is no longer valid for the subnet upon which it presently resides.

One of the most common applications requiring a mobile-node approach is a wireless VoIP phone. Maintaining an IP connection while roaming is required to maintain the call, and therefore the IP address must stay the same while roaming.

Mobile IP

Mobile IP has been around for many years, but it has really never gotten much play in the enterprise industry because it relies on the mobile node using specialized Mobile IP client software. This means replacing the IP stack with a special version, different from the supplied Microsoft IP stack or other OS-supplied IP stack. This software provides the intelligence to communicate with other Mobile IP entities, such as home agents and foreign agents, and the capability to generate registrations as appropriate.

For a mobile node to successfully roam across subnets, it must first be anchored to its home network by the home agent router. The home agent router contains a list of all devices, by IP address, capable of roaming from its network. When the mobile node roams to a new network, it registers with the home agent as being away from home. The home agent also maintains an association between the mobile node's "home" IP address and the *care-of address* (CoA) or "loaned address" on the foreign network. It also redirects and tunnels packets to the CoA on the foreign network.

The mobile node's registration is sent using the foreign agent router that is providing service on the foreign network. The foreign agent includes a CoA in the registration it sends to the home agent. This address is used as the termination address of the tunnel on the foreign router. A tunnel is then built between the home agent and foreign agent for all traffic destined for the mobile node. When the mobile node sends traffic to another device (known as the *correspondent node*, such as a web server), that outbound traffic can be routed directly to the destination device. The destination device replies to the source IP address. This results in the traffic being routed to the home agent because it is the default router for the subnet from which the mobile node originated. The home agent then forwards that traffic through the tunnel to the foreign agent, which then forwards it to the mobile node.

Figure 9-5 presents the key components and traffic flow of Mobile IP:

1   Traffic is sent from the mobile node directly to the correspondent host.

2   The host replies to the source address of the mobile node.

3   The traffic is routed to the home agent

4   The home agent tunnels the traffic to the CoA of the foreign agent.

5   The foreign agent forwards the traffic to the mobile node.

Figure 9-5   *Key Components of Mobile IP*

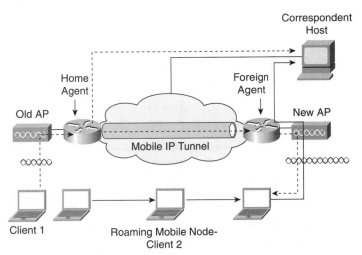

When the mobile node roams back to its home network, it drops its registration with the home agent and the tunnel is removed. If more than one node roams from the same home network to the same foreign network, a single tunnel is used to service traffic for all mobile nodes between those two tunnel endpoints. *Internet Control Message Protocol* (ICMP) *Router Discovery Protocol* (IRDP) is the protocol used to exchange information between the home agent, foreign agent, and mobile node. Extensions have been added to this protocol to accommodate Mobile IP operation.

Mobile IP Disadvantages

Some aspects of Mobile IP make it difficult to manage. The cost of the client software and the administration time required to load this software onto the devices might be a burden to the IT department. Also because the population of mobile nodes might change over time, management of Mobile IP can be a challenge.

In addition, the infrastructure devices must also contain support for Mobile IP. You must have at least one home agent on the overall network and at least one foreign agent per subnet. Typically, a home agent is located wherever clients are located for the majority of time (home location). This reduces the number of tunnels needed.

Another disadvantage is the roam time. The time it takes to build a tunnel can be in excess of 10 seconds. Although this long roam time might be okay for some applications, it poses a problem for session-persistent applications and VoIP systems.

Proxy Mobile IP

Proxy Mobile IP supports Mobile IP for wireless nodes without requiring specialized software for those devices. With Proxy Mobile IP, the wireless AP acts as a proxy on behalf of wireless clients, so the wireless clients are unaware they have roamed onto a different Layer 3 network. The AP handles IRDP communications to the foreign agent and manages registrations to the home agent. The Proxy Mobile IP scheme is less expensive, requires less administration overhead, and is faster to deploy than Mobile IP.

Any AP in the network might be designated as an authoritative AP. An *authoritative access point* is responsible for informing all other APs on the network about networks that have mobile nodes and specifies which home agent must be contacted to register a roaming mobile node.

Not all APs support Proxy Mobile IP, and its overall deployment is still very limited in the WLAN industry.

Before deploying Proxy Mobile IP, network design and implementation engineers should address these fundamental questions:

- Is there an alternative approach to using Proxy Mobile IP?
- What is the corporate policy with regard to device roaming?
- Should static or dynamic IP address assignment be used?
- Does an operational Mobile IP network currently exist or will a new Mobile IP network need to be built?
- If building a new Mobile IP network, is the correct software version and feature set available on existing routers?

The answers to these questions will vary depending on the network, desired applications, and environment. Several answers to these questions are presented in the next sections.

Most IT managers use dynamic IP address assignment with DHCP. However, when using DHCP with the Microsoft Windows 2000 or Windows XP operating systems, the operating system automatically sends a broadcast DHCP renew packet with its existing source IP address when the client roams to a new AP. If the operating system does not receive a response, it reverts to a standard Windows IP address and looks for a new address using DHCP. This capability to "sense the media" results in a failed Proxy Mobile IP connection.

NOTE   Most Windows CE devices do not support this media-sense logic for reacquiring and IP address like Windows 2000 or XP does.

Using a Registry entry, you can disable the operating system's search for a new address using DHCP. This procedure is detailed at the following Microsoft website: http://www. microsoft.com/WINDOWS2000/en/server/help sag_TCPIP_pro_DisableAuto Configuration.htm.

Generally, if the Proxy Mobile IP registration requests are processed within 7 to 10 seconds from the time the device begins to roam, media sense does not need to be disabled because registration typically completes before a new IP address is obtained. However, a roaming device might eventually need to release its IP address. At that time, the Proxy Mobile IP connection is broken, and the device obtains an IP address specific to the subnet it resides on.

An alternative to DHCP is to statically assign IP addresses to the wireless interfaces in devices that are allowed to roam between subnets. Using statically assigned IP addresses avoids the problem of the operating system automatically searching for a new IP address. Although there will be a momentary loss of connectivity as the device roams across subnet boundaries, connectivity is regained after Proxy Mobile IP has registered the device with the home agent and the tunnel to the foreign agent is built. If DHCP is in use in the rest of the network, static IP addressing for wireless clients might be viable on a separate subnet solely for mobile nodes.

Before adding Proxy Mobile IP, consider alternative approaches to providing mobility to roaming nodes. Once reviewed, if these solutions are either impractical or undesirable, Proxy Mobile IP might be the best solution for providing mobility to roaming nodes.

One alternative approach to Proxy Mobile IP is to design the wireless infrastructure so that all wireless devices are on a single subnet in the network. Many companies already deploy wireless in this fashion for security reasons or to identify a particular device as wireless based on its IP address. With this strategy, roaming devices never roam across subnets, because all APs support the subnet from which they originated.

The second alternative approach to Proxy Mobile IP is to use VLANs on APs. If the wireless community is broken into several subnets, with each AP supporting multiple VLANs, Layer 2 roaming can be provided without increasing the number of network APs. This provides native-subnet support for each device regardless of its origination or roaming location. You learn more about wireless VLANs later in this chapter in the section "Deploying VLANs over Wireless."

Layer 3 Wireless Switching

As discussed in Chapter 5, a surge of "wireless switches" has recently hit the WLAN market. Although these are truly not "switched wireless," where you create a unique collision domain (within your wireless RF channel), these systems use wired network switches to control the access ports and manipulate data traffic. Almost every vendor of enterprise-class WLANs has some type of integration between their wired switches and APs today.

The first type of these wireless switch products discussed is the appliance or wireless AP controller. Although not a switch (it does not do network switching of data, but just manages wireless traffic and configuration for the APs), these controllers provide the tunnels between appliances, which in turn forward data to the proper subnet. The client is actually sending data to the controller, which in turn is forwarding it with the proper addressing scheme for the subnet (see Figure 9-6).

Figure 9-6   *Wireless LAN Controllers*

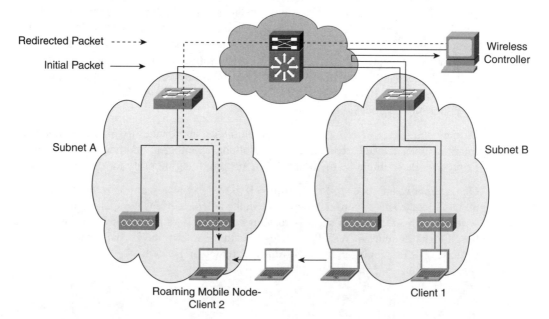

The second type of wireless switch that was discussed earlier does actual network packet switching, and handles traffic for the APs. This type of device, although very similar to the WLAN controller, incorporates both the controller and the network switch into one device (see Figure 9-7). One thing to note is that *all* wireless traffic must be routed through the controlling switch, as shown by the traffic flow from Client 2 to Client 3.

Figure 9-7   *WLAN Switches*

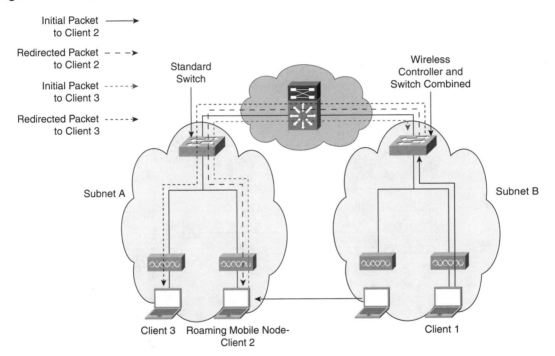

The downside of this type of device is that it usually requires a different type of network management than the existing network switches deployed for the wired part of the network, and requires the IT staff to learn yet another new interface and configuration utility.

Deploying VLANs over Wireless

The use of VLANs with WLANs is becoming more popular. Initially, VLANs were used only on the wired side, and all the APs were placed on a single VLAN. Many of the enterprise-class wireless devices today support VLANs over the RF. This enables you to place wireless devices into different VLANs, all while communicating to the same AP.

According to the IEEE, VLANs define broadcast domains in a Layer 2 network. Traditional networks use routers to define broadcast domain boundaries. Layer 2 switches create broadcast domains based on the configuration of the switch. Switches are multiport bridges that allow the creation of multiple broadcast domains. Each broadcast domain is a distinct virtual bridge within a switch.

VLANs have the same attributes as physical LANs with the additional capability to group end stations virtually to the same LAN segment regardless of the end stations' geographical locations. Figure 9-8 shows an example of two wired VLANs in logically defined networks that have been extended to the wireless.

Figure 9-8 *Extending VLANs Beyond the Wire*

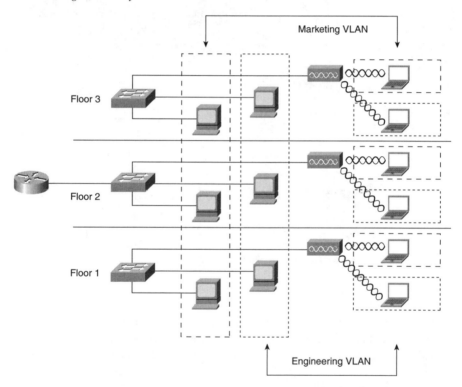

Single or multiple VLANs can be identified within most switches. Each VLAN created in the switch defines a new broadcast domain. Switch interfaces assigned to VLANs manually are referred to as *interface-based* or *static membership-based VLANs*. This type of VLAN is often associated with IP subnetworks. For example, when all the end stations in a particular IP subnet belong to the same VLAN, traffic cannot pass directly to another VLAN (between broadcast domains) within the switch or between two switches. Traffic between VLANs must be routed.

To interconnect two different VLANs, routers or Layer 3 switches are used. These routers or Layer 3 switches execute inter-VLAN routing, or routing of traffic between VLANs. Broadcast traffic is then terminated and isolated by these Layer 3 devices. (For example, a router or Layer 3 switch will not route broadcast traffic from one VLAN to another.)

The concept of Layer 2 wired VLANs has been extended to the WLAN with wireless VLANs. As with wired VLANs, wireless VLANs define broadcast domains and segregate broadcast and multicast traffic between VLANs. When VLANs are not used, an IT administrator must install additional WLAN infrastructure to segment traffic between user groups or device groups. To segment traffic between employee and guest VLANs, for example, an IT administrator must install two APs at each location throughout an enterprise WLAN network. In the 2.4-GHz band, however, there are only three nonoverlapping channels—an obvious limitation. This limitation restricts the number of VLANs and hinders the reuse of channels.

With the use of wireless VLANs, however, you can use one AP at each location to provide access to both groups. With most enterprise wireless products today, an 802.1Q trunk can be terminated on an AP, allowing access for up to as many as 16 wired VLANs and possibly more.

In addition, with WLANs, you can define a per-VLAN network security policy on the AP, providing different levels of security for users on different VLANs.

Wireless VLAN deployment is different for indoor and outdoor environments. For indoor deployments, the AP is generally configured to map several wired VLANs to the WLAN. For outdoor environments, 802.1Q trunks are deployed between bridges, with each bridge terminating and extending as an 802.1Q trunk and thus participating in the 802.1d-based *Spanning Tree Protocol* (STP) process.

Figure 9-9 shows an indoor wireless VLAN deployment scenario. Four wireless VLANs are provisioned across the campus to provide WLAN access to full-time employees (segmented into engineering, marketing, and human resources user groups) and guests.

Figure 9-9   *Wireless VLAN*

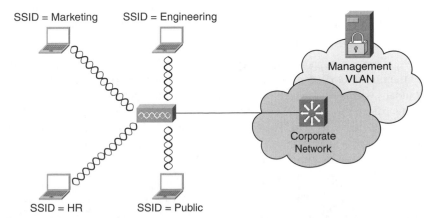

In the case of Figure 9-9, the SSID is used to define a wireless VLAN on the AP. Each SSID is then mapped to a VLAN ID on the wired side, with a default SSID to VLAN ID mapping. In other cases, the type of authentication or security used or even MAC addresses might be used to place certain users into specific VLANs.

If VLANs are intended as a feature for the WLAN, be certain that the routers or switches that the APs will connect to provide the necessary support.

QoS for WLANs

Some applications require the network to provide higher levels of services for proper performance. *Quality of service* (QoS) is used to assist this effort of adding varying levels of priority to traffic. The use of voice, video, and other very time-sensitive applications are driving this requirement into the WLAN products.

QoS on wired networks provides enhanced network service in several ways, including the following:

- Dedicated bandwidth for critical users and applications
- Limiting jitter and latency (required by real-time traffic)
- Minimizing network congestion
- Shaping network traffic to smooth the traffic flow
- Setting network traffic priorities

In the WLAN arena, not all of these advantages can be achieved because of the overall protocol and distinct differences between wired and wireless networks.

Wireless QoS Deployment Schemes

In the past, WLANs were used to transport low-bandwidth, data application traffic such as bar code information. Today, with the expansion of WLANs into enterprise and mainstream networking applications, WLANs are used to handle high-bandwidth, data-intensive applications as well as time-sensitive voice and multimedia applications. This requirement has led to the necessity for wireless QoS.

Several vendors support proprietary wireless QoS schemes for voice applications. To speed up the rate of QoS adoption and to support multivendor applications, the IEEE 802.11e standard will provide a unified approach to wireless QoS. The completion of the 802.11e standard should take place sometime in 2005, with available support on WLAN products following soon afterward. The QoS that is defined in 802.11e will provide methods for both upstream and downstream traffic, and will define ways to support options for power savings on clients while maintaining a level of QoS.

Downstream and Upstream QoS

Figure 9-10 illustrates the definition of upstream and downstream QoS. *Radio downstream QoS* refers to wireless traffic leaving the AP and traveling to the WLAN clients. *Radio upstream QoS* refers to traffic originating in the client and moving to the AP. In most APs today, radio downstream QoS is the only QoS supported. Support is currently proprietary or in development by WLAN vendors for radio upstream QoS. Both upstream as well as downstream QoS over the wireless are covered in the 802.11e specification.

Figure 9-10 *Upstream and Downstream QoS*

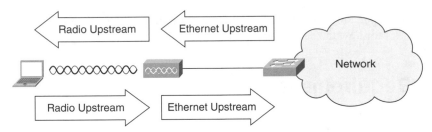

Ethernet downstream refers to wired traffic traveling to the AP. QoS can be used and applied at this point in the network to prioritize and rate-limit traffic to the AP. Configuring Ethernet downstream QoS is not discussed in this book.

Ethernet upstream refers to the wired traffic leaving the AP traveling to the network. The AP provides the classification of the traffic from the AP to the upstream network.

QoS and Network Performance

The performance improvement from the use of QoS might not be easily detected on a lightly loaded network. If latency, jitter, and packet loss are noticeable when the network is lightly loaded, it indicates a network fault or that an application's requirements are not a good match for the network.

QoS will start to provide improved application performance as traffic on the network increases. QoS helps to keep latency, jitter, and packet loss for selected traffic types within acceptable limits by providing downstream prioritization from the AP.

Until such time that 802.11e is completed and becomes available on clients, radio upstream (client) traffic is treated as best effort. A client has to compete with other clients for (radio upstream) transmission and compete for the radio waves with (radio downstream) transmission from the AP. Under certain traffic conditions, a client can experience radio upstream congestion and the performance of QoS-sensitive applications might be unacceptable despite the QoS features on the AP.

The same rules for deploying QoS in a wired network apply to deploying QoS in a WLAN. It is imperative that you understand the type of traffic and the requirements of that traffic as it moves across your network. The protocols, the application's sensitivity to delay, and traffic bandwidth all play an important part in using QoS and placing priority on the types of traffic.

It is also important to investigate the network to verify any limitations imposed by wired network infrastructure components (switched, routers, or hubs) that could impact the use of QoS. For example, having advanced QoS on the AP might be of little use if plugged into a 10-Mbps hub.

Also keep in mind that QoS does not create additional bandwidth, it just provides additional control for how the bandwidth is allocated.

Cabling Requirements

Typically, APs are connected to the network via some type of Ethernet cabling. This could be *Category* (Cat) 6 cable, Cat 5 cable, fiber-optic cable, or (in some of the older WLAN products) coax (although not many products support this today). In almost all cases, the same limitations apply to data cable that feeds an AP as would apply to feeding a wired client device. Limitations include distance, number of connections, plenum ratings, and so on.

Network engineers usually have a good understanding of Ethernet cabling, but an AP has one other requirement: power. Because APs are typically placed in the ceilings or other areas where the availability of AC power might not be easily accessible, vendors sought a way to use the same Ethernet cable to provide power to the AP.

Power over Ethernet

Most network devices require some form of power, whether central LAN infrastructure devices such as switches and routers, or peripheral components such as IP telephones and APs. *Power over Ethernet* (PoE) combines both data and power onto existing LAN infrastructure cabling, which is typically Cat 5 or Cat 6 cable.

PoE had a very high adoption rate for VoIP applications, and its usage in WLANs has recently been increasing (primarily because it can reduce installation cost by removing the need for local AC power at the AP and eliminates the need for extra cabling to feed power to the AP). In many cases, the cost of adding an AC power source (by a licensed electrician) for every AP location exceeds the overall cost of the AP itself.

PoE is used for many different applications. VoIP was one of the initial PoE applications, but now many other network devices benefit from this feature, including the following:

- Printers and print servers
- Web cameras and security devices

- Alarm systems
- Security locks/security door systems
- Any device connected to the LAN

You can provide PoE in three primary ways:

- Placing a standalone device anywhere on the Ethernet cable
- Using a multiport PoE device
- Using an end-span device

Placing a standalone device anywhere on the Ethernet cable provides a single Ethernet input and a single Ethernet with PoE output for connecting to a single device. Figure 9-11 shows examples of single-port power injectors.

Figure 9-11 *Single-Port PoE Power Injectors*

The second method for supplying PoE is through the use of a multiport PoE device. These come in several configurations, supporting as few as 6 or 8 devices (as the one shown in Figure 9-12) or up to 24 or more devices. Basically, these devices provide one Ethernet input and one Ethernet output with PoE for every device supported.

Figure 9-12 *Multiport Mid-Span Device*

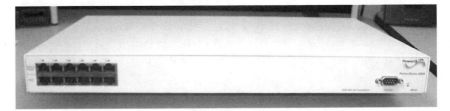

For both the single-port power injector and the multiport power injector, the Ethernet input for the injector comes from the wired network, usually the local Ethernet switch. The device is typically located in the same location as the Ethernet switch, where power is readily available. The output of the injector is connected to the Ethernet cable that feeds the device (such as the AP). Both of these types of devices are known as *mid-span devices* because power is injected in the middle of the Ethernet run. It is important to remember that this does not increase the length of the Ethernet run, and the limitation of the cabling applies to the total length of the cable between the switch or network connection and the end device. Figure 9-13 shows a typical connection for both a single-port power injector and a multiport power injector.

Figure 9-13 *Mid-Span PoE Applications*

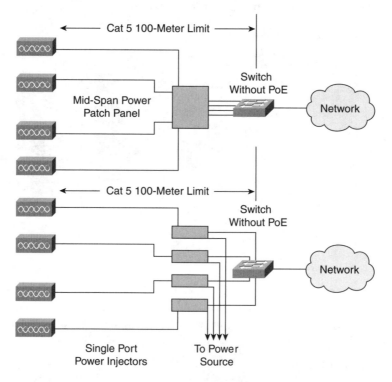

The third type of PoE-supporting device is the end-span device. This type of device is both the data source and the power injector. An Ethernet switch that provides power over the Ethernet without any external devices is such a product.

802.3af

The initial PoE implementations were proprietary and unique to certain vendors' products. The Cisco PoE format was the most widespread, with many vendors supporting it, and in some cases also supporting their own implementations. With the rapid acceptance of PoE, the IEEE determined that there should be a standard format for everyone to follow. Therefore, as part of the 802.3 Group, the 802.1af specification was developed. Although many companies were involved in the development of this standard, PowerDsine was a major driving force behind completing the standard.

The standard defines the following key elements:

- **The physical method for power distribution**—Defines the basic requirements for power delivery.

- **The voltage, power, and other parameters**—Defines the maximum current capacity, the minimum and maximum voltage, and the overall maximum power availability.

- **A standard method for end-device power request (signature recognition)**— Defines a specification to determine whether the end device requires PoE. This provides protection of non-802.3af devices. By the use of a physical "signature" on the end device, the power source will know whether power should be applied to the cable, protecting the end device from improper voltage on Ethernet cables.

Technical Specifications of 802.3af

Devices such as wireless switches that provide PoE power on either data pairs 1,2 (+) and 3,6 (–) or spare pairs 4,5 (+ve) and 7,8 (–ve).

Mid-span devices such as in-line power injectors provide power on spare pairs 4,5 (+) and 7,8 (–).

End devices (AP, phone, or camera, for example) using PoE must have the capability to accept power on both the data and spare pairs.

The maximum power of any PoE device is 12.95 watts.

Devices providing PoE must have the capability to supply a minimum current of 350 mA continuous, with a voltage between 44V DC and 57V DC. Average power capability must be, at a minimum, 14.4 watts continuous.

A signature recognition must be achieved by an impedance of 20k ohms to 30k ohms in the device requiring PoE.

A voltage between 2.8V DC and 10V DC will be used by the device providing PoE as the probe to discover end devices with the PoE signature.

Proprietary PoE Methods

As previously mentioned, it was only recently that 802.3af was ratified, even though PoE has been around for several years. Because many hardware vendors took it upon themselves to develop their own PoE solution, it is important to understand the basic differences between implementations to avoid integration and installation problems.

The Cisco PoE implementation was originally for supplying power to the IP Cisco IP phone products. The power requirements for the early IP phones were very minimal. Therefore, the Cisco PoE solution provided approximately 7 watts per port. When PoE became a requirement for Cisco APs, the same Cisco PoE scheme was used. At that time, the power consumption of the AP fell within the capabilities of most Cisco PoE-supplying switches. However, as new APs were developed, power requirements increased, requiring more power be made available. As a result, newer APs require either in-line power injectors or the use of newer PoE-capable switches.

When designing and installing PoE for APs, you must verify that the intended PoE switch can support the power required by the AP model that will be used (today, and in the future with upgrades). If not, you might have to find an alternative method such as the single-port power injectors.

Cisco Aironet power injectors provide an alternative powering option to local power or using a PoE switch. The single-port Ethernet power injector provides the required 48V DC power and carries it over the same cable as the data signal, by utilizing the unused pairs of the cable.

Cisco took the idea of power injectors one step further. Many networks today use fiber-optic connections, especially for long runs in places such as manufacturing facilities and warehouses. However, providing power over fiber is not possible (at least today). It is possible, however, to provide power from a location near the factory floor or warehouse, but again that is not where the AP is likely to be mounted.

The Cisco Media Converter converts fiber media to Cat 5 media and combines the resulting data signal with power for delivery to the AP or bridge. The power-injector media converter accepts 48V DC power from either the barrel connector of the local power supply or an alternative 48V DC power source. When powered by an alternative 48V DC power source connected using the provided power-supply pigtail, the power injector media converter is UL2043 certified and suitable for installation in plenum areas.

This device enables you to run the fiber to a location in the factory where AC is available, and from that point you can run a Cat 5 cable to the AP location (see Figures 9-14 and 9-15).

Figure 9-14 *Fiber Converter/Power Injector*

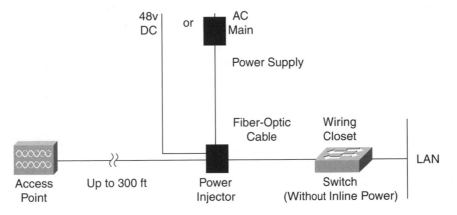

Figure 9-15 *Fiber Converter/Power Injector Application*

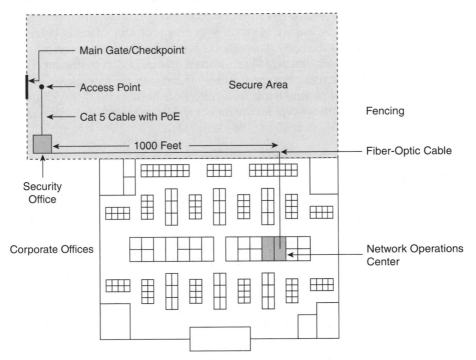

There are other possible PoE schemes, and you need to be aware that not all PoE schemes are created equal. Cisco PoE uses 48V DC over unused pairs of the Cat 5 cable, whereas the PoE scheme offered by 3Com provides 24V DC power over the spare pins in standard Cat 5 cable.

Because the 3Com devices use 24V rather than 48V, and the Cisco devices use a different pin-out for the power than an 802.1af system uses, both APs require a converter to receive power from an 802.3af source. PowerDsine and 3Com offer converters for this requirement.

If you are dealing with an existing network for which it would be financially unacceptable to swap or install new LAN switches to add APs, you might find that using a mid-span device is a more feasible and cost-effective option. When purchasing equipment for either mid-span application or for powered switches, ensure that there is an easy and practical upgrade path.

Summary

Just selecting the wireless devices used to be all that was necessary prior to installing a WLAN. With the services and features available today, however, it is now necessary to think of the WLAN as an integral part of your wired network. Many of the features and functions found on today's WLAN products require support from many of the wired components on the network, including switches, routers, and management platforms. Therefore, you must verify that these wired infrastructure devices support the necessary features. Such support means the difference between having a WLAN system that operates according to the initial concept and intentions and having one that just provides wireless connectivity to a computer.

References

Cisco Systems, "Wireless Quality of Services Deployment Guide," http://www.cisco.com/en/US/products/hw/wireless/ps430/prod_technical_reference09186a0080144498.html.

Cisco Systems, "Cisco Aironet Power Injectors Data Sheet," http://www.cisco.com/en/US/products/hw/wireless/ps430/products_data_sheet09186a00800f927d.html.

This chapter covers the following topics:

- Types of Site Surveys
- Manual Site Survey Tools
- Automatic and Assisted Site Survey Tools
- Theoretical Survey Tools

CHAPTER 10

Using Site Survey Tools

Since the first deployment of WLANs, the topic of how to do a site survey and even discussions regarding the necessity of doing site surveys have served to stem many a controversy. The question of "Should a site survey be done?" has been discussed, and this book has shown that in most cases, yes, it should. Therefore, this chapter concentrates on *the tools available* to do a survey. This topic alone is broken down into several sections. First you learn about the different types of surveys. Second, you learn about the utilities and features needed for performing a site survey. Then Chapter 11, "Performing a WLAN Site Survey," covers the topics of survey procedures and what thresholds are needed to define the cell coverage.

The tools selected for performing a survey depend on the level of completeness of the site infrastructure. Some tools require an existing wired LAN and the installation of at least some of the wireless infrastructure. Other tools can be used with little or no infrastructure in place. With any of the tools, the data rate will need to be configured for the minimum data rates required by design (based on applications to be used). Placement of *access points* (APs) will vary based on the type of survey, as will the transmitter power settings.

Another factor that needs to be incorporated into the site survey plan is the client capability. Not all clients have the same antenna gain, antenna performance, transmit power, or receiver sensitivity. Before beginning any survey, you must determine the "worst-case" client that will be used at the site. Here, the term *worst case* describes the performance of the client, included in the site's design, that will exhibit the poorest range. You might need to test to determine which client that will be. For example, many clients offer 100 mW of transmitter power; but as mentioned in Chapter 5, "Selecting the WLAN Architecture and Hardware," many of the 802.11b and 802.11g clients on the market today only provide 30 mW. A search of the vendor's website might produce a data sheet with specifics about the radio performance. Virtually all devices with a radio will have an FCC ID (if sold in the United States). The FCC website stores PDF files of the radio transmitter specifications, which are public information. To access the information, use the first three characters of the FCC ID to search for the radio vendor's files. The site is https://gullfoss2.fcc.gov/prod/oet/cf/eas/reports/GenericSearch.cfm.

The actual client radio used with the selected survey tool (if a client is used) should be configured to emulate the worst-case client radio performance as closely as possible.

Types of Site Surveys

Among network engineers, RF knowledge has been something that is typically not understood deeply. As WLANs have evolved, there has been a push to simplify deployment, making it easier for non-RF engineers to install and manage an RF WLAN network. Part of this push has been in deployment tools, or site survey tools. Today there are three general categories for such tools, as described in the following sections:

- Manual
- Automated and assisted
- Theoretical

Manual

The manual site survey has been the main method for determining how to deploy a WLAN. This type of survey requires physically being at the location and taking actual RF readings throughout the site. Using logical methods for working through the site, an AP is placed in the site with the associated antenna, and a physical walkabout is performed.

This type of survey is by far the most accurate because it provides real data transfer in a live environment in a manner similar to that of the actual WLAN user. The survey engineer moves from location to location (within the site) and takes readings to verify RF connectivity.

The downside to a manual survey is the time required to walk the site, move APs from place to place, and verify the coverage. In addition, understanding the results of the survey requires a high level of RF knowledge.

Automated

In an attempt to make installing WLANs easier (and more attractive to those with little or no RF knowledge), the concept of eliminating the necessity for a site survey altogether is being promoted heavily. In an ideal situation, a network engineer could walk into a site, drop APs in the site based strictly on location and density of users, and have the network "self-configure." A great idea, but automated site surveys require some on-site survey work to prevent either putting in too many APs (and increasing the overall system cost) or leaving holes in the RF coverage.

Some automated survey vendors claim that APs that must be located (in the site) and configured manually are bad. Instead, some management system could identify the requirement for RF coverage. And after the APs have been physically installed, this system could then configure the APs to provide the desired coverage.

But, one question continues be raised to those who have looked at this concept in depth: Where do I physically place the APs, and what antennas should I use? The concept for the automated survey is that you just place APs wherever it makes sense to achieve the type of coverage desired—coverage based on performance, high availability, resilience, and so on—and standardize on one simple antenna. In some cases (such as the "coffee cup" survey discussed in Chapter 8, "Discovering Site-Specific Requirements"), this might work just fine. For many types of sites, however, it will not work efficiently or economically.

Consider a warehouse or factory floor where there are certain types of obstacles impeding the RF coverage paths. Directional antennas and critical placement of APs is a requirement. The automated site surveys are not intended to work for these types of installations.

Consider also that sites that need a maximum coverage area but not necessarily maximum bandwidth, such as for data acquisition, RFID, or bar code scanning, present problems for an automated site survey. One common thread is needed for automated site surveys: user density. One vendor describes it as *overengineering*, or placing more APs than needed in the site. The WLAN management station can just turn down the power of the APs to achieve the required overlapping coverage. If the goal is to have maximum coverage, this method is not economical and can elevate the cost of the WLAN as much as double or triple the actual requirement. The argument here is that the cost of WLAN gear is less than hiring a wireless solution provider to perform a manual survey.

Another downside to most automated survey systems is that there is no feedback from the client. The system uses RF signal information received by APs, from the surrounding APs, to determine what the power levels should be set to. It does not provide a guarantee that there are no dead spots in certain areas, especially along the perimeter of the site, where there may not be another AP there to evaluate the RF levels.

One possible advantage to a system that offers automated surveys is that it provides some ability to reconfigure the RF if the environment changes. If walls are added, new equipment is brought into the factory, or inventory type changes for a certain location, the system might be able to compensate for these changes. However, this can happen only if the APs were installed properly in the first place and the APs are not currently running at full power.

Assisted

Assisted site surveys are a mix between a totally manual survey and a totally automated survey. Assisted site surveys take advantage of the best features from both. However, in doing so, you still have some of the downsides from both methods as well. Some manual surveying is still required, and some minimal RF knowledge of antennas and RF propagation is needed for the initial design. In addition, assisted site surveys are not suited for some sites due to lower RF coverage and the resulting higher cost of systems installed using automated or assisted survey methods.

The concept here is to take a manual survey process and determine optimum coverage in the site for each different type of area. The engineer takes manual measurements in selected areas and then logically extends those results to the remainder of the site. Then a configuration system is used to test and make preliminary adjustments of the APs. Finally a walkabout is done with a client that will work in conjunction with the configuration system, passing data to the configuration system on overall link performance, so that the configuration system can make final changes to the APs configuration.

Although this method comes closer to manual survey results, in most cases it will still result in somewhat more APs than a totally manual survey will, because part of the facility will be overengineered to guarantee coverage. The final walkabout is done to ensure no dead spots.

The assisted survey only works in areas where the user density or application bandwidth requires the AP's coverage area be lower than the maximum capability of the AP and the areas to be covered are somewhat uniform.

Theoretical Surveys

A few companies have developed tools that provide theoretical RF coverage plans for WLANs. For the most part, these tools are intended to remove the necessity for walkabout surveys.

To use a theoretical tool, input such as an aerial photo or scaled or scanned drawing of the site is required. Some permit the inputting of standard graphic files such as BMPs or AutoCAD drawings, whereas others might require the user to actually draw the facility in the supplied software package. The site needs to have a description of the construction and contents, as well as the attenuation factors entered into the system, and specifics about the radios and antennas that are going to be used.

From there the tool enables the design engineer to interactively place APs with a click of the mouse, and the system will determine theoretical RF patterns for the site. The resulting coverage and capacity can then be viewed in a graphical representation.

Most of these tools have already loaded the specifications for the more popular WLAN products, as well as a large assortment of antenna specifications. If the antenna and radio specification are not provided, however, this can be a big issue. Antenna polar plots are not easily obtained, and certain characteristics for radios can be difficult for non-RF engineers to understand.

These types of tools also usually offer features that keep complete and easy-to-use records of all technical and maintenance details for each job. Because most indoor and campus networks involve hidden APs and wiring that are not easy to find and can be lost over time, these graphical model documents can prove very useful for troubleshooting. This is a great aid in the final documentation stage (as discussed in Chapter 13, "Preparing the Proper Documentation").

Although these types of tools actually do work fairly well, they come with a drawback: higher overall cost. First is the initial purchase price of the tool; they tend to be very very expensive. And second, you need to input every piece of the site into the map (including building-wall construction and contents, and attenuation factor assignations for every piece). An experienced survey engineer can usually perform the survey in less time than it takes to import every detail, run the program, and then perform the walkabout verification.

Although these tools make accurate modeling of the site propagation, link budgeting, and modeling of the RF performance a closer reality, successful completion of these tasks is more than just a simple click of the mouse away. They come at a cost, both in dollars and time. And nearly all the theoretical tools recommend some type of final field walkabout to verify the installation.

Manual Site Survey Tools

This section discusses the popular survey tools that are available for performing manual WLAN surveys, how they operate, and what they offer the survey engineer. Most WLAN vendors offer some type of client device for taking at least a signal-strength reading, whereas some go into much more detail. Standalone site survey software tools are also available, intended to be used with any 802.11 radio device and offering a wide variety of information and capabilities.

Cisco Systems Aironet Client Utility

The Cisco *Aironet Client Utility* (ACU) has long been used for manual surveys and is well known. However, it is usable only with the Cisco 802.11b radio devices. It does not function with the newer Cisco 802.11a/g radio clients.

As with many tools, the signal-strength readings obtained with the Cisco ACU are in a percentage value rather than an exact RF level. One helpful feature of this Cisco tool is that it displays the actual dBm values rather than percentages, providing the experienced survey engineer a much better evaluation of the RF signal. The tool also enables the monitoring of noise floor, which in turn enables a *signal-to-noise ratio* (S/N or SNR) reading, both of which are critical to proper communications.

When using the Cisco ACU tool, the first thing you must do is set up the client to communicate to an AP. With the Cisco ACU site survey tool, the only thing that *must* be configured is the proper SSID. However, it is recommended that other parameters be configured when performing the actual survey. Whereas Chapter 11 discusses these parameters and settings, this chapter concentrates just on the features of the survey tools themselves.

Starting at the main screen of ACU, shown in Figure 10-1, notice the two key areas on the top toolbar. One is used to launch the site survey tool, and the other sets the preferences for reading values.

Figure 10-1 *Cisco ACU Main Screen*

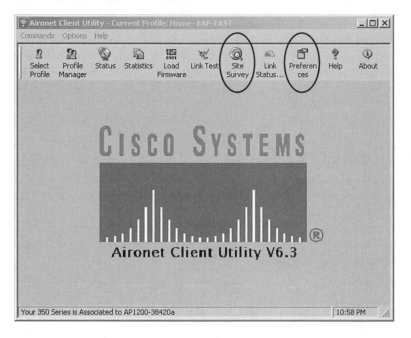

Change the default setting showing percentages to dBm via the Preferences button. (See Figure 10-2.) In the box titled Signal Strength Display Units, click the dBm (*decibels per milliwatt*) button.

From this screen, you can also choose to have seconds displayed on the clock in the status bar on the main screen as well as how often the screen updates. By default, the screen update parameter is set to one second (the lowest available setting) to ensure that the information read is as accurate as possible.

Next select the site survey utility from the toolbar. The ACU site survey tool offers two modes: active and passive. In passive mode, the ACU does not initiate any RF network traffic; it only listens to any other RF network traffic that the Cisco WLAN adapter hears (from the associated AP). The active mode is actually transferring packets between the AP and the client devices and evaluating packet performance. Active is more representative of an actual application because it has directed packets to and from the AP, and therefore is recommended for use in surveys.

Figure 10-2 *Cisco ACU Setting Readout Units*

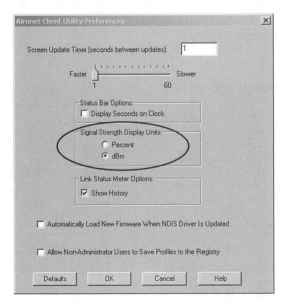

To set up active mode, you must first click the Setup button at the bottom of the screen (see Figure 10-3).

Figure 10-3 *Cisco ACU Passive Screen*

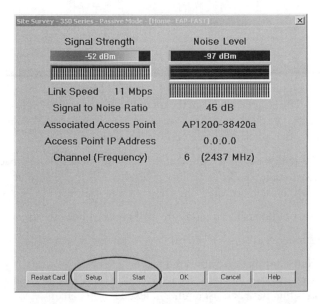

In the Site Survey Active Mode Setup screen, the destination MAC address should be that of the AP you want to test coverage to (see Figure 10-4). This keeps the client from roaming to another AP. When using a Cisco client to survey a non-Cisco AP, uncheck the Destination Is Another Cisco Device field.

Figure 10-4 *Cisco ACU Active Setup Mode*

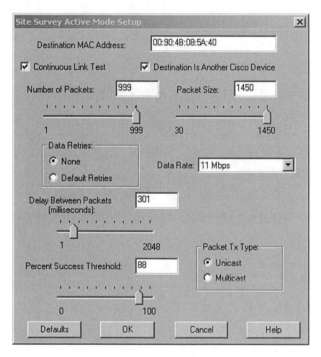

Set the packet size to a size representative of the packet size required for the applications used at the site. Pick the largest packet size used for any of the applications to be used on the WLAN. The larger the packet, the more likely the packet will become corrupted in noisy environments. Set the data rate to the lowest data rate desired by the customer. The higher the data rate, the smaller the size cell for the modulation type.

One helpful setting here is the number of times the client will send packets. (Inherent in this is the ability to continually run a survey test by selecting Continuous Link Test.) When satisfied with the settings, click the OK button to return to the Site Survey screen.

Use the **Start** button (shown in Figure 10-5) to start the site survey in active mode.

After the survey starts, it will provide the following information:

- **Percent Complete**—Shows the percentage of packets that have been sent. If Continuous Link Test has been selected, it shows the percentage of the number of packets that have been sent until it reaches 100 percent, and then starts over again.

- **Percent Successful**—Shows the number of packets that have been successfully sent and received. Notice the threshold line. If the percentage drops below this line, the bars will become yellow.

- **Lost to Target**—Shows the number of packets that were lost in the transmission from the client and the AP.

- **Lost to Source**—Shows the number of packets that successfully reached the AP but did not reach the client.

To stop the survey, click **Stop** or **OK**.

Figure 10-5 *Cisco ACU Active Mode Survey Results*

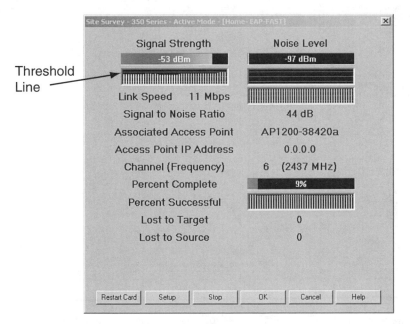

When performing the site survey, monitor the signal level and S/N ratio and stay above a predetermined value, which is based on data rate and application usage (as discussed more fully in Chapter 11). The signal and the noise levels might fluctuate, but if the S/N ratio remains at or above the given level, the signal can usually be considered reliable.

The packet-loss count is also a key parameter to watch when performing the survey. Sometimes the signal level or S/N might be acceptable, but packets are still being lost. Typically, this loss results from interference in the area; without some type of communication monitoring tool, such as packet count or retry count, such loss can be hard to account for. For these reasons, a survey tool that does not provide a packet-loss count is not as effective as one that provides these details.

Cisco Systems Aironet Desktop Utility

When Cisco released the 802.11a/g radio card, it was based on a different internal chip set and therefore required totally new drivers and utilities. Cisco decided to provide only a limited (and comparable to most other vendors) survey tool in the client utilities, relying instead on standalone, third-party site survey tools such as AirMagnet (discussed later in this chapter). In its basic reading mode, signal strength in the *Aironet Desktop Utility* (ADU) is displayed in a relative mode (see Figure 10-6). To get more details, use the Advanced selection.

Figure 10-6 *Cisco Aironet Desktop Utility (ADU)*

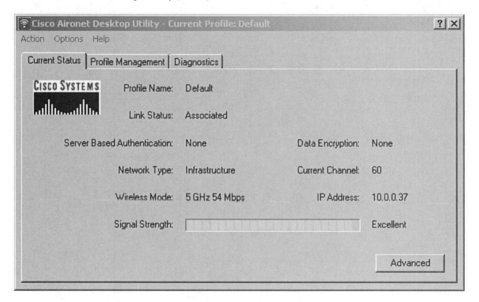

Compared to the Cisco ACU, the Cisco ADU provides only signal-strength and noise-floor readings, as shown in Figure 10-7. The actual transfer of data between the AP and the client is not available, and therefore packet-loss counts are also not available. This puts the ADU tool at a disadvantage for surveying, when compared to the ACU tool for the 802.11b cards.

Figure 10-7 *Cisco ADU Advanced Results*

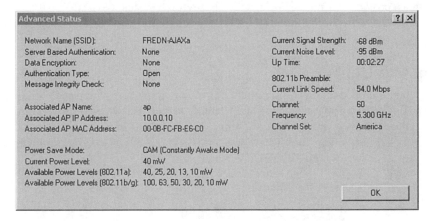

An additional feature of the Cisco ADU is its capability to scan and report other 802.11 systems in the area, which makes it a good tool for searching for interfering systems and rogue APs. Figure 10-8 shows a list of systems that have been found, the SSID associated with them, whether security is used, signal strength, channel numbers, and the frequency band.

Figure 10-8 *Cisco ADU WLAN Scan Results*

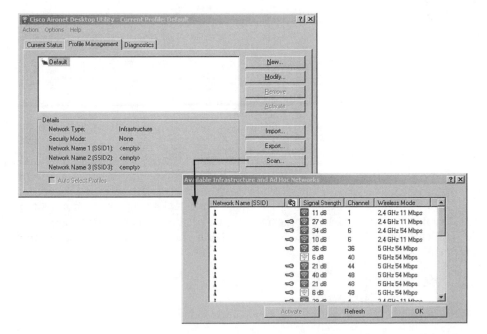

The Cisco ADU provides the signal strength and noise level for any given AP, but does not have provide any method of viewing data retries or packet loss, making it useful for checking installed systems and verifying signals but minimally useful as a site survey tool.

Intel Centrino Utility

Upon the introduction of the Intel Centrino program, many PC vendors moved quickly to adopt it. Today a vast majority of the laptops that are 802.11 equipped use a Centrino-based radio, and hence the utilities that come with it. As shown in Figure 10-9, the main page of the Centrino utility displays a simple graphical indication of signal strength, as well as a few statistics about the association parameters.

Figure 10-9 *Intel Centrino Association Statistics*

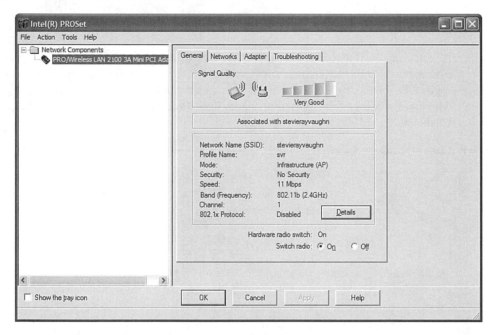

The Centrino utility Statistics page offers both signal-strength and noise-floor readings, as well as transmitter retries, beacons missed, and throughput, as shown in Figure 10-10. These values do provide a minimum level of usefulness as a true site survey tool.

Figure 10-10 *Intel Centrino Troubleshooting Screen*

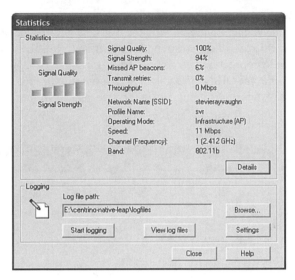

The Centrino utility also enables you to scan for multiple WLAN systems, as shown in Figure 10-11. Selecting an AP out of the list and then clicking Connect causes an attempt to associate with that AP.

Figure 10-11 *Intel Centrino Scanning Utility*

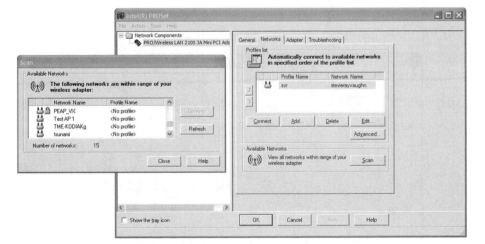

ORiNOCO Survey Utility

The ORiNOCO products come with a client utility offering two features to assist with site readings: Client Manager and Site Monitor. The Client Manager, as shown in Figure 10-12, offers a graphical scale of signal strength, indicating five different levels of signal strength, as well as a radio connection description (based on signal strength). Like many of the other utilities available, the ORiNOCO Client Manager Site Monitor function enables you to view signal statistics of different APs in the area, as shown in Figure 10-13.

Figure 10-12 *ORiNOCO Client Utility*

Figure 10-13 *ORiNOCO Site Monitor*

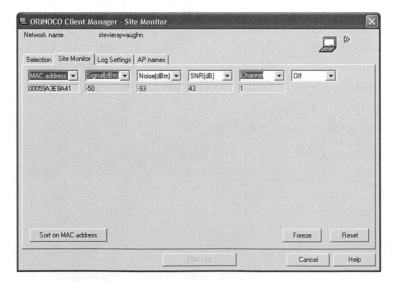

Similar to the Cisco ADU, this utility, does provide the signal strength and noise level for any given AP, but also like the Cisco utility, the ORiNOCO survey utility does not enable you to view transmit retries or packets lost, making it useful for checking installed systems and verifying signals but minimally useful as a site survey tool.

Netgear Clients

It is not unusual to find some of the inexpensive client cards, initially designed for the consumer market, in the corporate world. The Netgear client is one such device, and its utilities are very similar in looks and function to many others found on the market. From its initial screen, shown in Figure 10-14, the Netgear client utility shows signal strength as well as association parameters.

Figure 10-14 *Netgear Client Utility*

When you select the site survey utility, as shown in Figure 10-15, a list of all APs that have been found displays. You have an option to select and connect to any of the listed APs, much like with the Centrino utility. This screen provides the signal strength for any of the APs from which the client can hear beacons, but little else. As with many of the utilities, this is fine for troubleshooting WLANs that are already installed, but for performing surveys it lacks some key features.

Figure 10-15 *Netgear Site Survey Utility*

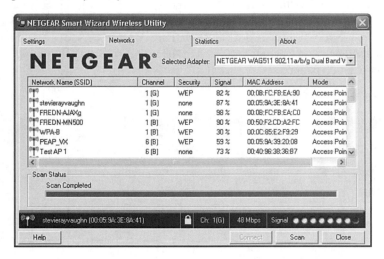

Wireless 802.11 Phones

The adoption of WLANs in the enterprise and several other areas is bringing with it the demand for wireless, noncellular phones. Several 802.11b phones are available today. These include products from Spectralink, Symbol, and Cisco, which come with some type of survey tool as well. However, these phones do not have a tool that is what most survey engineers would consider adequate. Again, the phones just provide the ability to report signal strength from the AP and do not test any type of communications or link between the two devices with actual data (or voice packets). The Cisco 7920 phone does enable you to view the overall loading of the RF channel, referred to as *channel utilization* (CU). Although this feature proves useful when reviewing overall performance of a working system, it does not help in the task of performing surveys for yet-to-be-installed WLANs. The utilities on the phones are best used as troubleshooting tools, to be used after the system is fully installed, up, and running.

AirMagnet

The AirMagnet utility surfaced in the WLAN market in 2002. It was introduced as a WLAN sniffer tool and quickly became a tool of choice by many WLAN administrators for troubleshooting and monitoring WLANs and detecting rogue APs. The site survey portion of this tool is adequate for most requirements, but the overall cost of the tool makes it prohibitive for many smaller companies.

The AirMagnet sniffer tool, as shown in Figure 10-16, is available for use on both a laptop (called AirMagnet Laptop) as well as the Compaq Ipaq (AirMagnet Handheld), and according to AirMagnet will be made available on other PDA devices as well. The handheld version makes it a convenient tool for carrying around a site and performing surveys with a PCMCIA card. However, with the onslaught of 802.11a/g cards, which use a Card-bus interface rather than a PCMCIA interface, and the lack of Card-bus support in *Compatible Extension* (CE) devices, this is not always a feasible solution.

Figure 10-16 *AirMagnet Laptop Main Screen*

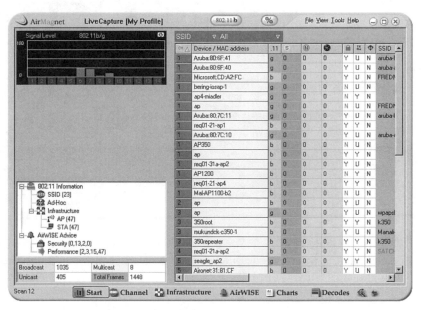

The AirMagnet tool provides many useful troubleshooting and surveying tools. Figure 10-17 shows the channel monitor mode, in which it can view a single channel and display signal strength of all APs heard on that given channel. This capability enables the engineer to view given channels to determine whether the signal from nearby APs (or neighboring systems) will be a problem. It also helps to determine where rogue APs might be located.

Figure 10-17 *AirMagnet Channel Scanning*

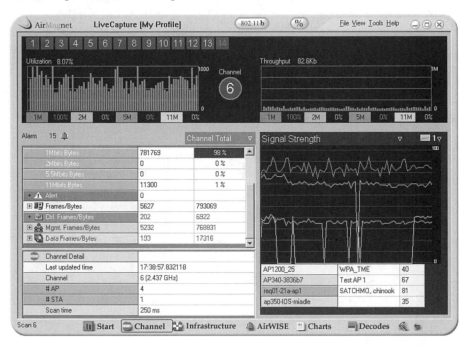

As shown in Figure 10-18, when selecting the infrastructure mode, you can select a single AP from the list on the left side (all APs that are heard), and you can view the S/N ratio in both a graphical and text display.

Figure 10-18 *AirMagnet Laptop Single Channel Scan*

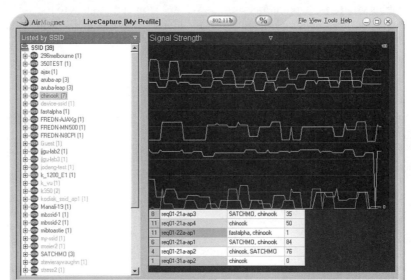

With the AirWISE selection, AirMagnet can display security information concerning the AP and its selections. Figure 10-19 shows the utility displaying an AP that has been set with no encryption, as explained in the text box on the upper right. To the left is a list of all APs and their basic settings. On the lower right you again see the S/N ratio.

Figure 10-19 *AirMagnet Laptop AirWISE Mode*

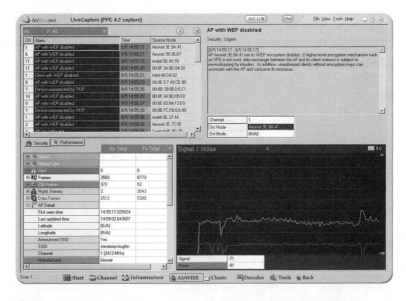

A useful troubleshooting tool, the 802.11 packet-tracing capability, shown in Figure 10-20, enables you to trace problems with the WLAN. You can use this to locate malicious RF, to troubleshoot authentication and association issues, and to view retries and other RF communication problems.

Figure 10-20 *AirMagnet Laptop Packet Sniffer*

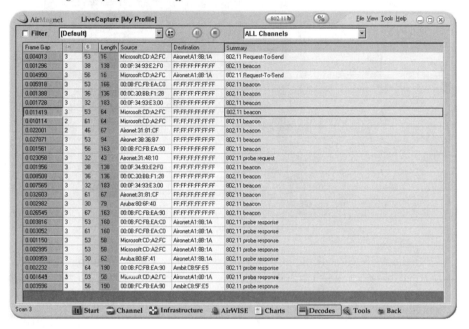

The site survey tool provides configuration for the AP *Media Access Control* (MAC) address in which the test will be run, the packet size for data transfer, and the delay between packet transmissions. Figure 10-21 illustrates the survey in action, using the AirMagnet Handheld utility. This provides a display for signal strength, noise level (and hence S/N ratio) packet loss, as well as basics about the RF communication link (SSID, channel, and so on).

Figure 10-21 *AirMagnet Laptop Site Survey Utility*

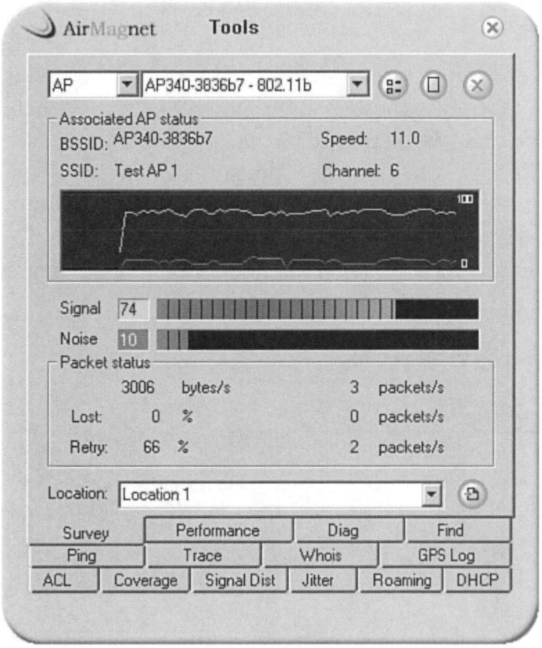

AirMagnet Site Survey Utility (SiteViewer)

Because of the lack of overall site survey tools available and the higher cost of the AirMagnet sniffer tool, the company decided to develop a standalone site survey tool, AirMagnet SiteViewer. With assistance from a few select companies in the WLAN industry, the AirMagnet Site survey tool was developed into one of the best available today.

The cost of the AirMagnet SiteViewer is reasonable, and the features it brings to a survey and troubleshooting engineer are excellent. The ability to not only survey but also document the results makes it exceptional for delivering the required survey reports. Some of the screens in the GUI look similar to the original AirMagnet Laptop (sniffer) tool, but do not be misled. AirMagnet SiteViewer provides a much-improved tool for surveys.

AirMagnet SiteViewer is used as a walkabout survey tool, as are most client-side tools. From the information collected during the walkabout, AirMagnet can develop several views.

The SiteViewer opening screen shown in Figure 10-22 presents the three main areas of the workspace. On the lower toolbar are the control buttons to toggle between the Survey (data collection) mode and the display (data presentation) mode. The upper left is the data catalog area, where different sets of survey data are listed and can be individually enabled or disabled in display mode. The lower left is the Survey Tool Control area, where depending on the mode, the data collection or data manipulation controls display. The main area on the right is the window for displaying the floor or building plan graphics, with overlays for the AP locations and survey data rendering.

Figure 10-22 *AirMagnet SiteViewer Survey Tool*

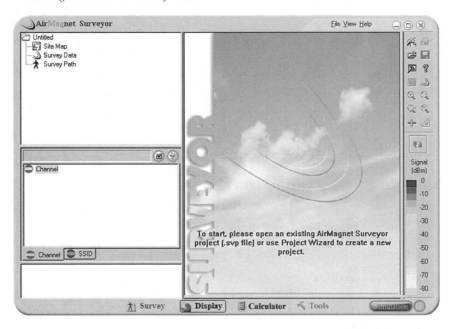

The first step for creating a new project is to import the floor or building plan graphics file(s) and specify the scale. Many popular graphics file formats are supported (BMP, JPEG, and so on). After importing the graphic, you must place the overall dimensions into the tool. This provides a very good approximation of the dimensions within the site. This screen also allows the setting of packet size and delay between packets for the testing (see Figure 10-23).

Figure 10-23 *Starting a New Project*

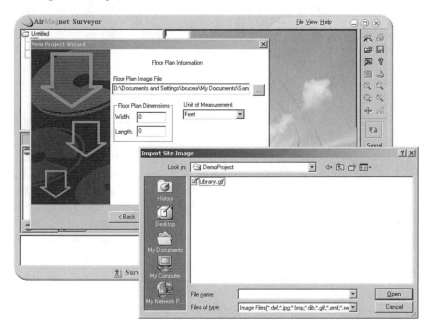

Figure 10-24 shows an example of importing graphics for a typical office building.

Figure 10-24 *Data Collection Mode Setup*

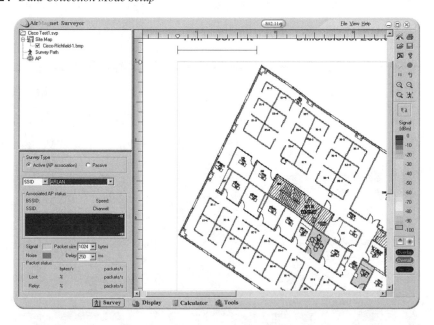

There are two modes for collection of survey data:

- **Active mode**—The SiteViewer *network interface card* (NIC) associates to an AP and sends round-trip data packets to the AP. Active mode most closely simulates a real WLAN environment, so it is strongly recommended that active mode be used for initial AP surveys. Active mode allows the resulting survey data to be displayed in several different views, including by the link speed achieved at each location. Active mode supports two connection methods:

  - **Specific AP**—The NIC will associate only to a specific AP, which is selected in the AP drop-down menu.

  - **SSID**—The NIC will associate to the "best" AP it can observe, the one that matches the SSID chosen in the drop-down menu. In this mode, the NIC roams between APs that have the same SSID, in the case where more than one AP is active in the area being surveyed. This mode most closely simulates the actual behavior of a client in the real network. The Survey tool status panel always displays the SSID and MAC of the AP that is currently associated.

- **Passive mode**—Where the SiteViewer NIC measures the *received signal strength indicator* (RSSI) of the packets coming from the AP and records this signal strength data. This mode is most often used for auditing the coverage of an existing network, but can also be used in conjunction with active mode in an initial survey.

Figure 10-25 shows a completed walkabout path taken for this coverage area. The path includes a section outside of the perimeter walls of the building. This is done to measure the possible propagation outside of the building, where is it usually desired for the signal level to be as low as possible without compromising connectivity to the interior areas, making any unauthorized connection to the WLAN as unlikely as possible.

Figure 10-25 *Active Mode Walkabout Completed*

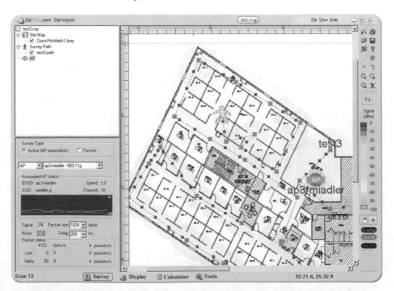

If you select the display mode toggle button on the lower toolbar, SiteViewer can display data collected from the survey in different manners (see Figure 10-26). Two new panels appear in this mode: the filter area in the center left panel, and the map zoom box in the lower left. Selection of one or more survey data sets to display is accomplished by clicking the appropriate check boxes in the data catalog area in the upper left of the screen.

Figure 10-26 *Signal-Level Display*

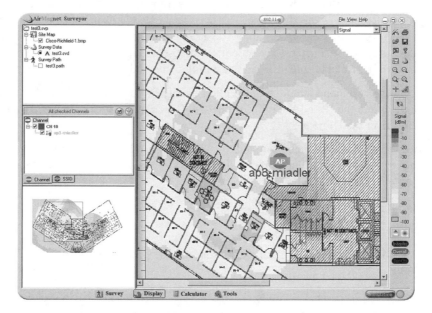

To display parameters for the data sets, select from the drop-down menu in the upper-right corner of the floor plan display area. The choices are as follows:

- Signal
- Noise
- Speed
- S/N ratio

You can also enable appropriate filters to the data based on several different parameters, providing a wide variety of display options. The survey data displays as color-coded zones tied to the legend shown. For signal level, shown in Figure 10-26, the different colors represent 10-dBm levels.

DOS and Other Systems That Do Not Support Standard Utilities

It is not uncommon to find clients that offer few or no utilities to assist with site surveys, especially in the markets where devices such as bar code scanners, devices with custom operating systems, PDAs, and so on are common. For these situations, it is recommended that an alternative device, such as a PDA that supports a survey utility or a laptop, be used for the survey. However, this might not provide the best possible survey results, because the actual clients will have different performances from those of the PDA or laptop used for the survey. Because of this difference, some coverage comparisons must be made before surveying. Using the PDA or laptop, do a sample survey of an area, noting where coverage edges are. Then using the actual client, attempt some type of connection. Most often a DOS window is available, and you can use a **ping** command for this.

From the command interface of the client, verify the IP address of the client. It should be static and in the IP address range of the AP. The client must be associated to the AP to run pings over the RF to the AP.

Use the ping options that allow setting multiple transmits of the ping packet and setting the packet size to a value that is representative of the customer application. An example of a ping command is as follows:

  ping –t –l 256 192.168.200.1

Where:

- –t runs the ping until the escape sequence of Ctrl-C is entered.
- –l sets the length of packet to send.

When the **ping** command ends, the success rate of completed packets and other statistics such as TX/RX (transmit and receive) packets and approximate round-trip times display in milliseconds.

The size of the packet defined to send to the AP from the client is echoed back to the client by the AP. To evaluate the performance, record the ping times in milliseconds while near the AP and compare those times as the client is moved about the cell. As the ping times start to increase, this indicates that the communication link between the AP and the client is starting to have problems. This method provides a good comparison between a laptop or PDA with a survey utility and the specific client device.

Figure 10-27 shows an example of the **ping** command.

Figure 10-27 *Ping Testing*

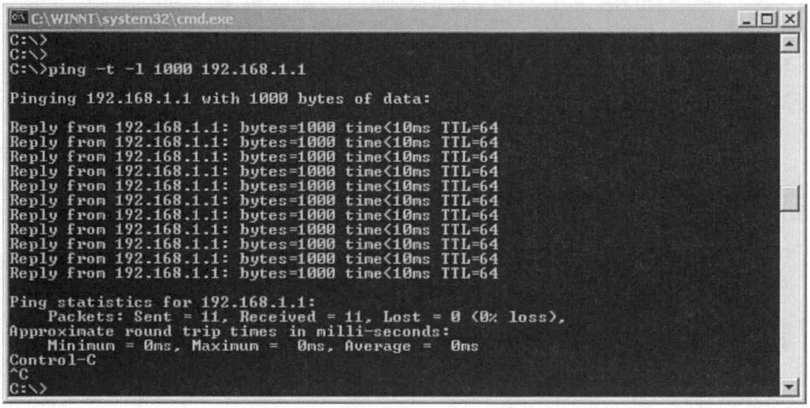

```
C:\WINNT\system32\cmd.exe                                              _ □ ×
C:\>
C:\>
C:\>ping -t -l 1000 192.168.1.1

Pinging 192.168.1.1 with 1000 bytes of data:

Reply from 192.168.1.1: bytes=1000 time<10ms TTL=64
Reply from 192.168.1.1: bytes=1000 time<10ms TTL=64
Reply from 192.168.1.1: bytes=1000 time<10ms TTL=64
Reply from 192.168.1.1: bytes=1000 time<10ms TTL=64
Reply from 192.168.1.1: bytes=1000 time<10ms TTL=64
Reply from 192.168.1.1: bytes=1000 time<10ms TTL=64
Reply from 192.168.1.1: bytes=1000 time<10ms TTL=64
Reply from 192.168.1.1: bytes=1000 time<10ms TTL=64
Reply from 192.168.1.1: bytes=1000 time<10ms TTL=64
Reply from 192.168.1.1: bytes=1000 time<10ms TTL=64
Reply from 192.168.1.1: bytes=1000 time<10ms TTL=64

Ping statistics for 192.168.1.1:
    Packets: Sent = 11, Received = 11, Lost = 0 (0% loss),
Approximate round trip times in milli-seconds:
    Minimum = 0ms, Maximum = 0ms, Average = 0ms
Control-C
^C
C:\>
```

Automatic and Assisted Site Survey Tools

Automated surveys include both assisted and totally automatic surveys. As suggested earlier, the assisted survey is really a mix between a manual and a totally automatic survey, providing benefits of both. Here the discussion focuses on only one of each type, using the Aruba Networks to discuss automatic surveys and the Cisco SWAN framework for discussing the assisted survey. Although the actual implementation of these types of surveys will vary somewhat between vendors and is unique to each product type, they are similar. The intention of this section is to give an idea of how they work in general terms, and the pros and cons of each type.

Aruba

Aruba Networks offers a WLAN system that includes a network switch acting as the WLAN controller, and APs that are managed by the switch. When installing an Aruba network, you must first install the APs and WLAN. The initial reaction to an installation like this is often, "Where do you place the APs? Isn't that what a site survey is for?" The answer is to use a best-guess process based on user density and location (similar to the coffee cup survey discussed earlier), and to place enough APs to feel certain there will be more than enough RF coverage in the desired areas. This means using more APs than might be necessary based on user density. This overengineering enables you to cover any RF holes that might result from RF shadows and multipath interference.

After installing the network and APs, perform a calibration of the APs. The *calibration* is a process typically performed first at the time of network installation and then periodically as the physical environment changes significantly. Normally this is performed on a per-building, per-band type (2.4/5-GHz) basis. All 802.11a radios in a given building are calibrated at the same time, and all 802.11g radios are calibrated at the same time with negligible impact on the availability of the WLAN.

During calibration, all APs and *access monitors* (AMs; AP type of device used only for monitoring and not for communication to clients) communicate with each other at the various data rates and different transmit power levels. This process allows the Aruba switch to build an RF-based map of the network topology, learning about environmental characteristics such as attenuation, interference, and reflection. When calibration is finished, Aruba's Wi-Fi switch automatically configures AP/AM mode of the APs, transmit power levels, and channel selection to minimize interference and maximize coverage and throughput.

Because such a system is not truly bullet proof and there is a high probability of RF holes, Aruba provides a feature called Coverage Hole Detection. Coverage Hole Detection looks for clients that have been unable to associate to any AP (not sure how this feature works, because the device is not associated to an AP and therefore the AP does not know the client is even there), or associating at low data rates or low signal strength. These symptoms indicate areas of a building where holes in RF coverage exist. When the system detects such coverage holes, the administrator is notified of the condition via the event log. At that point, the administrator must go into the facility and place another AP.

Cisco Assisted Survey Utility

The Cisco Assisted Site Survey tool is a cross between the automated survey and the manual survey. In most cases, there is a need to perform some initial testing at the site before using the WLAN manager site survey tool, and hence the name *Assisted Site Survey*. The tool is a part of the *Wireless LAN Solution Engine* (WLSE).

The first step is to determine the area (using the floor plan) that will cover the desired number of users. This must be done in the different types of areas where densities will vary, such as conference rooms, lunch rooms, and so on, because these require a higher number of APs to provide the ratio of users to APs specified in the design.

After determining that the cell size of a full-power AP, at the defined minimum data rate, is greater than needed to provide coverage for the maximum number of users for a single AP, you can use the floor plan to determine locations for the APs. Some areas (such as conference rooms) will use a smaller cell size to maintain the proper ratio of users to APs. After the AP locations have been determined, the installation must be done. After installing the APs, you can begin the assisted site survey.

If there are areas for which the maximum power and minimum data rates cell size are insufficient to provide coverage for the proposed ratio of users to APs, a manual site survey will provide a better economics of scale for the network. Manual surveys enable you to more accurately determine cell sizing, select the appropriate antennas, and accurately provide coverage while using the minimum number of APs. If some areas use unusual antennas (such as the Yagi), a manual site survey provides more guarantees for coverage in desired areas.

The Cisco Assisted Site Survey tool requires the use of the Cisco WLSE on the network, and the survey is completed in three parts. The first part is an AP scan, which takes control of all APs and performs a scan by each AP, listening for all other APs. When this is completed, there is a mode (it is optional, but highly recommended) known as the *client walkabout*. This is where a Cisco client (or Cisco CE client) is walked throughout the facility, usually around the perimeter, and throughout the internal area. The client in turn reports back to WLSE regarding the signal levels it reads from the APs as it moves about.

In the final step, radio-management-assisted configuration, the WLSE uses the data information from the client walkabout and AP scan to adjust to the signal levels reported by the clients at each data point. WLSE then increases or decreases the transmit power of the AP to provide an adequate S/N ratio.

Clients in most applications are 3 feet to 4 feet off the floor and are generally subject to a good deal more attenuation than an AP. For this reason, the WLSE optional client walkabout mode will factor in the results of the survey data collected by the clients, providing a much more robust survey than one that uses the AP scan only. Another factor that is missed in an AP-scan-only type of utility is that the S/N ratio changes depending on the modulation type and data rate (and depending on the location in the facility and even within a single cell). The client walkabout takes this into account.

Theoretical Site Survey Tools

The most common of the theoretical tools comes from Wireless Valley (http://www.wirelessvalley.com). Their overall survey package, LANPlanner, combines the theoretical survey and the manual survey and has the provides three different tools to assist in WLAN deployment:

- The Predictor tool
- The LAN Fielder tool
- The Optimatic tool

The Predictor tool enables you to visualize in full color the theoretical performance of a wireless network, including estimated information such as RSSI, S/N ratio, bit error rate, end-user throughput, and a full link budget and bill of materials.

The LAN Fielder tool is used in conjunction with an actual 802.11a/b/g WLAN card, and is used to quickly verify and record network performance statistics directly from the WLAN card. RSSI, throughput, packet error rate, and even jitter and latency are a few of the parameters that LAN Fielder can collect. It also can detect rogue APs.

The Optimatic tool enables you to use field measurement data taken with LAN Fielder to optimize the wireless system predictions.

With tools such as LANPlanner, WLANs can be designed from an engineer's desk. To confirm that you have the best possible network, however, it is vital to use the LAN Fielder tool to verify coverage and make changes as necessary.

Summary

This chapter has discussed several survey methods—automated, assisted, theoretical, and manual—and now you might be asking which one is the best. There is no definitive answer. Each has advantages and disadvantages. Most require some sort of actual walkabout to verify performance. Areas such as warehouses and factories floors will likely still need a manual survey because they typically are looking for maximum range per AP and utilize directional-style antennas, making assisted and automated surveys less economical (because you need more APs). A theoretical survey requires you to input the attenuation factors of all the contents of the facility, something most non-RF engineers will not know or understand, and something difficult to do at many factories and warehouses.

For facilities that have public exposure, or where aesthetics are critical, placement possibilities of the APs might not fit into an automated or assisted survey model.

Totally automatic surveys, although they might work in some instances, most often result in at least one of two negative effects on a WLAN: A much higher number of APs is required to ensure no missed coverage; and at the other end of the risk spectrum, you risk not having enough (or incorrectly placed) APs and therefore dead spots. In such cases, a manual survey is needed to determine where these dead spots are and why they exist. This in turn requires additional APs (or, at least, new AP placement).

For carpeted offices and other areas where the typical range of an AP is greater than needed for the AP-to-user density specified in the design, an assisted site survey can be effective. However, the effectiveness is contingent on the environment being very consistent. If the arrangement of users or of the environment varies widely, assisted surveys might be only partially effective. In either case, a manual survey for user density is needed (hence the term *assisted* site survey).

A combination of theoretical, automatic, and manual survey techniques is ideal. (Assisted is already a combination of manual and automatic.) Each offers its own advantages, but the bottom line is that there is a need to have expertise in manual survey techniques, regardless of which survey method is chosen.

This chapter covers the following topics:

- Steps in the Site Survey Process
- Surveying with the AirMagnet Tool
- Assisted Site Surveys
- Site Surveying for Repeater Usage
- Dual-Band Surveys
- Site Surveys for Voice
- Final Verification

CHAPTER **11**

Performing a WLAN Site Survey

The ultimate goal of an RF site survey is to supply enough information to accurately locate, install, and configure the RF parameters of the *access points* (APs) and antennas, which in turn will provide the required coverage and performance defined in the WLAN design. In most implementations, coverage and performance include some minimum throughput value at all defined user locations. As a secondary task, a site survey should include a report detailing other RF signals, including other WLANs, as well as any competing RF signals and interference. Recommendation for proper placement, mounting, and configuration of APs and antennas to counter these competing RF signals is another requirement of the site survey.

The overall need for a complex survey, or a simple test and verification, will vary depending on the site and the requirements of the users and applications. A small two- or three-room office might not need a survey, because one or two APs might provide adequate coverage. In this case, a simple verification might be all that is needed when installing the WLAN. When the site includes multiple APs, unique coverage areas, or large numbers of users, however, a survey is highly recommended.

Steps in the Site Survey Process

RF engineering for specific sites is not an exact science, and therefore neither is the practice of doing site surveys. There are many, many ways to perform a site survey, and of all these different methods many are just fine. Because one engineer prefers method one but another engineer prefers method two does not necessarily make one method better or more correct than the other. However, both methods should provide similar results—that is, adequate coverage and performance.

The general steps (some of which have been discussed in various chapters in this book already) that should be part of a site survey include the following:

Step 1 Obtain a floor plan or facility blueprint.

Step 2 Visually inspect the floor plan.

Step 3 Identify user areas on the floor plan.

Step 4   Identify potential problem areas on the floor plan.

Step 5   Identify AP locations and antenna types.

Step 6   Document the findings.

These are general steps, and each one builds on the other to complete a quality survey. Skipping any of these steps can make for problems during the installation or the actual implementation of the WLAN. Several topics have been discussed previously, and in this chapter details of the remaining topics are covered.

Obtain a Floor Plan or Facility Blueprint

You have learned about obtaining a floor plan or facility blueprint in Chapter 6, "Preparing for a Site Survey," and more details are included in Chapter 13, "Preparing the Proper Documentation," so the discussion of such is kept brief here.

Many survey tools, such as the AirMagnet Surveyor and Cisco *Wireless LAN Solution Engine* (WLSE), enable you to import many types of standard graphic formats such as JPEG and BMP files. This makes importing easy. If a drawing is not available, you should generate one, even if it is somewhat simplistic.

Make this drawing available in a printed version so that the engineer can easily make notes throughout the survey. Without this capability, it will be difficult to capture all the necessary information needed.

Inspect the Facility

When possible, personally visit the site before the survey begins. On-site visits enable you to understand the working conditions under which the WLAN will be used and the conditions under which you will perform the survey. A site visit will also help you determine which types of antennas might be used in a facility, determine whether any particular pieces of equipment might be needed for the survey, and give you a chance to inspect the overall site for unusual issues or concerns that could inhibit the completion of the survey.

This is the time that safety issues should be analyzed, and determinations made as to whether safety equipment or special clothing is required. It also gives you the chance to meet the on-site personnel and learn of any issues or concerns they have regarding your survey work.

Identify User Areas on the Diagram

User density should have already been specified in the initial WLAN design. Understanding the location of the users—where they gather in numbers and where the WLAN is not needed—is critical. These parameters should be well defined on the facility diagram. Make note of areas such as lunch rooms, conference areas, informal gathering areas, and even outdoor areas where users gather in numbers.

Another portion of this documentation task is to identify areas that have the common characteristics for physical user areas and density. For example, cubical areas tend to be similar in physical size and distribution in the same facility, making these areas very similar for user density. Similarly, conference rooms, meeting rooms, and so on, if similar in physical size, can be considered as like areas. Note any areas where the contents, applications to be used, number of users, and geographic location of users are similar. This helps when performing the user-density testing and is vital for using assisted site survey tools. The different types of areas might have different requirements for cell size and bandwidth.

Another task here is to identify areas where users require a constant connection while roaming from one point to another. In most cases, laptops are not used when physically in motion and represent a very small issue here. However, *voice over IP* (VoIP) phones, PDAs, bar code scanners, and other similar devices are commonly used while moving through some facilities, and you need to consider their requirement for constant connection.

Identify Potential Problems Areas on the Diagram

One of the first steps in a survey is a walk through the facility, which is needed to search for potential problem areas. From the diagram itself, you often can identify building-structure items such as elevators shafts, stairwells, and fire doors. These items tend to cause RF shadow areas and dead spots. If coverage is needed in these areas (as may be desired for seamless roaming with voice, for instance), take special care to place APs strategically for coverage.

Also note other wireless equipment or devices in the facility that might cause interference. This information can help you reduce problems that might occur if you place APs too close to these devices or systems (or prevent placement on the opposite side or a wall, hidden to the eye, but not the RF).

It is also a good idea to note items that might have RF reflections, which in turn might cause multipath signals, such as large metal doors, metal cabinets, or, as commonly found in many warehouses, secure areas that use a metal meshing as the walls. (See Figure 11-1.) This notation helps explain why an AP is placed in a particular location, or why a particular type of antenna is used.

Figure 11-1 *Potential Building Problem Areas*

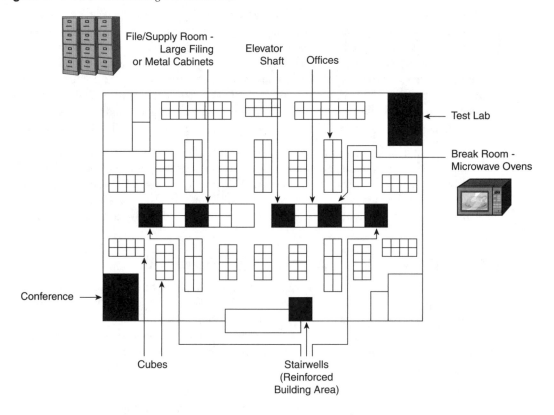

TIP	While noting potential problems, be aware of things that can change in the environment. For instance, large metal doors might be open at the time you perform the survey, but might be closed at other times. Normally you want to perform a survey with all doors closed, even if they are usually kept open. In general, it is better to have a little extra overlapping coverage via open doors than to have closed doors blocking the RF signal and causing dead spots.

Identify AP Locations and Antenna Types

Identifying AP locations and the antennas to be used is the heart of any site survey project. Exactly how you identify these particulars will vary from one type of survey to another and from one site survey tool to another, but the overall results (that is, coverage and user performance) should be similar.

As you perform a survey, you need to have a good understanding of RF issues in the site, such as RF signal attenuation and how to identify RF interference. This knowledge will assist in identifying problem areas in the site. To determine where to place the AP and what antenna to use, a walkabout is performed and RF measurements are taken. These measurements are used to determine the RF coverage, identifying the edges of the APs' cell boundaries. This step also helps to identify the overlap needed between cells to ensure continuous RF coverage with no dead spots. Each of these topics is discussed in detail in the following section (and the differences between manual and automated/assisted survey methods are noted).

RF Issues in the Site

As discussed in Chapter 2, "Understanding RF Fundamentals," one of the first issues to be understood regarding WLAN site surveys is that distance between the AP and client affects WLAN bandwidth and therefore capacity. Unfortunately, when deploying any radio system, including WLANs, the laws of physics apply. RF signals propagating through the air are subject to attenuation, losing signal strength while encountering obstacles, both natural (including the atmosphere) and manmade.

To effectively deploy a WLAN, technicians must understand the causes of RF attenuation and what applicable countermeasures are available. This knowledge is extremely important to the site survey engineer as well.

As a rule, as the distance between a client and an AP increases, the signal strength decreases. And at some point the bandwidth has to decrease to maintain the connection. The actual attenuation will vary widely, and without testing and verification it is impossible to determine exactly the overall effect of all the objects in most sites.

As described in Chapter 2, as the frequency increases, the amount of attenuation produced by the atmosphere increases, reducing range. Unlike outdoor line-of-sight applications based on straightforward path-loss calculations, attenuation for indoor systems is much more difficult to calculate. The main reasons for this difficulty are the multipath signals that occur in most indoor sites and the different attenuation effects created by the various materials found indoors.

The algorithms used to estimate path loss are very complex and are used in the theoretical site survey tools. These algorithms differ from indoor to outdoor, and the attenuation of RF signals also vary. In Figure 11-2, notice that at distances up to 50 feet attenuation is very similar. Beyond this distance, however, the path loss indoors increases much faster. Even so, you can estimate that indoors approximately 100 dB of attenuation occurs over distances of 150 to 200 feet for 2.4-GHz signals. Remember, however, that attenuation is not linear and it increases exponentially as range increases.

Figure 11-2 *Indoor Attenuation at 2.4 GHz*

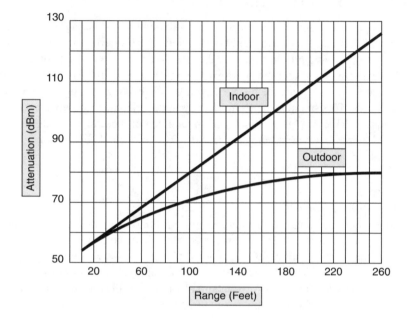

Typical obstacles found indoors, such as walls, doors, and office furnishings, offer fairly consistent levels of attenuation. Some standard items can be estimated for attenuation, as shown in Table 11-1.

Table 11-1 *Attenuation for Standard Building Obstacles*

Building Obstacle	Attenuation Level
Drywall	– 3 dB
Plaster and lathe wall	– 4 dB
Cement-block wall	– 4 dB
Typical glass window (nonmetallic tint)	– 2 dB
Steel-reinforced preformed concrete wall	– 9 dB

Some obstacles in the site might offer such a high level of RF attenuation that little or no RF penetrates it. Such a scenario usually results in an area with a high concentration of metallic content, such as steel floor pans, steel reinforced walls, metal mesh behind the stucco walls, elevators shafts, and so on. However, a high concentration of paper, card-board, or other materials that contain a high level of moisture can causes serious problems for RF penetration, especially at 2.4 GHz. Even some types of tinted glass or energy-efficient glass can cause a high level of attenuation or RF shadows.

When performing a walkabout survey, note areas where the signal drops off rapidly. This generally indicates some type of RF shadow effect and might require a different placement of the AP and antenna so that the area has adequate RF coverage. In some cases, you might need to actually add an AP if the area is totally blocked (such as an x-ray room, metal-walled freezer area, or steel-reinforced section of a building).

Identifying these areas is critical for full coverage and for proper roaming with devices such as wireless phones. Site surveys techniques that do not use a client walkabout to assist in the survey often do not identify areas that will exhibit poor roaming. A totally automated survey just cannot guarantee there are no RF shadows and dead spots associated with shadow effects.

One possible problem mentioned earlier is fire or hazard doors. These are doors that must remain open during normal business hours, but close automatically to restrict the spread of a fire or other hazard. Although many sites do not anticipate using the WLAN during such an emergency, some sites might want to use voice or even PDAs to assess the hazard problem. Surveying with the doors open will likely lead to dead spots when the doors are closed. Obtain permission (and use signage to indicate work is in progress) to close the doors if the survey is being performed during business hours.

While moving throughout the facility during the survey process, you will find that the signal levels vary in strength. However, the amount of variation should not be pronounced over small movements. Because RF is an analog signal with many influences on its strength and propagation, the overall level will be somewhat linear over small movements, unless acted upon by an obstacle. Dramatic variations that occur when moving only short distances (inches and feet) can indicate a high level of multipath interference. For such areas, there are several possible solutions:

- Use diversity antennas (recommended in any case)
- Verify diversity is set to on in the AP
- Move the AP (actually the antennas) farther away from any metal structures
- Use a more directional antenna

Detecting Interference

As discussed in Chapter 6, the pre-site survey form should have a place to identify any known RF systems that are used on the site. However, not all sites will have a single document or even someone who knows all of the RF equipment that is in use. Most enterprise WLAN equipment has the capability to look for other WLAN devices (usually referred to as *rogue AP detection*), and some can even report other interfering signals. The drawback to such features is that the APs for the new WLAN need to be installed first. If the installer is not aware of the other WLANs, he might install an AP in very close proximity to an interfering device. This will in turn require a relocation of the AP, possibly affecting other AP locations as well.

It is vital to identify all other possible interference in the site before starting any RF survey work (through a walkabout survey, for example). Even if the survey to be used is an automated survey, it is a vital part of an installation to first look for and identify any interfering signals.

There are a number of methods to identify potential interference. The most accurate is to use a spectrum analyzer. Spectrum analyzers enable you to view the entire spectrum, looking for signals that might not only be within the frequency range of the intended WLAN system, but could be near or at a frequency that could cause interference.

Interference from Non-802.11 Equipment

Interference can come in many flavors. You have already learned about the problems with microwave ovens at 2.4 GHz, and wireless phones at either 2.4 or 5 GHz. Many other devices can cause interference, too; and although some of these will be in the same band as the WLAN, some might not be.

Many vendors now offer wireless cameras, wireless security systems, wireless theft-detection systems, and even wireless projectors. Because the 2.4- and 5-GHz bands are unlicensed, these devices often fall into these bands. Efforts should be taken to identify and document the frequency and power output as well as the level of interference that these devices create for the WLAN. When evaluating the interference, be certain that the device is running at full RF capacity.

There are also devices that might be in a totally different part of the RF spectrum but can cause RF interference. One fundamental characteristic of an RF signal is known as the *harmonic of the signal*. When a signal is generated (and transmitted in the case of an RF signal), harmonics are also created. These harmonics are multiples of the desired signal, and although at a much lower level (both by design and by regulation limits) they can at times cause interference. The odd harmonics or multipliers are the strongest, with most often the third harmonic (three times the transmitted frequency) being the problem. As the harmonics climb in frequency, the signal level of the harmonic usually decreases very quickly.

Consider, for example, an installed 802.11g WLAN that is using channel 6 (2442 MHz). The site is a small-city office building where the police department and government offices are combined. Located at the same site is the citywide communication tower, which is attached to the building for support (and therefore very close in proximity to the WLAN in the building). Also located on that same tower are other wireless services that lease space from the city. If that tower happens to have an 814-MHz transmitter on it, there is the possibility of interference to channel 6 (814 MHz * 3 = 2442 MHz = 802.11g channel 6). A WLAN system with rogue AP detection would never find this problem because it is not an 802.11 signal. Therefore, a spectrum analyzer would likely be needed. However, a spectrum analyzer in the hands of an inexperienced user might not reveal it either, because the interference would be there only when the 814-MHz transmitter is actively transmitting RF, and might be easily overlooked if the analyzer is not set up properly.

It is vital to the quality of interference detection to become proficient with a spectrum analyzer. To locate any possible interference from some non-802.11 transmitter (see the "Interference from Non-802.11 Equipment" sidebar), use a higher-gain antenna on the analyzer, a peak hold function to capture any signals that are on line for a short period of time, and proper resolution and video bandwidth settings.

Existing WLAN devices represent another common source of interference. If the existing device uses a separate band (900 MHz, for instance), then this should not cause an issue. However, it is still recommended to keep some minimum distance between any two RF devices (minimum of 3 feet, or about 1 meter) even if they are on different bands.

When installing a system in the same facility that has competing RF on the same band, exercise extreme caution during the installation to keep interaction to a minimum. For example, when adding an 802.11b or 802.11g system to a site that has an existing *frequency-hopping* (FH) system, maintain a minimum of 10 feet (3 meters) between the 802.11b or 802.11g and the FH system RF components.

Another common issue with regard to interference is the rogue AP (that is, the AP that some employee has brought in and put into the network without the consent of the IT staff). This type of AP can cause several issues, with the number one being security (because rogue APs typically do not conform to the IT security requirements).

The second issue is interference with the properly installed WLAN. If not identified before the walkabout portion of the survey begins, it can cause missed packets and higher noise-floor readings, which in turn might trigger the need for another AP in that location. These devices should be "sought and destroyed" before starting a survey.

Some WLANs systems offer rogue AP detection utilities, but require the WLAN to be fully installed and operational before they can be used. Therefore these utilities are more for maintaining a WLAN and identifying rogue APs in an operation WLAN and not for use as part of a site survey.

You might feel like there is far too much to think about regarding interference, but that is not necessarily the case. Although 2.4 GHz does have many more possibilities of interference (because of more devices on the market), in reality you will have few interference problems with a WLAN when surveyed and installed correctly.

The Walkabout Test

The walkabout is one step in performing any site survey and completing any WLAN design. Although the process is nothing more than actually walking through a facility, taking measurements, and verifying coverage levels, it is a vital step that must not be overlooked, and it must be done logically. During the walkabout, you verify the signal attenuation of objects, define cell boundaries, identify noise-floor problems, and verify communication between a client and an AP at the appropriate data rate, all of which help to determine where to place an AP and what type of antenna to use. As stressed throughout this book, skipping the walkabout test will result in a WLAN with one of two problems: dead spots or a highly overengineered, and therefore highly expensive, WLAN. A proper walkabout mixed with other survey techniques and appropriate design is the only way to guarantee the best performance, efficiency, and economy. But how is this vital step completed? Take a look at the steps to identify the boundaries of a wireless cell, as well as to verify the proper overlap of coverage between cells.

Defining the Cell Boundaries

When you start to do either a user-density test (discussed later in the section "Performing a User-Density Test") or a manual survey, you need definitions for the cell boundaries—that is, what constitutes the edge or limitation of the cell. To establish the cell boundaries, you first need to define the following parameters:

- **Packet size**—As discussed in Chapter 10, "Using Site Survey Tools," one of the parameters that needs to be set correctly is the packet size. Packet size is dependent upon the applications that will be used in the site. This should be set to the largest packet that will be used. If the system will be used for standard Ethernet access, the packets size should be set to 1400 bytes (or as high as 1518 depending on the limitations of the site survey tools).

- **Data rate**—The AP should be set to the minimum data rate permitted in the design.

- **Transmitter power**—TX power needs to be set to either the maximum transmitter level of AP (if you are using the same AP model for the survey as for the installation) or to the maximum level of the AP intended for deployment.

So now that you have set the appropriate parameters in the AP for performing the RF tests, it is time to place the AP in a location in the site and take some measurements. Before proceeding, however, you need to define the measurements and RF test results that will determine the cell boundaries.

As mentioned in Chapter 10, you use three major items to determine whether the signal is adequate for proper WLAN performance:

- Signal strength
- Noise level
- Packet retry counts

Together these three can provide not only a good indication of cell boundaries, but also assist the survey engineer to understand why communication issues exist at certain points.

As the client is moving away from an AP, the signal level will be getting lower overall. There will be some fluctuations because of multipath signals, but in overall scope the signal level should gradually decrease. To determine the edge of the coverage for a data network, refer to the values listed in Table 11-2.

Table 11-2   *Cell Boundary Recommendations for 2.4-GHz Data Surveys*

Data Rate	Absolute Minimum RX Threshold	Recommended Minimum RX Threshold	Absolute Minimum RX Signal to Noise (S/N)	Recommended Signal to Noise (S/N)
54	−71	−61	25	35
36	−73	−63	18	28
24	−77	−67	12	22
12/11	−82	−72	10	20
6/5.5	−89	−79	8	18
2	−91	−81	6	16
1	−94	−84	4	14
Packet Retry Rate	Less Than 10% Packet Loss			

The table includes four columns of RF signal-level values. The absolute minimum RX threshold (receiver sensitivity) indicates the absolute minimum performance of the receiver at the given data rate. This particular table contains the values for the Cisco Aironet 802.11a/b/g combo card. These values should be set according to the equipment that will be used (the worst-case device). Notice that the minimum recommended RX threshold is 10 dB greater (less negative) than the RX threshold. This provides a 10-dB margin for fluctuations produced by multipath, body movement, body shadows, and so on.

As you understand by now, signal strength alone is not adequate to determine coverage. The table also defines the absolute minimum S/N values for the device to receive and decode a signal properly. Again in this case the values are for the Cisco Aironet 802.11a/b/g combo card, but they are similar to most other devices for the 2.4-GHz band. Next to this column is a recommended minimum S/N value. It is also easy to see that this has the same 10-dB ratio when compared to the minimum S/N value.

Now that you have defined the signal parameters, the final step is to look at overall communications link quality. That is determined by the packet performance. The minimum loss of packets should never exceed 10 percent. Although 10 percent might sound high to engineers who have been working in a wired network world, for RF it is normal to have a few percentage points of lost packets. That is the nature of RF. And at 10 percent for the edges of the cell, the retry mechanism for the data retry protocol will ensure there is no noticeable performance impact to the user in a data environment.

If the packet loss is higher than 10 percent, and the signal strength is also high, verify the noise floor and S/N values. A high noise floor can cause loss of packets. If the noise floor increases, the minimum signal level will also need to increase. Watch for large fluctuations in packet loss and signal strength, indicating an area where multipath is very likely.

Notice that Table 11-2 is for data communications. Wireless voice is a whole different beast than data and requires different minimum recommended values for cell boundaries. If the WLAN system is going to be using voice, overall cell boundaries need to be a bit stronger. Table 11-3 shows some changes to the recommended values.

Table 11-3 *Cell Boundary Recommendations for 2.4-GHz Voice Surveys*

Data Rate	Absolute Minimum RX Threshold	Recommended Minimum RX Threshold	Absolute Minimum RX S/N	Recommended S/N
54	−71	−56	25	40
36	−73	−58	18	33
24	−77	−62	12	27
12/11	−82	−67	10	25
6/5.5	−89	−74	8	23
Packet Retry Rate	Less Than 1% Packet Loss			

In Table 11-3, notice that the margin for the recommended minimum signal level and S/N values has increased to 15 dB. This is due to the nature of voice, and the critical necessity for maximum performance in packet transfer. Missed packets in voice are immediately noticeable to the user's ear. Therefore, not only has the minimum recommended value been increased, the maximum packet loss has been reduced to a much lower limit.

Finally, notice that the data rates below 5.5 Mbps are missing. Although it is recommended in most voice applications to maintain an 11-Mbps or higher data rate, a few vendors of wireless voice products do suggest allowable usage of data rates as low as 5.5 Mbps, but nothing lower.

Figure 11-3 shows the defined cell boundaries.

Figure 11-3 *Cell Boundaries*

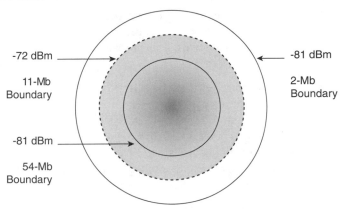

-72 dBm

11-Mb
Boundary

-81 dBm

54-Mb
Boundary

-81 dBm

2-Mb
Boundary

For different devices or different bands, these signal level and S/N values will change. It is important to understand the devices' technical specifications so the criteria can be defined. Using the same Cisco Aironet 802.15 a/g combo card, and looking at the 5-GHz performance as shown in Table 11-4, it is easy to see the differences from the 2.4-GHz band shown in Table 11-3. Although the overall margins have been kept consistent (for the data networks), the overall levels have changed because of differences in the radio capabilities.

Table 11-4 *Cell Boundary Recommendations for 5-GHz Data Surveys*

Data Rate	Absolute Minimum RX Threshold	Recommended Minimum RT	Absolute Minimum RX S/N	Recommended S/N
54	−68	−58	20	30
36	−73	−63	14	24
24	−77	−67	12	22
12	−82	−72	7	17
6	−85	−75	5	15
Minimum packet performance should be greater than 90% successful packet transfer (10% lost).				

Using the parameters defined in Tables 11-2, 11-3, and 11-4, you can define or verify the boundaries of a cell. In defining a cell, however, you must determine where one cell ends and another begins. To put it another way, how much overlapping coverage should occur between cells, and how do you verify that? The next section addresses these issues.

Overlapping Cell Coverage

Just as important as cell boundaries is the concept of overlapping cell coverage. Excessive overlap of coverage can result in some channel interference, unnecessary AP-to-AP roaming (by client devices that have a limited roaming algorithm), and added expense because of more APs being required.

A typical overlap in coverage is set to about 10 percent to 15 percent of the overall cell coverage area. Some engineers try to place a minimum signal level for both APs. Suggesting that the cell boundary of AP 1 is at –72 dBm (for some given data rate) and the signal level of the other AP at that point is –57 dBm seems to indicate some amount of overlap. However, this can be difficult to correlate to a percentage of overlap. Because signal levels vary from site to site, the signal strength of adjacent cells is very much dependent on the contents of the site.

Using a site map, as shown in Figure 11-4, with correct dimensions, you can define what the 10 percent or 15 percent overlap is. When performing the final walkabout, verify not only cell boundaries, but also that cell overlap is within the acceptable range.

Figure 11-4 *Recommended Cell Overlap*

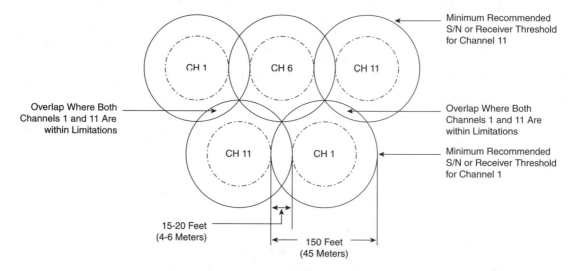

To summarize, cell boundaries for a 2.4-GHz 11-Mbps cell for data use only (using the data for the Cisco Aironet 802.11a/b/g card) can be determined by the following parameters:

- At the edge of the coverage area, the lowest signal strength should be –72 dBm or higher.
- At the edge of the cell, the minimum S/N should be 20 dB.

- Packet loss should be no more that 10 percent.
- Overlapping overage should be defined by the site map, and verification should be made that the adjacent AP can be heard with values greater that the minimum recommended thresholds.

Also it is important to remember that the client settings used in this cell boundary test process should match the actual network application scenario, as well as emulate the RF performance of the worst-case client that will be used in the WLAN system.

Performing a Manual Survey

The manual site survey is still by far the most popular and the most accurate, but it is also the most time-consuming and work intensive (but then again you don't get quality work without a little effort!). There are many ways to get started with a manual survey, but one that is very common is the "outside-in" survey method. This is where you start at the outside of the area and work toward the center. It is logical and accurate and provides for a very smooth workflow.

It is recommended that an analysis of the ambient RF environment be performed. After that, set the test AP on a channel that has no activity in the desired area.

Consider, for example, a typical retail site. In such, maximum range is needed, because there are only a minimum number of users; user density is not an issue. To start, an AP is placed near a corner of the facility, as shown by reference point A in Figure 11-5. Next, using the parameters defined for cell boundaries, perform a survey and determine where the edge of the coverage is. Mark this on your site plan for a temporary AP location, as shown in Figure 11-5.

Figure 11-5 *Outside-In Survey Starting Position*

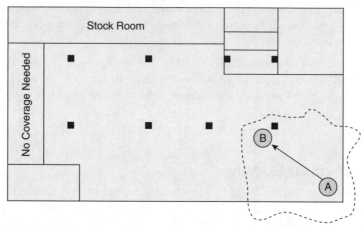

You might wonder why the AP is placed in the corner. Well, 75 percent of the signal is outside the facility, and that is what we *do not* want! However, this is not where the AP will get installed; this is just for a starting point. Here the AP is located in the corner along with a standard antenna (in this case, placed at ceiling level with a 5.2-dBi omni antenna hanging down from the ceiling).

On the site map, locate the approximate center of the coverage arc, as shown by reference point B in Figure 11-5. This will be the new location of the AP for testing. The rationale here is that if the client can communicate from point B to the AP at point A, they should still be able to communicate when the devices are reversed (with the AP at point B and the client at point A). And a minimum amount of signal will extend beyond point A outside the facility, but there will be adequate coverage at point A. Just guessing where point B needs to be based on the site map could result in more energy outside the facility than necessary (or desired), or not enough signal to reach the inside corner, resulting in a dead spot.

Figure 11-6 shows the revised location of the AP with the associated coverage area. Notice the corner of the facility is fully covered as well.

Figure 11-6 *Outside-In Survey First Cell Location*

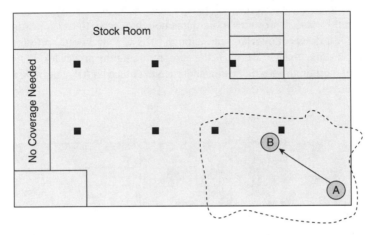

Repeat the same effort for points C, E, and G, as shown in Figure 11-7. After you complete this step, you might need to fill in the center areas if there is still more coverage needed. Because the number of users were defined to be higher in the stockroom, the two area APs (F and H) were slid back slightly to provide adequate overlap and to provide more signal into the storeroom (which results in fewer main store users on these APs because less area of the main store is covered by these APs).

Figure 11-7 *Outside-In Survey—Four Corners*

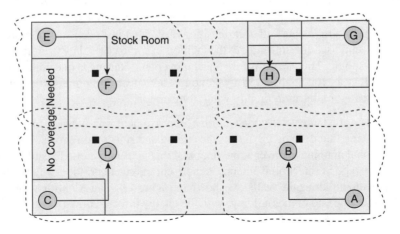

Knowing the average coverage ranges, you can make an estimated guess as to where to place the next AP. In Figure 11-8, point J is selected and its overall coverage tested and noted. In this case, it provides more than enough overlap to the adjacent cells. Take care to verify that it does not overlap with enough cells so that it could interfere with some other cell on the same channel. If this is the case, reducing the power level on this AP (or moving to a smaller antenna) should be considered. Next place an AP at point K and test to complete the site coverage.

Figure 11-8 *Outside-In Survey—Filling In*

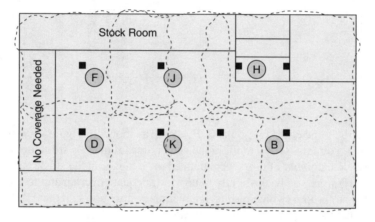

Retail stores are typically one of the easiest sites to survey because of their physical nature and contents. So what happens when things get a bit more congested, less open, and coverage requirements and user densities vary? That just takes a little more work. You can use the same scheme throughout the facility. In some cases, however, it requires a little different logic. This can be a more linear movement, starting at one point and moving across the facility as you might do in a warehouse, or just working one section at a time (for a health-care or education facility wing, for example).

Now look at a large do-it-yourself home-improvement warehouse. This type of facility has tall racking that extends up to near the ceiling and runs in long rows. Using an omni-directional antenna to cover something like this is usually not a feasible solution. The use of some type of directional antenna is more common and provides a fairly easy installation by placement along the walls. As shown in Figure 11-9, an AP with a patch antenna is placed at one end of the building, with the energy directed down the aisle. The coverage is then tested to see how much coverage is obtained, and exactly how well the RF extends down the aisles.

Figure 11-9 *Warehouse Survey Using Patch Antennas*

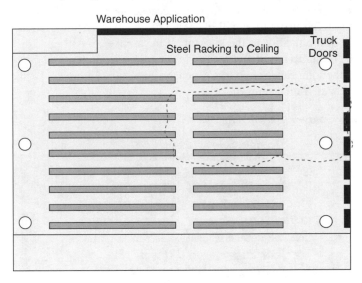

In this particular case, notice that one AP and a patch antenna provides about 3 to 4 rows of coverage, a little more than 50 percent of the way down the building. Placing another AP several rows over, as shown in Figure 11-10, would provide verification of coverage for adjacent aisles. Using this test, you could analyze that placing APs in the locations shown in Figure 11-10 would provide coverage for the entire facility.

Figure 11-10 *Warehouse Survey Completed*

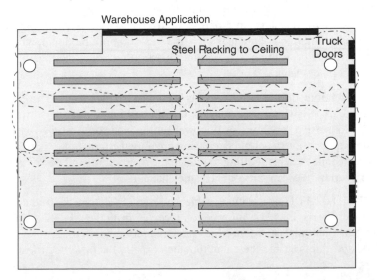

However, it might be worthwhile to test another alternative before deciding on the final approach. Exchanging the patch antenna (8.5 dBi) for a higher-gain (13.5 dBi) Yagi antenna might provide enough range to fully reach down the aisles. This might eliminate the need to place APs at the back of the facility. Because the higher-gain antennas have a narrower beam width, however, they will likely not cover as many rows, requiring more APs along the front of the facility. In the long run, if the number of APs ends up being identical, it might be easier to install and require fewer cable runs to have all the APs on a single wall. This, in the long run, can be less expensive to install. Figure 11-11 shows the coverage obtained with Yagi antennas.

Figure 11-11 *Warehouse Survey Using Yagi Antennas*

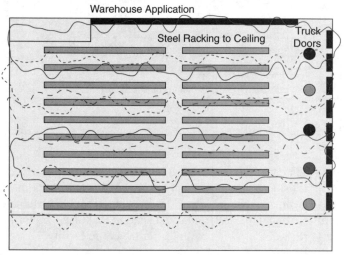

For certain types of facilities (education and health care, for example), you confront several issues. The first is the exposure of the products, or the physical security. In most of these cases, the AP and antenna have to be secured either out of sight or with some type of locking mechanism. Therefore, antennas such as Yagis or omnidirectional, which hang down from the ceiling, are typically not an option. This requires some thought as to possible antenna types and placements.

In some schools, the determination has been made to place one AP in every classroom. This gets quite expensive, but provides the overall best bandwidth performance. Such installations use a very low 1-mW power setting, and some even go beyond that and install an attenuator on every antenna, reducing not only the transmitter power, but also the ability to hear distance clients. Failing to reduce the overall radiated power would create far too much overlap between APs on the same channel.

The IEEE 802.11d specification enables the client to change the frequency of operation and the power levels, based on information received from the AP. This is primarily done to provide a client that can roam from one regulatory domain to another. In some cases, a few WLAN products enable the client to match exactly the power settings of the AP.

For health-care facilities, in some areas the required bandwidth varies drastically. For normal hallways and patient rooms, where the network is used for patient records or perhaps bar code scanning of medicines, bandwidth and redundancy are not critical to patient life and death. In most cases, the WLAN is a requirement for normal operation; if there is a location where the WLAN has failed, however, the user could revert back to the old paper and pen method. If the WLAN goes down, it only affects the overall efficiency of the work that is being done. However, in *cardiac care units* (CCU) or *intensive care units* (ICU), where the WLAN is used in the monitoring of the patients' vitals, this is very different. The WLAN is used as a life-monitoring system, and it must be up at all times. In these situations, there should be enough overlap of APs to provide absolute redundancy of coverage. (See Figure 11-12.) In these cases, some overlap of the same-channel cells might be necessary. There should be no area where a client cannot hear at least two different APs.

Another way to ensure redundancy is to use APs that perform hot standby. In a hot standby setup, two APs are mounted at each location. One AP is in standby mode and monitors the other AP. If a problem occurs, the standby unit takes over.

When trying to survey something such as a hospital wing or office building with long hallways and identical offices, your best bet is not the use of omnidirectional antennas. In many cases, low-gain patch antennas might work well. In the case of the five floors depicted in Figure 11-13, the patch antenna would not radiate down the hallway totally. Because it had a wide angle of radiation, however, it did cover some of the floors above and below, so alternating ends of hallways allowed enough coverage to "bleed over" so that full coverage was obtained. In this case, a Yagi might have worked, but the aesthetics of the Yagi were not conducive to the facility.

Figure 11-12 *Redundancy Using Overlapping Coverage*

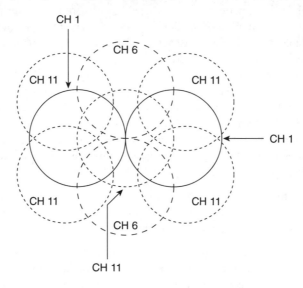

Figure 11-13 *Vertical Survey Using Patch Antennas*

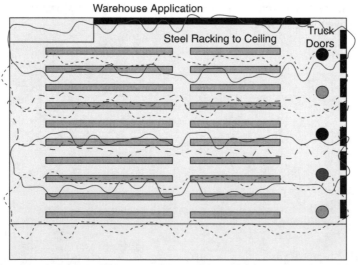

While surveying, you need to consider another dimension: vertical. RF is three-dimensional in that it radiates in all directions. Facilities that are more than a single floor need special attention. In these situations, it is important to survey on floors above and below to verify where coverage comes into play. You can reduce undesired floor-to-floor coverage by using specific antennas. However, be sure to rotate channels of APs so that the same channel is not used directly above or below an AP on the same channel. (See Figure 11-14.)

Figure 11-14 *Multifloor Deployment*

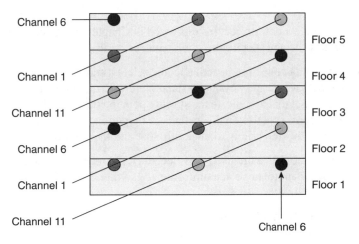

Documenting the Site Survey

As you complete every cell, stop and document the coverage area, AP location, and antenna type. You can use this information for notes for the final documentation (discussed in Chapter 13); this information also proves useful as you move to the next cell area to survey, helping you judge well where to place the AP to start the survey process for the next area. This is also a good time to make any notes about issues or possible problems that you discovered but were not included in the pre-site survey documentation.

Surveying with the AirMagnet Tool

In Chapter 10, you learned about the AirMagnet Surveyor tool. The recommended technique for use of the AirMagnet Surveyor tool is very similar to the inside-out survey methodology. The AirMagnet Surveyor tool measures all the critical values for determining cell boundary locations and provides graphical assistance for collecting and documenting the survey results.

After you create a new project (as discussed in Chapter 10), import the floor or building plan graphics file and specify the scale—you are ready to start collecting data.

To begin the data collection in active mode, select a starting position near the perimeter of the area to be covered and physically stand there with the survey tool. Click on this location in the AirMagnet tool to indicate the starting point on the floor plan map. A small stick man will appear at this spot. Begin the walkabout by moving at a smooth pace to the next checkpoint in the path; stop briefly to click this spot and then continue.

The more locations that are used to collect data, the more accurate the survey data will be. It is also important to move at a uniform pace so that the collected data is similar for all parts of the facility.

The Survey tool control area displays various real-time data as the walkabout proceeds, which is used to monitor the instantaneous state of the link. The signal-strength, noise-level, link-speed, and packet-loss statistics all display. You can use these indicators to monitor the signal conditions from the test AP and make decisions about the coverage boundary for a given service level specification.

If each AP cell of coverage is specified to support a minimum link rate of 5.5 Mbps (for 802.11b), for example, the coverage boundary can be found by walking to points where the Speed indicator crosses from 5.5 Mbps to 2.0 Mbps. Then move back into the solid 5.5-Mbps area to determine the edge of the cell where the performance is stable and record that location. As recommended previously, the initial configuration of the active mode survey tool should set the packet size to most closely resemble the data payload of the real WLAN applications.

The next step is to place icons representing the test AP or existing APs in a network. A drop-and-drag tool enables you to easily add the graphics display. The view in Figure 11-15 shows this simple process. First click the Add AP Icon button on the graphics toolbar on the right side of the screen. The dialog box displays, enabling you to add a name. Then drag the AP icon to the appropriate location on the floor plan.

Figure 11-15 *Adding AP Locations to a Floor Map*

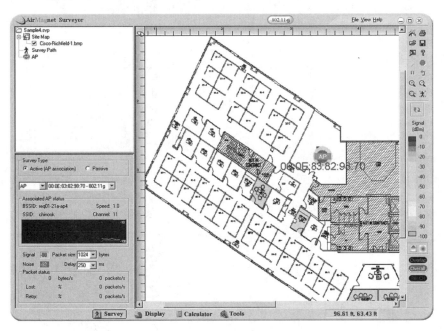

If you select the display mode toggle button on the lower toolbar, Surveyor will display data collected from the survey. Two new panels appear in this mode: the Filter area in the center-left panel and the map zoom box in the lower left.

First, choose one or more survey data sets to display by clicking the appropriate check-box(es) in the data catalog area in the upper left of the screen. Then choose the display parameter for the data sets, by making a selection from the drop-down menu in the upper-right corner of the floor plan display area. You have the following choices:

- Signal
- Noise
- Speed
- S/N ratio

Finally, enable appropriate filters to the data.

The survey data will then display as color-coded zones tied to the legend shown. For signal level, shown in Figure 11-16, colors represent 10-dBm levels.

Figure 11-16 *Displaying Survey Results*

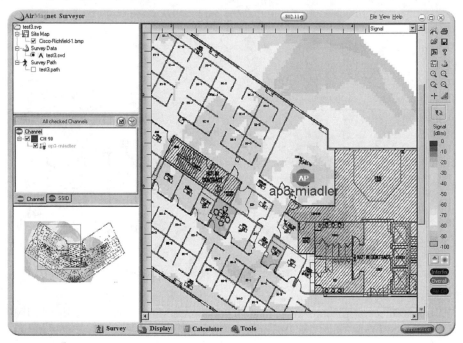

Assisted Site Surveys

In an assisted site survey, you first need to determine how big a cell needs to be for the user density defined in the design. This might vary in different locations throughput the site, and this test will need to be performed in all the similar areas. An assisted site survey helps to ensure that an AP can cover the amount of area needed, without any dead areas. In most cases, you use an assisted survey when the power of the AP provides cell coverage greater than desired for the user density.

Performing a User-Density Test

Using the facility diagram survey method, locate the center (if using an omniantenna) of a common type of area in the facility, such as a group of cubicles. Place an AP at that location, in a similar position to how it would be installed. Define the number of users, and their locations should be serviced by this one AP, and note this information on the facility diagram (see Figure 11-17).

Figure 11-17 *Density Testing*

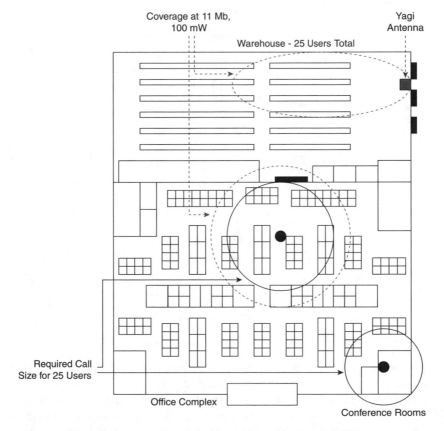

Then perform a walkabout test for that one AP, using the values defined earlier in this chapter, and determine where the cell boundaries are. Compare this cell boundary to the desired coverage areas defined on the site map. Reduce the power of the AP, and perform the walkabout test again. Once more, compare the cell boundary to that of the desired coverage. When the coverage area is at the desired range, note the power setting on the facility diagram.

After completing this step for all identified area types, you can use this information to estimate on the facility diagram where APs should be placed (see Figure 11-18).

Figure 11-18 *Placing APs for an Assisted Site Survey*

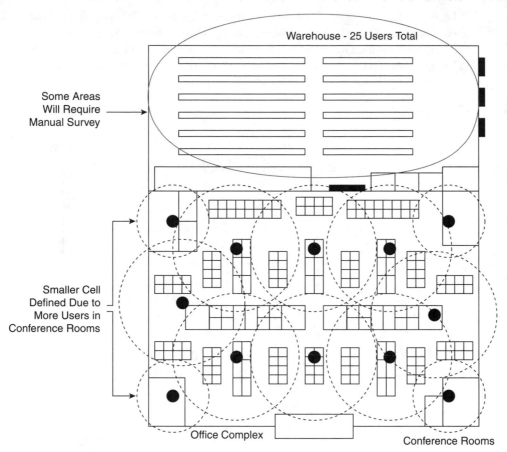

If the area requires a unique antenna such as a Yagi, patch, or other "nondefault" antenna, you might need to survey it entirely using the walkabout method. (Such a need sometimes arises because many assisted or automated survey tools do not account for anything other than omnidirectional antennas.) The same holds true for areas in which the desired coverage is the maximum size possible with the AP and antenna combination at full power. This would normally occur in a facility such as a warehouse with only a handful of wireless bar code scanners, or an outdoor site where the system is used by a limited number of security guards for wireless VoIP and the coverage area is very large.

Using the Assisted Site Survey Tool

After completing the density test, you can progress to the initial installation of APs. Using the estimated location of the AP (see Figure 11-18), install the AP and set to full power.

Assisted site survey methodologies vary from vendor to vendor. In general, however, you complete the following steps after performing a density test:

1 Install the APs based on the density test and floor plan.

2 Perform an AP scan.

3 Perform a client walkabout.

4 Generate the radio parameters based on the AP scan and walkabout.

In an AP scan, you use one AP's receiver to hear the surrounding APs. The system records all surrounding AP signal strengths and determines what the power setting of the AP should be. In many cases, this will provide coverage in all areas, but there might still be some dead spots. One key point to remember about this method is that the APs are typically mounted in the ceiling. Therefore, the path loss between APs is typically less than the loss occurring between the AP and a client, which is located much lower, and possibly behind cube walls, desks, and so on. This is exactly why it is vital to perform a verification walkabout, looking for dead spots, RF shadows, and so on.

The Cisco WLAN products enable the client to participate in the assisted survey process (via a client walkabout). The client sends data from a walkabout up to the management system, providing not only AP-to-AP signal strengths but also client-to-AP signal strengths.

RF Configuration Parameters

After completing the site survey, you must select the proper channels for the APs so that channel reuse is properly implemented (to reduce same-channel overlap and improve performance). Some systems allow automatic channel selections. In such a case, you must verify that there are no adjacent cells on overlapping channels after you have installed and configured the system.

Any other parameters that need to be set, such as packet size, diversity antennas, or RTS/CTS, should be identified and documented as part of the survey. It is important to configure and verify the coverage after the installation.

Some products offer the feature to have the AP set power and channel schemes as an ongoing task. Although this might seem like a desirable feature, it can sometimes cause a network to become unstable. If RF interference or a network glitch causes an AP to drop off line for any length of time, the network will start to reconfigure the APs, for both power and channel scheme. When the "down" AP comes back on line, the reconfiguration takes place again.

Although this automatic reconfiguration feature might sound great for a failed AP, if the AP is intermittent, or the interference that is causing the problem is intermittent, the systems will go through constant reconfiguration, disrupting normal usage. To prevent the constant changes to configurations, take care to ensure reconfiguration parameters filter out these fluctuations and temporary situations.

Site Surveying for Repeater Usage

Repeaters are supported by many of the WLAN products available today. However, the use of repeaters is recommended in only two scenarios:

- Locations where there is no possible way to wire the device
- If the installation will be temporary

The reason for this limited recommended use of repeaters is that a 50-percent reduction of bandwidth is typically introduced. The overlap on a repeater and its wired AP partner has to be, at a minimum, 50 percent. This is required so that the two APs have full communication with each other (see Figure 11-19).

Figure 11-19 *Repeater Overlap*

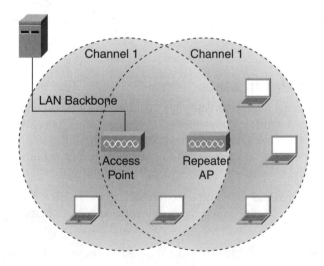

Dual-Band Surveys

When you survey a site that includes dual-band APs, providing both 2.4-GHz and 5-GHz support, set up two client profiles, one for each band. It is also recommended that different SSIDs be used for the different bands if a dual-band card is used for the survey client. Using the same SSID can cause confusion if the client actually is using 2.4 while you are trying to survey at 5 GHz.

When conducting a dual-band site survey, the survey itself is typically done at 5 GHz, which has a smaller coverage area. Before making this assumption, however, perform a test using the actual components that will be installed. Follow the density test and determine the cell boundaries for each band. From that information, select the product that has the lowest coverage. This will typically be 5 GHz.

Then reduce the power of the other larger-coverage radios (typically 2.4 GHz) in the APs until the cell boundaries are similar for both bands. When performing the survey itself, use these settings to start. When a location has been determined for an AP, run a test for both bands and document the results. In some locations where multipath is high or certain contents affect the signal (such as high moisture content of materials stored in the facility, which hinders 2.4-GHz signals more than 5-GHz signals), you might have to alter the power levels. You *must* document these differences for the installer and the IT staff.

Site Surveys for Voice

As discussed previously in this chapter, WLANs used for voice require a little different survey approach. Table 11-3 indicated that the recommended signal strength, S/N ratio, and packet loss were much more conservative than those values used for a data-only WLAN. There is also more concern for same-channel cells that can overlap, or be close to overlapping. Figure 11-20 shows yet another parameter that should evaluated when installing a WLAN that will use wireless voice devices. That parameter is the signal level from the closed same-channel AP.

In Figure 11-20, a client that is placed at the edge (or anywhere in) Cell B should receive a signal from Cell A with a signal strength no greater than –87 dBm. This provides enough same-channel isolation to maintain a quality voice connection.

Figure 11-20 *Same-Channel Isolation*

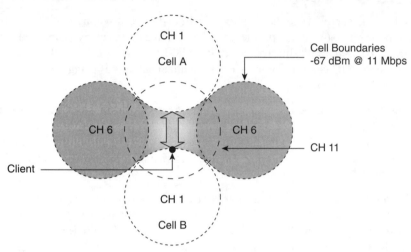

Because of the critical nature of interference from adjacent same-channel cells, as well as the more stringent requirements for signal strength and S/N, it is highly recommended that assisted or automated site surveys are not used for WLANs that will include voice. If there is the remote chance that voice will be added to the WLAN at a later date, the survey should be performed with voice parameters. This normally requires a bit more work and possibly more APs, but this trade-off is necessary for a properly working voice system.

Final Verification

Regardless of which site survey method you choose, conduct a walkabout for verification after the system has been installed. For this task, use the same tools and guidelines for boundary values as the manual survey uses. Perform a walkabout of the perimeter, as well as any locations that might cause RF shadows, interference, or multipath areas. Test whether you can roam from one AP to another without dropping below the recommended cell boundary values, including packet retry counts. The use of a tool such as AirMagnet Surveyor helps to document this task for addition to the final report and documentation.

Summary

Performing a survey is a logical process. Understand the site, evaluate the site, note possible problem areas, perform a manual or assisted survey, configure the APs based on the survey results, and perform a final verification. (Installation of APs is done after the manual survey or after a density test.) Following this logical flow makes the overall survey process seem very simple.

The heart of a high-quality survey is understanding how to use and interpret the results of the survey tools and what the parameters need to be to cell boundaries (essential information to define AP coverage areas).

Sites vary, and so will the type of survey used and approach to the survey. Warehouse, manufacturing, and large retail surveys typically use manual surveys, whereas facilities containing only offices and cubicles might use an assisted site survey. Small, single-AP sites such as a small retail store might not need a structured survey. Sites with wireless voice require more attention to specifics. In all cases, understanding and applying the fundamentals covered in this chapter will enable you to conduct a survey that results in a quality WLAN appropriate for the intended wireless applications.

PART III

Installing WLAN Components

Chapte 12   Installing WLAN Products

Chapte 13   Preparing the Proper Documentation

Chapte 14   Outdoor Bridge Deployments

This chapter covers the following topics:

- Understanding Installation Issues
- Proper AP Mounting
- Proper Antenna Mounting
- Ethernet Considerations

CHAPTER 12

Installing WLAN Products

This chapter focuses on the physical installation of WLANs and the issues and problems that you might encounter during a WLAN install. Throughout this book, installation concerns have been discussed when they were relevant to the particular topic. This chapter ties together and summarizes these issues.

After the WLAN project team completes the installation, the WLAN needs to be configured, the performance verified with the final walkthrough survey (see Chapter 11, "Performing a WLAN Site Survey"), and the WLAN documented (see Chapter 13, "Preparing the Proper Documentation").

Understanding Installation Issues

In many cases, the installation team is not the same individual or group of individuals who set down the initial design or performed the survey. However, the installation of a WLAN has to be closely tied to the WLAN design and survey, and therefore the documentation stage of the survey is critical. If important details are left out, or not explained fully, the installer might make assumptions, and the resulting WLAN installation might not be what the survey team or the design engineers had in mind.

The installer must take into account many different concerns, including overall type of facility (public or private), aesthetics, the physical security that will be needed, the environmental conditions, the local building codes, and fire regulations. These considerations are in addition to the general items such as mounting and connecting the WLAN components to the network.

The actual installation usually falls into two separate tasks:

- Installing the WLAN hardware
- Connecting to the network

These two tasks must be worked on hand in hand, but are often separated based on the expertise or job functions of the individual. For larger sites, the tasks are often divided.

Above all, take care to ensure the installation does not alter the design set down by the site survey team. The site survey step was critical to finalizing the design of the WLAN, and alterations at this point in the project need to be discussed with the survey engineer and tested if necessary.

Facility Construction

The facility construction and its effect on a site survey and WLAN operation were discussed in detail Chapter 8, "Discovering Site-Specific Requirements." After the survey has been conducted, the WLAN is designed to deliver the necessary performance with the facility construction in mind. That process partially dictates where the *access points* (APs) and antennas will be located. In the installation phase, the type of construction again plays a role in how easy or difficult it is to install a system.

The difficulty of installation varies widely with the building type. In most warehouses or manufacturing facilities, mounting is usually straightforward because the APs and antennas are attached either to the wall or the ceiling rafters. For facilities with enclosed ceilings, mounting can become in issue. How much of an issue depends on physical security, aesthetics, and the type and height of the ceiling. Survey engineers who are familiar with installation procedures can make the installation process easier by identifying in their surveys optimal AP locations.

Aesthetics

Many facility managers are extremely concerned about building aesthetics. To maintain the look and feel of the surroundings, the installer needs to be creative, but still work within the boundaries of the site survey. An experienced survey team can make the install easier by testing and recommending solutions that work well from the aspect of aesthetics. Survey engineers with minimal experience might overlook this step and leave it up to the installer to figure a way out of the problem. Therefore, a survey engineer should be part of an installation team, at least for some short period of time. This helps the survey engineer understand the potential problems that might arise during the installation process.

In some cases, even when aesthetics are important, a wall-mounted AP in plain sight might be acceptable. In Figure 12-1, a nonintrusive AP is mounted to an office wall. This particular AP uses internal omnidirectional antennas, keeping the overall look very clean.

Figure 12-1 *Unobtrusive Wall Mount*

Much of the aesthetics are directly related to the AP itself, as well as the desired antennas. Some APs are just cleaner looking and can fit well into the environment, whereas others just do not blend well into the surroundings. Adding external antennas exacerbates the problem with aesthetics. In some cases, a little logic and imagination need to be used. For example, Figure 12-2 shows one way to use external patch antennas while still maintaining a clean look. In this case, the AP is placed next to the picture to just indicate there is an antenna behind the picture. In most cases, however, the AP would be placed on the backside of the wall or above the ceiling and the cable run down through the center of the wall, exiting to the antenna behind the print.

Figure 12-2 *Hidden Antenna*

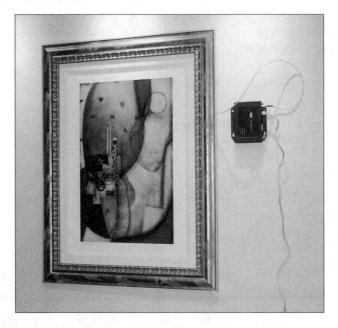

The particular photo shown in Figure 12-2 was taken during a site survey. Testing showed that the print had no effect on the performance, and the photo was used in the site survey report to indicate exactly where to place the antenna.

In some cases, antennas cannot be hidden easily, and the installer will need help to keep the aesthetics clean. Theme parks, for example, are extremely sensitive about the looks of their environment. In one scenario, a theme park contained a remote beach with an old aircraft environment. The WLAN required that a Yagi antenna be installed outdoors to enable communications from a building on the remote beach. To blend into the environment, the Yagi was mounted to a mast and then covered with a fake windsock.

Health-care locations also want to maintain a clean aesthetic. In these cases, you can paint many of the antennas (using, of course, a nonmetallic paint) to assist in blending APs into the environment. In one case, the customer even went to the extent of using patch antennas mounted to the hallway walls and covered the antennas with vinyl wallpaper that matched the wall covering used in the hallway.

Appendix C, "Alternative Antennas," describes a ceiling-tile antenna. This antenna is attached to the top of a ceiling tile, and therefore is totally hidden from view. The downside to a ceiling antenna is the need for adaptor cables (and tying to match to existing ceiling tiles). As an alternative, Figure 12-3 shows a mounting system from Maxrad that provides a very unique mounting, for both an AP and for antennas. The entire fixture can be assembled and installed as a complete system. It contains a 2.4-GHz diversity omnidirec-tional antenna with an outward radiation pattern. In addition to that, the bracket is designed to hold the AP just high enough above the ceiling tile to permit an attached 5-GHz dipole or patch antennas to radiate as well as possible (for being above the ceiling). Of course, the survey engineer should first test with this type of antenna to ensure accurate deployment. This is just one reason why it is a great idea for survey engineers to understand installation issues.

Figure 12-3   *Blending the Antenna with the Environment*

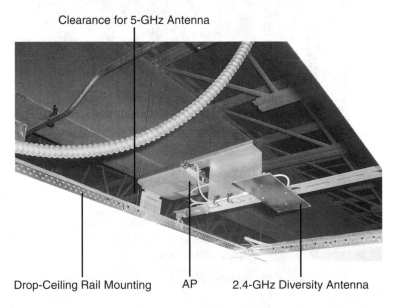

Physical Security

The physical security of an AP is sometimes based on the old adage "out of sight, out of mind." In some situations, APs placed above ceiling tiles seem to meet this level of "security." In environments with heavy public traffic but inconstant monitoring, such as a school or other public building, however, this practice is not adequate. Although one would hope that students and others would not be prone to mischief, you must plan for just such mischief.

The mounting of the antenna must be such that it is secure and cannot be removed easily. However, the real security threat is the AP itself. Securely mounting the AP and the radios modules within the AP is critical.

Some devices, such as the Cisco Aironet 1200, provide a security slot that enables you to attach a Kensington-type locking cable (identical to the ones used for securing laptops). Some APs also offer unique mounting brackets that enable you to use a small padlock (see Figure 12-4).

Figure 12-4 *Physically Securing APs*

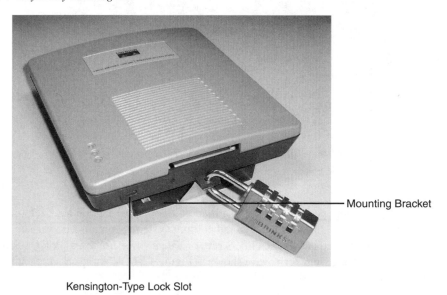

Mounting Bracket

Kensington-Type Lock Slot

At times you might need to provide a totally secure box for the AP (which is often the case when APs are mounted for public access and you do not have a secure location in which to mount the AP). Various boxes are available to enclose an AP. These can be as simple as a small plastic lock box available at any electrical-supply outlet or even some home-improvement stores. Plastic can be drilled easily (for cable entry) and, in some cases, the antenna might even work well through the plastic (but this should be tested as part of the site survey).

Environment

A few APs can handle outdoor or harsh environmental conditions (for example, the Intermec WA21 or Cisco Aironet 1300, shown in Figure 12-5), but the vast majority of APs available today are not up to such tasks. If you plan to place an AP in an outdoor area such as an open-air patio for public access or a beach house where salt spray and humidity are very common, you typically need some type of extra enclosure.

Figure 12-5 *Environmentally Sound AP*

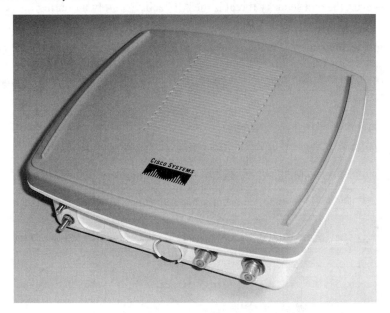

Several different enclosures are on the market today. They vary in size, features, and material. Some might offer heating and cooling systems, contain a power supply, or have AC line voltage fed into them. Others rely on *Power over Ethernet* (PoE), as do the enclosures available from TerraWave shown in Figure 12-6. When specifying enclosures, look for features such as these:

- NEMA ratings. Some enclosures are intended for indoor use to provide a degree of protection against dust, falling dirt, and dripping noncorrosive liquids; others are intended for outdoor installation.
- A opening large enough to facilitate component installation and maintenance.
- A method for direct mounting or optional external mounting feet.
- A seamless one-piece gasket to provide oil-tight and dust-tight seal.
- A lockable door.
- Dual antenna connections for external diversity antennas.

Figure 12-6 *Environmental Enclosures for APs*

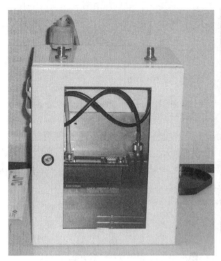

In many cases, these environmental enclosures are used for more than just environmental protection. For example, in many cases you can physically secure the AP by using the lockable door.

Building Codes

Building codes vary widely from location to location. This can be a problem for a company that is trying to standardize on an implementation for multiple sites located in different municipalities. There are different regulations regarding cable usage, fire ratings, accessibility to plenum areas, and so on. Although this section touches on a few of the issues, this is a topic that is beyond the scope of this book. Consult local authorities or use local contractors to guarantee that the installation meets the local regulations.

The *National Electric Code* (NEC) defines a plenum space as a compartment or chamber where one or more air ducts are connected and form part of the air distribution system used for ventilation into locations where people reside.

The space above acoustic ceiling tiles can be classified as plenum if the space extends beyond a single room. Typically, this space is common to the majority of the building (or at least to a particular floor). This type of construction is common. The reason for rating this as a plenum area is that in the case of fire, any smoke or fumes in the plenum area can travel through the air ventilation and into other inhabited areas. Therefore, equipment placed in the plenum must meet certain requirements for fire and smoke. If the walls extend above the ceiling tile and seal off the space, the area above the ceiling might be exempt from the plenum rating.

To meet the requirements of the NEC, you must use cables rated for plenum spaces (labeled as *Communication Plenum Cable*, or CPM). Similarly, any equipment—including APs, antennas, and antenna cables—installed above the ceiling must meet the plenum ratings.

Although the NEC defines the plenum ratings, and most cities use these same ratings, some localities have defined their own local codes. This is something that the installer must research before installing any equipment into a plenum area.

Another regulation in some localities concerns certification of the individuals accessing the plenum areas. Some regulations specify that any person accessing a plenum area must hold a valid *heating, air conditioning, and ventilation certification* (HVAC). This regulation might impact well beyond the installation portion of a WLAN project. If an HVAC contractor is used for the installation (installing the APs and running cables), what happens if an AP fails sometime down the road and needs to be replaced? If such a regulation applies in this locality, it is illegal for an IT person (unless HVAC certified) to access the AP above the ceiling.

One company had a custom AP enclosure made to meet this HVAC certification requirement, as well as any plenum requirements. Figure 12-7 shows the enclosure, which once installed is totally isolated from the plenum air space and opens from the user side of the ceiling. This permits anyone (with keys to the boxes) to access the AP for installation and maintenance. The box itself had to be installed by an HVAC contractor, but once installed and wired, the IT staff could handle all the necessary maintenance.

Figure 12-7   *Ceiling Enclosure for Plenum Area—Working View*

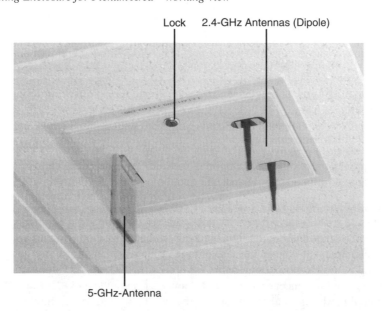

Lock   2.4-GHz Antennas (Dipole)

5-GHz-Antenna

Proper AP Mounting

There are endless ways to mount APs. Some APs come with versatile mounting brackets that provide many options (see Figure 12-8a and 12-8b); others might offer only a simple keyhole mounting option (see Figure 12-8c), in which case mounting possibilities are limited unless you fabricate some type of bracket.

Figure 12-8 *AP Mounting Methods*

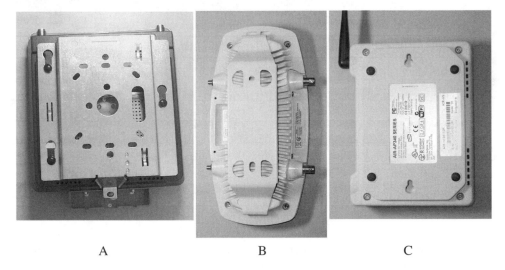

A B C

For antenna mounting, the style of antenna dictates the available methods. You may need to purchase different antenna mounting brackets for your particular site. Antenna mounting hardware is available from many different vendors, or even the local two-way radio shop or hardware.

The reliability of the mounting (of both the APs and the antennas) is a primary concern. The last thing that a customer wants is to have something fall from the ceiling or wall and cause injury (or cause damage to the WLAN devices) because of improper installation.

Some mounting methods are as simple as placing the AP on top of a cabinet, desktop, cubicle wall, and so on, as shown in Figure 12-9. Such simple methods are common for small sites that just require one or two APs.

NOTE   Make sure the antenna is not located next to the metal portion of a cabinet or desk. In Figure 12-9, the antenna sticks up vertically above any metal objects, so this is not an issue.

Figure 12-9 *Desktop- or Cabinet-Mounted AP*

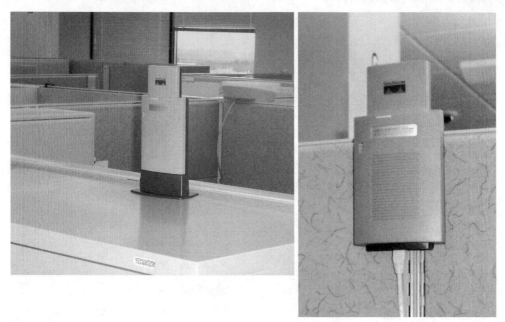

Other mounting options include wall mounting and ceiling mounting, as described in the next sections.

Wall Mounting

Wall mounting of APs is very simple, particularly when using the standard type of antennas. Here you can use the small keyhole-type mounts if the AP does not need to be mounted more securely. In some cases, the installer will have a standard electrical box placed in the wall, with the Ethernet cable run through the wall to the box. In such a case, a mounting bracket can be screwed to the box and the AP mounted to the bracket (and secured, if necessary). The AP covers the mounting screws and provides a bit more security.

Figure 12-10 shows two mounting examples. In both cases, the AP is mounted to a junction box in the wall, where the Ethernet cable exits and attaches to the AP without being seen.

Figure 12-10 *Wall-Mounted AP ExamplesB*

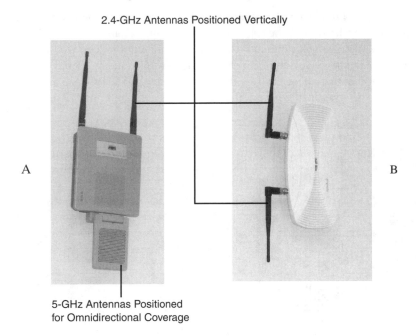

2.4-GHz Antennas Positioned Vertically

A

B

5-GHz Antennas Positioned
for Omnidirectional Coverage

When mounting to a wall, you generally place the AP as high as possible. However, you need to be aware of a few issues when wall mounting an AP. First, if the AP is using an omnidirectional antenna, as is the case with both APs in Figure 12-10, try to position the antennas between the wall studs so that there is limited interaction with the studs (especially if they are metal studs). Second, position the antennas vertically. If the AP is mounted like the example in Figure 12-10a, one dipole will point up and one will point down. This positioning provides omnidirectional coverage and diversity support.

Another issue to investigate is what is behind the wall. If you install an AP with omni-directional antennas on a wall that has something on the other side of it that might create multipath signals or interference, AP coverage and performance might be detrimentally effected.

Finally, when wall mounting an AP, do not place the AP so far up the wall that the antennas are close to the ceiling. In the case of drop ceilings, the metal support structure can cause the antenna performance to drop off. If the ceiling is made of drywall, there might be metal corner beads at the ceiling and wall junction. It is best to have the antennas at least a few inches below the ceiling.

Ceiling Mounting

The most common type of mounting is ceiling mounting, which provides the best overall coverage for the AP and the easiest access for running cables. If the AP has self-contained antennas (nonmovable antennas), the product might not radiate well when placed on the ceiling. The site survey engineer should address this issue by identifying the mounting orientation in the site survey report. If the AP uses a standard-type dipole, the antennas should hang straight down from the ceiling, as shown in Figure 12-11.

Figure 12-11 *Ceiling Mounting*

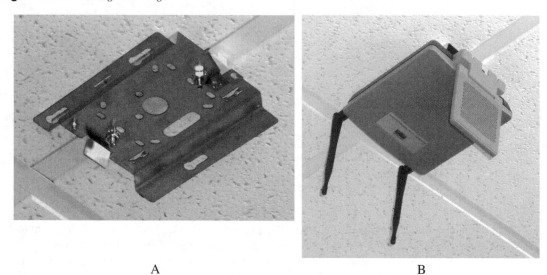

A   B

In many cases, the APs will be mounted above the ceiling tile and the antennas below the ceiling. When mounting in this fashion, you need to attach the AP to some structure, not just place it on top of a ceiling tile (which is actually quite common). The best method is to mount the AP to the building structure, such as to an I-beam. You can buy clamps at any electrical-supply outlet and even some home-improvement centers to securely attach WLAN products to an I-beam.

Proper Antenna Mounting

Antennas come in many different styles and form factors, and you have even more choices with mounting brackets. Some antennas are designed to be mounted to a mast, others to a drop ceiling, and others to a custom bracket. Most antenna manufacturers provide some type of mounting for the antennas. However, not all "standard" mounting solutions will work in all situations. A number of companies offer a wide variety of accessories for mounting antennas. Most of these are designed for outdoor applications, but work just fine for the indoor WLANs. However, some antennas are not sealed for outdoor use. Prior to using any antenna outdoors, verify that the antenna is rated for outdoor exposure. Also verify that any outdoor antenna is mounted properly to prevent water from entering any vent holes that might exist. Another concern with antenna mounting is to be certain they are positioned properly and they are secure in that position. Failure to secure an antenna properly can result in poor performance, or even the possibility of falling and causing damage or injury.

At some sites, installation will be easy. In Figure 12-12, the Yagi antenna, the AP, and all connections are mounted to a single piece of plywood, which in turn is mounted to the wall. This particular installation is located at a large home-improvement store.

Figure 12-12 *Indoor Yagi Antenna Mounting*

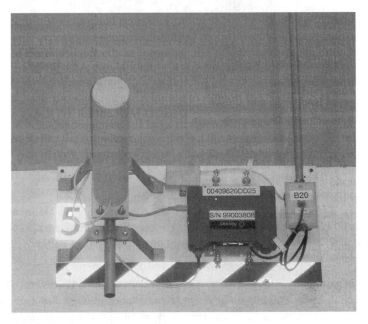

Likewise, not all sites require a large number of APs and antennas. If the application bandwidth requirement is minimal, user density is low, and minimum bandwidth is fine, you can use a minimum number of APs to provide adequate coverage. In Figure 12-13, the installation for a retail appliance store uses a single AP with a single patch antenna mounted on the front wall.

Figure 12-13 *Simple Patch Antenna Installation*

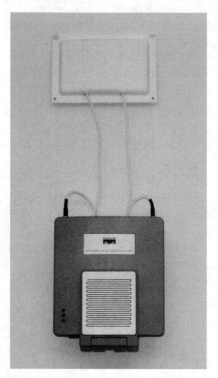

Although the previous two installations do not offer a very aesthetically pleasing system, the location of the APs and antennas is about 25 feet off the floor and most customers never know the devices are there.

Inexperienced survey engineers and installation teams commonly use conventional omni-directional antennas. The antennas works well for some sites, but as explained in Chapter 8, these antennas tend to attract attention in sites where the public is present. Antennas that can be either hidden well (behind the ceiling or wall) or blend into the environment (low-profile, ceiling-mount antennas) are better suited for this scenario.

One simple installation example is to take an AP, poke a hole in the ceiling tile, and stick the dipole through the tile. The AP sits on top of the tile, and the antenna hangs down as shown in Figure 12-14a. However, this method is not recommended unless the AP is secured above the ceiling in some fashion to prevent it from falling through the ceiling tile. A better solution is to use a conventional omni antenna and drop-ceiling mount, as shown in Figure 12-14b.

Figure 12-14 *Conventional Omnidirectional, Ceiling-Mounted Antennas*

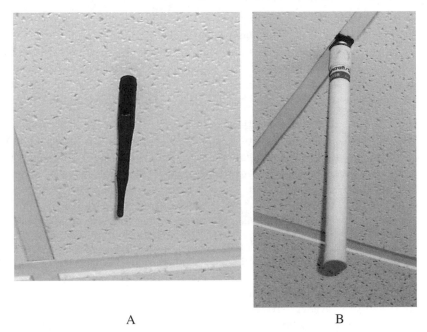

A   B

Both of the omnidirectional antennas might entice a passer-by to grab, pull, or otherwise disturb the antenna. Other antennas are designed to be "stealthy" and blend in; such antennas are designed to create minimum disturbance to the surroundings while still providing the level of performance of a dipole antenna. Figure 12-15 shows a profile antenna designed to clip to the grids of a drop ceiling.

Figure 12-15 *Low-Profile, Ceiling-Mounted Antenna*

Ethernet Considerations

When installing the APs, it is imperative to understand cable limitations for the data cable. If *Category* (Cat) 5 cable is going to be used, the AP must be located within 100 meters of the hub or switch to which it will be connected. The survey engineer should be aware of this, and part of the pre-site survey is to investigate where these infrastructure devices are located. If the survey report does not contain this information, the installer must verify the information and determine whether the AP is within that distance limitation.

For APs that will exceed the 100-meter limitation, consider using fiber-optic connections. You can use a number of converters to provide Ethernet-to-fiber translation. Although this cures the distance issue, it does introduce an issue with power. With fiber, you cannot send power over the optic cable. Because of this, many installers order an AC main outlet for AP location when using fiber. However, most of the APs that support PoE offer some type of power injectors (discussed in Chapter 9, "Discovering Wired Network Requirements"). You can resolve this issue by using a combination of fiber converters and a power injector.

Figure 12-16 shows a scheme that uses both PoE and fiber. In this particular example, the Ethernet switch is Cat 5 only and feeds an Ethernet-to-fiber converter placed in the same location as the switch. The other end of the fiber cable is located where there is AC power. This location must also be within 100 meters of the AP. At this location, the AC is fed to both the fiber converter and the power injector. From here, Cat 5 cable connects to the AP, carrying the necessary PoE as well as Ethernet. If the Ethernet switch supports fiber directly, you can eliminate one fiber converter.

Some vendors now offer a *fiber injector*. It combines the Ethernet-to-fiber converter and the power injector in a single package, making the installation even simpler.

Figure 12-16   *Using Fiber Optic for Distant APs*

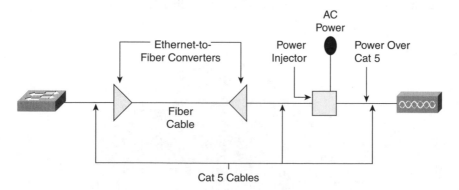

Summary

Proper installation of the WLAN infrastructure is as important to the system operating properly as any part of the design or survey. The installation is tied very closely to the site survey, and is much easier if the same team actually performs both (and hence brings continuity between the two tasks). Details of the survey should be very accurate and descriptive so that the installation can be performed properly. Some of the installation concepts should be tested when performing a survey so that the installation model is verified to work properly.

After the WLAN has been installed, you must update the document; at that point, the system is ready to be configured for operation.

This chapter includes the following topics:

- Final Site Survey Report
- Documenting the Work
- Site Survey Report-Generation Programs

CHAPTER 13

Preparing the Proper Documentation

You've probably heard the saying "The job is not complete until the paperwork is done." This saying holds true for site surveys. For site surveys, you need to complete several documents. As discussed in Chapter 6, "Preparing for a Site Survey," the pre-site survey should be completed before the survey begins, and the final survey report is developed as the survey progresses and finished as the final step. As with any network project, the more complete the documentation, the easier the network is to manage, troubleshoot, and expand. Missing, incomplete, or faulty documentation can lead to time-consuming tasks for the IT management, expansion, and maintenance teams.

During the survey, the site survey engineer must keep accurate notes and later record detailed information on the site survey document that gets delivered to the customer. In most cases, this document is the final product for the site survey team, and is what the customer is really paying for. This chapter details the final site survey documentation that will be delivered to the customer.

Final Site Survey Report

The customer needs the final site survey report to move forward with the WLAN installation. The customer and the installation team depend on the site survey engineer to provide them with all the information they need to be able to gather the materials and make the necessary adjustments to the network. A sample site survey report has been included in Appendix D, "Sample Forms." Most site survey engineers create their own template and from there create a unique site survey document that fits the customer's needs.

The survey should be as specific as possible in the report. It is very common that the survey engineer will not be the same person doing the installation, and therefore the report should be as clear, concise, and easy to understand as possible.

The engineer should think of the report as protection for both the engineer and the customer. In the event of a disagreement or problem, a good site survey report can prove that the site survey was completed per the customer's requirements at the time of the survey.

A typical site survey report includes the following sections:

- **Objective**—The objective should describe what work was performed, when and where it was performed, and so on. Basically this section reviews the scope of work from the pre-site survey and defines what other actions were done.

- **Site description**—This is a simple description of the site. It should include floor plans, coverage areas (from the pre-site survey documentation), the type of construction, the number of floors, the number of buildings, and so on. All the general site information belongs in this section of the report.

- **Survey dates**—An installer might be handed a site survey report and asked to install the equipment without much else to go on. If there is a date on the survey that indicates the survey is a number of months or years old, he may question the survey's integrity. Facilities change, as do the equipment that will be installed. When deciding what to put into the report, consider what an installer would want to see in a site survey report.

- **Testing procedure**—The method of testing is something that should be included in any survey document. It provides the customer with a description of what tools (both hardware as well as software versions) were used to do the testing, and how it was done. This helps in troubleshooting the network if necessary.

- **General network description**—This is a general description of the preexisting wired network and infrastructure. Define the types of connections (Token Ring, Ethernet, ATM, fiber, and so on), the types of connecting devices (Nortel Baystack 350 switch, Linksys 2400 hub, Cisco 2600 router), and general information (such as the number of wireless users and the location of the connection points). Review Chapter 8, "Discovering Site-Specific Requirements," for more details about what should go in this section.

- **Proposed WLAN components**—This section details the components that will be used for the survey and installation. Included here would be a complete parts list needed for the wireless system. Some survey engineers even estimate cable lengths, but many leave this up to the installation engineer. In any case, the AP must be located within 100 meters of the hub or switch, if *Category* (Cat) 5 cable (which is the most common) will be used.

- **Existing wireless system definition**—Detail any present wireless systems on the site. If possible, list the frequencies, the power levels, modulation types (spread spectrum, frequency hopping, narrow-band FM), and applications for the wireless (paging, wireless phone, video monitors, and so on). It is also a good idea to note locations of other wireless systems components on the site plan if possible.

- **Wireless sniffer traces**—The report should include some type of RF sniffer tracing showing what other 802.11 devices might be seen on the site. In many cases, there will be no other devices; however, it is desirable to verify whether there are neighboring systems to be aware of.

- **RF spectrum analyses results**—As part of every site survey, a review of the RF spectrum at the site is required. Document any RF that you discover, noting frequency, signal strength, type of signal, location of transmitter (if known), and any possible interference it may have on the WLAN.

- **Area-by-area analyses**—This is the "meat" of the report. This section is where the actual information for AP location, type of antennas, data rates, transmit power, and mounting instruction are placed. The use of a digital camera is ideal here. Photographs can be a time-saver and make the exact location of the AP or antenna unquestionable.

- **Contact list**—The report should include contact information for all parties involved. Include information for the survey engineer, the survey company sales or account representative, the customer contact, and any others who were involved in completing the survey.

Documenting the Work

The site survey report describes the details that were completed as part of the survey and what might need to be done in the installation and configuration processes. When documenting the actual work, include specific details about the following in the report:

- Analysis of the RF spectrum at the site
- AP location and mounting methods
- Antenna type and mounting methods
- AP configuration for RF (when applicable)
- Coverage map for each AP

Including detailed descriptions about these items in a final report will ensure that the details necessary for a properly installed and easy-to-maintain WLAN are available.

Detail about the location, the type of mounting, the antennas used, and the recommended cabling methods enhance the chances for an error-free, easy install. Here you can use photographs to great effect (with little text required). Use photos whenever possible.

When describing *access point* (AP) locations, the site survey engineer should be as specific as possible. It is recommended to use objects and identifiers to explain exactly where the AP is to be located. Use a photo to identify this in the report, and label the photos so that they correspond to the site map (see Figure 13-1).

Figure 13-1 *Documenting AP Locations*

If the AP is to be located in an aisle or hallway, specify which aisle or hallway, and where it is located in the facility. If possible, use some type of marking method (flagging tape or marker flags, for example) to identify the exact location. This provides the installer with a defined location and eliminates any question as to exactly where it goes.

Do not use as markers objects that might be temporary. If the object has moved before the installer arrives, the installer might not be able to find the location and might mount the equipment improperly.

Even more important than the AP location, the engineer must specify with as much exactitude as possible where the antenna is to be located. See the photograph in Figure 13-2.

Just stating "place the antenna on the wall above the doorway" is not enough. The installer might not be aware of RF characteristics and might place it behind the exit sign, so it is out of sight, thinking that this would look better. "Place the antenna on the wall above the doorway, a foot left of exit sign" is a better explanation. You can also use a picture to spell out exactly what the description means (see Figure 13-2). Notice the duct tape used to temporarily mount the antenna for the site survey. The AP and battery pack are placed above the ceiling on the wall edge.

Figure 13-2 *Using a Photo to Document Location*

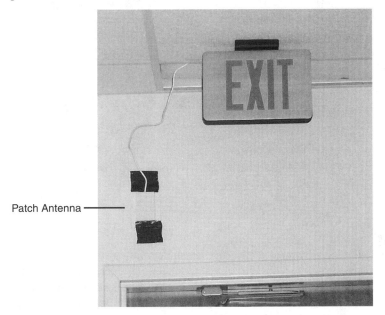

A detailed description of how the antenna is to be oriented must be included. Whereas correctly positioning an antenna might seem simple to some who have a basic understanding of RF and antennas, many others just do not have such an understanding of proper positioning. In some cases, the installer might have no knowledge of RF (or even networking for that matter). In one case, a university installed APs with 2.2-dBi dipoles that both swiveled and had a flexible 90-degree coupler. The installer assumed the energy from the antenna was radiated out the end of the antenna, as with an LED pointer. Therefore, he placed the antennas in a horizontal mode, as shown in Figure 13-3, so that the energy was "radiated out both ends." The end result was great performance on the floors above and below, but poor performance on that floor itself.

Figure 13-3 *Defining Antenna Position*

If the antenna is omnidirectional, the engineer might mention that the antenna is to be mounted vertically, with the cable or connector at the top or bottom. If the antenna is directional, describe the direction in which the antenna should be oriented. A patch antenna might be described as "facing north" or "directed at the nursing station at the end of the hall," but unless the installer has an understanding of that particular antenna, it might not be installed properly. Again, a good photo can provide tremendous assistance here. The more directional the antenna, the more important this description.

Another entry in a survey report should be parameters and settings of an AP that can affect coverage. It is important to identify the parameters that were used in the survey, including transmitter power levels (of both the client and AP), data rates, channels, packet size, and thresholds. All of these parameters can affect the overall survey results, and may or may not be the same throughout a facility. If there is both a warehouse and an office environment in the same site, the warehouse might only need support for a few users, over a very wide area, with minimal bandwidth. For the warehouse, therefore, maximum power and minimum data rates would be used. In the office area, however, there may be a need to keep the data rate set to 11 Mbps, and the transmit power to some lower value to stay within the user density defined in the design.

The report should also detail the coverage of each AP and define that coverage at desired data rates in an included diagram. Electronic diagrams can be generated easily and make any report look more professional. Microsoft Visio is available with templates that include items such as APs.

The report should also indicate areas where WLAN coverage is not needed. This helps to prevent misunderstandings or the customer complaining later that there is no coverage in an area he believes was missed, even though the original design did not include coverage for that area. Without documenting no-coverage areas, you cannot prove that the survey was done properly and that the original design did not include these areas for coverage.

The report should detail the specifications for providing power to the APs. It is not uncommon for the survey engineer to discuss the proposed cabling runs with the site maintenance team (power and networking), including where and how they will attach to each system. A list of the system components, the network media type, and the network cabling methods recommended for connecting should also be documented.

Site Survey Report-Generation Programs

Some programs offer report generators to assist in developing the necessary documentation, including site map coverage plans and equipment lists. This is one of the unique features to the AirMagnet tool that was discussed in Chapter 10, "Using Site Surveying Tools." The AirMagnet SiteViewer site survey tool can provide coverage maps generated based on SSID, channel, AP coverage, and so on, as shown in Figure 13-4. The AirMagnet Reporter tool can generate reports in various formats, making it easy to import data into the site survey final report.

Figure 13-4 *AirMagnet SiteViewer Coverage Report*

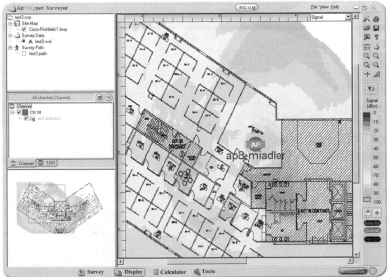

Other tools such as the Cisco Assisted Site Survey tool used with the *Wireless LAN Solution Engine* (WLSE) provide some graphical documentation on site coverage. If the site survey is completed using a tool such as WLSE, the final report should include a coverage map generated by this tool.

Regardless of which tool you use, a couple variations of the coverage diagrams can provide a great deal of assistance to anyone using the survey report when installing or maintaining a WLAN. Two variations are as follows:

- Coverage and signal strength for each AP at the minimum data rate
- Combined coverage with signal strength of all APs for the minimum data rate

Summary

The final site survey report should contain every detail needed to install the wireless portion of the WLAN. The more detailed this report, the easier the installation, and the more exact the installation will be based on the survey testing. This is the deliverable to the customer, and providing the most accurate and complete report should be the goal of any survey engineer.

If the customer discusses future expansions or WLAN client upgrades, that should be explained in the report, as well as any problems that the upgrades might pose.

It is highly recommended that the customer and survey engineer sign and maintain a copy of the report for their respective records. This provides a record of acceptance by the customer of the survey and its results.

This chapter covers the following topics:

- Understanding Bridge System Characteristics
- Understanding Bridge Topologies
- Using Common Applications Over Bridges
- Feasibility Study
- Interference Study
- Installing Bridges

CHAPTER 14

Outdoor Bridge Deployments

This chapter covers outdoor bridge deployments (both point-to-point and point-to-multipoint) and discusses various issues such as interference, survey techniques, installation, and troubleshooting tips. Wireless bridges are typically used to connect two networks (usually in different buildings) but can be used for a variety of purposes from mobile networks, such as on a ship or crane, to trains and police cars.

Understanding Bridge System Characteristics

Ranges for bridge systems vary as a result of frequency, transmitter power, and available antennas. Ranges of a couple miles or less cover the vast majority of bridge installations; however, longer ranges can be activated with appropriate selection of antennas, clear line of sight, and proper Fresnel zone clearance. (Refer to Chapter 2, "Understanding RF Fundamentals," for an introduction to Fresnel zones.) Note that typically only bridges, not *access points* (APs), have this extended range capability. The 802.11 specification was based on a presumption that a WLAN communication link (keeping in mind this is defining a local-area network) would be not more than 1000 feet. Therefore, distances for AP-to-client communication are limited to shorter distances for quality performance, irrespective of transmit power, cable, and antenna combinations. This is because timing restrictions in the 802.11 protocol, which synchronize the timing of the communications to support delays induced by the distance. Although most bridges might follow the 802.11 protocols, they do not strictly adhere to the timing parameters, or they have the ability to alter the timing (or distance) capability.

The data rate capabilities of bridges also vary. If a bridge follows one of the 802.11 specifications, the available data rates will be defined by the specifications, and throughput will be similar to a WLAN using the same technology. However, some bridges use proprietary modulation and, although they might be in the same frequency bands as 802.11 systems, they use proprietary channelization, which can enable higher throughput and data rates.

As discussed in Chapter 3, "Regulating the Use of 802.11 WLANs," you must adhere to various regulations when installing WLANs. The same is true for bridging. There are different *Effective Isotropic Radiated Power* (EIRP) limitations for different countries, as well as differences in available channels and even modulation schemes permitted. Review Chapter 3 for these regulations.

Understanding Bridge Topologies

Two types of bridge topology are normally deployed. A large number of the systems are point to point, connecting just two locations together. Figure 14-1 shows a typical bridge topology for point-to-point systems.

Figure 14-1 *Point-to-Point Bridge Topology*

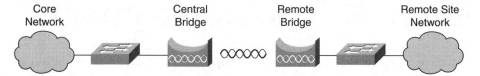

An increasing number of multipoint systems are being installed today. In most systems, one bridge is usually defined as the central, or master, bridge. This provides the central point of data flow from the remote sites. (See Figure 14-2.)

Figure 14-2 *Point-to-Multipoint Bridge Topology*

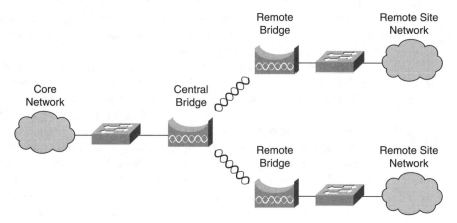

In some cases, the bridges might also act as an AP permitting individual wireless clients to associate to the bridge.

The number of possible remote sites is based on the vendor, but the actual limitation should be addressed by the overall bandwidth needed by each end user. The central or master bridge is the limiting point. In some cases, it is desirable to have multiple master bridges, operating on separate, nonoverlapping frequencies, as shown in Figure 14-3.

Figure 14-3 *Point-to-Multipoint Bridge Topology*

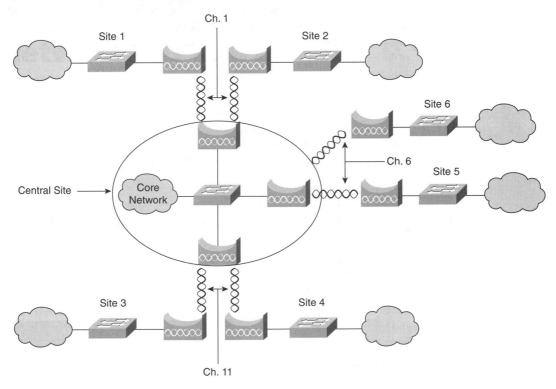

Most bridges operate on a Layer 2 level (MAC layer). If the networks that are being tied together are on different subnets, some type of router must be installed in at least one site to separate the segments and route traffic properly. Many installations use routers at every site, permitting not just segmentation, but also the use of *virtual private network* (VPN) tunnels over the RF links for a more secure system. This can also permit some types of traffic filtering to improve the throughput of the wireless link.

Using Common Applications over Bridges

In the service provider arena, bridges are often used to tie multiple companies back to a single point of presence. However, the traffic needs to be separated for security and privacy reasons. Here, you can use *virtual LANs* (VLANs).

Because bridges are also used to replace T1 lines, fiber links, or other hard-wired systems, they are expected to carry any and all of the same type of network traffic between sites. In many cases, this can include time-sensitive traffic, for which *quality-of-service* (QoS) implementations should be used to improve performance. Bridges are increasingly replacing certain types of leased lines, and one common application used in such scenarios is VoIP.

VLANs

A VLAN is a group of end stations with a common set of requirements, independent of their physical location. A VLAN has the same attributes as a physical LAN, but enables you to group end stations even if they are not located physically on the same subnet.

802.1Q VLAN support is provided to work in conjunction with the switch or router attached to the wireless bridge. Both the wired Ethernet and wireless radio interface should support VLAN trunking. Native Ethernet and 802.1Q tagging is supported on many of the available bridges today.

Thus, the bridge participates in the 802.1d Spanning Tree Protocol process of bridging two networks together. VLANs can be extended into a WLAN by adding IEEE 802.1Q tag awareness to the bridge. The basic wireless components of a VLAN consist of two or more bridges communicating using wireless technology. The bridge is physically connected through a trunk port to the network VLAN switch on which the VLAN is configured. The physical connection to the VLAN switch is through the bridge's Ethernet port.

Figure 14-4 shows a typical VLAN bridge topology.

Figure 14-4 *Bridge Topology Using VLANs*

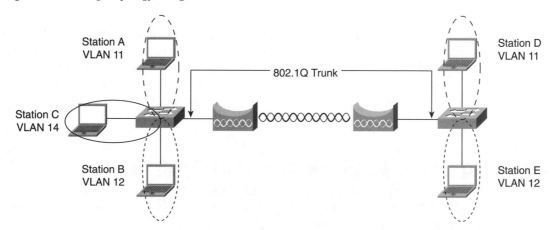

QoS

Implementing QoS in your wireless link makes applications run more predictably and bandwidth utilization more effective. By using QoS features, you can prioritize specific types of traffic instead of sending packets in a purely *first in, first out* (FIFO) manner. When subject to delays, voice and video traffic causes very unfavorable behavior in phone conversations (major lags or even dropped phone calls). The objectives of a QoS feature on a bridge would include providing 802.1p priority bits and 802.1Q VLAN tag-based QoS, and priority services for VoIP traffic, based upon IP TOS (*type of service* bits in the IP protocol header) / DSCP (differentiated services code point).

Many bridges can only classify traffic based on IP TOS precedence and DSCP values and put it into the correct priority queues. Devices that follow the 802.11e priority values have eight priority queues. The *class of service* (CoS) values associated with the eight priority queues are the same as in 802.1p.

User priority values are carried in an Ethernet frame, an 802.1Q priority tag, or an 802.1Q VLAN tag. The CoS value is used to select the appropriate 802.11 transmit queue.

A bridge can use the priority tag to calculate back-off times for each packet, enabling high-priority packets to have short back-off times, setting them up for transmission before lower-priority packets.

Voice over IP

When using QoS, you should prioritize voice traffic by defining a policy and assigning that policy to the VLAN carrying the voice traffic. Many bridges support QoS only in point-to-point links. Voice in a point-to-multipoint configuration gets a bit tricky, because over-the-air QoS coordination between endpoints is difficult if they cannot hear each other. In point-to-multipoint systems, it is typical that one remote site can hear the central site but cannot hear other remote sites, because of distance or even antenna type and direction. This is commonly referred to as a *hidden node*. A protocol called *Point Coordination Function* (PCF) enables the central site to control when each endpoint has access. Voice in point-to-multipoint networks is possible if PCF mode is implemented, but not many products support this today.

The typical number of voice lines for an 802.11a or 802.11g 54-Mbps bridge link operating in a point-to-point topology can vary based on the coding of voice traffic. For a typical 54-Mbps link, up to 15 calls can be handled when using G.711, and as many as 40 calls may be possible when using G.729 protocol. These numbers take into account some data traffic also running on the link. The number of voice lines has been calculated by using a maximum jitter of 25 ms.

Security

Security is a major part of any enterprise deployment, and as such the design should ensure the security of not only the wireless links as a whole but also the bridge itself. Multiple types of security levels are available in different bridges, including a variety of proprietary schemes, WEP, WPA, and 802.1x authentication schemes. One very common method is just to put a router behind each bridge that supports VPN tunneling, or to use a VPN hardware device behind each bridge (but be aware some VPN tunnels hide any 802.1Q tag). It is advisable to review some good security references before selecting the product to install.

Feasibility Study

This section explains what is required to determine whether a successful bridge link can be accomplished.

When determining the feasibility of a successful bridge link, you need to define how far the bridge link is expected to transit, at what frequency, and at what radio data rate. Very close bridge links (such as 1 mile or less) are fairly easy to achieve assuming there are no obstructions. This is referred to as a clear *line of sight* (LoS).

If both sites are very close, a link might be attained from a window by using one of the upper floors of the building, avoiding the need to install the bridge outdoors. This might work fine for a temporary event or in a pinch to get a link up when time or weather conditions do not allow for a more permanent solution. Keep in mind that some windows have metallic content for tinting or conductive gas for insulation to prevent fogging, and such materials might impede the radio signal, preventing a working link, even for short distances. Therefore, links through glass are not a preferred method, but could work for very short links.

In one real-world case, two bridges were used as a temporary link between two buildings. Because it was temporary, the bridges were placed in unused areas of the buildings, with the antennas located in the windows. The bridges had no problem achieving a connection through windows, but the network soon started to have troubles at a similar time each day. It turned out that the areas in which the bridges were located at this time of day, and the office inhabitants were closing the blinds (made of aluminum) each day to keep the sun's glare out.

When preparing for a bridge system, you need to consider several factors. LoS is a must for any outdoor bridge link of more than 100 feet or so. You must also consider two distance parameters: the Fresnel zone and the earth's curvature or bulge. These two factors impact you antenna height choices. Environmental condition such as rain, fog, and snow do not have a big effect on 2.4-GHz or 5 GHz-links.

Determining Line of Sight

Because radio waves used by 2.4-GHz and 5-GHz bridges are very high in frequency, the radio wavelength is relatively small. As a result, the radio waves do not travel nearly as far (given the same amount of power) as radio waves on lower frequencies. This fact also has an advantage: It makes the bridge ideal for unlicensed use because the radio waves do not travel far unless a high-gain antenna that can tightly focus the radio waves in a given direction is used, reducing interference possibilities. Remember from Chapter 2 that high-gain antennas focus radio waves, allowing them to go much farther, similar to adjusting the focus of a flashlight from a flood type light into a tight beam. This not only provides greater range, it provides a much smaller focus for both transmit and receive, reducing also the possibility of interference to other systems as well as from other systems. This in turn also means they are more critical to proper alignment.

The higher the frequency used, the more dependent a system becomes upon LoS. Therefore, longer distances (more than a couple hundred feet) using 2.4- or 5-GHz products require LoS for successful operation. It is also very difficult to acquire a good communication link when attempting to transmit 2.4- or 5-GHz Z radio waves through objects such as trees, foliage, hills, or other buildings because these objects can absorb or reflect radio signals away from the intended target. Distances greater than 6 miles (9.6 km) generally require radio towers or high locations to overcome the LoS obstruction caused by the curvature of the earth.

As frequency increases, so does signal loss through the atmosphere. This is known as *free-space loss* or just *path loss*. As the signal propagates from the antenna, its power level decreases at a rate that is inversely proportional to the distance and proportional to the wavelength of the signal. You can use this variable to determine the maximum distance a bridge link can go. You can find utilities available on the web that have been developed to assist in this calculation. One such utility is the Cisco Outdoor Bridge Range Calculation Utility available on the Cisco website.

Calculating Distances for Outdoor RF Links

You can calculate the theoretical maximum distance for an RF system in an outdoor environment before ever stepping outside the office by using the following equations:

Distance = (300 / Freq) * (Conversion from metric to miles) * EXP ((System gain –First wavelength loss –margin) / 6 * Natural log (2))

TO measure a wavelength in miles, the first part of the formula is used:

(300 / Frequency) * (39 / 12) * (1 / 5280).

Then the overall system performance based on antennas, cables, and radio capabilities is calculated:

System gain = Transmitter power + Antenna 1 gain – Cable 1 loss + Antenna 2 gain – Cable 2 loss + Receiver sensitivity

Make sure to add in any losses for other devices such as lightning arrestors or splitters.

The efficiency of an antenna to convert electrical energy to radiated energy is –22 dB:

Distance = (300 / 2442) * (39 / 12) * (1 / 5280) * EXP ((Ant / Radio parms –22 –10) / 6 * LN(2))

The system gain determines how much overall path loss is possible. It takes into account the gain of antennas at both ends of the RF link, the transmitter power and minimum receiver sensitivity, and any associated RF cables. Subtracting from this value, the efficiency of an antenna to convert signals into radiated signals (the –22 in the formula) provides the signal strength at a distance of one wavelength from the antenna. The –10 in the formula provides an extra 10 dB of margin (fade margin) in the event of environmental condition changes.

But the most useful item of this mathematical formula is that 6 * LN(2) provides the doubling of distance for every 6 dB. After a system is designed and working, you can make "rule of thumb" estimates. Every increase of 6 dB (higher antenna gain, shorter cables) will double the distance. With every decrease of 6 dB (loss such as cables or lower antenna gain), the range will be cut in half.

Consider, for example, a system designed to operate at 18 miles at a given data rate with given antennas. A change in length to the RF cables on each end, adding 3 dB more cable loss per end, results in a total change of 6 dB in the system gain parameter. This means that the overall range will drop to 9 miles (6 dB less).

If the antennas on each end of the link change from a 21-dBi antenna to a 13.5-dB antenna (7.5 dB change on each end, for an overall change of 15 dB), the range will drop to less than 4 miles. This is calculated by reducing the distance in half for the first 6-dB drop (9 miles) and in half again for the next 6-dB drop (4.5 miles). The remaining 3 dB will reduce the range a bit farther, for an estimation of 3.5 to 4 miles.

The same can be done for increasing antenna gain. If a system has a maximum range to 10 miles using two 13.5-dBi antennas, and one antenna is replaced with a 21-dBi antenna (increase of 7.5 dB), the range will double for the first 6 dB increase (20 miles) and a slight amount more for the next 1.5 dB. You could make an estimate of 22 miles or so.

This 6-dB/range-doubling estimation is only for outdoor ranges. Indoor ranges vary dramatically, but in many cases 9 dB can be substituted for a similar estimation.

Although you can use a *Global Positioning System* (GPS) and topographical maps to determine whether any hills or obstructions are in the way, it is always best to first visit the site and physically assess the site to determine whether the sites to be linked can be visually connected. An on-site assessment can answer many questions up front, but accessing the rooftop of the building or climbing a tower might be necessary to successfully perform this task.

When conducting a visual inspection, check whether the remote site is behind trees or other obstructions. This is where some simple logic can come into play. To determine whether you need a tower, you can just raise a small weather balloon (or any other type of balloon that you can raise the appropriate distance) at one site and look for the balloon from the other site. Even the low-cost helium foil balloons available at any party shop might work if the wind is minimal. You might need binoculars or a telescope to view the balloon for longer-distance links. You could use strobe lights if doing this task at night. Measuring the string used to float your "spotter balloon" would give you an idea about how high a radio tower or other structure would need to be to support your bridge antenna. Another method of spotting is to raise a bucket truck or vehicle with a telescoping mast.

If all the sites have visual connection from the central site, installing the links might be a simple matter of determining the distances and data rates desired. If the buildings do not have LoS directly between them, you might be able to install a radio tower or use a nearby radio tower or mast to get above the obstruction. Another possible approach is to find a location that both sites can see and install a bridge pair or repeater. As shown in Figure 14-5, you could use another building or structure, such as a water tower, for this purpose.

Figure 14-5 *Using a Remote Site for Connection*

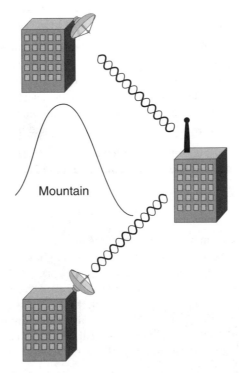

Mountain

One drawback with this type of solution is the reduction of throughput (50 percent) that occurs when using a single radio device as a repeater. An alternative design, as shown in Figure 14-6, uses two separate RF links on separate channels to reduce this throughput degradation.

Figure 14-6   *A Repeater Site with Full Bandwidth*

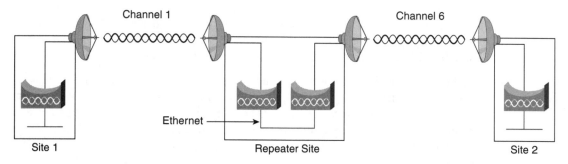

Environmental Issues

Now that you have learned about how free-space path loss and LoS can affect the distance of a bridge link, you need to examine a few other variables that can degrade a bridge link.

You might have heard that rain, snow, fog, and other high-humidity weather conditions can obstruct or affect the LoS, introducing a small loss (sometimes referred to as *rain fade* or *fade margin*). Generally, these weather conditions have minimal effect on RF links running at frequencies under 10 GHz. If you have established a good stable connection, such weather will almost never be an issue; however, if the link was poor to begin with, bad weather could degrade performance or cause loss of the link.

For this reason, most path-loss calculations should include some type of fade margin error. Usually 10 dB is sufficient for data networks running 2.4- or 5-GHz systems.

Fresnel Zone

A Fresnel zone is an imaginary ellipse around the visual LoS between the transmitter and receiver (see Figure 14-7). If radio waves (or even light waves) encounter an obstruction in the Fresnel area as the signal travels through free space to their intended target, it can be attenuated, sometimes severely. The best performance and range is attained when there is no obstruction of this Fresnel area. Although this is not always completely unavoidable, engineers should try to maintain a clear zone for 60 percent of the Fresnel area. Also keep in mind that a Fresnel zone is not only vertical, but actually surrounds the signal in a 360-degree zone. Fresnel zone clearance in all directions must be maintained.

Figure 14-7 *Fresnel Zone*

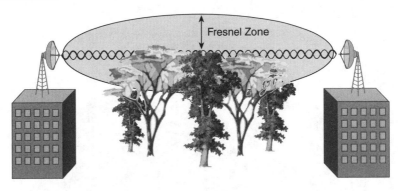

To improve a Fresnel zone impeded by an obstruction, it might be necessary to get above (or away from, if the obstruction is on the side of the LoS such as very tall building) the obstruction, which usually requires mounting the antenna higher. This might be a simple matter of mounting the antenna at another point on the building, such as an elevator room, or other structure higher on the building's roof. However, it might also mean adding a taller mounting structure.

It is possible to calculate the radius of the Fresnel zone (in feet) at any particular distance along the path using the following equation:

$$F1 = 72.6 * SQRoot (D / 4 * f \text{ in GHz})$$

In this equation, F1 = the first Fresnel zone radius (ft.), D = the total path length (mi.), and f = frequency (GHz).

Normally 60 percent of the first Fresnel zone clearance is all that is required for a good, stable link. As such, you can modify the preceding formula for 60-percent Fresnel zone clearance as follows:

$$0.6\,F1 = 43.3 * \sqrt{(D / 4 * f \text{ in GHz})}$$

Of course, it is much easier to forget the math and rely on several of the tools available via the Internet. Try doing a Google search for "Fresnel Zone calculation." Make sure you are using a Fresnel zone calculator that provides 60 percent clearances (otherwise the Fresnel value will be much larger). The Cisco Outdoor Bridge Range Calculation Utility mentioned previously provides this calculation.

One thing to remember is that these theoretical range calculations are based on the flat earth. As Christopher Columbus learned back in the year 1492, the earth is not flat. So the earth curvature (also known as the earth bulge) must be taken into account when planning for paths longer than approximately 7 miles. To calculate the approximate earth bulge, you can use the following formula:

$$H = D^2 / 6$$

Where D = distance in miles, and H = the earth bulge in feet.

Figure 14-8 *Earth Bulge*

Looking at Figure 14-9, you can see that at the midpoint, the LoS clearance needs to take into account the maximum earth bulge and the maximum Fresnel zone clearance (or 60 percent of it).

Figure 14-9 *Antenna Height Requirement*

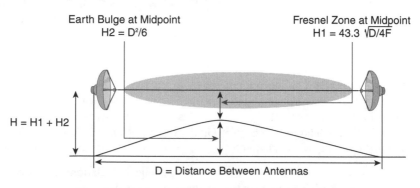

The required antenna height can add up quite quickly. As the distance between antennas increases, the overall required height increases as well. For example, two sites separated by 20 miles would have an earth bulge of approximately 70 feet, and the 60-percent Fresnel zone value would be approximately 63 feet. Adding these two values results in a required antenna height of around 133 feet. Keep in mind that is the height *above* any obstructions in the center of the path!

Determining the Possible Coverage Distance

Determining the maximum distance in a strictly point-to-point bridge link is fairly easy. As you can imagine, when linking only two sites your antenna choices become easier because you need to concentrate your radio signal only in one direction at the central bridge and vice versa.

When two or more remote sites are connected to the central site, the central bridge might require an antenna with a much larger field of view. Unlike a point-to-point link, the central site now has to transmit in more than one direction to establish a radio path with the other remote bridges. Directional antennas are not practical unless all remote sites are in the coverage pattern of a directional antenna. (If this is the case, the rules require the maximum EIRP to be less than 36-dBm EIRP. See Chapter 3 for point-to-multipoint system regulations.)

A site survey can flush out problems such as interference, Fresnel zone issues, or logistics problems that occur when installing a bridge system. A proper site survey should involve temporarily setting up a bridge link and taking some measurements to determine whether your antenna calculations proved accurate and that you have picked the right location and antenna before you spend a lot of time drilling holes, routing cables, and mounting equipment.

Before attempting a site survey, you should have already determined the following:

- How far is the bridge link?
- Is there clear line of sight?
- What is the minimum acceptable data rate at which the link will run?
- Is this point to point or point to multipoint?
- Are the proper antennas available for testing?
- Has a path-loss analysis been performed (or some calculation utility used to check figures)?
- Is there physical access to both of the bridge locations?
- Have the proper permits, if any, been obtained?
- Will there be two engineers available for this survey? (Never attempt to survey or perform work on a roof or tower alone.)
- Have the products been configured prior to any on-site visit?
- Are the proper tools and equipment available to complete the survey?

Interference Study

Although the unlicensed spectrum offers the benefit of no licensing fees, users pay a penalty in terms of interference. There are no restrictions on the types of devices that operate in these bands, provided that they all conform to a common set of rules. Although the 5-GHz band is less crowded than the 2.4-GHz band today, over time the 5-GHz band will likely become equally crowded with more and more interference-causing devices.

The *Industrial, Scientific, and Medical* (ISM) frequencies can contain emissions from microwave ovens, heaters, plywood laminators, medical diathermy, and other noncommunication devices. Although most of these types of devices usually pose no threats of interference to bridge links (because they are low-power, indoor devices), the engineer must be aware that the possibility exists of some industrial high-power system (such as a 10-kilowatt industrial oven next door) that wipes out any attempted communications use of that band. Equipment operating in this type of environment is subject to FCC rules and regulations as well.

Amateur radio operators are also licensed to use parts of the bands in which bridge products are designed to be used. Although not many amateurs use these bands, a few full-time (on the air continually) point-to-point amateur microwave links operate in this band.

There is also the possibility of interference from other data systems in the same bands. In any case, it is necessary to do an interference analysis using a spectrum analyzer to make sure you have an interference-free radio link.

Installing Bridges

Bridges typically fall into one of three general design categories: single-piece outdoor devices, single-piece indoor devices, or two-piece indoor/outdoor devices. Some systems have the entire bridge designed to withstand outdoor installations. This also permits the antenna to be attached directly to the bridge, reducing cable loss and increasing possible range. The downside to this type of device is that if the bridge happens to fail, it might mean climbing a tower or other structure for replacement, which is particularly difficult in bad weather.

The second bridge design is not intended to withstand weather, and must be mounted indoors, or at least in some type of controlled environment. This has the advantage of physical access to the bridge devices, as well as reduced cost (no need for weatherproof enclosures, temperature-stability circuits, and so on). However, in these cases, some type of RF coax cable is almost always required between the bridge and the antenna, increasing installation cost slightly and reducing overall path capabilities.

The third design style lies between these two. It splits the bridge into two devices. One is the indoor digital portion, referred to as the *indoor unit* (IDU). The radio section, or *outdoor unit* (ODU), gets mounted outdoors with the antenna. Actually, this type of device has the advantages of the outdoor units for range, but keeps at least part of the system (usually the CPU and digital components) indoors. However, this approach is typically the most expensive, and in many cases requires special cabling between the IDU and ODU.

It is a good idea to configure the bridges and verify RF connectivity before installing them. By doing so, you can document any potential configuration problems you might encounter. In addition, you might save time by knowing the devices can link and are configured and working correctly before going on site.

At the survey of the site where the bridges will be mounted, address the following issues:

- Is the mounting location structurally sound, and will it hold the weight of the bridge? (Some of the outdoor units can be heavy.)
- If the mounting location is on a rooftop, will the roof itself not affect the Fresnel zone? (Moving the devices closer to the edge of the building might assist in this effort.)
- Is there a good source of electrical or earth ground available (for grounding the antenna structure)?
- Is there access to route the cables inside the building or will holes need to be drilled?
- Will additional resources, such as a bucket truck or the services of others (some sites require union workers or the use of licensed electricians) be required?
- If a tower is used, will it handle the extra wind load and weight of the bridge and/or antennas? (When using a tower, it is recommended to use a professional installer to climb the tower.) Will the mounting structure be strong enough to prevent movement or oscillation in the wind?
- Is there a source of electrical power (assuming power is needed) for power tools such as drills test equipment, or for the bridge (if required)?

Are there other RF systems in the same vicinity? Some systems can be licensed to run very high power, and close proximity to such might be hazardous. Verify with the site owner as to other systems located at the site. When in doubt, employ or seek assistance from a professional installer.

Lightning Protection

Lightning is caused by the buildup of electrical potential between cloud and ground, between clouds, or between clouds and the surrounding air. During thunderstorms, static electricity builds up within the clouds. A positive charge builds in the upper part of the cloud, while a large negative charge builds in the lower portion. When the difference between the positive and negative charges becomes large enough, the electrical charge jumps from one area to another, creating a lightning bolt. Most lightning bolts actually occur from one cloud to another, but the difference of potential can also occur between a cloud and the earth, or items that are located on the earth.

One step in preventing lightning strikes is to prevent static energy from building up on the antennas and supporting structures. Metallic objects that are not grounded can build up electrical charges and attract lightning strikes. Providing a good ground path will assist in bleeding off this energy.

However, most damage to equipment does not come from direct lightning strikes, but rather from nearby strikes. As a lightning strike occurs, a very large current moves from one location to another. This current can cause electrical energy to be coupled (inductive coupling) into nearby conductors (such as coax cable, electrical wires, and antennas). This inductive coupling can be great enough to cause severe damage to any device on the attached cables (see Figure 14-10).

Figure 14-10 *Induced Energy*

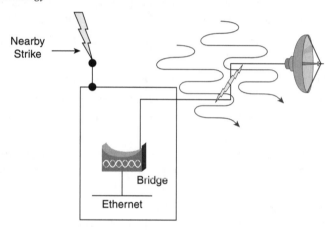

The first step in protecting against potential lightning damage is to ground all mounting structures and devices. Second, ground all cables through appropriate means. If using coaxial cable, place a lightning arrestor near the cable entrance to the building, or between the building entrance and the bridge itself. Placing the arrestor at the antenna does not provide protection to the cable on the bridge side of the arrestor (see Figure 14-11).

Figure 14-11 *Proper Lightning-Arrestor Placement*

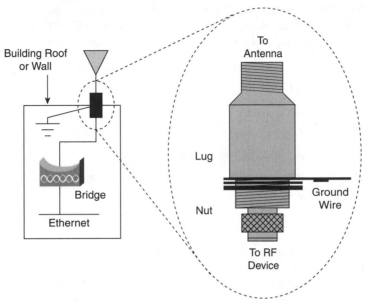

For outdoor devices, the manufacturer usually provides some type of grounding block. The Cisco BR1400 recommends grounding in a manner shown in Figure 14-12.

Figure 14-12 *Outdoor Device Grounding Example*

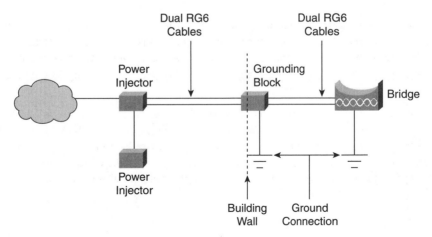

For the most effective grounding, use a heavy-gauge wire and keep ground wire as short as possible. The use of a good ground lessens the chance of damage because of a nearby strike and/or helps to bleed off any static charges that might build up on the cable. The National Electrical Code handbook recommends a #6 copper wire for grounding.

Suitable grounds include (but are not limited to) the following:

- Ground rod buried into the earth
- Electrical panel ground
- Building structural steel such as I beams (providing the building has a good ground)
- Professional grounding systems that may already be installed
- Metal air-conditioner units (attached to the building), provided they are grounded
- Metal radio tower (assuming the tower is grounded)

NOTE   Some towers, especially AM radio towers, are not grounded because the tower is actually isolated from ground and is used as the antenna itself. This is known as a *hot tower*, and you must isolate the bridge and all grounds from this type of tower.

If you are working in an older building, sometimes you can use a cold water pipe (if metallic, and not plastic) for a ground connection. Make certain the water system has the proper bypassing on meters, hot-water tanks, and so on, in accordance with the local electrical codes.

There is no known or guaranteed protection from a direct lightning strike. A direct hit will almost always damage the device. This can also cause repercussions to the network itself. Because the bridge is usually attached to a switch or router on the network, it is possible for the energy surge to move through the bridge (usually causing catastrophic failure) and affect the switch or router.

One way to protect the network is to use a length of fiber-optic cable to isolate, from a DC voltage point of view, the network and the bridge (see Figure 14-13). Because fiber is a glass material, it does not conduct electricity and would stop any surge from reaching the network. If you use two Ethernet-to-fiber converters, make certain the converters are powered from different AC circuits to prevent the electrical surges from following that path.

Figure 14-13 *Using Fiber-Optic Cable for Protection*

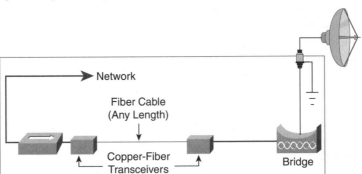

Indoor Testing Before Installation: Understanding Maximum Operational Receive Level

When performing testing in a lab or indoor environment and the bridge antennas happen to be located in close proximity, you could encounter throughput issues because of receiver overload. When performing an indoor test, it is recommended that when possible to set the RF devices to operate at their lowest power setting and use the lowest-gain antenna possible. Physical separation of the antennas is also required.

WARNING   Under no circumstance should two RF devices be directly connected from antenna port to antenna port without the use of a proper attenuator. Should it be required to connect directly (because of interference or some other issue), keep in mind that the maximum survivable receive level is typically 0 dBm or less for most receivers. Exceeding a product's limit can cause damage to the receiver. A maximum receiver level of –50 dBm is a very good level for most systems when performing configuration and lab testing. To determine the suitable attenuation, just take the transmitter power and subtract –50 from it. If the transmitter is +20 dBm, you would need 70 dB of attenuation (+20 minus –50 equals 70.)

To determine how much attenuation is needed when using antennas in lab testing, just add the transmitter power to the antenna gain and then add the gain of the other receiving antenna. This assumes the antennas are focused at each other. Suppose, for example, the transmitter is set to +20 dBm. The antenna on the transmitter is 13.5 dBi, and the antenna on the other bridge is 21 dBi. This provides a total of 54.5 dBm maximum possible power (20 + 13.5 + 21 = 54.5). To obtain a –50-dBm signal level at the receiver, approximately 100 dB of attenuation (54.5 dB – [–50] = 104.5) is required.

The conversion from electrical to radiated energy for an antenna provides approximately a 22-dB loss, when measured at the first wavelength from the antenna. As explained in the "Calculating Distances for Outdoor RF Links" sidebar earlier in this chapter, for every doubling of this distance an extra 6 dB of loss occurs. Using this, you could calculate the minimum distance you need to provide the necessary attenuation. That means that a distance of between 64 and 128 wavelengths would be required. Because the wavelength of a 2.4-GHz signal is approximately 4.7 inches and at 5.8 GHz a wavelength is approximately 1.9 inches, this would result in distances of 50 and 20 feet respectively for 128 wavelengths. Of course, this might not be practical in a lab, based on the size of the facility. Therefore, adding in attenuation via RF attenuators between the radio and antenna might be necessary.

Aligning the Antenna

When first setting up the system, align the antennas first, using known direction and LoS. A compass and GPS is an ideal way to start here. Most systems offer some type of *receive signal strength indication* (RSSI) measurements for antenna alignment. Using these utilities, make very minor adjustments until the RSSI peaks. Some systems have a slight delay in reporting the RSSI, so make minor adjustments slowly.

Weatherproofing the Connectors

After you have aligned the antennas and configured everything physically, it is time to weatherproof the connectors. Failure to weatherproof the coaxial cables and antenna connectors can result in failure over time because of corrosion or water ingress. Weatherproofing your connectors on the nice warm day you install the bridge can prevent the need to troubleshoot the link in the dead of winter.

Use a good electrical joint compound on the connector threads and grounding points because it serves as a water repellent and anti-seizing thread lubricant. Teflon or silicon grease is a suitable compound.

For sealing, one of the most common, inexpensive products is called Coax-Seal, a form of moldable plastic from Universal Electronics (http://www.universal-radio.com/catalog/cable/1194.html). To completely cover the connectors, wrap in a spiral direction up the connector (opposite of the way the water would flow).

Many installers use a layer of high-quality electrical tape, such 3M Scotch Super 88 or 88T PVC electrical tape, to weatherproof the connectors. The 88T PVC electrical tape has a better temperature range. A thin layer of electrical tape followed by Coax-Seal and then another layer of tape is sometimes used so that the weatherproofing can be undone easily using a simple utility knife.

Avoid using poor-quality electrical tape or other forms of weatherproofing such as rubber silicones, RTV, or liquid rubber-type spray-on coatings. These types of sealants can contain acetone or other chemicals that can eat the rubbers or gaskets found in some connectors, or cause connector corrosion. These types of products might also break down in ultraviolet light (sunlight), destroying the sealing properties. If you need to use something like this for whatever reason, always cover it with a good-quality electrical tape first.

If the connection will be underground, use tape layers and Coax-Seal and then apply a rubber coating such as Plastic Dip spray-on or dip coating over the final tape layers.

One word of warning: If an RF cable has suffered water intrusion into the connector, it is very likely the water has found its way into the cable itself. The braid and shield of coax can act like a wick and pull water far up into the cable itself. This changes the velocity factor of the cable, affecting the cable impedance. This in turn will increase losses in the cable. If there has been water intrusion, you should replace the entire length of cable.

Parallel Bridge Links for Increased Throughput

In some installations, you might want to install two parallel bridge wireless links between two buildings to increase the throughput.

Systems such as this require that the links operate on nonadjacent, nonoverlapping RF channels. This "stacking" of bridges can provide higher bandwidth, redundancy, and load balancing. This is possible, but minimum physical separation criteria must be followed when installing the antennas so that mutual interference between the systems does not influence performance. (See the sidebar "Receiver Desensitization" in Chapter 5, "Selecting the WLAN Architecture and Hardware").

Figure 14-14 shows a conceptual diagram.

Figure 14-14 *Parallel Links for Increased Throughput*

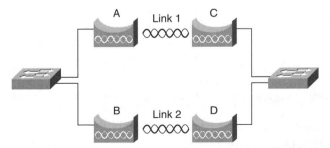

Sufficient isolation must exist between redundant links, and you can create such by physically separating the antennas. When using 802.11a or 8902.11g products, this is even more important because of the large amount of energy in the OFDM sideband. Another way to add isolation is to change antenna polarization, which can add up to 20 dB more isolation. You can use an RSSI reading to verify isolation.

Also note that the bridge needs to work in an integrated system environment, wherein the attached switches or routers use aggregation protocols such as *Fast EtherChannel* (FEC) and *Port Aggregation Protocol* (PagP). FEC and PagP are used to provide up to 100 Mbps of combined bandwidth. In particular, if the bridges provide 802.1d spanning tree, one link might be shut down if the switched network is not correctly designed and configured.

Summary

Outdoor links are increasing in popularity and are being installed in ever-increasing numbers. Proper site selection, site surveys, configuration, and installation are key to ensuring a successful bridge deployment, to provide a system robust to interference, and to keep interference potential with others minimal. Failure to take into account issues such as LoS, Fresnel zone, or path loss can cause a system to run poorly or not at all.

If logic is followed and details are defined, a successful bridge system can provide a communication link superior to most hard-wired systems available today, at a fraction of the cost.

Appendixes

Appendix A   WLAN Product References

Appendix B   Antenna Radiation Patterns

Appendix C   Alternative Antennas

Appendix D   Sample Forms

WLAN Product References

There are many WLAN manufacturers and thousands of different WLAN products. This appendix identifies several of the more popular manufacturers, listing company information, product style, and target markets. This first section lists many of the common corporate and enterprise WLAN vendors, followed by some of the most common *small office/home office* (SOHO) product vendors.

WLAN Equipment: Enterprise Class

Wireless equipment intended for the corporate and enterprise markets have certain features and functions sought after by the IT staff of most corporations—things such as 802.1x authentication, *Wi-Fi Protected Access* (WPA) certification, VLAN capability, *Power over Ethernet* (PoE) and external antennas to name a few.

Airespace Networks

Founded in 2002 and originally known as Blackstorm Networks, Airespace Networks is headquartered in San Jose, California. The Airespace Wireless Enterprise Platform provides advanced RF management capabilities, comprehensive end-to-end security, and mobility. It supports both switched wireless and controller/appliance-based approaches. The product line includes wireless switches, security appliances, and *access point* (AP) hardware. Airespace products started shipping to the WLAN market in 2003.

For more information, visit http://www.bstormnetworks.com/.

Aruba Wireless Networks

Founded in late 2001, Aruba Wireless Networks, like so many networking companies, is also headquartered San Jose, California.

The Aruba Wireless Networks product line is based around its wireless switch products, with several switches for various applications, as well as a line of limited-feature APs. The Aruba product line started shipping in mid-2003.

For more information, visit http://www.arubanetworks.com/.

Cisco Systems

A well-known name in networking, Cisco moved into the WLAN market in 2000 with the acquisition of Aironet Wireless Communications. Aironet was founded in 1994, from a company with roots back to 1986 founded as Telesystems SWL, making this one of the oldest companies in commercial spread-spectrum communications.

The Cisco Aironet product line includes APs, clients, management and WLAN switching hardware, and wireless bridging products. Aironet products started shipping wireless products in 1988 under the previous company name of Telesystems SWL.

For more information on Cisco Aironet products, visit http://www.cisco.com and search for Aironet.

Enterasys

As a well-known networking company, Enterasys entered the WLAN industry by working with an *original equipment manufacturer* (OEM) vendor for WLAN hardware and adding features to the existing firmware and software. The Enterasys hardware line includes intelligent AP and client hardware, and management software.

For more information, visit http://www.enterasys.com/home.html.

Extreme Networks

Extreme Networks was founded in 1996, and is headquartered in Santa Clara, California. The primary target market for Extreme has been enterprise Ethernet switches. In 2003, Extreme introduced a line of WLAN gear, consisting of Ethernet switches for controlling their feature-limited (or sometimes called dumb) APs.

For more information, visit http://www.extremenetworks.com/.

Foundry Networks

Founded in 1996 in San Jose, California, Foundry Networks entered the networking business with Ethernet switch products. The same founders also previously started Centillion Networks (acquired by Bay N/W).

The Foundry WLAN products provide RF management capabilities, security, and mobility. Foundry supports both switched wireless and appliance-based approaches. The product line includes wireless switches, security appliances, and limited-feature AP hardware. Foundry WLAN products started shipping into the WLAN market in 2003.

For more information, visit http://www.foundrynetworks.com/.

Nortel Networks

Headquartered in Brampton, Ontario, Canada, Nortel Networks is one of the well-known networking companies providing all types of wired network gear from routers and switches to packet, optical, wireless, and voice technologies.

Nortel moved into the WLAN market several years ago, and has recently also signed a WLAN compatibility partnership agreement with Symbol Technologies.

The Nortel WLAN solution includes intelligent APs as well as switches that provide management and support of the APs.

For more information on Nortel Networks, visit http://www.nortelnetworks.com/index.html.

Proxim Corporation

One of the older companies in the WLAN market, Proxim, Inc. was founded in 1984 to develop spread-spectrum wireless technologies for military applications. Proxim entered the commercial market in 1989. The present Proxim Corporation was created by the merger between Proxim, Inc. and Western Multiplex Corporation in March 2002. Western Multiplex was founded in 1979, and has traditionally designed and manufactured point-to-point and point-to-multipoint licensed and unlicensed products for outdoor bridging applications. When Western Multiplex Corporation and Proxim, Inc. completed their merger of equals, the combined company took the name Proxim Corporation.

Very shortly after the Western Multiplex merger, Proxim Corporation completed the acquisition of Agere Systems' WLAN equipment business, adding the ORiNOCO product line in August 2002.

Proxim was the first to market an Ethernet controller-based (switched) wireless product with its Harmony product line using limited-feature APs and a centralized controller. With the addition of the ORiNOCO product line they also support the intelligent AP solutions as well as client and bridging products.

For more information, visit http://www.proxim.com/.

Symbol Technologies

Symbol Technologies started as a bar-code scanner manufacturer. With their acquisition of MSI Data Corporation in the late 1980s, Symbol Technologies moved into the bar-code terminal market. As wireless products were developed in the data-acquisition market, Symbol Technologies developed its own radio group and manufactured WLAN products geared for the retail and other bar-code markets.

In recent years, Symbol has moved from its traditional vertical markets such as retail, warehousing, and manufacturing, and has released new products geared for the more horizontal markets such as small and medium corporate offices, enterprise campus offices, and education facilities. Symbol provides intelligent APs and limited-feature APs, wireless switches, and client and wireless bar-code scanners.

For more information, visit http://www.symbol.com/.

3Com Corporation

3Com Corporation was founded in 1979 in the San Francisco Bay area by Bob Metcalfe, the principal inventor of the Ethernet technology, and primarily marketed wired network components from *network interface cards* (NICs) to routers and switches.

3Com moved from the traditional wired networking product market into the WLAN market initially by entering into an OEM partnership with Symbol Technologies and reselling Symbol's intelligent access point products. In 2002, 3Com released another generation of wireless products, no longer based on the Symbol radio technology. These new devices had limited security and options.

3Com offers APs and various client devices for both the enterprise and SOHO markets.

For more information on 3Com, visit http://www.3com.com.

Trapeze Networks

Trapeze Networks, located in Pleasanton, California, was founded in March 2002. Trapeze Networks is strictly a WLAN company, with the entire product line based on WLAN solutions. Its product line includes the wireless mobility switch, limited-feature APs, and management software.

For more information on Trapeze, visit http://www.trapezenetworks.com/HomePage.html.

WLAN Equipment: SOHO and Personal Use

Many wireless products have been designed with the home office or small office in mind. Features and versatility required for enterprise and large corporate use are typically missing. Even the Wi-Fi Alliance has started distinguishing between such devices with labeling of WPA certification that differs between intended products usage. WPA-Personal depicts a product intended for SOHO usage, and WPA-Enterprise indicates products intended for usage in large corporate networks. This section describes some of the more popular products that historically have been geared for the SOHO market.

Buffalo

Founded in 2000, Buffalo Technology (USA), Inc. is a subsidiary of Buffalo, Inc. (JAPAN). The company's mandate since inception has been to support an easy-to-use computer network, and most recently, to make the Internet easier to use.

Buffalo offers a few wired products (four- and eight-port switches) appropriate for the home or small-office market. Buffalo also offers WLAN products, including APs, client devices, and wireless bridges. As with its wired products, the features and capabilities of the Buffalo WLAN products are a bit limited for use in medium-size business and enterprise networks. The WLAN products, however, support numerous features that are attractive to home and small office users.

For more information, visit http://www.buffalotech.com/wireless/index.php.

D-Link

D-Link manufactures many different products, from silicon chips for Ethernet and WLAN technology to switching, routing, and WLAN network devices. D-Link entered the market in 1998, and offered its first wireless devices in 2000 (a home 802.11b wireless system). D-Link makes very good WLAN products for the home networking environment, but for corporate and enterprise environments the WLAN line leaves out many desired features, such as dynamic security and enterprise-class features.

For more information, visit http://www.dlink.com/.

Linksys

Linksys, founded in 1988, developed and marketed networking products that were an affordable commodity, enabling anyone to share documents, files, and e-mail. Over the past 14 years, Linksys has become the market leader in sales of wireless, routers, network cards, and USB adapters to the home user through retail and e-commerce channels. In 2003, Linksys was acquired by Cisco Systems, but remains a totally separate business unit. The Linksys products and Cisco Aironet products are marketed, sold, and supported as totally different product lines. The Cisco Aironet product line is geared for the corporate and enterprise market, whereas the Linksys products are targeted toward the home user.

Linksys provides various wired and wireless devices. For the home WLAN user, it provides residential gateways, APs with embedded switches, and numerous client devices.

For more on Linksys, visit http://www.linksys.com/.

SMC Networks

As a highly recognized name for networking products over the past 30 years, SMC Networks has been best known for its standards-based connectivity products, including Ethernet NICs, hubs, and switches. With the wireless revolution, the movement into the WLAN market was a natural progression.

SMC offers a variety of WLAN products, including APs, client devices, and home gateways. The SMC product line supports features desired by home users, but lacks many of the features sought after by enterprise and corporate IT engineers.

For more information on SMC, visit http://www.smc.com/.

WLAN Accessory Vendors

Several other key products tie directly into WLAN networks. Such products include PoE devices, antennas, cables, and other accessories. This section provides just a sampling of some of these product offerings.

PowerDsine

PowerDsine leads the fast-growing PoE technology that allows power to be transmitted over the same network cable as data. PowerDsine has spearheaded the development of the PoE market from its inception.

The company first developed its PoE technology in 1998, and has subsequently delivered its solutions through communications companies such as Avaya, 3Com, Nortel, Siemens, and Ericsson, and has even marketed its own midspan solutions.

Founded in 1994, PowerDsine is headquartered in Israel, along with its research and development facilities, and has offices in Farmingdale, New York. The company was the driving force behind the IEEE 802.3af standard for sending data over Ethernet cabling.

For more information on PowerDsine, visit http://www.powerdsine.com/.

Times Microwave Systems

Times Microwave Systems (TMS), a division of Smiths Interconnect, was founded in 1948 as the Times Wire and Cable Company. TMS is an engineering-oriented organization specializing in the design and manufacture of high-performance flexible and semirigid coaxial cable, connectors, and cable assemblies for RF transmission from HF through microwave frequencies.

Although many cable companies manufacture RF cabling, TMS is one company that not only sells various cables, but also handles many of the hard-to-find connectors (as well as all other cabling accessories).

For more information on TMS, visit http://www.timesmicrowave.com/; in particular, refer to http://www.timesmicrowave.com/telecom/connectors/selection/ for connector information, including availability of the reverse-polarity connectors (such as the RP-N, RP-TNC, and RP-SMA).

TerraWave Solutions

TerraWave Solutions, a sister company to GigaWave Technologies (a training company specializing in wireless networking technologies), was founded in 2000, and distributes WLAN infrastructure and accessory products. Included in its product line are WLAN "standard" accessories such as site survey tools, various antennas, and cabling solutions for many of the unusual needs in corporate and enterprise environments. In addition, the product line includes AP enclosures for outdoor and harsh environments, unique AP and antenna mountings fixtures, and even lightning-protection products.

For more information on TerraWave Solutions, visit http://www.terra-wave.com/.

Antenna Radiation Patterns

This appendix contains many of the common WLAN antennas that are used in the industry today. Several companies produce antennas that are widely used by the various WLAN product vendors. Some *original equipment manufacturer* (OEM) antennas might have different company logos put on them, as well as proprietary antenna connectors.

Each antenna in this appendix is supplied with a polar plot chart, showing the radiation patterns, as well as physical specifications. Because physics convey how antennas radiate, antennas of similar style (omni, patch, and so on) and similar gain, from different vendors, will usually have similar attributes to those depicted here.

For those of you who are not familiar with a polar plot, they are very simple to use. As discussed in Chapter 2, "Understanding RF Fundamentals," linear antennas have two radiation planes, referred to as the *horizontal* and *vertical* planes. Omnidirectional antennas, which radiate in a full circle around them, have a 360-degree beam width in the horizontal plane (when installed properly). In many cases, an omni antenna will not include a horizontal plot if the radiation pattern is uniform in its horizontal plane for the full 360-degree plane.

Another specification that is sometimes listed in directional antennas is the front-to-back or front-to-side ratio. This is a ratio, measured in decibels, of the maximum signal level in the main lobe, compared to the maximum signal level either at 180 degrees (front to back) from the primary energy lobe, or at 90 degrees (front to side) from the primary lobe.

The antenna depicted in Figure B-1 and Figure B-2 is known as a Yagi antenna. A *Yagi antenna* is a unidirectional antenna commonly used in communications when a frequency is above 10 MHz, and consists of two or more straight elements, each measuring approximately $1/2$ electrical wavelength. The Yagi in Figure B-2 has a beam width of 25 degrees horizontal and 30 degrees vertical. When describing a beam width, the edges of the main beam are identified as the points where the energy is 3 dB below (Points A and B) the peak energy point (Point C).

Figure B-1 *Horizontal Polar Plot*

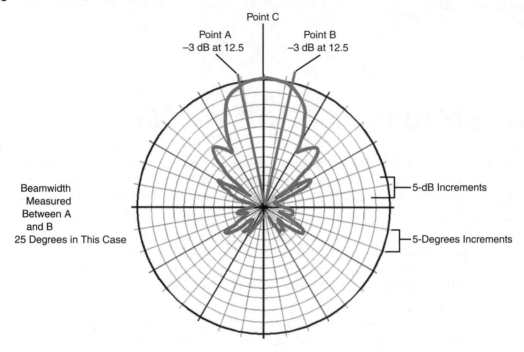

Figure B-2 *Vertical Polar Plot*

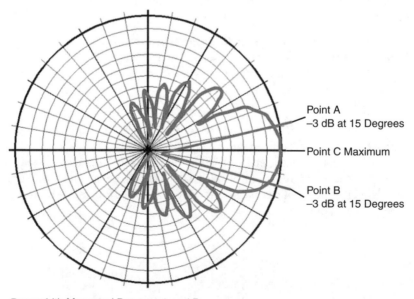

Dipole Antennas

Dipole antennas are, by far, the most common antennas used for *access points* (APs). Many vendors manufacture them, and they come in various form factors. Some are hinged so that they can be positioned straight or at right angles, whereas others are rigid with no adjustments at all. At 2.4 GHz, a dipole antenna will vary from 2.5 inches to as much at 6 inches, depending on manufacturing methods. A dipole antenna exhibits a gain of 2.14 dBi, but many vendors actually round up to 2.2 dBi. (As explained in Chapter 2, dBi is a reference of gain in dB, when compared to an isotropic antenna.) Typically, they are attached directly to the AP, but in some cases they might come with a weighted (or even magnetic) base and a short cable.

Table B-1 lists the specifications of a typical dipole antenna. The frequency range defines the maximum and minimum frequencies that the antenna was designed to operate at, and the *voltage standing wave ratio* (VSWR) indicates the maximum reflected power over the frequency range. The polarization of the antenna is important for proper installation, and therefore it is a requirement of any specification sheet. The Azimuth and Elevation ratings define the *beam width* (BW), or radiation-pattern angle, that is contained between the two points where the radiated power is reduced by 3 dB, when compared to the peak power point. See Chapter 2 for a detailed description of these parameters.

Table B-1   *Typical Specifications for a Dipole*

Parameter	Specification
Frequency range	2.4–2.483 GHz
VSWR	2:1
Gain	2.14 dBi
Polarization	Linear
Azimuth (3-dB BW)	Omnidirectional
Elevation (3-dB BW)	80 degrees

Figure B-3 illustrates a typical 2.4-GHz dipole antenna along with the vertical radiation pattern (polar plot). As with most omnidirectional antennas, the horizontal radiation pattern is assumed to be a 360-degree coverage pattern with only minor variations around the complete circle pattern.

Figure B-3   *Dipole Antenna Examples*

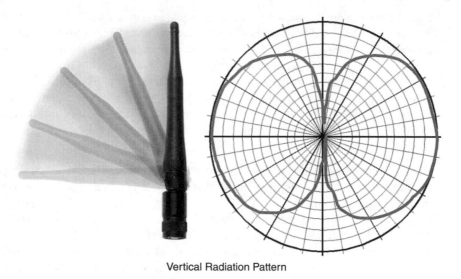

Vertical Radiation Pattern

Ceiling-Mount Antennas

One of the most common indoor mounting locations for an antenna is the drop-ceiling support grids. The AP can be located above the ceiling tiles, and the antenna placed below the ceiling (providing the AP has the proper ratings, as explained in Chapter 12, "Installing WLAN Products"). The most common such antennas are omnidirectional, with fairly low gain ranging from 2 dBi to about 5.2 dBi.

2-dBi Diversity Ceiling-Mount Antennas

An antenna that provides good coverage in offices and locations with fairly low ceilings, and yet has an excellent "stealth" capability, is a low-gain, low-profile ceiling-mount diversity antenna. Sometimes called a *squint antenna*, this blends into the ceiling very well. The antenna shown in Figure B-4 is manufactured by Cushcraft Corporation. When using antennas that mount to the ceiling grids, verify that the antenna mounting and the ceiling tiles are compatible. In some cases, the ceiling tile itself might extend down below the grid, causing interference for the antenna mounting.

Figure B-4   *Low-Profile, Ceiling-Mount Antenna*

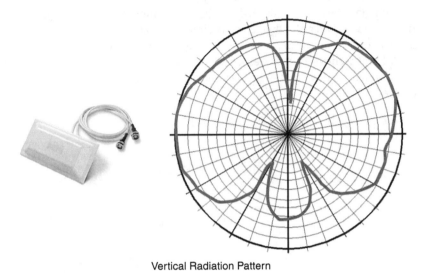

Vertical Radiation Pattern

Table B-2 lists the specifications for the Cushcraft 2-dBi squint antenna.

Table B-2   *Typical Specifications for a Squint Antenna*

Parameter	Specification
Frequency range	2.4–2.5 GHz
VSWR	1.7:1
Power	5 watts
Gain	2 dBi
Polarization	Vertical linear
Azimuth (3-dB BW)	Omnidirectional
Elevation (3-dB BW)	80 degrees
Dimensions	5.3" * 2.8" * 0.9"
Mounting	Drop-Ceiling Cross-Member Mount

5.2-dBi Omnidirectional Ceiling-Mount Antenna

The antenna shown in Figure B-5 is a 5.2-dBi ceiling-mount from Cushcraft Corporation. It is provided with a clip that attaches directly to the drop-ceiling support grids, and hangs down about 9 inches. This antenna is not a good selection for low ceilings because it invites meddling by curious fingers, especially in public areas. For higher ceilings such as retail environments, however, it is an economical antenna, providing 3 dB of gain over a standard dipole.

Figure B-5   *5.2-dBi Ceiling-Mount Antenna*

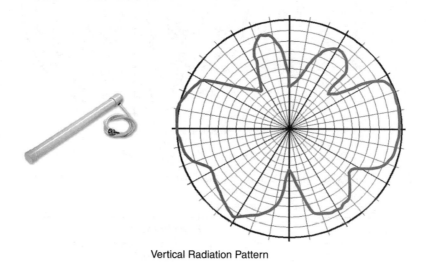

Vertical Radiation Pattern

Table B-3 lists the specifications for the Cushcraft 5.2-dBi ceiling-mount omni antenna.

Table B-3   *Typical Specifications for a Ceiling-Mount 5-dBi Antenna*

Parameter	Specification
Frequency range	2.4–2.83 GHz
VSWR	2:1, 1.5:1 nominal
Gain	5.2 dBi
Polarization	Vertical
Azimuth (3-dB BW)	Omnidirectional 360 degrees
Elevation (3-dB BW)	50 degrees
Dimensions	9" * 1.25"
Mounting	Drop-ceiling cross member (indoor only)

Mast-Mount Antennas

Mast mount antennas come in many different styles, gains, and mounting capabilities. A mast-mount antenna can be used either indoors or outdoors. Be aware, however, that hanging a mast-mount antenna from a ceiling upside down might not work as well as desired if the antenna is designed with some "down tilt" to the radiation pattern. (For more on downtilt, see Chapter 2.) Antennas used indoors typically have gains of 7 dBi or less. Gains higher than that tend to have shadows of dead spots directly under the antenna.

For short-range outdoor and some indoor applications, a 5.2-dBi antenna works very well. The antenna pictured in Figure B-6 is manufactured by Cushcraft Corporation and mounts to a mast using two band clamps (also called *worm clamps*).

Figure B-6   *5.2-dBi Mast-Mount Antenna*

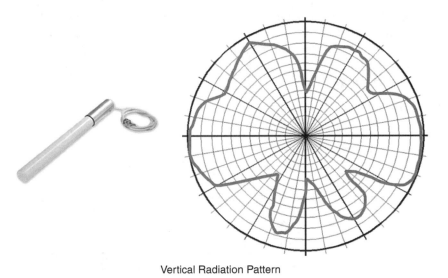

Vertical Radiation Pattern

Table B-4 lists the specifications for a typical 5.2-dBi mast-mountable omni antenna.

Table B-4   *Typical Specifications for a Mast-Mount 5.2-dBi Antenna*

Parameter	Specification
Frequency range	2.4–2.83 GHz
VSWR	2:1, 1.5:1 nominal
Gain	5.2 dBi
Polarization	Vertical

continues

Table B-4   *Typical Specifications for a Mast-Mount 5.2-dBi Antenna (Continued)*

Parameter	Specification
Azimuth (3-dB BW)	Omnidirectional 360 degrees
Elevation (3-dB BW)	50 degrees
Dimensions	13.5" * 1.25"
Mounting	Mast mount (indoor/outdoor)

Pillar- or Wall-Mount Omni Antennas

Designed with the retail market in mind, the pillar-mount antenna pictured in Figure B-7 comes from Telex Communications. It was designed to be mounted to a building-structure pillar or to an inner-building wall. It also works well when placed on an outside corner of two walls. It has a fabric covering over it, allowing it to blend into the surrounding environment extremely well. This antenna supports diversity and is provided with dual-feed cables for the AP.

Figure B-7   *5.2-dBi Pillar-Mount Antenna*

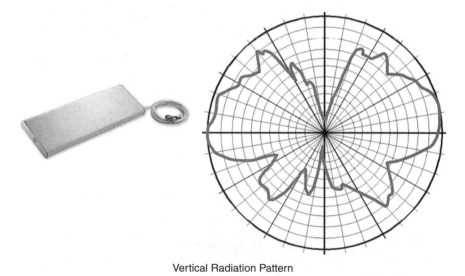

Vertical Radiation Pattern

The specifications listed in Table B-5 for the pillar-mount antenna are similar to most typical 5.2-dBi antennas.

Table B-5   *Specifications for a 5.2-dBi Diversity Pillar-Mount Antenna*

Parameter	Specification
Frequency range	2.4–2.83 GHz
VSWR	2:1 Nominal
Gain	5.2 dBi
Polarization	Vertical
Azimuth (3-dB BW)	Omnidirectional 360 degrees
Elevation (3-dB BW)	25 degrees
Dimensions	12" * 5" * 1"

High-Gain Omni Antennas

The antenna shown in Figure B-8 is a high-gain 12-dBi omni antenna from Mobile Mark Antennas. It is designed with no down tilt for use in long-range communication between sites with similar elevations. If the gain is very high, the antenna has a very narrow vertical beam width resulting in poor performance for indoor applications or those installations where there is a height disparity. An example would be an antenna located on top of a high building, which is intended to provide "local" coverage on the ground.

Figure B-8   *12-dBi Omni Antenna*

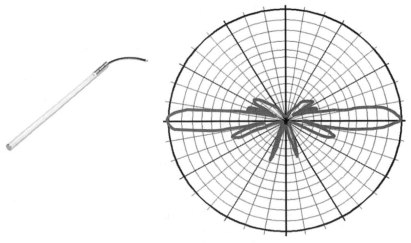

Vertical Radiation Pattern

Table B-6 lists the specification for a typical 12-dBi omni antenna. Note the very narrow vertical beam width.

Table B-6   *12-dBi Omni Specifications*

Parameter	Specification
Frequency range	2.4–2.83 GHz
VSWR	2:1 nominal
Gain	12 dBi
Polarization	Vertical
Azimuth (3-dB BW)	Omnidirectional 360 degrees
Elevation (3-dB BW)	7 degrees
Dimensions	40" * 1.25"
Wind rating	100 mph

Panel or Patch Wall-Mount Directional Antennas

Panel or patch antennas are designed to mount to a wall and provide coverage to an area such as an auditorium or large meeting room. They are fairly small in size and can even be painted to blend in with the wall (as long as the paint is nonmetallic). Figure B-9 shows a 6-dBi diversity patch antenna from Cisco Systems.

Table B-7 lists the specifications for a 6-dBi patch antenna.

Table B-7   *6-dBi Diversity Patch Antenna Specifications*

Parameter	Specification
Frequency range	2.4–2.5 GHz
VSWR	1.7:1 nominal
Gain	6 dBi
Polarization	Vertical
Azimuth (3-dB BW)	80 degrees
Elevations plan (3-dB BW)	55 degrees
Dimensions	6.65" * 4.78" * .82"
Mounting	Wall mount

Figure B-9   *6-dBi Diversity Patch Antenna*

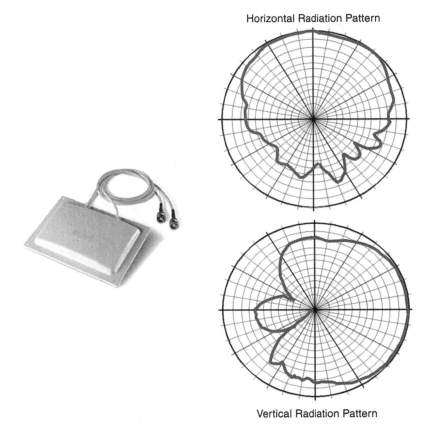

Horizontal Radiation Pattern

Vertical Radiation Pattern

Longer-Range Directional Antennas

Although most indoor systems do not require high-gain directional antennas, in some circumstances you might use a 10- or 13-dBi Yagi indoors to cover areas such as long corridors or long runs between high shelving (such as in a do-it-yourself homeowners' warehouse). In these cases, the Yagi can provide the necessary long-range, narrow-focused beams.

For longer outdoor links, a parabolic dish antenna might be required. For both the Yagi and parabolic dish antennas, when mounting, be sure to not only consider the horizontal beam width, but also the vertical beam width. Most dish antennas are provided with adjustments for vertical alignments, and some Yagi antennas have optional mounts to permit vertical alignment as well.

Figure B-10 shows a Cisco 13.5-dBi Yagi antenna. This might look similar to antennas you have seen from Telex, Proxim, and others, because it is sold by many different manufacturers as an OEM product.

Figure B-10   *13.5-dBi Yagi Antenna*

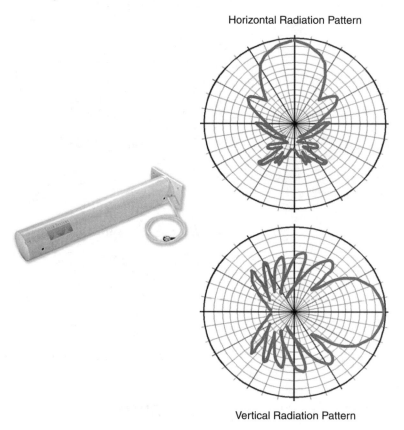

Horizontal Radiation Pattern

Vertical Radiation Pattern

Table B-8 lists the specifications for the Telex 13.5-dBi Yagi antenna.

Table B-8   *13.5-dBi Yagi Antenna Specifications*

Parameter	Specification
Frequency range	2.4–2.83 GHz
VSWR	2:1, 1.5:1 nominal
Gain	13.5
Front-to-back ratio	30 dB

Table B-8   *13.5-dBi Yagi Antenna Specifications (Continued)*

Polarization	Vertical
Azimuth (3-dB BW)	30 degrees
Elevations (3-dB BW)	25 degrees
Dimensions	18" * 3"
Wind rating	110 mph

Figure B-11 shows a Cisco 21-dBi solid parabolic dish antenna. As with the Yagi, this particular antenna is sold by many different vendors as an OEM product.

Figure B-11 *21-dBi Parabolic Dish Antenna*

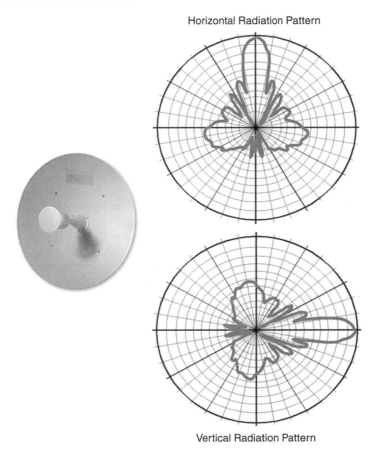

Horizontal Radiation Pattern

Vertical Radiation Pattern

Table B-9 lists the specification for the 21-dBi dish antenna.

Table B-9 *21-dBi Parabolic Dish Antenna Specifications*

Parameter	Specification
Frequency Range	2.4–2.83 GHz
VSWR	1.8:1, 15:1 nominal
Power	5 watts
Gain	21 dBi
Front-to-back ratio	25 dB
Maximum side lobe	−17 dB
Polarization	Vertical
Azimuth (3-dB BW)	12.4 degrees
Elevation (3-dB BW)	12.4 degrees
Dimensions	24" * 15.5"
Wind Rating	110 mph

5-GHz Antennas

Although most indoor 5-GHz products use permanently attached antennas, there is a big push to move 5 Ghz to the bands permitting external antennas. Presently, only a few antennas are available for the 5-GHz WLAN products, and many of them are similar to those found in 2.4 GHz. As a comparison, a 5-GHz 28-dBi parabolic dish is shown in Figure B-12. This particular antenna, from Maxrad, is about the same physical size as the 21-dBi 2.4-GHz dish antenna. Notice, however, that the gain is quite a bit higher for the same size, and the beam width is drastically reduced (12 versus 4 degrees). This will continue to be the case for 5-GHz antennas. For similar-gain antennas, a 5-GHz antenna will be approximately half the physical size.

Figure B-1   *28-dBi 5-GHz Parabolic Dish Antenna*

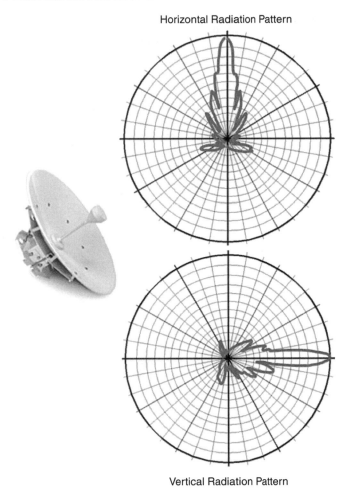

Horizontal Radiation Pattern

Vertical Radiation Pattern

Table B-10 lists the specifications for a high-gain (28-dBi) 5-GHz dish antenna.

Table B-10 *28-dBi 5-GHz Antenna Specifications*

Parameter	Specification
Frequency range	5.725–5.825 GHz
VSWR	1.5:1 nominal
Gain	28 dBi
Polarization	Vertical or horizontal
Azimuth (3-dB BW)	4.75 degrees
Elevation (3 dB BW)	4.75 degrees
Maximum power	4 watts
Temperature (operating)	–30C min, +60C max
Mounting	1.5–2.5" mast mount
Wind speed (operational)	100 mph
Wind speed (survival)	125 mph
Dimensions	25" diameter

Alternative Antennas

Occasionally, standard antennas just do not meet the requirements of a particular environment. At times, issues concerning differing coverage areas arise, such as aesthetics or mounting concerns that prohibit some of the more standard type of antennas. This appendix identifies three different types of alternative antennas that you can use (as long as they fall within the legal usage for the regulatory agencies): leaky coax, sectorized panel, and ceiling-tile antennas.

Leaky Coax Cable

A leaky coax cable is very similar to normal coaxial cable in its construction. The major difference is in the cable's outer conductor. Normal coaxial cables use outer conductor shields that are designed to minimize RF leakage. The outer conductor of a typical leaky coax cable has holes or openings in the outer conductor to allow a controlled amount of RF signal to leak out into the surrounding environment. Although most of the signal still travels through the cable, these openings allow the signal to radiate out from the cable or currents to travel on the outer conductor surface, creating an RF field around the cable.

Leaky coaxial cables have been used for many years as wireless feeders in coalmines and vehicular tunnels. More recently, leaky coax has been used as a base-station antenna for in-building wireless systems for hard-to-cover areas such as elevator areas, and for building-to-building tunnels.

Figure C-1 shows the two major kinds of radiating coax (more commonly known to as leaky coax). The type of leaky coax known to many, called *coupled mode*, has closely spaced slots milled in a corrugated outer conductor of a rigid type of coax (often referred to as *hardline*). One such brand name is Radiax, manufactured by Andrew Corporation. More recently, a new type of leaky coax has been developed. This newer kind, called *radiating mode*, typically has a foil outer conductor with nonuniformly spaced slots arranged in a periodic pattern. In free space, its external fields are closely bound to the cable and do not radiate, except for minor end effects. Radiation depends on scattering of the local fields by nearby random objects.

Figure C-1   *Radiating ("Leaky") Coax*

Coupled Mode Cable

Radiating Mode Cable

Radiating-mode cable with a nonuniform periodic slot pattern will radiate in free space. However, radiating-mode cable also has strong local fields, and it is probable that in any environment where coupled-mode cable radiates effectively by random scattering, the principal mechanism by which radiating-mode cable works is also random scattering.

It is unpromising to look for a detailed model of scattering, because directional or point-source antennas, by design, have strong signal levels near the antenna. Signal levels get weaker as you move away from the antenna. They also tend to yield more line-of-sight radiation characteristics. This effect creates shadowing and uneven signal distribution. Leaky coax cable emits a low-level signal and actually provides a uniform distribution of signal around the cable. Point-source antennas such as omni or patch and panel antennas are very practical and recommended for distribution of RF signals in large open areas. For more congested areas such as narrow aisles, tunnels, and confined environments, however, leaky coax can resolve some difficult coverage problems.

Leaky coax comes in various diameters, and the major difference from one to another has to do with the insertion loss of the cable. Similar to coaxial cables, as the leaky coax cable length or operating frequency increases, so does the insertion loss for that cable. To minimize losses or their impact on the overall system performance, you can use a larger-diameter cable for longer lengths or higher frequencies. Another difference in leaky coax is the outside jacket on the cable. Many applications require the cable to have a fire-retardant jacket (outside covering) to meet building fire codes.

The performance of leaky coax depends on the environment it is installed in. In general, specifications provided in manufacturer catalogs apply to in-building applications and environments. If you install the cable outdoors, you might experience fewer coupling effects and slightly lower insertion loss (because outdoors is similar to free space). If the cable is installed in a tunnel, the different types of tunnels (concrete versus steel) have different impacts on the cable's performance. Some tunnels enhance coupling effects, whereas others dramatically increase insertion loss.

Sectorized Panel Antenna

Although there are many different style of antennas possible for WLANs and wireless bridging, one specific antenna is particularly well suited for local outdoor coverage: a sectorized panel antenna (see Figure C-2). Many of the cellular telephone base-station sites use a type of sectorized antenna.

Figure C-2   *Sectorized Antenna*

Front View   Side View   Back View

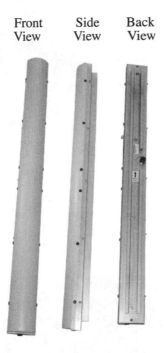

Wall-mounted omnidirectional antennas can suffer from multipath components created by the wall itself. Covering a large area for local coverage, such as a parking area, neighborhood, or educational or industrial campuses, can also be a challenge for an omnidirectional antenna placed on a building. Sectorized antennas, although similar in nature to omni antennas, offer a solution for these situations. These antennas use a wide horizontal coverage angle with ranges from as little as 60 degrees to as much as 180 degrees. Figure C-3 shows how using three 120-degree sectorized antennas can provide a 360-degree range of coverage providing higher gain than possible from an single omni, while having a very broad vertical radiation angle.

Figure C-3 *Using Sectorized Antennas for Increased Coverage*

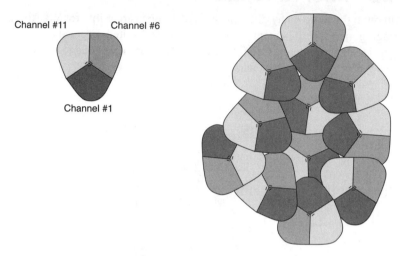

Figure C-4 depicts the use of three sector antennas on a single mounting mast. Notice that you can angle the antennas slightly downward with the mounting brackets to obtain down tilt (discussed in Chapter 2).

Figure C-4 *Mounting Sectorized Antennas*

Notice also the possibility of physical space between the antennas; this space helps to eliminate the receiver de-sense issues discussed in Chapter 5, "Selecting the WLAN Architecture and Hardware." An alternative method is to mount these at some greater physical distance apart, such as at the edges of a building, or separate them using longer horizontal support arms similar to those found on cellular phone towers.

Ceiling-Tile Antennas

In some cases, antennas must be totally hidden. This makes for an extremely tough installation. One possible solution is called a *ceiling-tile antenna*. Centurion Wireless Technologies offers such an antenna (see Figure C-5).

Figure C-5   *Armstrong Centurion Ceiling Tile Antenna*

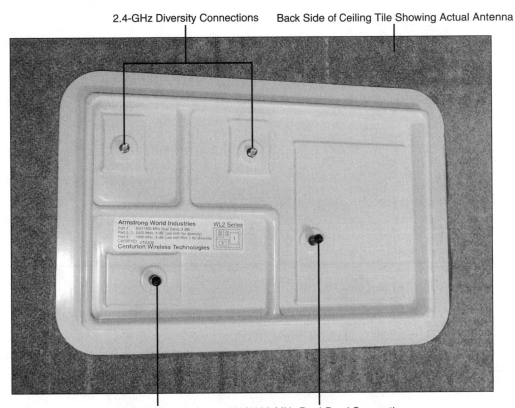

Although the antenna is pleasing aesthetically, it does have reduced coverage when compared to a typical "below-the-ceiling" antenna. Some of these ceiling-tile antennas come in multiple frequencies, offering a single antenna for servicing of paging systems, wireless phones, and wireless LANs, for example. The gain of ceiling tile antennas is usually fairly low, with 3 dBi being typical.

Sample Forms

This appendix provides samples of two pre-site survey documents that will help you create your own pre-site survey template, which you learned about in Chapter 6, and a sample site survey report, which you learned about in Chapter 13.

Pre-Site Survey Forms

The first form was provided by a professional site survey company, NeTeam Corporation. Some readers may be surprised by a few items in this document, but in many cases items such as drug testing or insurance certificates can delay any work to be performed until these items are completed.

This particular pre-site survey report is just one example (this one is for an 802.11b survey). Most survey engineers will add many other items that they find useful to performing the needed tasks.

The second pre-site survey form, from Ohio Wireless, is a bit more detailed. A combination of the two samples, along with some additions and deletions to suit the desires of the survey engineering team, can create a very useful tool.

Site Specific Information

Type of Business?		Type of Facility?	

☐ Union Facility   ☐ Insurance Certificate Needed   Fax # to Send Insurance Certificate: ☐ Drug testing required prior to arrival on site?

☐ Floor prints or blueprints available? (soft copy preferred: .dwg, .dxf, .vsd, .bmp, .tif, or ,jpg)   Where:

Required Equipment	☐ Lift ☐ NeTeam to Obtain Height: Feet: Width: Feet: Type:
	☐ Ladder ☐ NeTeam to Obtain Length: Feet:

Saftey Considerations   ☐ Shoes   ☐ Hard-Hat   ☐ Glasses   ☐ On-Site Safety Course   ☐ Other   ☐ None

Square Footage of Facility: Feet: Square Footage of Coverage: Feet: Number of Floors:

Number of Buildings: ☐ Buildings Detached   Distance Between Buildings:

If multiple buildings or floors, please detail in scope of work.

Ceiling Height: Feet: Rack Height: Feet: Distance Between Ceiling and Stock: Feet: Distance between racks: Feet:

☐ Multiple LANs?   If so, how many?   ☐ Mezzanines

Basic RF Design   (2000-6000 sq. ft.)_____ Micro (6000-12000 sq ft) _____ Macro (large outside coverage)

Areas with high user volume:

What areas require 11 Mbps coverage?

What areas require 5.5 Mbps coverage?

What areas require 2 Mbps coverage?

Areas Not Requiring Coverage: Micro Cell Overlap:

List any known RF-based systems (existing equipment, security systems, cell phone towers, wireless phones, etc.)

Building	Equipment	Frequency

Network Information

Current Topology: ☐ Ethernet   ☐ Token Ring   ☐ Other, Describe:

Special Site Considerations: (Please mark all that apply and describe constraints.)   ☐ **Check Here For None**

☐ Clean Room?	☐ Intrinsically Safe?
☐ Security Systems/Secure Area?	☐ Medical Equipment?
☐ Hazardous Area?	☐ Hazardous Material?
☐ Outdoor Coverage?	☐ Other?
☐ Any Asbestos in Facility?	Describe Where Asbestos Is:
☐ Freezer?	Temperature:

Resource Requirement Projection

Skill Level	Number of Engineers	Project Days

Skill Levels: MP = Managing Partner / Sr. Sys. Design Engr. / System Design Engr. II / Sys. Design Engr. I / System Technician

NeTeam Services Request Form

Statement of Work / Special Site Considerations

If any of the following apply, you must include a Statement of Work detailing the requirements and constraints.
Also note any requirements that are not covered in the form but are necessary to meet customer expectations or policies.

- Specific points of contact for work coordination and contact order, that is, primary, secondary, and so on.
- A specific radio type to be used, for example, the customer will be using FH radios and so we have to be concerned with co-existence issues.
- Corporate or site cabling specifications, for example, plenum or PVC-coated cable, cables in specific colors, fiber run requirements, and so on. (Please attach.)
- Required standard antenna types for a roll out.
- Required standard AP mounting brackets and/or enclosures.
- Minimum or maximum equipment mounting heights.
- Required local permits (include contact details).

(Paste Statement of Work here.)

Sample Site Survey Report

As you learned in Chapter 13, a detailed site survey report is critical to the person or team installing and troubleshooting the WLAN. This sample is from Ohio Wireless. Use it for ideas when creating your own report template.

8056 Seasons Rd, Streetsboro, Ohio, 44241

Pre-Site Survey Form

Filling out a pre-site survey forms helps us in our preparation prior to our arrival at your site and helps us ensure that we design a wireless LAN (WLAN) that will meet your needs and requirements. Please fill in the form and fax to (Company Name) at (123) 456-7891. If you have any questions regarding this form please contact your (Company Name) representative at (123) 456-7891.

Customer:	Contact:	
Site Adress:	Department:	
Phone:	Pager:	Mobile:
Fax:	E-mail:	

Total Number of Sites:	(Please fill out one form for each site.)	
Site Number: of	Number of Buildings at the Site:	802.11 Compliant?
Hours of Operation:	Approximate Square Footage:	Redundant WLAN?
Hours during which site survey may be performed.		
List models of wireless devices to be used.		Total Number of Users:
Packet Size:	Average:	
Minimum:	Maximum:	
Will WLAN be used for wireless voice? ☐ Yes ☐ No	Number of wireless VoIP devices	

RF Coverage

Coverage
Complete Inside ☐   Selective Inside ☐   (Please provide diagram of facility indicating desired coverage)
Complete Outside ☐   Selective Outside ☐   (Please provide diagram of facility indicating desired coverage)
Using WEP Encryption ☐ Yes ☐ No   Desired Link speed(s): ☐ 11 Mb ☐ 5.5 Mb ☐ 2 Mb ☐ 1 Mb
Utilize Rate Shifting ☐ Yes ☐ No   (Please indicate areas where desired linkspeed will be needed)

8056 Seasons Rd, Streetsboro, Ohio, 44241

Existing Network

Existing Network Topology:	☐ Ethernet	☐ Token Ring	☐ Other
All sites use same topology?	☐ Yes	☐ No	Explain

Application type(s) to be used on WLAN:

If Emulation, what type?	If other, explain
Protocol(s)	Host Environment

WAN Connectivity:

LAN Connectivity: (check all that apply)	Media: (check all that apply)
☐ 10 Mbps ☐ 100 Mbps	☐ Coax ☐ Copper ☐ Fiber
	If Copper: ☐ Cat 5 ☐ Cat 7 ☐ Gigabit

Existing WLAN   ☐ Yes   ☐ No   If yes, explain:

Site Information

Ceiling Height: ☐ 8-10 feet   ☐ 10-20 feet   ☐ 20-30 feet   ☐ 30+ feet
Is lift available?   ☐ Yes   ☐ No   If no, will customer provide lift?   ☐ Yes   ☐ No
Racking/Shelving   ☐ Yes   ☐ No   If yes, please describe construction.
Clearance Above Storage Level: ☐ < 4 feet   ☐ 4-8 feet   ☐ 8+ feet
Any hazardous areas?   ☐ Yes   ☐ No   (Please indicate hazardous areas on the diagram.)
If yes, please describe.

8056 Seasons Rd, Streetsboro, Ohio, 44241

Site Information (continued)

Temperature Range Inside Facility:	Temperature Range Outside Facility:
Any freezers? ☐ Yes ☐ No (Please indicate freezer areas on the diagram.)	
Temperature (check all that apply) ☐ 30 feet ☐ 15-30 feet ☐ 0-15 feet ☐ < 10 feet	
Special Safety Requirements: ☐ Steel-Toed Boots ☐ Hard Hat ☐ Safety Glasses ☐ Other	
Other non-WLAN RF Equipment installed at facility? ☐ Yes ☐ No (Please indicate on diagram)	
If Yes, please describe Frequency	
Frequency	
Frequency	
Material Stored at Site:	
Do stock levels fluctuate? ☐ Yes ☐ No Explain:	
Current Stock Levels: ☐ High ☐ Average ☐ Low Floor Construction:	
Any conveyors? ☐ Yes ☐ No (Please indicate location on site diagram.)	
Available Power: ☐ 110V AC ☐ 220V AC	
Does site experience power problems? ☐ Yes ☐ No	
If Yes, please explain	
Site Construction: Building: Ceiling: Walls:	

Projected Survey Start Date:	Projected Installation Date:
Date received at (Company name):	Representative:
Date Received by SE:	Initial call placed on (date):

Green Cross Hospital
Northampton Hills, Ohio, 44223

802.11b Wireless LAN Project
Site Survey Report
March 2004

NOTE: This is a sample site survey report, with only excerpts of a full survey report. It provides only three AP locations. A typical hospital this size may, in fact, require as many as 300 APs, depending upon the number of rooms and the number of users. This is to be used as a training aid only and may be reprinted as needed.

Table of Contents

1.0 Objective 382

2.0 Site Description 382

3.0 Test Procedure 382

4.0 Proposed Components 383

5.0 Existing Wireless Assessment 386

6.0 Wireless Sniffer Trace Analysis..386

7.0 Access Point/Antenna Information Locations 387

8.0 Infrastructure Notes 390

9.0 Site Plan 391

10.0 Required WLAN Hardware Overview 392

11.0 Contact Information..393

12.0 Customer Acceptance 393

1.0 Objective

On February 17 – 18, 2004 Ohio Wireless performed a Site Assessment for Green Cross Memorial Hospital (GCMH) at the request of the GCMH IT department. The primary objective was to assess all patient floors, as well as ER, ICU, CCU, the Easy Street facility, New Horizons Facility, and radiology, for installing an 802.11b WLAN system.

2.0 Site Description

Location Specific Description

1 Site is a hospital environment with multiple floors (3)

2 All areas of the hospital require 11-megabit data-rates.

3 Symbol Technologies Frequency Hopping and 2.4-GHz access points are deployed in the ER and ICU areas.

4 The deployment must be aesthetically pleasing if installed in areas visible by the public. Any antennas that are visible must have approval from the IT staff before being selected for use.

5 Construction of the building is typical brick, steel stud drywall walls, and steel pan re-enforced concrete floors.

3.0 Test Procedure

1 A site spectrum analysis was performed and found an existing 2.4-GHz wireless system already in place. The system identified was a Symbol 2.4-GHz Spread Spectrum Frequency Hopping system.

2 A network wireless sniffer was introduced into the testing procedures to accurately assess the existing network and determine an overall wireless evaluation as the network was constructed at that time.

3 Upon completion of the initial assessment, a floor-by-floor assessment and an RF survey was performed to determine location of access points, as well as location, mounting, and type of antennas.

4 Survey was performed between the hours of 8 am and 7 pm.

5 The RF System Design procedure was performed using AirMagnet software running on a PDA to assess performance.

6 The site evaluation was performed for this area on the dates specified in this report. Changes in building structure or new construction will affect the results of this site evaluation. Changes in RF coverage resulting from anything out of the control of IWS may result in additional site evaluation costs at the customer's expense.

4.0 Proposed Components

Cisco Systems 802.11b Access Point

The Cisco Aironet® 1200 Series is the flagship of the Aironet line, designed for high-performance, secure, manageable, and flexible wireless local-area networks (WLANs). The modular design of the Cisco Aironet 1200 allows single or dual radio configuration for up to 54 Mbps connectivity in both the 2.4- and 5-GHz bands and is fully compliant with the IEEE 802.11a, 802.11b, and 802.11g standards. The model used for this survey included only the 802.11b radio module.

6.5-dBi Spatial Diversity Antenna (proposed)

This 6.5-dBi spatial antennas was provided to the GCMH IT staff for approval to be used in areas where the antenna will be visible to the public. It is an ideal solution for places where 2.4 GHz is deployed and maximum interference rejection is required due to the effects of multipathing. The Cisco Aironet 2.4-GHz radio with Diversity Antenna Ports will take advantage of this antenna's dual radiating elements. Its radiation pattern makes it perfect for large gathering areas, auditoriums, and so on.

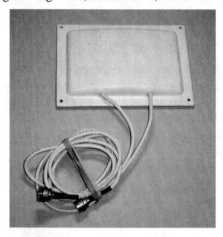

5-dBi Sector Directional Antenna

This 5-dBi spatial antenna was provided to the GCMH IT staff for approval to be used in areas where the antenna will be visible to the public. It is a perfect solution for places where large coverage areas are needed outdoors. It is designed for outdoor deployment and is low profile for unobtrusive outdoor wall mounting.

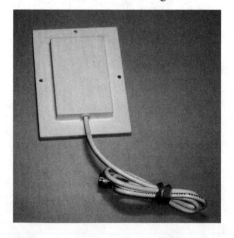

2-dBi Diverse Omni-Directional Antenna

This 2-dBi spatial antenna was provided to the GCMH IT staff for approval to be used in areas where the antenna will be visible to the public. It is a perfect solution for places where 2.4 GHz is deployed and maximum interference rejection is required due to the effects of multipath. The AP 1200s 2.4-GHz radio with Diversity Antenna Ports will take advantage of this antenna's dual radiating elements. This antenna is perfect for deployment in the drop ceilings found in GCMH, because it is unobtrusive and blends well into the ceiling.

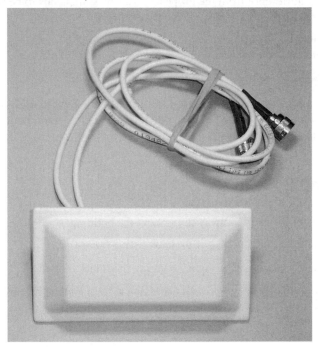

5.0 Existing Wireless Assessment

2.4-GHz Patient Monitoring system

1 Symbol Technologies Frequency Hopping access points were deployed in the ER and the ICU and are used for patient monitoring systems. It is vital that these units receive no interference from the proposed WLAN. Care needs to be taken to insure there is adequate isolation between the two systems.

2 The majority of these access points were deployed with the 2-dBi omni-directional antenna (ceiling tile grid mount) within 3 feet of the access point.

3 Access points were set at 100 mW output power.

4 Testing showed that the Cisco AP 1200 and the Symbol FH APs were installed with a minimum of 10 feet between the devices. There was no noticeable interference between the two systems.

Wireless Phone System

1 Spectralink 900-MHz phones are deployed throughout the facility with base stations located in every hallway throughout the building.

2 The transmitter power of these phones is 600 mW.

3 The phones use a frequency hopping modulation mode.

There is no interference between the phone system and the proposed 2.4-GHz WLAN system.

6.0 Wireless Sniffer Trace Analysis

1 Using the AirMagnet tool, throughout the survey, only the Symbol 2.4-GHz Frequency Hopping system was discovered. No other 802.11 WLAN devices were found to be active anywhere in the facility. The only RF that was found to be in the same band as the proposed WLAN was the patient monitoring system.

7.0 Access Point/Antenna Information Locations

Access Point #1

Access Point

Hardware: Cisco Systems 802.11b Access Point

Access Point Location:

ER wing, first floor. Mounted above ceiling tile located at intersection of ICU entrance and ER wing, two ceiling tiles west of exit sign (between two light fixtures).

Antenna Type: (1) 2-dBi Diversity Omni.

Antenna Location:

Mounted to the ceiling cross member, centered in the hallway, two ceiling tiles away from the exit sign, on the west side of the sign (below AP).

Antenna Installation Orientation: N/A

Channel: (One 2412 MHz)

Power: 100 mW out of radio

Misc.: N/A

AP above ceiling tiles, antenna on cross member at hallway intersection—in center of intersection

Access Point #2

Access Point

Hardware: Cisco Systems 802.11b Access Point

Access Point Location: Mounted to the wall directly above the surgery waiting area reception desk door.

Antenna Type: (1) 6.5-dbi Spatial Diversity Patch Antenna.

Antenna Location:

Mounted on the wall to the left of the access point by 6 inches.

Antenna Installation Orientation: Toward the hallway.

Channel: (Six 2437 MHz)

Power: 100 mW out of radio

Misc.: N/A

AP/Antenna mounting

Access Point #3

Access Point

Hardware: Cisco Systems 802.11b Access Point

Access Point Location:

First floor—Mounted to the wall above the ceiling tile directly above the exit doors for emergency entrance

Antenna Type: (1) 5-dBi Sector Antenna.

Antenna Location:

Mounted under overhang on brick wall. Cable routed through wall above ceiling.

Antenna Installation Orientation: Mast mount vertical

Channel: (Eleven 2462 MHz)

Power: 100 mW out of radio

Antenna Cable: (1) 10 feet LMR600 cable

Misc.: N/A

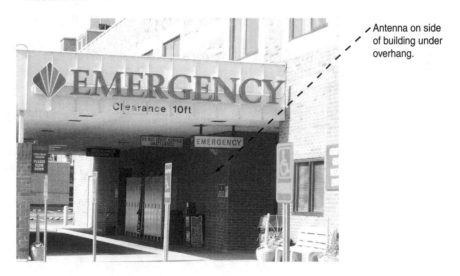

Antenna on side of building under overhang.

8.0 Infrastructure Notes

1   Access point power schemes

The Cisco Aironet AP 1200 provides the ability to accept power over the CAT 5 Ethernet cable. This particular site does not have Ethernet switches that support this Power over Ethernet feature; therefore, power will be provided via the Cisco In–line power injector. These should be located in the wiring closet where the Ethernet switch is located for the given AP. For more on this, refer to the installation documentation from Cisco for the AP 1200.

2   AP mounting hardware

Cisco provides a mounting bracket for the AP 1200 that offers multiple mounting capabilities, as well as the ability to secure the AP to the mounting bracket with a lock. This should be used in all locations.

3   Antenna mounting

Each antenna has a unique mounting requirement. Refer to the survey document for the description of mounting.

a   Use the provided brackets for the 2-dBi diversity omni-directional antenna and mount to the drop ceiling grid work, running the cables up through the ceiling to the AP.

b   The 6.5-dBi patch antenna is designed to be mounted flat against the wall, positioned so that the cables running out of the top or the bottom of the antenna. This can be mounted to the wall with small (#6) screws.

c   The 5-dBi sector antenna is designed to be mounted flat against the wall with the cable exiting on the bottom side.

9.0 Site Plan

9.1 ER and OR wings

(Note: this is an example showing only partial information for three APs.)

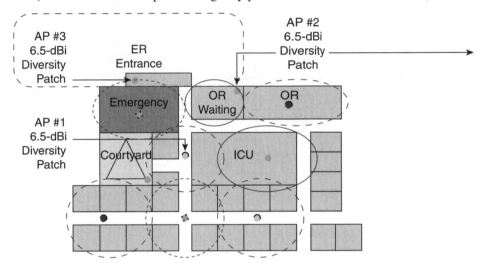

10.0 Required WLAN Hardware Overview

Ohio Wireless Part Number	Description	Qty
AIR-AP1200-802.11b	Cisco AP 1200 2.4-GHz 11 Mb AP	143
AIR-AP1200 MTGBKT	Cisco AP 1200 Mounting Bracket	143
AIR-AP1200 PWR INJ	Cisco AP 1200 In-Line Power Block	143
47211443	2.2-dBi Ceiling Mount Diversity Omni-Antenna	131
47211419	6.5-dBi Diversity Wall Mount Patch antenna	9
47211402	5-dBi Sector Antenna 160°	1
47211400	2.2-dBi Dipole Antenna (Rubber Duck)	6
47211100	LMR400 Cable (ft)	20
47211801	RP-TNC-Female/LMR400	2
47211802	RP-TNC-Male/LMR400	2

11.0 Contact Information

Ohio Wireless-	Bruce Alexander
	K8DGV@aol.com
	1863 7th Street
	Cuyahoga Falls, OH 44261
	330-52x-xxxx
Green Cross Memorial-	Kyle Lynch
	Kyle.Lynch@GCMH.rr.org
	2100 Main Street
	Northampton Hills, OH 44224
	330-92x-xxxx

12.0 Customer Acceptance

By signing this report, both parties agree to its contents and verify that the work has been completed in accordance with prior agreements and within the defined design.

Ohio Wireless-_____

Bruce Alexander

_____

Date

Green Cross Memorial-_____

Kyle Lynch

_____

Date

NUMBERS

802.11. The IEEE standard that specifies a carrier sense Media Access Control and physical layer specifications for 1- and 2-Mbps WLANs.

802.11a. The IEEE standard operating in the 5-GHz license-free frequency band, providing data rates up to 54 Mbps.

802.11b. The IEEE standard for the physical layer for 2.4-GHz DSSS WLANs with data rates up to 11 Mbps.

802.11d. The IEEE standard enabling WLAN client devices to determine what regulatory domain the AP is located in and to automatically change parameters to the associated regulatory domain requirements.

802.11e. The IEEE proposed standard for link-layer quality of service for 802.11 networks.

802.11f. The IEEE proposed standard protocol for AP-to-AP roaming.

802.11g. The IEEE standard operating in the 2.4-GHz license-free frequency band, providing data rates over 20 Mbps.

802.11h. The IEEE standard for controlling transmitter power and providing dynamic selection of frequency (channels) to avoid interference to and from radar and navigational systems.

802.11i . The IEEE standard for link-layer security for 802.11 networks.

802.1Q. Specification for tagging packets with VLAN.

802.1x. The IEEE standard for port-based network access control capability. Uses the EAP framework for authentication of users using a variety of methods.

802.3. The IEEE standard for wired Ethernet topologies. This specification encompasses Ethernet, Fast Ethernet, and Gigabit Ethernet today.

802.3af. The IEEE standard for supplying power over the Ethernet cable.

A

adjacent cell. A coverage area of an AP that is physically located next to an existing AP's coverage area.

adjacent channel. A channel or frequency that is directly above or below a specific channel or frequency.

AES. Advanced Encryption Standard. A next-generation encryption function approved by the *National Institute of Standards and Technology* (NIST) for use with WLAN. The encryption mechanism to be used in 802.11i and is likely to replace DES and 3DES.

aggregate throughput. A measure of the maximum amount of data a network or other communications system can carry in a given timeframe. Basically a total summation of all data rates of all simultaneous transmissions possible at one instance on the system. If a system could support five simultaneous transmissions of 2 Mbps, for example, it would have an aggregate throughput of 10 Mbps.

amplitude. The magnitude or strength of a varying waveform.

amplitude modulation (AM). A technique whereby the voltage level or amplitude of a carrier is varied to transmit digital or analog information.

antenna. The part of a radio communications system intended to radiate and/or collect RF energy.

antenna gain. A relative measure of an antenna's capability to direct or concentrate RF energy in a particular direction or pattern. Typically measured in dBi or dBd. *See also* dBi and dBd.

AP. access point. The central point of communications for all stations in a WLAN. An AP provides connection between wireless devices as well as between the wired network and the wireless network.

attenuation. A reduction in strength or deterioration of a radio signal as it passes through a transmission medium. Attenuation generally increases with frequency, cable length, and the number of connections in a circuit. Attenuation is measured in *decibels* (dB).

attenuator. A device that reduces the level of a transmitted signal, in terms of current, voltage, or power.

authentication. In WLAN usage, a process by which a user must present some form of identifying credentials to be permitted access to a resource. In *mutual authentication*, a user must validate his identity to the network and the network's identity must be validated by the client.

bandwidth. The frequency range necessary to convey a signal, measured in units of *hertz* (Hz). For example, voice signals typically require approximately 7 kHz of bandwidth, and data traffic typically requires approximately 50 kHz of bandwidth, but this depends greatly on modulation scheme, data rates, and how many channels of a radio spectrum are used.

B

beam antenna. *See* Yagi antenna.

beamwidth. The area of radiation a directional antenna provides. This is typically measured in degrees, and is usually rated from between the two closest points where the signal level is 3 dB below the maximum level.

bit. The term is a contraction of *binary digit*, which is the smallest possible unit of information a computer can handle.

Bluetooth. A short-range wireless technology designed to create personal-area networks.

BPSK. Binary Phase Shift Keying. BPSK is a digital frequency-modulation technique used for sending data over a coaxial cable network or wireless networks. This type of modulation is less efficient—but also less susceptible to noise—than similar modulation techniques.

bridge. In wireless networking, a wireless system for connecting two or more separate Ethernet networks. In general networking, typically used to describe a component of a communications network, this spans the network from one physical medium to another, such as from a wired Ethernet to wireless.

broadcast domain. An internetwork of devices that are capable of sending and receiving broadcast frames to and from one another.

C

captured antenna. A wireless device that contains a nonremovable antenna.

Card Bus. A 32-bit interface standard for PC card devices. Similar form factor to PCMCIA, and typically provides support for older 16-bit PCMCIA PC cards.

carrier frequency. The base frequency of a transmitted signal that would be transmitted if it were not modulated by information. A carrier "frequency" can be either a single frequency or a range of frequencies carried at one time between the transmitter and receiver.

CCA. Clear Channel Assessment. Wireless devices can be configured to a particular background interference level found in a specific environment, for reduced overhead contention with other wireless systems.

CCK. Complementary Code Keying. A physical layer modulation technique used by the 802.11b standard to achieve 5.5- and 11-Mbps data rates.

CCX. Cisco Compatible Extensions. Provides tested compatibility with licensed Cisco infrastructure innovations.

CDMA. Code-Division Multiple Access. A technique associated with spread-spectrum systems that is used to increase channel capacity. Typically, each user is given a different pseudo-random spreading code. To communicate with a particular user, the sender must select the code assigned to that user. This technique can permit many users to operate simultaneously on the same frequency.

cell. In wireless networking, the coverage area of a single wireless AP or wireless bridge. This is also known as the *basic service area* (BSA).

chip. In spread spectrum, the time it takes to transmit a bit or single symbol of a *pseudo-random noise* (PN) code (a single element of the spreading code).

coaxial cable (coax). A concentric two-conductor cable in which one conductor surrounds the other, separated by an insulator.

coax seal. A type of moldable plastic that is used for weatherproofing and sealing radio connectors.

collision domains. A collision domain is where one or more devices are connected to a single network, and only one device on that network may transmit at a time. Often referred to as an *Ethernet segment*.

collisions. In network systems, when two nodes transmit simultaneously, causing destruction of a data packet's information.

compression. In RF amplification, an amplifier is said to be "in compression" (distorting) when the output is no longer a linear representation of the input signal, typically at the operational limits of the amplifier.

CSMA/CD. carrier sense multiple access/collision detection. The LAN access method used in Ethernet. When a device wants to gain access to the network, it checks to see whether the network is free. If it is not, it waits a random amount of time before retrying. If the network is free and two devices access the line at exactly the same time, their signals collide. When the collision is detected, they both back off and each waits a random amount of time before retrying.

CTS. clear to send. A signal or frame of data indicating that the receiver has "permission" to send data. In 802.11 WLANs, a device sends a CTS control packet to indicate to the WLAN network a data packet is about to be sent.

CW. continuous wave. An analog signal that is always "on" (100 percent duty cycle).

D

dB. decibel. A logarithmic representation of magnitude relationships commonly used in radio and sound measurement. A ratio of decibels to an isotropic antenna that is commonly used to measure antenna gain. As a rule, the greater the dBi value, the higher the antenna gain value. This results in a more acute angle of coverage.

dBd. dB dipole. The gain an antenna has over a dipole antenna at the same frequency. A dipole antenna is the smallest, least-gain practical antenna that can be made. To convert from dBd to dBi, just add 2.14 to the number (0 dBd = 2.14 dBi).

dBi. dB isotropic. The gain a given antenna has over a theoretical isotropic (point-source) antenna. Unfortunately, an isotropic antenna cannot be made in the real world, but it is useful for calculating theoretical fade and system operating margins.

dBm. dB milliwatt. A signal strength or power level. 0 dBm is defined as 1 mW (milliwatt) of power into a terminating load such as an antenna or power meter. Smaller signals are expressed as negative numbers (for example, –83 dBm).

DBPSK. Differential Binary Phase Shift Keying. Modulation technique used by IEEE 802.11-compliant WLANs for transmission at 1 Mbps.

dBW. dB relative to 1 watt. *See also* dB.

DDP. Datagram Delivery Protocol. The protocol used to facilitate communication among wireless devices such as the AP to client communication.

demodulate. To convert a modulated signal back to the original signal.

DES. Data Encryption Standard. An encryption standard issued by the National Bureau of Standards. The 3DES protocol uses a version of this encryption that carries three times the encryption protection.

de-spreading. The process used by a correlator to recover the information from a spread-spectrum signal.

dipole antenna. Antenna with the gain, pattern, and impedance defined at and near resonance of one-half wavelength. The antenna is split at its electrical center for connection to a transmission line. The radiation pattern is maximum at right angles to the axis of the antenna. Cisco dipole antennas are made of rubber; therefore, this antenna is sometimes referred to as a *rubber duck*. This started a long time ago when a very popular dipole manufacturer once referred to them in this manner and to this day still uses the duck logo in advertisements.

direct sequence (DS). A spread-spectrum modulation technique where a pseudo-random code directly phase modulates a carrier, increasing the bandwidth of the transmission. The resulting signal has a noiselike spectrum. The signal is de-spread by correlating with a pseudo-random code identical to and in synchronization with the code used to spread the carrier at the transmitter. Sometimes referred to as *DSSS*.

directional antenna. An antenna that concentrates transmission power into a direction thereby increasing coverage distance at the expense of coverage angle. Directional antenna types include Yagi, patch, and parabolic dish.

diversity. The intelligent system of two antennas continually senses incoming radio signals and automatically selects the antenna best positioned to receive it. This feature proves useful for operating in areas susceptible to the affects of multipath interference.

down tilt. The angle difference between perfectly horizontal (compared to the earth) and the center of the vertical beam width of an antenna.

DQPSK. Differential Quadrature Phase Shift Keying. Modulation technique used by IEEE 802.11-compliant WLANs for transmission at 2 Mbps.

DSSS. direct sequence spread spectrum. This transmission technology spreads a signal across a wide range of frequency spectrum. The data signal is broken up into several bits (known as a chipping sequence) and sent across the medium. The receiving station can reassemble the bits into the original information, even if some of the bits are missing due to interference.

dual band. Referred to when a WLAN device has more than one radio or a radio capable of operating on more than radio band (set of channels). The Cisco 1200 series AP is a dual-band unit.

E

EAP. Extensible Authentication Protocol. A mechanism for encapsulation of authentication credentials within a PPP-formatted frame. 802.1x uses a special format of EAP (EAPOL, or EAP over LAN) to send EAP authentication messages within Ethernet-type frames between an authenticator (for example, an AP) and a RADIUS server.

EAP-TLS. An EAP type defined by IETF (RFC 2284) that uses client and server digital certificates to authenticate users.

EIRP. Effective Isotropic Radiated Power. A term for expression of the performance of an antenna in a given direction (main lobe of the transmitter antenna) relative to the performance of a theoretical (isotropic) antenna; it is expressed in dBm. EIRP is calculated by adding the sum of the antenna gain (in dBi) plus the power (in dBm) into that antenna minus any loss (attenuation) caused by antenna cable, connectors, and so on.

electromagnetic spectrum. The full range of electromagnetic (same as magnetic) frequencies, a subset of which is used in commercial RF systems.

elevation plane (E-plane) of the antenna. Pertains to antenna gain. The E-plane depicts how the RF energy propagates looking at the side of the antenna. The E-plane correlates to the vertical beam width. *See also* down tilt.

EMI/RFI. electromagnetic interference/radio frequency interference. Broad spectrum noise or interfering signals.

encryption. Modification of a bit stream so that it appears random. Encryption is used for security purposes. The sender and receiver must both use the same encryption method.

ERP. Effective Radiated Power. The product of the transmitter peak envelope power, expressed in watts, delivered to the antenna, and the relative gain of the antenna over that of a half-wave dipole antenna.

Ethernet. Ethernet is a type of wired network that supports high-speed communications among devices over a specified cable.

ETSI. European Telecommunications Standards Institute. The standards body responsible for regulating telecommunications. The role of ETSI is develop technical standards aimed at achieving a large unified European telecommunications market.

F

fade margin. Additional signal level required to prevent the loss in signal along a signal path caused by environmental factors such as terrain, atmospheric conditions, and so on.

fading. Occurs when the power level of the signal drops because of various environmental factors.

Fast Ethernet. Extension of the Ethernet standard, IEEE 802.3u; defines the transmission of data over copper wire or fiber-optic cable at a rate of 100 Mbps.

fast roaming.
Roaming between or changing connections from one AP to another in a timeframe suitable for time-sensitive applications. Typically this is under 150 ms.

FCC. Federal Communications Commission. The government agency responsible for regulating telecommunications in the United States.

feedhorn. The part of a parabolic or grid reflector antenna that contains the driven element.

filter. A device used to block or reduce signals at certain frequencies while allowing others to pass through.

frequency. The rate at which an electrical current alternates, expressed as the number of cycles per unit of time (from crest to crest in a sine wave pattern); frequency is typically measured in hertz (Hz) or cycles per second (cps). For example, a 1-MHz frequency would have a full cycle (a complete sine wave) pass a given point in space at the rate of one million cycles per second. A 1-GHz frequency would have sine waves pass a given point in space at the rate of one billion times per second, and so forth.

frequency hopping (FH). A spread-spectrum modulation technique where the transmitter frequency hops from channel to channel in a predetermined but pseudo-random manner. The signal is tracked at the receiver by a frequency synthesizer controlled by a pseudo-random sequence generator synchronized to the transmitter's pseudo-random generator.

frequency modulation (FM). An analog modulation technique whereby the frequency of a carrier is varied to encode information.

Fresnel effect. A phenomenon related to line of sight, whereby an object that does not obstruct the visual line of sight obstructs the line of transmission for radio frequencies.

Fresnel zone. The area around the line of site between two points caused by the Fresnel effect. In WLANs, the critical area is 60 percent of the overall Fresnel area.

full-duplex transmission. A channel that allows transmission in two directions.

G

gain (antenna). The relative increase in power or magnitude of a signal, typically measured in decibels. A method of increasing the transmission distances of a radio by concentrating its signal in a single direction, typically through the use of a directional antenna. Gain does not increase a radio's signal strength, but just redirects it. Therefore, as gain increases, the decrease in angle of coverage is inversely proportional.

GHz. gigahertz. One billion cycles per second. This is a unit of measure for frequency.

grid antenna. A type of antenna that uses an open-frame grid as a reflector rather than a solid one. The grid spacing is sufficiently small to ensure that waves of the desired frequency cannot pass through, and are hence reflected back toward the driven element.

ground. A connection between a device or circuit and the earth or some device serving as the earth.

H

half-duplex transmission. A channel that allows transmission in only one direction at a time, switching back and forth between transmit and receive. Most spread-spectrum WLAN equipment is half duplex.

harmonic. The frequencies generated by a transmitter that are multiples of the primary frequency.

HiperLAN. A set of WLAN communication standards primarily used in European countries. There are two specifications: HiperLAN/1 and HiperLAN/2. Both have been adopted by the *European Telecommunications Standards Institute* (ETSI). This is similar to 802.11a, but is not the same specification.

horizontal plane (H-plane) of the antenna. Pertains to antenna gain. The H-plane depicts how the RF energy propagates looking down from the top of the antenna.

hub. A half-duplex Ethernet device with multiple ports. A hub allows a single Ethernet signal to be repeated out many ports. A hub provides a single collision domain between all devices attached to the hub.

Hz. Hertz. The international unit for measuring frequency, equivalent to the older unit of cycles per second. One *megahertz* (MHz) is one million hertz. One *gigahertz* (GHz) is one billion hertz. The standard U.S. electrical-power frequency is 60 Hz, the AM broadcast RF band is 0.551.6 MHz, the FM broadcast RF band is 88,108 MHz, and wireless 802.11 LANs operate at 2.4 GHz.

I

IAPP. Inter-Access Point Protocol. Protocol used by APs to communicate with one another.

IEEE. Institute for Electrical and Electronics Engineers. A professional organization that sets standards for telecommunications and computers.

impedance. The opposition to the flow of alternating current.

initialization vector. A value used with WEP security (or other stream-cipher implementation) to "initialize" or alter the RC4 key stream to ensure uniqueness. The IV is 24 bits in length in standard 802.11 WEP and 48 bits in WPA.

in-line. Power or signal passage through a device that is in series with the line.

ISA card. Industry Standard Architecture card. This card was the original form for PC expansion circuits such as modems, network adaptors, and other peripherals attached directly to the PC motherboard. It was based on a slow 8-bit architecture and migrated to a 16-bit architecture over time. The ISA card architecture has been replaced by the faster PCI bus architecture.

insertion loss. The loss in signal strength due to the insertion of a device in series with a signal path. Typically measured over the intended operating frequency range of the device.

interference. Unwanted communication noise that decreases the performance of a link or prevents a link from occurring.

intermodulation (intermod). The distortion product of an amplifier caused by the interaction of different signal products within the amplifier.

IP address. Internet Protocol address. A 32-bit address assigned to host on an IP Internet. The IP address has a host component and a network component.

IPSec. Internet Protocol Security. A protocol defined by the *Internet Engineering Task Force* (IETF) that provides security via authentication and encryption over the Internet.

isotropic. A theoretical "isotrope" is a single point in free space that radiates energy equally in every direction.

isotropic antenna. A hypothetical antenna that radiates or receives energy equally in all directions. Used as a 0-dB gain reference in directivity calculation (gain). The isotropic antenna provides a convenient reference for expressing the directive properties of actual antennas. This is the standard by which gain from other antennas are measured against.

K–L

key stream. A stream of characters used as a security key in various data encryption algorithms

L2TP. Layer 2 Tunneling Protocol. A protocol used for securely connecting VPNs over unsecure transmission media such as the Internet.

LAN. local-area network. A local group of computers and other network devices connected together in one area.

Layer 2 roaming. Roaming between or changing connections from one AP to another where the APs are connected to the same IP subnet.

Layer 3 roaming. Roaming between or changing connections from one AP to another where the APs are connected to different IP subnets.

LEAP. The Cisco proprietary Extensible Authentication Protocol.

lightning arrestor. A protective device that provides a very low-resistance path to any voltage above its rated value. It is designed to protect against nearby lightning strikes or static, sending the energy to the ground to prevent damage to equipment.

linear amplifier. A device that accurately reproduces a radio wave in magnified form.

link budget. A mathematical model of a wireless communications link that accounts for a wide variety of factors that affect operating range and performance. Sometimes called a *path budget*.

LNA. low-noise amplifier. Typically a small-signal amplifier for RF receiver applications.

local-area network. *See* LAN.

LoS. line of sight. An unobstructed straight line between two transmitting devices. Line of sight is typically required for long-range directional radio transmission. Because of the curvature of the earth, the line of sight for devices not mounted on towers is limited to 16 miles (26 km).

low-pass filter. A signal filter that passes all frequencies below a certain frequency and attenuates all higher frequencies.

M

MAC. Media Access Control. In a WLAN network card, MAC is a radio controller protocol. It corresponds to the ISO network model's Layer 2 (data link layer). The IEEE 802.11 standard specifies the MAC protocol for medium sharing, packet formats and addressing, and error detection.

MAN. metropolitan-area network. Similar to a LAN, but typically over a larger area such as a city.

MHz. megahertz. A unit of measure for frequency equal to one million cycles per second.

MIB. Management Information Base. A collection of network operational information residing in a virtual store that may be accessed, typically through an SNMP-compliant system, for analysis.

microwave. Usually refers to all radio frequencies above 2 GHz or so.

mini-PCI. miniature Peripheral Component Interconnect. A standard developed by Intel Corporation that defines a method to connect high-speed peripherals to a system. The WLAN radio inside the Cisco 1100 Series AP is a mini-PCI radio.

modulate. To vary the amplitude, frequency, or phase of an RF wave in accordance with the information to be conveyed.

modulation. Process by which the characteristics of electrical signals are transformed to represent information.

multipath distortion. Caused by the transmitted signal reaching the receiver via more than one path. A common cause is reflected signals bouncing off metal objects in a room. The reflected signal (having traveled farther) reaches the antenna at a slightly later time period, mixing with the original signal and causing interference.

multipoint. A communications circuit interconnecting several nodes (usually more than two).

N–O

NEMA enclosure. An enclosure that conforms to one of the National Electrical Manufacturers Association's many different types. Typically used in WLAN systems for dust, water, and temperature protection of an AP.

OFDM. orthogonal frequency-division multiplexing. A modulation technique used to provide very high data rates for 802.11a and 802.11g.

omnidirectional antenna. An antenna that radiates RF energy in a 360-degree pattern about an axis. An omni antenna can pick up signals from all directions; that is, it does not have to be pointed directly at the source of the signal to pick it up. Typically, this type of antenna is used when the specific direction of the signal is not known, as in a mobile application or when point-to-multipoint operation is desired.

open authentication. An authentication algorithm defined in the IEEE 802.11 specification where a client is permitted to "authenticate" to the network, regardless of whether it possesses the correct WEP key. Open authentication is typically used in conjunction with 802.1x authentication to establish initial client 802.11 connectivity prior to submission of EAP authentication.

oscillator. A device that produces a "vibration" or variation in signal level at a given frequency.

P

parabolic dish antenna. An antenna that uses a dishlike reflector to focus radio energy of a specific range of frequencies on a tuned element.

parabolic grid antenna. An antenna that uses an open-frame grid rather than a solid dish reflector. *See also* grid antenna.

Part 15 rules. The FCC regulation that regulates unlicensed use of the *Industrial, Scientific, and Medical* (ISM) bands for wireless networking and other uses.

patch antenna. Typically a flat, rectangular or round antenna having a hemispherical pattern.

path budget. A mathematical model of a wireless communications link that accounts for a wide variety of factors that affect operating range and performance. Sometimes called a *link budget*.

path loss. The weakening of a signal over its path of travel due to various factors such as terrain, obstructions, and environmental conditions.

PCMCIA. Personal Computer Memory Card Association. This is a standard for PC expansion cards used on laptop computers and other portable devices. It is often used for memory and data storage as well as communication devices, and uses a 16-bit interface. Often referred to as *PC card*.

PEAP. Protected Extensible Authentication Protocol. Provides an EAP activity in a protected tunnel. Two types exist today, which were defined by Microsoft and Cisco and are not compatible with each other.

peer-to-peer network. All nodes on the network have equal access to and control of the network medium.

physical layer (PHY). Provides for the transmission of data through a communications channel by defining the electrical, mechanical, and procedural specifications for IEEE 802 LANs.

PN. pseudo-noise. A digital signal with noiselike properties.

point to multipoint. A communications channel that runs from one point to several other points.

point to point. A communications channel that runs from one point to another.

polling. A process in which a device polls the terminals connected to it, asking whether they have data to be sent to the host.

power meter. A device used to measure radio energy.

professional installer. Someone who has been trained in the applicable rules and regulations, is receiving compensation for his or her work, has knowledge of radio emissions, and can verify that a site that deviates from the standard product set requirements meets the limitations of the FCC rules.

propagation. The travel of a signal through a medium such as air or free space.

Q–R

QAM. quadrature amplitude modulation. A method of combining multiple *amplitude-modulated* (AM) signals into a single channel, thereby doubling the effective bandwidth. QAM is used with *pulse amplitude modulation* (PAM) in digital systems, especially in wireless applications. Variations of QAM include 16QAM, and 64QAM, where the numbers of modulation points increase to 16 or 64 per symbol.

QoS. quality of service. The capability to treat different types of network traffic differently to ensure required levels of reliability and latency according to the type of traffic. Certain kinds of traffic, such as voice and video, are more sensitive to transmission delays and are therefore given priority over data that is less sensitive to delay.

radiation. Electromagnetic energy, such as radio waves, traveling into space from a transmitter.

radio wave. A combination of electric and magnetic fields varying at an RF and traveling through space at the speed of light.

raw data rate. Typically refers to the number of bits per second that can be transmitted, not accounting for overhead associated with error correction and other protocol-related factors.

receive gain. A measure of received signal boost contributed by an amplifier or antenna system, and typically measured in dBi.

receiver sensitivity. The minimum acceptable value of received power needed to achieve an acceptable *bit error rate* (BER) or performance. It takes into account the thermal noise of the receiver. Generally expressed in dBm using negative numbers. For example, the Cisco 350 series bridge has a receiver sensitivity of –85 dBm at 11 Mbps.

repeater. Any device that regenerates a signal to continue its propagation, usually increasing total distance or coverage area.

RF. radio frequency. Typically a frequency from 20 kHz to 3 GHz. RF is usually referred to whenever a signal is radiated through the air. Literally, any and all frequencies that can be radiated as an electromagnetic wave.

roaming. Typically used to describe a portable communications device moving its network connection from one fixed AP to another.

rogue access point. An unauthorized AP being used on a network. May be implemented by legitimate network users or an intruder attempting to compromise a network.

RPI. received power indicator. A measurement of how much power is being transmitted by wireless devices, which is a critical measurement for radio monitoring.

RP-TNC. Reverse Polarity Threaded Navel Connector. A Threaded Navel Connector with a reversed center connection (when compared to a standard TNC connector). This connector type is unique to certain wireless radios and antennas. Part 15.203 of the FCC rules covering spread-spectrum devices limits the types of antennas that may be used with transmission equipment. In compliance with this rule, WLAN providers equip radios and antennas with a unique connector to prevent attachment of unapproved antennas to radios.

RSSI. receive signal strength indicator. A parameter used in the location estimation of unknown radios.

RTS. request to send. A signal or frame of data indicating that the transmitter has data ready to be sent. In 802.11 WLANs, a device sends an RTS control packet to ask for a clear time to send the packet.

rubber duck. *See* dipole antenna.

S

S/N ratio. signal-to-noise ratio. Signal-to-noise ratio, often written S/N or SNR, is a measure of signal strength relative to background noise. The ratio is measured in *decibels* (dB). A higher S/N ratio indicates better channel performance.

saturation. In amplification, a term that describes the point at which the amplifier is producing the most output power it is capable of, basically in an overdriven situation. Typically, a device driven to saturation is no longer performing in a linear fashion or distortion-free manner. *See also* compression.

scalability. The ability to increase the availability capacity of any system, including wireless, security, and so on.

sector antenna. Typically an antenna similar to a patch antenna. Most sector antennas are designed with a horizontal beamwidth between 60 and 120 degrees. Many times sector antennas are used in groups of three or four to provide a complete 360-degree antenna.

Shared Key Authentication. An authentication algorithm defined in 802.11 in which the client is asked to respond back to the AP with a valid WEP key. It is considered less secure than open authentication, because the initial authentication challenge is clear, which could permit both the challenge and the response to be captured and compared, yielding the key.

single band. Referred to when a WLAN device has a single radio capable of operating on only one radio band (set of channels). The Cisco 1100 Series AP is a single-band unit.

sinusoidal signals. An electrical signal that varies with time proportionally to the sine of an angle. An example is *alternating current* (AC).

SNMP. Simple Network Management Protocol. A standard protocol for collecting statistics from networked devices.

spectral efficiency. The measurement of how much information is placed on a transmitted signal compared to the RF bandwidth required to transmit that signal.

spectrum. A series of radiated energies arranged in order of wavelength. The radio spectrum extends from 20 kHz upward.

spectrum analyzer. An instrument that can be used to view signals across a wide range of frequencies.

splitter/combiner. A transmission component that divides or sums power between two or more ports.

spread spectrum (SS). A wideband modulation that imparts noiselike characteristics to an RF signal. This communications technique spreads a signal over a wide range of frequencies for transmission and then de-spreads it to the original data bandwidth at the receiver.

spurious emissions. Unwanted RF signals, emitted from a transmitter, that sometimes cause interference.

SSID. service set identifier. In the 802.11 standard, an identifier string of up to 32 characters that is used to uniquely identify a WLAN. Sometimes referred to as *network name.*

STP. Spanning Tree Protocol. A protocol defined by the IEEE 802.1d standard to prevent packets from looping indefinitely in a network that contains loops in the transmission paths.

stream cipher. An encryption architecture that generates a key stream from small "seed" values. This key stream is combined with the plaintext (data) to generate the "ciphertext" or encrypted data. The key stream may vary with same "seed," but streams will match at encryptor and decryptor, because they use the same algorithm.

switch. A multiport Ethernet bridge that typically has hardware acceleration to increase the performance of switching Ethernet frames between collision domains.

T

throughput. A measure of the volume of data that can be transmitted (typically per second) through a given communications system.

TKIP. Temporal Key Integrity Protocol. In WPA and 802.11i standards, TKIP is a mechanism for protecting the encryption key data used to secure 802.11 traffic. WPA TKIP includes per-packet keying and a message-integrity check. Per-packet keying generates a unique, one-way encrypted key per 802.11 packet.

transceiver. A combination radio transmitter and receiver.

Type N connector. Named after Paul Neill of Bell Labs after being developed in the 1940s. The Type N connector was developed to satisfy the need for a durable, weatherproof, medium-size RF connector with consistent performance through 11 GHz. This connector is used as the antenna connector for the Cisco BR1400 series bridges.

U

UHF. ultra high frequency. Ultra high-frequency radio waves that are in the range of 300 to 3000 MHz.

ultra-wide band. A new technology provides very high data rates through the use of very short duration and very low-power pulses.

UNII. Unlicensed National Information Infrastructure. Refers to IEEE 802.11a standard for operating in the 5-GHz radio band. There are currently three such UNII bands for a total of 300 MHz of spectrum allocated within the United States. Different FCC rules and regulations cover each of the UNII1 through UNII3 bands.

V

VHF. very high frequency. Very high-frequency radio waves that are in the range of 30 to 300 MHz.

VLAN. virtual local-area network. A VLAN is a group of clients situated at different physical locations but that communicate with each other as if they were all on the same physical LAN segment.

VoIP. Voice over IP. Enables a device to carry voice traffic (for example, telephone calls and faxes) over an IP network. In VoIP, the device segments the voice signal into frames, which are then coupled and stored in voice packets.

VPN. virtual private network. A network that uses public, unsecure transmission media such as the Internet, but is set up securely and limited for use by a group of defined authorized users.

W–Y

WAN. wide-area network. Connects LANs together. Typical WAN interfaces include plain old telephone (POT) lines, digital subscriber lines (DSL), broadband cable, ISDN, and T1/T3.

wavelength. The distance that an electromagnetic wave travels in one complete cycle.

WEP. Wired Equivalent Privacy. WEP data encryption is defined by the 802.11 standard to prevent access to the network by intruders using similar WLAN equipment and capture of WLAN traffic through eavesdropping. WEP enables the administrator to define a set of respective keys for each wireless network user based on a key string passed through the WEP encryption algorithm. Access is denied by anyone who does not have an assigned key.

wide-area network. *See* WAN.

Wi-Fi Alliance. A nonprofit group that develops and institutes interoperability testing and certification for 802.11 WLAN products.

wind loading. A characteristic of an antenna or other structure that is a measure of the forces applied to the structure due to wind.

WLAN. wireless local-area network. A short-range, computer-to-computer wireless data communications network.

WLCCP. Wireless LAN Context Control Protocol. The protocol used to facilitate communication between wired infrastructure devices such as APs and networks management stations, for radio management.

WPA. Wi-Fi Protected Access. The Wi-Fi Alliance specification for certification of authentication and encryption of WLANs in advance of the IEEE 802.11i standard. It was intended to solve known security problems with 802.11 WEP. WPA was intended for implementation in software to provide security capability for the majority of existing hardware platforms.

Yagi antenna. A directional antenna named for one of its inventors, which consists of a boom supporting a series of elements (typically, aluminum rods). Often called a *beam antenna*.

INDEX

Numerics

2.4-GHz frequency band, 60
    ETSI channel scheme, 66
    Japan channel scheme, 67
    NA channel scheme, 65
5-GHz frequency band, 62, 64–65
    ETSI channel scheme, 67
    Japan channel scheme, 67
    NA channel scheme, 66
802.11
    direct-sequence channels, 8
    direct-sequence spread spectrum, 7
    frequency hopping, 8–9
    overview, 6
    working groups, 9–10
802.11a, 10
802.11b, 11, 60, 94
802.11f IAPaP, 194–195
802.11g, 11
802.3af, 211
900-Mhz frequency band, 59

A

access point (AP) selection
    dual-radio architecture, 131, 133
    overview, 131
    radio styles, 134–135
    single-radio architecture, 131, 133
access points (AP), 16, 57
    documentation, 306
    mounting
        ceiling mounting, 296
        overview, 293–294
        wall mounting, 294

    site surveying, 158–160
accessories, 21–22
aesthetics and installation, 286, 288
AirMagnet SiteViewer, 237, 239, 241, 270, 272, 309
AirMagnet utility, 233, 235–236
amplifiers, 75–76
amplitude modulation, 28
antenna connectors, 76–77
antennas
    directional properties, 38
        directional antennas, 40
        omnidirectional antennas, 38–39
    diversity, 42–45
    documentation, 307
    examples, 40
        dish antenna, 41
        patch antenna, 41
        sectorized antenna, 41
        Yagi antenna, 41
    gain, 37
    identifying types, 253
    mounting, 296, 298–299
    omnidirectional antennas, 163
    outdoor bridge deployments, 332
    overview, 36
    polarization, 40
    site surveying, 163–164
AP locations, identifying, 253
applications
    environments
        education facilities, 93, 95
        enterprise offices, 89–91
        health care industry, 91–93
        hotel, conventions, and hospitality systems, 97–98

environments *(Continued)*
    manufacturing facilities, 95–96
    overview, 83
    public hotspots, 98–99
    retail/bar coding, 84–89
    SOHO sites, 99–100
    requirements
        overview, 100–101
        technology requirements, 101–104
architectures
    centralized intelligence
        overview, 117–118
        packet flows, 120–122
    core device, 118, 120
    distributed intelligence
        overview, 115, 117
        packet flows, 120–122
    dual-radio, 131, 133
    edge device, 123
    free-space optics (FSO), 130
    mesh networking, 129
    overview, 114–115
    single-radio, 131, 133
    switched antenna
        overview, 124
        phased array antenna extends range, 126–128
        phased array antenna technology, 125–126
area-by-area analyses, 305
Aruba network, 243–244
assisted site survey tools
    Aruba network, 243–244
    Cisco Assisted Site Survey utility, 244–245
    overview, 243
assisted site surveys
    overview, 219, 273
    RF configuration parameters, 276–277

assisted site surveys
    tools, using, 276
    user-density test, 274
assisted survey and installation tools, 113
attenuators, 166
automated site surveys, 218–219
automatic site survey tools
    Aruba network, 243–244
    Cisco Assisted Site Survey utility, 244–245
    overview, 243

B

bandwidth, 26, 49
bar code scanners, 85
battery packs, 170–171
binary phase shift keying (BPSK), 30
Bluetooth, 12
bridge system characteristics, 313
bridge topologies, 314–315
bridges, 18, 20
building codes, 291–292
building construction, 179–180
building contents, 180, 183–184
building-to-building connectivity, 107–108

C

cables
    overview, 45–46
    site surveying, 165–166
cabling requirements
    802.3af, 211
    overview, 208
    PoE
        overview, 208–210
        proprietary methods, 212, 214

capabilities label, 14

ceiling mounting of APs, 296

cell boundaries, defining, 258–261

cell coverage, overlapping, 262–263

centralized intelligence architecture

    overview, 117–118

    packet flows, 120–122

channel selections

    ETSI domain channel scheme

        2.4 GHz, 66

        5 GHz, 67

        overview, 66

    Japan channel scheme

        2.4 GHz, 67

        5 GHz, 67

        overview, 67

    NA domain channel scheme

        2.4 GHz, 65

        5 GHz, 66

        overview, 65

    other countries and, 67

    overview, 65

channel utilization, 232

Cisco Aironet Client Utility (ACU), 221–222, 224–225

Cisco Aironet Desktop Utility (ADU), 226, 228

Cisco Assisted Site Survey utility, 244–245

Cisco Wireless LAN Security (Sankar & Sundaralingam), 113

client devices

    overview, 17

    site surveying, 160–161

client product selection

    Ethernet client, 137

    overview, 136–138

    PCI card, 137

clients, roaming, 195–196

complementary code keying (CCK), 31

connectors

    overview, 45

    site surveying, 162

    weatherproofing, 332–333

contact list, 305

cookie cutter designs, 188

core device architecture, 118, 120

coverage

    bandwidth compared, 49

    distance, determining possible, 325

    documentation, 308

    map, 152

    modulation compared, 50

current network and communications information, 147–148

    current equipment installed, 147

    LAN connectivity, 147

    security, 147

    type of wired network installed, 147

    WAN connectivity, 147

customer information

    address, city, state, zip code, 145

    company name, 145

    date of delivery, 145

    e-mail, 146

    mobile phone, 146

    phone and fax number, 145

    PO date, 145

    point of contact name, 145

    purchase order number, 145

    work-order number, 145

customer restrictions, 186

D

data rates, 33–34, 258

decibels (dB), 35

demilitarized zone (DMZ), 120

device roaming, developing policy for, 193–194

digital cameras and site surveying, 172

dipole antenna, 37

directional antennas, 40

directional properties, 38

    directional antennas, 40

    omnidirectional antennas, 38–39

direct-sequence channels, 8

direct-sequence spread spectrum, 7

dish antenna, 41

distributed intelligence architecture

    overview, 115 117

    packet flows, 120–122

diversity antenna systems, 42–45, 134

documentation

    final site survey report

        area-by-area analyses, 305

        contact list, 305

        existing wireless system definition, 304

        general network description, 304

        objective, 304

        overview, 303

        proposed WLAN components, 304

        RF spectrum analyses results, 305

        site description, 304

        survey dates, 304

        testing procedure, 304

        wireless sniffer traces, 305

    of actual work

        antenna locations, 307

        AP locations, 306

        coverage issues, 308

        overview, 305–306, 308–309

        of actual work

        overview, 303

        site survey, 270

        site survey report-generation programs, 309–310

dual-band surveys, 278

dual-radio architecture, 131, 133

Dynamic Frequency Selection (DFS), 64

E

earth bulge, 51–52

edge device architecture, 123

educational facility, 93, 95, 268

Effective Isotropic Radiated Power (EIRP), 68

enclosures, 290

enterprise offices, 89–91

environmental issues

    concerns, 187–188

    feasibility study, 322

    installation and, 290–291

environments

    education facilities, 93, 95

    enterprise offices, 89–91

    health care industry, 91–93

    hotel, conventions, and hospitality systems, 97–98

    manufacturing facilities, 95–96

    overview, 83

    public hotspots, 98–99

    retail/bar coding

        overview, 84

        retail, 85–87

        warehousing, 88–89

    SOHO sites, 99–100

equipment installation limitations

    customer restrictions, 186

    environmental concerns, 187–188

equipment installation limitations *(Continued)*

overview, 185

regulatory limitations, 186–187

ethernet

client, 137

installation, 300

ETSI, 57

ETSI domain channel scheme

2.4 GHz, 66

5 GHz, 67

overview, 66

ETSI regulatory power levels

2.4 GHz power levels, 72

5 GHz power levels, 73

overview, 72

existing wireless system definition, 304

F

facility, inspecting, 250

facility documentation

building construction, 179–180

building contents, 180, 183–184

overview, 177

site map, 178

user areas and density, 184–185

FCC, 57

FCC Class B regulations, 57

feasibility study

coverage distance, determining possible, 325

environmental issues, 322

Fresnel zone, 322–323, 325

line of sight, determining, 319–320, 322

overview, 318

features of WLAN

assisted survey and installation tools, 113

mobility, 113

overview, 111

features of WLAN *(Continued)*

remote debugging, 114

rogue AP detection, 112

self-healing systems, 114

software upgrade capabilities, 112

final site survey report

area-by-area analyses, 305

contact list, 305

existing wireless system definition, 304

general network description, 304

objective, 304

overview, 303–304

proposed WLAN components, 304

RF spectrum analyses results, 305

site description, 304

survey dates, 304

testing procedure, 304

wireless sniffer traces, 305

floor plan or facility blueprint, obtaining, 250

free-space optics (FSO) architecture, 130

frequencies of operation

2.4-GHz frequency band, 60

5-GHz frequency band, 62, 64–65

900-MHz frequency band, 59

overview, 58

frequency, 25

frequency hopping (FH), 8–9

frequency modulation, 29

Fresnel zone, 51–52, 322–323, 325

G-H

gain, 37

general network description, 304

hazardous areas

overview, 151

site-specific requirements, 188

health and safety regulations, 77–78

health-care facility, 91–93, 268

hemispherical antenna, 41

hertz (Hz), 25

Hertz, Heinrich, 25

HiperLAN, 13

Home RF, 13

hotel, conventions, and hospitality systems, 97–98

I-L

IAPP (Inter-Access Point Protocol), 194–195

installation

    aesthetics, 286, 288

    antenna mounting, 296, 298–299

    AP mounting

        ceiling mounting, 296

        overview, 293–294

        wall mounting, 294

    building codes, 291–292

    environmental conditions, 290–291

    ethernet considerations, 300

    facility construction, 286

    overview, 285

    physical security, 289

installation of bridges

    antenna alignment, 332

    indoor testing before, 331–332

    lightning protection, 327, 330

    overview, 326–327

    parallel bridge links for increased throughput, 333–334

    weatherproofing connectors, 332–333

Intel Centrino utility, 228

intentional radiators, 56

interference

    detection, 255–257

    SOHO sites, 99

    study, 326

interoperability, 107

IP subnet roaming, 106

isotropic antenna, 37

Japan channel scheme

    2.4 GHz, 67

    5 GHz, 67

    overview, 67

Japan domain power levels

    2.4 GHz, 73

    5 GHz, 74

    overview, 73

LAN Fielder tool, 246

Layer 2 roaming, 196–197

Layer 3 roaming, 197

Layer 3 wireless switching, 202–203

lightning protection, 327, 330

line of sight, determining, 319–320, 322

load balancing, 107

M-N

manual site survey tools

    AirMagnet site survey utility (SiteViewer), 233, 235–237, 239, 241

    Cisco Aironet Client Utility (ACU), 221–222, 224–225

    Cisco Aironet Desktop Utility (ADU), 226, 228

    Intel Centrino utility, 228

    Netgear clients, 231

    ORiNOCO survey utility, 230–231

    overview, 221

    standard utilities, systems that do not support, 242

    wireless 802.11 phones, 232

manual site surveys

    overview, 218

    performing, 263, 265–266, 268, 270

manufacturing facilities, 95–96

Maxwell, James Clerk, 25

mesh networking architecture, 129

milliWatt (mW), 35

Mobile IP
  disadvantages, 200
  overview, 198–199
  Proxy Mobile IP, 200–201

mobile node roaming, 198

mobility, 113

modulation
  amplitude modulation, 28
  coverage compared, 50
  data rates, 33–34
  frequency modulation, 29
  orthogonal frequency division multiplexing, 32–33
  overview, 26, 28
  phase modulation, 29–30
    binary phase shift keying (BPSK), 30
    complementary code keying (CCK), 31
    quadrature phase shift keying (QPSK), 31
  quadrature amplitude modulation, 31–32

mounting hardware, 172–173

multipath distortion, 42–43

multipath fading, 33

National Electric Code (NEC), 291–292

Netgear clients, 231

network performance, 207–208

network switch, 114

noise, 48

nomadic node roaming, 198

non-802.11 equipment and interference, 256

North American (NA) domain channel scheme
  2.4 GHz, 65
  5 GHz, 66
  overview, 65

North American regulatory domain, 57

North American regulatory power levels
  2.4-GHz power levels, 68
  5-GHz power levels, 71–72
  overview, 68

O

omnidirectional antennas, 38–39, 163

Optimatic tool, 246

ORiNOCO survey utility, 230–231

orthogonal frequency division multiplexing, 32–33

outdoor bridge deployments
  applications
    overview, 316
    QoS, 317
    security, 318
    VLANs, 316
    Voice over IP, 317
  bridge system characteristics, 313
  bridge topologies, 314–315
  feasibility study
    coverage distance, determining possible, 325
    environmental issues, 322
    Fresnel zone, 322–323, 325
    line of sight, determining, 319–320, 322
    overview, 318
  installation
    antenna alignment, 332
    indoor testing before, 331–332
    lightning protection, 327, 330
    overview, 326–327
    parallel bridge links for increased throughput, 333–334
    weatherproofing connectors, 332–333
  interference study, 326

outdoor bridge links
    antennas, 153
    building exterior construction, 153
    existing towers, 153
    line of sight, 153
    roof access, 154
    site-specific information, 153
outdoor RF issues
    earth bulge, 51–52
    Fresnel zone, 51–52
    overview, 50
    propagation and losses, 51
outdoor tools, 170

P

packet flows
    centralized intelligence architecture, 120–122
    distributed intelligence architecture, 120–122
packet size, 258
panel antenna, 41
parallel bridge links for increased throughput, 333–334
patch antenna, 41
PCI card, 137
personnel requirements, 152
phase modulation, 29–30
    binary phase shift keying (BPSK), 30
    complementary code keying (CCK), 31
    quadrature phase shift keying (QPSK), 31
phased array antenna extends range, 126–128
phased array antenna technology, 125–126
physical measuring devices, 167
physical security, 289
ping command, 242

plenum locations
    installation, 292
    regulations, 79
PoE (power over Ethernet)
    overview, 208–210
    proprietary methods, 212, 214
point-of-sale (POS) device, 86
point-to-multipoint (PTMP) systems, 69–70
point-to-point systems, 69–70
polarization, 40
portable analyzer tools, 169–170
power ratings, 35
power values
    decibels, 35
    overview, 34
    power ratings, 35
Predictor tool, 245
pre-site survey form information
    coverage map, 152
    current network and communications
        information, 147–148
        current equipment installed, 147
        LAN connectivity, 147
        security, 147
        type of wired network installed, 147
        WAN connectivity, 147
    customer information
        address, city, stae, and zip code, 145
        company name, 145
        date of delivery, 145
        e-mail, 146
        mobile phone, 146
        phone and fax number, 145
        PO date, 145
        point of contact name, 145

customer information *(Continued)*
    purchase order number, 145
    work-order number, 145
outdoor bridge links
    antennas, 153
    building exterior construction, 153
    existing towers, 153
    line of sight, 153
    roof access, 154
    site-specific information, 153
    overview, 143–145
personnel requirements, 152
scope of work, 152
site information, 149
    ceiling construction, 150
    ceiling height, 150
    floor construction, 150
    hazardous areas, 151
    lift availability, 150
    plenum ceiling, 150
    stock levels, 150
    temperature ranges, 151
    wall construction, 150
site survey location
    name of sites, 146
    number of sites, 146
    point of contact information, 146
    working hours, 146
WLAN equipment requirements
    AP manufacturer, 148
    AP model number, 148
    coverage areas, 149
    end-user devices, 148
    minimum data rates, 148
    packet size, 149
    rate shifting, 149
    redundancy, 149

WLAN equipment requirements
    special needs, 149
    total number of users, 149
price-verifier scanning device, 85
problem areas on diagram, identifying potential, 251
proposed WLAN components, 304
proprietary WLANs, 4–5
Proxy Mobile IP, 200–201
PSP (power-savings protocol), 197
public hotspots, 98–99

Q
QoS (quality of service), 105
    deployment schemes, 206
    downstream QoS, 207
    network performance and, 207–208
    outdoor bridge deployments, 317
    overview, 206
    upstream QoS, 207
quadrature amplitude modulation, 31–32
quadrature phase shift keying (QPSK), 31

R
radio frequency (RF)
    antennas
        dipole antenna, 37
        directional properties, 38–40
        diversity, 42–45
        examples, 40–41
        gain, 37
        hemispherical antenna, 41
        isotropic antenna, 37
        overview, 36
        panel antenna, 41
        polarization, 40

radio frequency (RF) *(Continued)*

   bandwidth, 26

   cables, 45–46

   components

      frequency, 25

      modulation, 26, 28–34

      overview, 25

      signal strength, 34

   configuration parameters, 276–277

   connectors, 45

   outdoor environment, calculating distances for, 319–320

   overview, 25

   power values

      decibels, 35

      overview, 34

      power ratings, 35

   site propagation

      coverage versus bandwidth, 49

      frequency versus coverage, 47

      material absorption, reflection and refraction, 47

      modulation versus coverage, 50

      noise, 48

      outdoor RF issues, 50–52

      overview, 46

      reflection, 47

      signal, 48

      signal-to-noise ratio, 48

   site survey and, 253–255

radio management, 114

radio styles, 134–135

receive threshold, 34

receiver desensitization, 132–133

reflection, 47

regulations

   amplifiers, 75–76

   antenna connectors, 76–77

   channel selections

      ETSI domain channel scheme, 66–67

      Japan channel scheme, 67

      NA domain channel scheme, 65–66

      other countries and, 67

      overview, 65

   frequencies of operation

      2.4-GHz frequency band, 60

      5-GHz frequency band, 62, 64–65

      900-MHz frequency band, 59

      overview, 58

   health and safety, 77–78

   overview, 55

   plenum locations, 79

   remote antennas, 76–77

   RF regulatory domains, 57

   spread-spectrum regulations, 55

   technology requirments, 104

   transmitter power levels

      EIRP, 68

      ETSI Regulatory power levels, 72–73

      Japan domain power levels, 73–74

      North American Regulatory power levels, 68, 71–72

      overview, 67

      world mode (802.11d), 74

regulatory limitations, 186–187

remote antennas, 76–77

remote debugging, 114

repeater usage, 277

requirements

   overview, 100–101

   technology requirements

      AP location, 102

      bandwidth, 101–102

      client devices, 103

requirements *(Continued)*
> other systems, 104
> overview, 101
> physical areas, 102
> regulatory issues, 104
> RF signal, 104
> user density, 101
> vendors, 103
> VoIP connections, 102

retail environment, 85–87

retail facility, 263, 266

retail/bar coding
> overview, 84
> retail, 85–87
> warehousing, 88–89

RF analyzers
> site surveying
> > overview, 168
> > portable analyzer tools, 169–170
> > spectrum analyzers, 169

RF regulatory domains, 57

RF spectrum analyses results, 305

roaming
> clients, 195–196
> device roaming, developing policy for, 193–194
> IAPP, 194–195
> Layer 2 roaming, 196–197
> Layer 3 roaming, 197
> Layer 3 wireless switching, 202–203
> Mobile IP
> > disadvantages, 200
> > overview, 198–199
> > Proxy Mobile IP, 200–201
> mobile node roaming, 198
> nomadic node roaming, 198
> overview, 192–193

rogue AP detection, 112

S

Sankar, Krishna, 113

scope of work, 152

sectorized antenna, 41

security
> outdoor bridge deployments, 318
> overview, 106
> physical security, 289
> SOHO sites, 99

self-healing systems, 114

services
> interoperability, 107
> IP subnet roaming, 106
> load balancing, 107
> overview, 105
> QoS, 105
> security, 106
> VLANs, 105

signal, 48

signal strength, 34

signal-to-noise ratio, 48

sine waves, 26

single-radio architecture, 131, 133

site description, 304

site information, 149
> ceiling construction, 150
> ceiling height, 150
> floor construction, 150
> hazardous areas, 151
> lift availability, 150
> plenum ceiling, 150
> stock levels, 150
> temperature ranges, 151
> wall construction, 150

site map, 178

site propagation
    coverage versus bandwidth, 49
    frequency versus coverage, 47
    material absorption, reflection, and refraction, 47
    modulation versus coverage, 50
    noise, 48
    outdoor RF issues
        earth bulge, 51–52
        Fresnel zone, 51–52
        overview, 50
        propagation and losses, 51
    overview, 46
    reflection, 47
    signal, 48
    signal-to-noise ratio, 48
site survey
    AirMagnet site survey utility (SiteViewer), 270, 272
    assisted site surveys
        overview, 273
        RF configuration parameters, 276–277
        tools, using, 276
        user-density test, 274
    dual-band surveys, 278
    final verification, 279
    for voice, 278–279
    overview, 249
    process
        AP locations and antenna types, identifying, 253
        cell boundaries, defining, 258–261
        cell coverage, overlapping, 262–263
        documentation, 270
        facility inspection, 250
        floor plan or facility blueprint, obtaining, 250
        interference detection, 255–257
        manual survey, 263, 265–266, 268, 270
        overview, 249
        potential problem areas on diagram, identifying, 251
        RF issues, 253–255
        user areas on diagram, identifying, 251
        walkabout test, 258
    repeater usage, 277
site survey kits, 173, 175
site survey location
    name of sites, 146
    number of sites, 146
    point of contact information, 146
    working hours, 146
site survey preparation
    balancing wants, needs, and capabilities, 154–155
    pre-site survey form information
        coverage map, 152
        current network and communications information, 147–148
        customer information, 145–146
        outdoor bridge links, 153–154
        overview, 143–145
        personnel requirements, 152
        scope of work, 152
        site information, 149, 151
        site survey location, 146
        WLAN equipment requirements, 148–149
    user input, 154
site survey report-generation programs, 309–310
site survey tools
    assisted site survey
        Aruba network, 243–244
        Cisco Assisted Site Survey utility, 244–245
        overview, 243

automatic site survey
    Aruba network, 243–244
    Cisco Assisted Site Survey utility, 244–245
    overview, 243
manual site survey
    AirMagnet site survey utility (SiteViewer), 233, 235–237, 239, 241
    Cisco Aironet Client Utility (ACU), 221–222, 224–225
    Cisco Aironet Desktop Utility (ADU), 226, 228
    Intel Centrino utility, 228
    Netgear clients, 231
    ORiNOCO survey utility, 230–231
    overview, 221
    standard utilities, systems that do not support, 242
    wireless 802.11 phones, 232
overview, 217
ping command, 242
site survey kits, 173, 175
theoretical site survey
    LAN Fielder tool, 246
    Optimatic tool, 246
    overview, 245–246
    Predictor tool, 245
types of site surveys
    assisted site survey, 219
    automated site survey, 218–219
    manual site survey, 218
    overview, 218
    theoretical site survey, 220–221
WLAN equipment
    access points, 158–160
    antennas, 163–164
    attenuators, 166

    battery packs, 170–171
    cables, 165–166
    client devices, 160–161
    connectors, 162
    digital cameras, 172
    mounting hardware, 172–173
    outdoor tools, 170
    overview, 157–158
    physical measuring devices, 167
    RF analyzers, 168–170
    two-way radios, 170
site surveys
    types of
        assisted site survey, 219
        automated site survey, 218–219
        manual site survey, 218
        overview, 218
        theoretical site survey, 220–221
site-specific requirements
    cookie cutter designs, 188
    limitations affecting equipment installations
        customer restrictions, 186
        environmental concerns, 187–188
        overview, 185
        regulatory limitations, 186–187
    recommended facility documentation
        building construction, 179–180
        building contents, 180, 183–184
        overview, 177
        site map, 178
        user areas and density, 184–185
small office/home office (SOHO) sites, 99–100
software upgrade capabilities, 112
spectrum analyzers, 169
spread-spectrum regulations, 55
standards-based WLANs, 5–6
Sundaralingam, Sri, 113

survey dates, 304

switched antenna architecture

    overview, 124

    phased array antenna extends range, 126–128

    phased array antenna technology, 125–126

T

technology requirements

    AP location, 102

    bandwidth, 101–102

    client devices, 103

    other systems, 104

    overview, 101

    physical areas, 102

    regulatory issues, 104

    RF signal, 104

    user density, 101

    vendors, 103

    VoIP connections, 102

TELEC, 57

theoretical site survey tools

    LAN Fielder tool, 246

    Optimatic tool, 246

    overview, 245–246

    Predictor tool, 245

theoretical site surveys, 220–221

Transmit Power Control (TPC), 64

transmitter power, 258

transmitter power levels

    EIRP, 68

    ETSI Regulatory power levels

        2.4-GHz power levels, 72

        5-GHz power levels, 73

        overview, 72

    Japan domain power levels

        2.4 GHz, 73

        5 GHz, 74

        overview, 73

    North American Regulatory power levels

        2.4-GHz power levels, 68

        5-GHz power levels, 71–72

        overview, 68

two-way radios, 170

U-V

ultra wideband, 13

unintentional radiators, 56

Unlicensed National Informatin Infrastructure (UNII) bands, 62

user areas and density, 184–185

user areas on diagram, identifying, 251

user input, 154

user-density test, 274

verification, 279

VLANs, 203, 205

    outdoor bridge deployments, 316

    overview, 105

Vocera Communications Badge, 92

voice over IP (VoIP) phones, 86, 317

voice site surveys, 278–279

W-Y

walkabout test, 258

wall mounting of APs, 294

wants, needs, and capabilities, balancing, 154–155

warehouse facility, 266–267

warehousing environment, 88–89

Wi-Fi

    capabilities label, 14

    certifications, 14

    overview, 14

wired network requirements

    cabling requirments

        802.3af, 211

cabling requirments *(Continued)*
    overview, 208
    PoE, 208–210, 212, 214
overview, 191
QoS
    deployment schemes, 206
    downstream QoS, 207
    network performance and, 207–208
    overview, 206
    upstream QoS, 207
roaming
    802.11f IAPP, 194–195
    clients, 195–196
    device roaming, developing policy for,
        193–194
    Layer 2 roaming, 196–197
    Layer 3 roaming, 197
    Layer 3 wireless switching, 202–203
    Mobile IP, 198–201
    mobile node roaming, 198
    nomadic node roaming, 198
    overview, 192–193
VLANs, 203, 205
wireless 802.11 phones, 232
wireless fidelity network, 3
wireless LAN. *See* WLAN
Wireless LAN Interoperability Forum (WLIF), 5
Wireless LAN Solution Engine (WLSE), 310
wireless sniffer traces, 305
wireless standards
    Bluetooth, 12
    compared, 11–12
    evolution of, 4
        802.11, 6–11
        proprietary WLANs, 4–5
        standards-based WLANs, 5–6

HiperLAN, 13
Home RF, 13
ultra wideband, 13
WLAN
    802.11, 6
        802.11a, 10
        802.11b, 11
        802.11g, 11
        direct-sequence channels, 8
        direct-sequence spread spectrum, 7
        frequency hopping, 8–9
        working groups, 9–10
    access points, 16
    accessories, 21–22
    bridges, 18, 20
    client devices, 17
    components
        access points, 16
        accessories, 21–22
        bridges, 18, 20
        client devices, 17
        overview, 15–16
WLAN equipment
    access points, 158–160
    antennas, 163–164
    attenuators, 166
    battery packs, 170–171
    cables, 165–166
    client devices, 160–161
    connectors, 162
    digital cameras, 172
    mounting hardware, 172–173
    outdoor tools, 170
    overview, 157–158
    physical measuring devices, 167
    RF analyzers, 168

WLAN equipment (Continued)
>   portable analyzer tools, 169–170
>   spectrum analyzers, 169
> two-way radios, 170
WLAN equipment requirements
> AP manufacturer, 148
> AP model number, 148
> coverage areas, 149
> end-user devices, 148
> minimum data rates, 148
> packet size, 149
> rate shifting, 149
> redundancy, 149
> special needs, 149
> total number of users, 149
work documentation
> antenna locations, 307
> AP locations, 306
> coverage issues, 308
> overview, 305–306, 308–309
working groups, 9–10
world mode (802.11d) 74
Yagi antenna, 41

CISCO SYSTEMS

Cisco Press

SAVE UP TO 25%

Become a member and save at **ciscopress.com**!

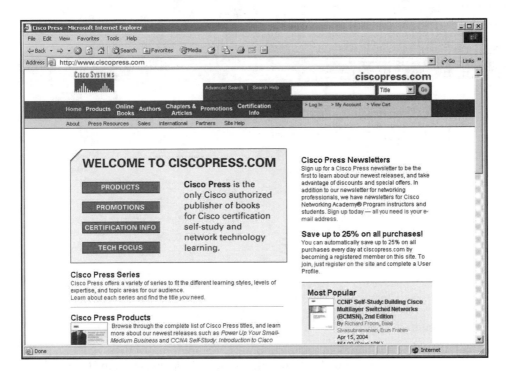

Complete a **User Profile** at ciscopress.com today to become a member and benefit from discounts of up to **25% on every purchase** at ciscopress.com, as well as a more customized user experience. You can also sign up to get your first **30 days FREE on InformIT Safari Bookshelf** and **preview Cisco Press content**. With Safari Bookshelf, you can access Cisco Press books online and build your own customized, searchable electronic reference library. And don't forget to subscribe to the monthly Cisco Press newsletter.

Visit **www.ciscopress.com/register** to sign up and start saving today!

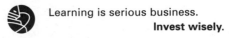

Learning is serious business.
Invest wisely.

SEARCH THOUSANDS OF BOOKS FROM LEADING PUBLISHERS

Safari® Bookshelf

Safari® Bookshelf is a searchable electronic reference library for IT professionals that features more than 2,000 titles from technical publishers, including Cisco Press.

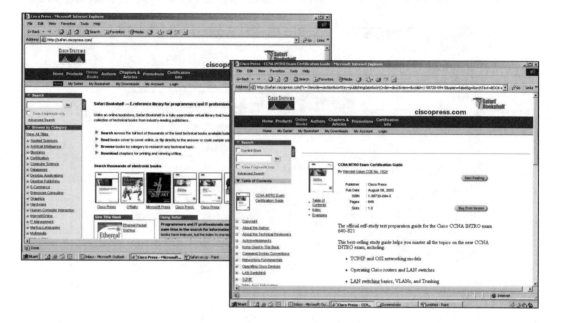

With Safari Bookshelf you can

- **Search** the full text of thousands of technical books, including more than 70 Cisco Press titles from authors such as Wendell Odom, Jeff Doyle, Bill Parkhurst, Sam Halabi, and Karl Solie.

- **Read** the books on My Bookshelf from cover to cover, or just flip to the information you need.

- **Browse** books by category to research any technical topic.

- **Download** chapters for printing and viewing offline.

With a customized library, you'll have access to your books when and where you need them—and all you need is a user name and password.

TRY SAFARI BOOKSHELF FREE FOR 14 DAYS!

You can sign up to get a 10-slot Bookshelf free for the first 14 days.
Visit **http://safari.ciscopress.com** to register.

CISCO SYSTEMS

Cisco Press

3 STEPS TO LEARNING

STEP 1

STEP 2

STEP 3

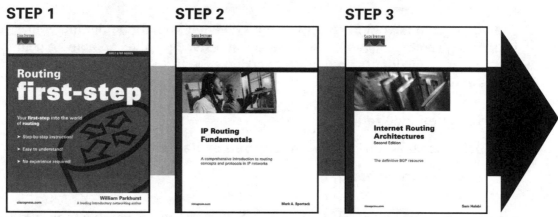

First-Step

Fundamentals

Networking
Technology Guides

STEP 1   **First-Step**—Benefit from easy-to-grasp explanations.
No experience required!

STEP 2   **Fundamentals**—Understand the purpose, application,
and management of technology.

STEP 3   **Networking Technology Guides**—Gain the knowledge
to master the challenge of the network.

NETWORK BUSINESS SERIES

The Network Business series helps professionals tackle the
business issues surrounding the network. Whether you are a
seasoned IT professional or a business manager with minimal
technical expertise, this series will help you understand the
business case for technologies.

Justify Your Network Investment.

Look for Cisco Press titles at your favorite bookseller today.

Visit **www.ciscopress.com/series** for details on each of these book series.